# Are We Really Going to Let Mum Backpack on Her Own?

## A Journal of My Gap Year Travelling Solo at Sixty

### HAZEL LOUTSIS

Copyright © 2018 Hazel Loutsis

ISBN: 9781729200957

All rights reserved, including the right to reproduce this book, or portions thereof in any form. No part of this text may be reproduced, transmitted, downloaded, decompiled, reverse engineered, or stored, in any form or introduced into any information storage and retrieval system, in any form or by any means, whether electronic or mechanical without the express written permission of the author.

Formatting by Rebecca Emin.

# Acknowledgements

There's a mass of information available on the Internet which is helpful for travellers, but in the interest of keeping life simple and not spending hours on my laptop, the following were my 'go to' sites.

I'd like to especially thank these organisations:

TRAVEL NATION, the online company who arranged my 'Round the World' ticket; they were always available to give advice about visas and flight changes and it gave me confidence knowing I had their support during the year.

GOOGLE MAPS were Invaluable; I used them everywhere and took mobile photos of map pictures on my laptop for the times when I was unable to access the Internet.

BOOKING.COM gave me instant access to accommodation in all countries. It was easy to book a day or two ahead and using their rating system and reviews I learned to find excellent hostels and homestays.

LONELY PLANET was brilliant for letting me know which tourist destinations would be right for me and for finding the best sights to see.

TRIP ADVISOR for reviews and conversations about all things from 'places of interest', tour organisers, public transport and restaurants.

The maps in this book were created using Google Maps

To my wonderful children,
Phil and Jo,
thank you for your encouragement and support.

# PREFACE

This is my journal of a year backpacking in eighteen countries, starting in India and ending in Brazil.

Writing this book has given me the joy of re-living my experiences and gaining clearer insights into how they shaped the person I am now.

Every day I feel massively grateful that I made the decision to travel and if the idea of exploring the world has ever entered your mind, I promise you, it's easier than you think.

## Contents

| | |
|---|---|
| A (Tooth Gap) Year | |
| India to Nepal | 1 |
| Nepal, on My Own | 29 |
| Darjeeling, West Bengal | 62 |
| Kolkata (Calcutta), India | 80 |
| Sri Lanka | 115 |
| Back into India -Palolem (Goa) and Mumbai | 139 |
| Singapore | 163 |
| Vietnam | 168 |
| Cambodia | 209 |
| Thailand | 227 |
| Malaysia | 236 |
| Kuala Lumpur, Malaysia | 246 |
| Bali, Indonesia | 251 |
| Gili Islands, Indonesia | 269 |
| Singapore to Australia | 278 |
| Sydney to Adelaide Road Trip | 284 |
| Adelaide to Darwin | 294 |
| The Kimberley Tour | 308 |
| Broome to Cairns | 318 |
| Cairns to Brisbane Campervan Trip | 325 |
| Fiji | 336 |
| New Zealand | 356 |
| Santiago, South America | 372 |
| Angelmo, Chile | 378 |
| Rupanco Farm, Chile | 385 |
| Argentina | 414 |
| Patagonia | 421 |
| San Pedro de Atacama, Chile to Bolivia | 436 |
| Cusco, Peru | 455 |
| 'Inca Trail' to Machu Pichu, Peru | 461 |
| Iquitos, Peru | 470 |
| Iguazu, Brazil | 484 |
| Rio de Janeiro, Brazil | 492 |

# *A (Tooth Gap) Year*

I'm standing in the kitchen and in my mind I see a farmyard. There's a chicken scratching around in the dirt, pecking at the ground looking for grain and I feel like the chicken, pecking about in life, looking for scraps. Then I see a fence and over the other side are vast fields of golden corn. I laugh as I realise all I have to do is hop over the fence.

******

My cat died. She'd been with me for twenty years and when she left she also left me without responsibility. I had incredible freedom. I could go anywhere, live anywhere. There was nothing and no-one to hold me back and I felt the need to do something with this freedom.

******

A visit to the dentist meant the loss of a back tooth. My vanity kicked in and I said to my dentist *"well you'll just have to put in a new tooth for me"*. When he told me it could cost around £3,000 I was shocked and blurted *"£3,000!! I could travel around the world for that kind of money"*. I think this was the first time I actually voiced the thought.

******

I can recall the day and the moment the decision was made. I was visiting my son on a warm day in August and we were walking in the Derbyshire Peak District. We'd been mulling over the possibility of me travelling on my own. We climbed up high and stood on some huge, grey rocks that looked out over the fabulous Derbyshire countryside and suddenly I knew, I knew this was what I was going to do. I turned to Phil and said *"I think I have to do it. I'm going to travel the world"* and he smiled and nodded. From that moment, I don't think I wavered.

******

There was a lot to do before I could leave. I 'closed' my home-based business that I worked with a network marketing company, handing my customers over to a colleague. I decorated my house from top to bottom and found tenants willing to take it on for a year, part furnished. All my personal stuff was ruthlessly cleared out, given away or put into storage. I had all the vaccines deemed necessary by the National Health Service and bought a stack of expensive malaria tablets. I put my affairs in order and as much paperwork 'on line' as I could and I sorted out banking and ways to manage finances from abroad.

I bought a new lightweight laptop, a small rucksack and a carry case for my ukulele which I decided to take with me. I was given an old iPhone to take as a 'spare' and a large backpack and I was good to go. It took four months from decision to departing.

I told my friends and family of my intention to travel solo for a year, and the more I talked about it, the more real it became for me. Phil and my daughter, Jo, were both very supportive, although I don't know how they felt inside. I did overhear my daughter say to my son *"are we really going to let Mum backpack on her own?"* I don't know if it was out of concern for my safety or my appalling lack of sense of direction.

Only one element caused me to hesitate. I'd just met a man, one I liked very much. Okay, let's be honest, I was dotty about him. Ben came into my life about the same time as my decision to travel. This felt a little unfair considering I hadn't let any man into my heart since my husband died twenty-one years ago. He never tried to influence my decision and I didn't know how he felt about me.

The day I left for the airport, Ben gave me a delicate silver horseshoe necklace for good luck and I fervently hoped that he would still be here for me when I came back.

# *India to Nepal*

## 9th December 2015

My good friend John is driving me to London Heathrow Airport. It's a cold, wet, dark evening on the 9th December. There's been considerable stress for me in the last few days leading up to my departure and I feel relief that at last the journey is about to begin. The moment has come. I'm in the Departure area of the airport. I'm wearing my big walking boots because they won't fit in my backpack and as I step away from John and out on my own, I look down at them. I feel surprisingly calm and tell myself *"it's okay, you only have to take one step at a time"*. I like being in airports and I know I'm capable of boarding an aeroplane, so all is well.

When I made the decision to travel, I started researching some of the world's most beautiful scenery. I had a vision of myself standing high on a rocky mountain looking out across an incredible landscape, the sort of image you see on travel websites. I spent many evenings looking on the Internet and came up with a vague personal itinerary, which amusingly turned out to be similar to every travel agent's suggested itinerary. Obvious now I think about it, we all like the same places!

With assistance from a helpful guy at an online travel company, my flight tickets were booked to the major countries I wanted to visit, starting in Delhi, India. I've no idea what was in my head when I picked India as my first destination. I recall the travel agent suggesting I might like to start somewhere a little less challenging, but India it was.

To ease myself into my solo adventure I booked a fifteen day 'Delhi to Kathmandu' tour, I felt this would be a good way to help me find my feet. I arrived in India two days before joining the tour group.

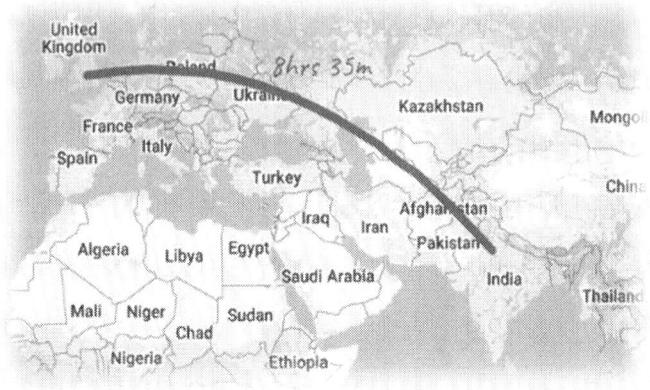

## 10<sup>th</sup> December

My flight, via Dubai, lands in Delhi at 3.30 pm local time, in a temperature of 27 degrees and fog, or maybe it's smog. It isn't possible to buy Indian rupees until arriving in India and I feel uncomfortable not having local currency in my purse. I'm very relieved to be met by a lady Tour Representative and have this concern resolved right away. I'm able to change my GBP for Indian rupees and from a counter in the 'Arrivals' area I can buy an Indian SIM for my spare phone. All good so far.

The taxi ride to the hotel, driven by the Lady Rep (her name I've forgotten) is extraordinary. There appears to be a lack of any road rules. The roads leading out of the airport are wide with several lanes of traffic all weaving in and out alarming close to each other, and there's no adherence to lines in the road at all. It sounds as though every car driver has their hand on the horn so it's incredibly noisy. I notice the majority of cars are white, which I later learned is because you can't see scratch marks on white so easily.

Each time our car stops at traffic lights, vendors and peddlers of all ages tap at the windows wanting to sell their wares. Some are skinny children, running in and out of the vehicles, selling goods or begging for money. It's now dark and it looks very dangerous, I wonder how many children get squashed in the chaos of traffic. It's heart-rending seeing their little faces appear at the car windows.

It's a long, slow ride to my hotel where I have to leave the taxi hastily, clutching all my clobber, big backpack, small front pack and ukulele bag, because the narrow road is stuffed with traffic of all kinds and there's nowhere for the taxi to stop. I feel sorry that I don't have any change to tip my driver.

'Hotel Perfect' isn't. It's rather shabby. The location is Karol Bagh, a district outside central Delhi. I check in, but before unpacking and before the evening gets too late, I'm keen to go out onto the street and see where I am.

It's an immediate assault on the senses. I've never experienced anything like this. The noise, the smells, the traffic. I don't move from the spot, just stand and watch as cars, motorbikes, pedal bikes, tuk-tuks, people, children and dogs, all mix together on the road, weaving in and out of each other accompanied by a continuous honking of horns.

I'm uncertain which way to walk or even how to negotiate a path through the chaos. The roads are uneven and although there are occasional footpaths, they're packed with sellers and peddlers of every kind.

Indians are cooking and preparing food at the side of the road and people are standing about eating or chatting. It's mayhem, but in a rather endearing way.

Undeniably fascinating and exhilarating, I don't want to stay out for long, I'm approached by every vendor to purchase their wares. I buy a bottle of water covered in road dust from a tiny street kiosk, and some peanuts from a man roasting peanuts over a fire. It's difficult to make the peanut seller understand that I only want a small quantity, so I'm grateful when a nearby English-speaking Indian, explains on my behalf. He's keen to talk to me and tells me that he's a teacher and I enjoy our conversation, but then he offers to show me around and I politely decline saying I'm meeting some friends. I'm not sure if it's okay to eat the peanuts because the seller scooped them up with his hand and put them in a bag made from old newspaper, but I'm hungry and eat them anyway.

I retreat to the hotel and my room. The water in the shower has one temperature - cold. My bedroom is roadside and the din is incredible. Noise from car horns continues until the early hours at which time the many stray dogs take over with a cacophony of barking and howling. I can tell India will be entertaining.

## 11th December

Asking about hot water at the reception desk I'm told that if I let them know when I want to bathe they will turn the boiler on.

Breakfast is on the quaint roof terrace and I'm surprised how chilly the morning air feels. I notice that I'm the only female here among about twenty Indian men who all seem know each other, they're standing around chatting and I wonder if they meet here for breakfast before going to work. I can see they're looking at me and I try not to feel awkward. The outside noise of traffic and hooting horns continues and to my ears it's very invasive, but I presume the locals are immune to it. Breakfast of banana, toast, jam and coffee costs the equivalent of £1.50 and I learn my first Indian word from the waiter, 'dhanya baad' which means 'thank you'.

I spend the morning sorting out techy stuff with some success, my new mobile SIM is connected, but I can't get my laptop to connect with the hotel Wi-Fi. I give up and go back up to the roof terrace for lunch. I have no idea what the dishes are on the menu, so take pot luck and order Aloo dum Bhojpuri, which turns out to be potatoes in a delicious spicy gravy, along with Palak Paneer which is bright green and sloppy. It's pureed spinach and I make a mental note not to order this again.

In the afternoon I'm keen to explore the surrounding area, but getting lost is a concern for me, so I walk down the street being super observant, then retrace my steps so I can be sure of finding the way back again. I do this with each street I walk onto and whilst it makes progress slow, since I have no agenda it really doesn't matter.

Everything I see is fascinating, the little shops and stalls and the people milling about. I notice how petite many of the Indians are, not only in height, but with very slender bodies. There's an old lady picking litter up from the street and putting it into a large cloth sack she's fashioned around her back; she looks far too old to be working. There are shoe-shine boys everywhere and I wonder how much trade they get since most people are wearing sandals or trainers. The streets are shockingly dirty, there's rubbish everywhere and I have to look

5

down constantly to watch where I'm treading. I've never been anywhere this messy before.

At a stall down a narrow side street an Indian man is passing sugar beet through a huge wringer. He winds it through the wringer several times collecting the juice, which he strains into glasses. He invites me to try some and it tastes delicious, very sweet, with a sort of vanilla flavour.

I realise I'm going to need comfortable walking sandals and with so many shoe shops here this seems like a good time to buy some. As soon as I show interest, every shop keeper is keen to sell me a pair. Eventually I try some on that I quite like. The sales assistant is a young boy, he asks me where I'm from and how old I am. The sandals cost me 250 rupees, less than £3.00.

## 12th December

## 15 Day Delhi to Nepal Tour

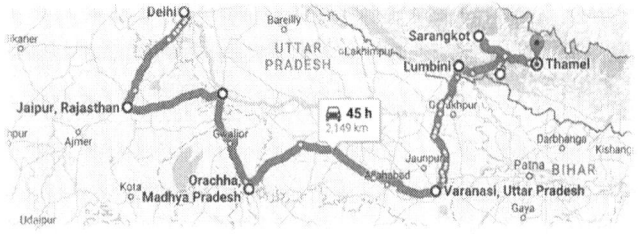

## Day 1

Shona from Scotland has arrived at the hotel, she's part of the tour group and will be my roommate for the next 15 days. She looks very suntanned and tells me she's been on a yoga retreat in Kerala in the south of India. I can tell we'll get along well. Later we meet our fellow travellers; Bruno, proud to tell us he's part Portuguese and part English; Patrick and Carmen from Germany, not a couple, just friends; Barney, a young music teacher from the U.K. and now living in Kuala Lumpar; Janine, South African, living in Australia and five months pregnant, and two friends, Amy and Jodie, also from Australia. Our tour guide is called Aura, he's from Delhi and I like him immediately. Aura gives us a briefing and it all sounds very exciting.

In the late afternoon Aura orders taxis to take us into New Delhi. We pull up outside The Rashtrapati Bhavan (The President's House), but we don't go in, only look through the tall, ornate, wrought iron gates. Afterwards we drive to India Gate and on to Connaught Place, a central area in busy Delhi with major roads leading off. We have some time to explore but having spotted a Starbucks my desire for a decent coffee over-rides my desire to look around. I'm not alone, some of the others come in with me.

Outside again, waiting for the taxi to return I'm amused watching a small boy, maybe six or seven years old begging, he's pretending to have only one arm, the other he tucks behind his back. Aura tells me that children here have free schooling and free school meals, there's no need for them to beg. I'm already impressed with Barney who not only sampled some local street food but walked the complete circuit of Connaught Place while we were drinking coffee.

We're all keen to get cash from the ATMs but each one we try refuses to spew out any money, presumably they're all empty.

## 13th December

### Day 2

A private bus drives us 280 kms to Jaipur and the drive is fascinating. I notice how beautifully decorated the lorries on the roads are, hand painted in bright colours. There are cows randomly wandering about, tumble down properties, or houses that don't look finished. There are 'one hump' camels carrying loads of logs, men washing at the side of a dual carriageway, people sitting in the dirt and the dust, a man pushing a motor bike; all very different sights from England.

Aura tells us there are three things a good Indian driver needs: a good horn, good brakes and good luck!

Driving into the city of Jaipur along a narrow, dusty street, I suddenly see ahead of us a huge elephant slowly walking towards our vehicle, his face painted in bright colours. It's such a surprising sight and I think *"only in India!"*.

Our hotel, Bissau Palace in Jaipur is Colonial style. It's beautiful and I love it. Jaipur is known as the 'Land of the Kings' and also called the Pink City because of the colour of the stones used in construction. In 1876, the Prince of Wales and Queen Victoria visited India on a tour and because pink denotes the colour of hospitality, Maharaja Ram Singh of Jaipur painted the whole city pink to welcome the guests. Imagine painting a whole city pink!

Our group go out to explore on 'cyclos', three-wheel bikes with a driver pedalling at the front and a passenger seat in the back wide enough to take three people. Poor guy pedalling. It's great fun, the colour, the noise, the people.

We walk around the streets, then up some steps onto

a roof where we're able to see the streets below. I notice there are children running along the top of the buildings in the distance, they're flying kites and it makes me think of the book 'The Kite Runner'. I notice tangles of kite strings on the ground and torn kites hanging in the trees, caught up in the branches. Kite flying must be very popular here.

Stopping at a street vendor, I have my first taste of Lassi, a beautiful yoghurt and sugar drink served in a small clay pot, which we throw and smash when we've finished. It seems a waste but much nicer than plastic cups. We also have the chance to drink Indian tea called Chai which is milky with spices and incredibly sweet. Indian portions are very small compared to U.K., which probably explains why many Indians remain skinny.

We're all relieved that the ATMs in Jaipur work so we can get cash and I take out 10,000 rupees, which is around £100. The wad of notes makes my purse very fat. It's hard to get my head around these high numbers.

## 14th December

### Day 3

We're out early to see the unusual Pink Palace (Hawa Mahal), also called the Palace of Breeze. It's the tallest building in the world without a foundation and remains standing because of its curved shape. We don't go in, just admire the outside. Then we pile into a couple of jeeps and have a fun ride, about 11 kms, through the cluttered, narrow streets, to see the incredibly beautiful Amber Fort.

Built out of marble and red sandstone in 1592 by Raja Mann Singh I, it's a real feast for the eyes, everything is on a grand scale. With the blue skies, the shimmering heat and the surrounding scenery everything looks very Indian and awesome. Our guide for the fort is Mr Vickers, he's proud to tell us he's been a guide here since 1959. I notice elephants are used to give rides to tourists and I feel sad for them, but I can't deny they make the place look amazing.

The last 'Royal' to live in the Palace was Gayatri Devi, listed by Vogue as *"one of the most beautiful women in the world, a charismatic woman with massive influence".* I've made a note of the name of her book of memoirs called 'A Princess Remembers', I'll get a copy when I can.

Afterwards we have 'free time' to explore. The area is full of stall holders selling touristy stuff, but also clothes, food and spices and everything looks interesting and colourful. Although the streets are filthy and at times smelly, I'm aware that I've already become fairly immune to the rubbish, noisy traffic etc.

In one of the shops I try on a typical Indian outfit; a tunic with matching trousers and scarf, all made from silk and cotton. I don't love it enough to buy it, even though the cost is only 3,500 rupees which sounds a lot, but in U.K. currency is less than £35.00.

Barney is keen to visit Jantar Mantar, an astronomical observation site built in the early 18th century (Mughal period) and a UNESCO World Heritage Centre. Shona and I are willing to go along too. My enthusiasm for scientific, geometric shaped structures "designed for the observation of astronomical positions with the naked eye" is limited, but with the blue sky as a backdrop, the white sculptures look beautiful.

Jaipur is famous for jewellery and I shop with Barney to help him choose a pendant for his girlfriend. I'm very touched by the care he takes to choose the right piece for her. There are postcards on sale here and

I buy one to send to Ben.

On our drive back to the hotel we stop to take pictures of a beautiful 'floating' palace on a lake which, strangely and sadly, is now abandoned. On the street a young boy does a magic trick for us, and I'm captivated by the quality of his skillful presentation. Naturally we all give him some money.

In the evening, Aura takes us to see a Bollywood film just for the experience. It's fun, but not having a clue what is being said by the actors, I don't mind at all when at the interval he suggests we don't need to stay for the second half.

I know I won't have much communication with Ben while I'm away, he has no interest in technology and manages very well without it. He has a basic mobile but doesn't care to use it much. Before I left, his sister kindly agreed to be our 'go between' via email. When I get back to the hotel I'm super-excited to find that I've received a short email from Ben, via his sister. Hooray, the line of communication is open! Shona wants to know why I'm grinning from ear to ear.

## 15th December

### Day 4

We're driving 240 kms, about six hours, to Agra and again I love the journey, the sights are fascinating and so different. Frustratingly, I find it hard to keep my eyes open, the bus makes me want to doze but I don't want to miss anything.

Our first stop is at Agra Fort, also known as the Red Fort, it's another UNESCO World Heritage Site. Built by Akbar and started in 1572, we're told it took 1,444,000 men 8 years to build! It's built mostly of red sandstone with marble added later and was originally inlaid with hundreds of precious stones. A shame they're no longer there, it must have looked stunning. It's actually a walled city and the defence system is so innovative and incredible that even I am fascinated, not to mention the remarkable water cooling and central heating system they created.

As we wander around the Red Fort we can see the Taj Mahal in the distance, we're going there next. I think it's ironic that the Emperor Shah Jahan, who had the Taj Mahal built in memory of his beloved wife, was imprisoned in the Red Fort for eight years by his son.

We're super-excited to visit the iconic Taj Mahal. Aura times our arrival near the end of the afternoon so we can catch the sunset. When we arrive, there are massive queues to get in and I'm very glad we're in an organised tour group which means we can walk straight through.

Seeing the Taj Mahal for the first time takes my breath away. Even the large number of people milling about doesn't detract from the awesome feeling it gives me. It's incredibly beautiful. I had always thought it was a palace so I'm surprised to learn that it's in fact a tomb, built as an expression of Shah Jahan's love for his wife. It took 22,000 people 17 years to complete.

I want to share the moment and write a text message to Ben telling him I'm standing in front of the Taj Mahal. It will 'send' when I get back on line.

The day couldn't be kinder, the sky is the bluest of blues making the beautiful creamy white of the Taj Mahal stand out. We have time to soak up the atmosphere and I'm happy to sit for ages gazing at the gorgeousness of the place, I can't quite believe I'm really here having this experience.

I spend time with Shona, Barney, Janine and the Aussie girls and we decide to get our photo taken as a group, with the Taj Mahal in the background. We laugh a lot because it takes three requests before we succeed in getting the photo we want. People are willing to take the picture but don't seem to understand that we want the Taj in the photo too. I'm especially amused when two families ask if they can have their photo taken *with* us and of course we agree.

By the time we're ready to leave, the sun is going down and the colour of the Taj Mahal changes to a warm, yellowy cream. I feel very privileged to have seen this iconic building.

At dinner this evening we sit outside the restaurant and we're entertained by some musicians. Barney teaches music at a school in Kuala Lumpar and Aura asks the musicians if he can have a go at playing the sita. The black lentil dish I ordered called Dal Makhani leaves my mouth on fire. I soothe it with a glass of the very decent red wine Aura has introduced me to, called Sula, a Cabernet Sauvignon and my first glass of red wine since leaving England.

After dinner I have my first experience of an Indian train station. We're taking an overnight train to Orchha. Porters greet us the instant we step down from the tuktuks and offer to carry our bags. I notice that even though some of the cases have wheels the porters still carry them on their heads. Our German friend has a suitcase the size of a small car, so I'm especially sorry for the porter carrying that one.

We're lucky we don't have to wait too long for our train, Aura tells us that it isn't uncommon for trains to be delayed by several hours (a piece of info I tuck away for future reference).

Climbing on board we're like excited schoolchildren, eager to see where we'll be sleeping. There are narrow 'pull down' beds with sheets and pillows, some you have to climb up to, and the carriages are open, so there isn't any privacy. The train seems okay, it's old, but fairly clean and I go to check out the toilets. There's an Indian squat style toilet on one side of the corridor and a western style one on the other, they're smelly and wet and standing in the tiny cubicle to clean my teeth over the washbasin isn't nice. Jodie declares that she won't be going to the toilet until we arrive in Orchha!

## 16th December

### Day 5

A very welcome breakfast comes early, omelette, toast with jam and lime water all served on the train before we reached Orchha. I'm not comfortable going too long without food so I'm always happy when a meal arrives.

The ride from Jhansi Station to Orchha and our hotel, The Orchha Resort, is just twenty minutes. It's a spacious and oddly beautiful hotel and appears out of place in this small medieval town which doesn't seem all touristy. From the hotel grounds, we can see the Betwa River and Shona and I sit in the garden and treat ourselves to gin and tonic, which feels like luxury.

In the late afternoon, we walk to some massive, wonderful old monuments. They're huge cenotaphs, strange and very atmospheric, an example of centuries old buildings on a very grand scale. We meander about exploring and my attention is taken by the many stray dogs, the river and the sky changing colour with the sunset. Aura adds to the surreal atmosphere by telling us that in this area of India, traditionally people didn't bury their dead but hung them from the monuments and allow the vultures to feed from the bodies. A gruesome thought.

Good fortune! We're told that this evening Orccha is

celebrating the annual festival of the wedding of Lord Ram. We walk a short distance into the town to join in the celebrations. Like everywhere I've seen in India so far, the place looks poor and messy but there's a fun, carnival atmosphere here with families milling about and vendors selling food and tat from wooden stalls.

Shona and I are standing at the side of the road waiting for a procession to come by and we become aware that we're surrounded by men. They're all standing looking at us. Shona looks at me questioningly and we start laughing. More men come. They don't say anything, just stare. Shona is also blonde so we presume they're looking at us because we're European. Then Aura arrives and we ask him *"why are they looking at us?"* Aura shrugs and laughs, then asks the crowd and one boy answers saying *"we can't go to other countries, so we like seeing people from other countries when they come here"*. It's a sweet reply. Anyway, Aura shoos the men away and we walk on.

We make our way to the town square where the main ceremony is about to take place. There's a large medieval style building as a back drop and hundreds of people are sitting or standing and milling about. An organiser comes up to Aura and to our amusement invites us to stand in an excellent high viewing place.

There's live music with drums and Aura persuades Shona to dance with him in front of the crowd. The crowd love it and Shona, wearing flowing culottes is dressed perfectly for the part. This causes a reporter with a video camera to come and interview Aura and the rest of us, they want to know where we are from and what we think of Orchha and their festival. The incident causes us much hilarity.

We have a long wait for the enactment of the wedding ceremony, then the bride and groom appear wearing masks and wigs. This is followed by a procession with men twirling big colourful umbrellas made from masses of real flowers. The procession moves slowly surrounded by a vast scrum of people and the area becomes so packed I feel concerned about getting lost or crushed.

A group of young men are dancing to some drums and as we stop to watch them they really turn it up and gyrate harder and faster, showing off their masculinity. A man in the street is making two horses dance, it looks cruel and I don't want to watch.

Walking back to our hotel in the dark, we realise the dogs have formed a pack and are following us. This makes me feel pretty tense and although I've seen dogs everywhere in India so far, this is the first time I've felt uncomfortable about them.

## 17th December

### Day 6

Aura greets us at breakfast with a copy of the local newspaper; there are pictures of us taken at last night's festivities on the front cover!

Today we explore more cenotaphs. They're called Chhatris Cenotaphs and there are fifteen of them in Orchha, each constructed over the funeral pyre of the rulers of the place, after the final rites were done. The architecture is amazing, and just as yesterday, the place has a wonderful, dreamy atmosphere. We're allowed to climb up high inside the cenotaphs and walk along corridors and between arches and experience the panoramic vista.

Outside I take a photo of an elderly Indian wearing gorgeous orange and red colours, he has a kitten on his head. His hand comes out for money at the same time as

I bring my camera out. I'm learning to always keep small change in my pocket for these occasions.

Aura invites us to take a small boat to go rafting on the River Betwa and a few of us take up the opportunity. The water is not exactly rapids but still quite fast flowing with large rocks here and there. We're each given a paddle. After paddling downstream for a while, Aura says we can take a swim. At first, I think he's joking, but when I realise he means it, I don't waste any time going over the side of the boat. I still have my clothes on but I'm only wearing a cotton skirt and blouse which will dry quickly. Janine is the only other one to join me. The water is cool but not freezing and with our life jackets on we bob about happily, much to the amusement of the others still in the boat.

Another new experience this evening. We visit a cooking class run by the Ranji. She gives lessons in her home and I'm fascinating to see inside an Indian home. It's very simple, not much furniture, and although old, the faded colours on the walls of red, ochre and aqua blue give the place a homely feel. There's a wonderful smell of spices.

Ranji demonstrates how she cooks several dishes inviting us to have a go as well. I'm fascinated when she roasts an eggplant over an open flame. From time to time children and people presumably from Ranji's family pop into the room, probably to see who we are.

When the cooking is over, our journey continues to the station with another overnight train, this time to Varanasi, a journey of 10 hours.

18th December

Day 7

We've arrived in Varanasi and it isn't at all how I thought it would be. I've heard it called a 'Spiritual City' and expected it to be a tranquil place but it's the opposite. It's the noisiest, most chaotic place I've ever been to.

Our group follow Aura through the narrow, dirty streets of Varanasi and I'm walking with childlike wide eyes full of wonder, everything is amazing and different. I watch a man standing on the pavement ironing sheets using a large heavy-looking iron that's heated with coals inside. Above our heads there are tangles of spaghetti-like electricity cables and wires, wandering from property to property. How anyone ever deciphers which wires belong to what defies the imagination and it looks like a serious health hazard.

Our accommodation is at the City Hotel and after checking in, Aura arranges for tuk-tuks to take us to The Ghats on the Ganges.

What a sight is laid out before me! Walking down the steps and seeing the Ganges for the first time and all the 'life' that is happening here, is extraordinary. A lady approaches us selling little cups made from leaves and decorated with flowers, each one has a candle inside and Aura buys several. A child holds out his hand asking for money, there are dogs and cows and goats milling about. An old bearded Indian leaning on a crutch hobbles along. Colourful boats bob about on the water. People are strolling about along the shore, some paddling in the river. Now I start to feel the spiritual side of Varanasi.

We get into a smallish wooden boat with a motor

and pootle along the river. People are bathing in the water, which doesn't bear thinking about, knowing that bodies are cremated daily at the water's edge, heaven knows what a health hazard it must be. Indians believe the Ganges to be sacred and hopefully with that belief in mind they are protected.

We stay on the river and watch the sun setting over the Ganges and when it becomes dark we light the candles with decorative leaves made into little 'boats' and with each one we make a wish and float them on the river. There are numerous boats and hundreds of pretty lighted candles bobbing about on the water and the Ganges looks wonderfully magical.

Along the banks of the Ganges cremations are happening. It's a surreal scene. Families are queuing up to cremate their dead. They take the body to the edge of the water and wash it, then place it on a pyre of wood. The more the family are prepared to pay, the more wood will go on the pyre. Columns of smoke rise into the night sky from the funeral pyres.

There are religious ceremonies taking place along the banks of the river with spiritual people dressed in orange and red, chanting prayers and waving incense. The lights and candles make the whole scene very mystical and there are many boats of all kinds moored alongside, watching the rituals. It reminds me of Henley Regatta, Indian style. Everyone, whether tourist or pilgrim is there to have an enjoyable time and it feels friendly and fun. This is such a good experience I don't want it to end.

Leaving our boat, we take tuk-tuks to a restaurant for dinner. This one is 'posh', our most expensive yet, the meal costs me the equivalent of £8 including wine. Most of our meals so far have been in very modest restaurants and although the food has been excellent everywhere, it feels nice to dine in relative luxury and we even have white table linen.

## 19th December

### Day 8

A very early start and I don't mind a bit because we take another boat on the Ganges, this time to see the sunrise.

Being a rowing boat, it's quiet and the whole scene is again unreal. There's a sort of mist, or maybe hanging smoke from the funerals, people are bathing in the murky water, the atmosphere is calm and peaceful.

On the other side of the river there is flat land and the horizon; no buildings, no people. In complete contrast, the side by the town where we are, is becoming busy; men are doing the washing (yes, men!), there are holy men walking about, children selling their wares, dogs, goats and cows meandering and I can hear the sound of chanting and bells ringing.

Watching the sun rise up through the haze across the river is a photographer's dream and we all take lots of pictures.

After the boat ride, some of us choose to stay in Varanasi to soak up more of the amazing atmosphere and we go back to the Ghats and saunter along by the river. I'm very happy to be here.

We see 'goats in coats' a phrase Shona comes up with; literally, goats are wearing sweatshirts or jumpers. I notice, not for the first time, that men urinate anywhere they feel like it. A young boy with a tiny baby fast asleep in his arms, asks for money. Being obviously foreign we are constant 'targets'.

Our walk takes us to the funeral area where a body lies by the water wrapped in gold and orange fabric. Some people, presumably relatives, are laying wood for the fire. An old Indian who's dressed like a religious man, approaches us and explains what the rituals mean. It feels odd standing around the ashes and pyres where bodies have been burnt only a few hours before. I don't want to breathe in the air, I feel like I'll be inhaling the ashes of dead people. We decide to move on and the Indian asks us for money. He's looking at the two young Aussie girls and they look at me to see if we should pay him. I shake my head 'no' and when we don't offer him money he becomes intimidating, saying to the girls *"if you want good karma you need to pay"*. I feel protective of them and put my arm out to move them on and keep him away, clearly, he's not as 'spiritual' as he appears.

In the afternoon, Aura takes us to a silk factory tucked away in one of the tiny side streets. The alleyways here are so narrow that when a motor bike comes, we have to squish up against the wall to let it pass. Watching our feet as we walk is essential, there are uneven paving slabs, cow and dog pooh, blotches of red spit from betel chewing Indians, and kite strings tangle themselves up in your shoes.

Inside the factory, I learn that silk fabrics can take two and a half months to make, they are so intricate. We watch looms being operated in a cramped and very noisy room where it's usual for the workers to go deaf from the constant din, and we see women and girls hand sewing tiny beads onto the beautiful silk.

We're invited inside the shop where white mattresses have been laid on the floor and we sit on them. It's time for the sales pitch and the owner unwraps silk shawls and bedcovers. As he unfolds each one he lavishly wafts it into the air with a flourish, showing off the most stunningly beautiful fabrics I've ever seen. He tells us that there are five levels of quality in silks and invites us to tell the difference with his samples. A gorgeously sumptuous collage bed spread captures my heart but at an equivalent price of £400 it's too extravagant and instead I buy a coral pink silk shawl.

Our dinner this evening is in a simple restaurant and we are fascinated to learn that on a nearby table there's an arranged marriage meeting going on between the betrothed and their families. I'm curious and surreptitiously watch the interaction between the girl and boy.

Aura advises us to take 10,000 rupees out of the ATM ready for Nepal tomorrow. The money comes from the machine as 1,000 rupee notes which he changes to 100 rupee notes for us, a 1,000 note is too big for Nepalese to accept. My purse is fit to burst with a massive wad of notes.

I'm in bed and I can't sleep. Midnight passes which is unfortunate because we have to be up at 3.45 am to catch another train.

## 20th December

### Day 9

The train to Gorakhpur takes about 14 hrs. Arriving at the station we're met by a small lilac-coloured bus which drives us for four hours to the border of Nepal.

I have butterflies in my tummy in case something goes wrong at the crossing, but I'm not the only one. Shona says *"everything's always alright in the end and if it isn't alright, it isn't the end"*. I love that quote. She tells me she heard it in a film about India called 'The Best Exotic Marigold Hotel'. Now I'm feeling excited, this is my first border crossing into another country on my trip.

Aura steers us through a confusing mass of people

into a basic little office and after a short wait and some stamping of passports, we're all happily allowed into Nepal.

Another hour and a half bus ride to the hotel and I notice the scenery change. My first impression is the houses are better quality, pretty colours and it seems quieter. On route we stop for a while at Lumbini, the birthplace of Buddha and also the place where he gave his first sermon. Lumbini is now a UNESCO World Heritage site.

Arriving at our hotel, we're surprised and amused to see a decorated Christmas tree in reception, presumably for the benefit of tourists since Nepalese are generally Hindu or Buddhist.

## 21st December

### Day 10

Another early start at 5.30 am but it isn't a problem, Shona and I have got this down to a fine art, packing before bed, it takes just 20 mins to wake, clean teeth, dress and leave the room.

We drive many miles again today in the small purple bus but I don't mind at all, there are so many interesting sights along the way. Our next destination, is Barauli Community Homestay in Tharu Village, Nawalparasi.

On arrival, we're welcomed by some very smiley local women who decorate us with flower garlands and a deka which is a small red mark dabbed onto our forehead.

For accommodation we share simple wooden cabins and in the afternoon sun the place is charming though I have a feeling it may be very cold tonight.

Our group is given bicycles and we pedal out in the early evening to explore our surroundings. Tharu

Village is the sweetest, quaintest village ever, like something from a story book. The small houses are painted in pastel colours and there are hens, cows and goats by old-fashioned hay stacks, two doves are cooing beside their wooden dovecote. All very picturesque and slightly unreal.

Cycling along the track and past fields, we come out to an open space and in front of us is the large Narayani River. The sun is low in the sky bathing the whole scene in a soft, hazy light and there's a small wooden boat on the river, with two people in it, fishing. Aura has brought flasks of hot chai with him and we stand watching the sun setting over the lake, bathing everything in a golden glow.

Dinner that evening is at the homestay and we're entertained with a demonstration of local dancing. Afterwards we drink mojitos and play our own music around the camp fire, I'm persuaded to play a couple of tunes on the ukulele, a challenge for me in the dark and without music.

## 22nd December

### Day 11

The morning temperature is very cold so I'm happy that there's hot porridge for breakfast.

Afterwards, a walk around the village takes us to a small school and we're allowed to look inside and meet some of the children working in their classrooms. I notice their little pairs of shoes are neatly placed outside, by the classroom door. The children are sitting on wooden benches and they're very smiley and friendly. The young, female teacher of the class is holding her baby, she tells us she's allowed to bring her baby in to class with her while she teaches.

In the afternoon, jeeps arrive to take us to Chitwan National Park which covers an area of 1000 sq. kms. We drive and bump our way through the jungle for about four hours looking out for animals, it's fun and I love feeling the hot sun again. We see a rhino, some deer and vultures and keep vigilant looking for the elusive tiger. On the drive back, another pretty, hazy, sun is setting over the river, but once the sun has gone the temperature takes a dramatic dive.

## 23rd December

### Day 12

Another early start and a long drive to reach Pokhara in Nepal.

This is a busy, touristy place, full of keen trekkers because lots of people come here to do the famous Annapurna trek. The main street is full of restaurants and pubs and is decorated for Christmas. Pokhara is built by the Phewa Lake which looks beautiful with mountains behind and quaint, coloured boats bobbing on the water.

We have free time to explore Pokhara and I go with Barney down to the lake where we buy a drink and sit for a while chatting. I'm glad to have the opportunity of getting to know him better.

## 24th December

### Day 13

Today is Christmas Eve and it starts with a short bus ride on roads that wind round hairpin bends, up very high. We're here to watch the sun come up over the Himalayas and we're not disappointed.

Gradually the darkness changes and we can make

out the soft layers of hills and mountains in the distance, first in black and grey, then the light changes to golds and oranges as the sun appears and we can see the beautiful Himalayas. We're lucky again to have a clear day and a glorious sunrise.

My tour is organised by G Adventures who support a project called Sisterhood of Survivors and this afternoon we're visiting the project. In Nepal, there's a lot of exploitation and trafficking of women and this worthy project, set up in 2008, is survivor-led and helps women get back into society and encourages them to take up careers.

Some of the ladies demonstrate how to make momos, a very popular food in Nepal. They're little steamed dumplings and can have different fillings and a variety of spicy sauces. We have fun moulding the dough into parcels, but the best part is eating them.

This is turning out to be an exciting day because five of us have chosen to paraglide. We drive back up the mountain, not a pleasant ride because travelling on the winding roads makes me feel nauseous. At the top I'm desperate for a toilet, but there isn't one. I'm introduced to my 'pilot' and kitted out with helmet and harness, my pilot is attached behind me.

The wind today, apparently, is not good for paragliding. We're standing high up on a hill and I'm given instructions to run to the edge when told to do so, but if the pilot changes his mind and yells 'stop', I have to run backwards! Really!! After three attempts at this, with intervals in between waiting for the right conditions, I'm becoming a nervous wreck. Finally, we take off and then I wish we haven't because motion sickness kicks in fast. The exhilarating experience of 'sitting' in the air, with a landscape of fields, the awesome Himalayas and a vast lake below isn't lost on me, but I only just manage to 'hold it together' before my pilot lands us safely on the ground. I feel as weak as a kitten.

It's surreal to think that this is Christmas Eve and I'm here in Nepal. We walk along Pokhara's main street in the evening and a jolly Father Christmas stops to shake hands with us, the street is celebrating.

The temperature is cold in Nepal and we've found it odd that there's so little heating in the shops and restaurants, even the shop keepers and restaurant workers are wearing coats and hats. The reason becomes clear when we learn that Nepal is currently in dispute with India, resulting in a serious shortage of bottled gas which they can't get across the border, and is predominantly used for cooking and heating. This means that menus are restricted because the chefs have to cook over open fires.

Fortunately, I've recovered from this morning enough to enjoy dinner at the 'Busy Bees' pub.

## 25th December

### Day 14

Christmas Day! We have a seven-hour drive from Pokhara to Kathmandu and on the bus Shona hands us each a bar of chocolate and for me she has a gift of a leather key fob she'd bought in Pokhara. I'm touched by her thoughtfulness.

We stop along the way to visit Swayambhunath, the Monkey Temple, which stands on a hill with a height of 1300 metres. It's another glorious blue-sky day and the clean white temple with its golden tower stands out beautifully. Surrounded by brightly coloured prayer flags, the whole scene looks gorgeous. Cheeky monkeys are everywhere, scampering about and clambering over walls, they're very entertaining. We can see far and wide from up here and I'm surprised to learn that the vast, built up area spread out in the distance is Kathmandu. I had always imagined Kathmandu as a small place in the hills.

We arrive in Thamel, the tour's final destination and book into Khangsar Guest House. For lunch we find a restaurant that serves pizzas and because today is Christmas Day I treat myself to a Marguerita and think how lucky I am that I'm not on my own.

I'm ecstatic! I've had a Happy Christmas message from Ben, the first text I've received from him since setting out. I've read it at least six times.

## 26th December

### Day 15

Aura has offered us the opportunity to take a special flight over Mt Everest and Shona, Barney and I decide to do it. It's an expensive option, but I can't resist the chance to fly over the magnificent Himalayas and see Everest. On board the small 'plane we're handed a glass of champagne, there are about a dozen of us inside and everyone's excited. The sheer magnitude of the mountain range is awesome and there it is, the iconic Mount Everest! An American woman in front of me is so emotional she's sobbing and says *"this is a dream come true for me"*.

And this is where the tour ends. I'm going to stay on in Thamel for a few days and happily so are Shona and the Aussie girls, so we've agreed we'll meet up. Saying goodbye to the others is hard, especially Aura who has been a genuinely excellent guide, knowledgeable and thoughtful.

# Nepal, on My Own

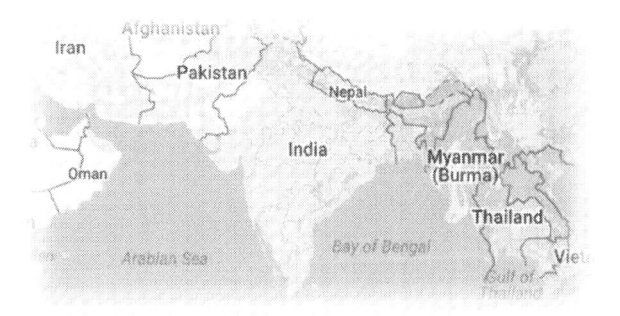

I consider staying at the same hostel that the Aussie girls are using, but the lack of gas in Nepal means there isn't any hot water or heating and it's cold here, especially at night, so I wimp out and book myself into the famous Kathmandu Guest House, recommended to me by a friend from back home. The price is a comfortable £25 a night.

Situated right in the heart of bustling, touristy Thamel, the guest house is an oasis of calm. A beautiful building, painted yellow and freshly decorated having recently undergone repairs from earthquake damage. My room is pleasant, on the ground floor with a door that opens out onto the attractive courtyard, but it's cold and I really wish I had a hot water bottle with me.

## 27th December

There's an excellent coffee shop in Thamel called 'Himalayan Java' which is like a trendy western coffee place, about a fifteen-minute walk from the Guest House and I settle in here with my laptop to do some research.

Since I started travelling I've been unable to connect my computer to the Internet which has been upsetting for me. Bruno from our group has shown me a 'backdoor' way to do it, by connecting my mobile to Wi-Fi and putting the same co-ordinates into my laptop. It's a nuisance, but at least I can connect. Without Bruno's knowledge my computer would be useless and I marvel how lucky I am that he's been able to help.

I've been given a recommendation by a friend back home to contact his friend Sanjay when I reach Nepal, so I give him a call. By amazing coincidence, he has a tour office just a few roads from The Kathmandu Guest House. Thamel is a maze of narrow streets and alleys and in the busy confusion of shops, eating places and advertising signs it takes me several attempts to find him. His tour company is called Drift Nepal and I instantly like Sanjay. I'm delighted to learn that he can arrange a trek for me.

Shona, Amy and Jodie are all staying nearby and we meet up in the evening for dinner. Afterwards I invite them back to The Kathmandu for coffee which is served in the outside courtyard. It's dark now and cold and there's a very inviting firepit alight so we choose a table next to it. Our coffee arrives and so do five members of staff, who all stand around the fire, blocking the heat from us, watching us and listening to our conversation. They're standing really close and don't seem to think it odd. I wonder if people living in such crowded places have a different spatial awareness.

## 28th December

I love the freedom of being on my own and choosing what I do and where I go. Walking around the little streets of Thamel is fun, there's continuous noise, different smells, people, bustle and traffic, mostly in the form of tuk-tuks, motor bikes and cycles. I'm constantly responding to people, calling out *'namaste'*, a lovely old Sanskrit word with a literal meaning of *"I bow to you"*, and used as a greeting or thank you.

A young man walks alongside me and asks *"where are you from?"* I tell him I'm from England and he says he likes talking to English people because he wants to improve his language skills. This isn't the first time this has happened and I'm never quite sure if they're leading up to sell me something, I'm willing to chat for a short while then make my excuse to move on.

There's an incident in a tiny street; a cycle rickshaw is turning into a narrow lane and his wheel catches a fruit seller's basket tipping the fruit into the road, a shout from the seller goes out and everyone turns to look, the bystanders are clearly amused and the situation is quickly resolved. In such a crowded place it amazes me that there aren't more accidents and scraps.

## 29th December

I've lost my spectacles! I can't believe I've been so stupid. I thought I had a good 'system' to ensure I don't lose stuff. Everything has a place in my rucksack, it has so many pockets I realised early on that if I didn't get organised I'd be constantly rummaging around trying to find things. Well my system clearly hasn't worked. I check again. I've just come back to 'The Kathmandu' after a couple of hours shopping for warmer clothes and accessing the ATM.

Before I left England, I had to change my glasses and I made the expensive decision to buy varifocals this time so I could avoid travelling with reading glasses and distance glasses. My vanity wouldn't let me purchase a cheap pair, I reasoned that since I'd be wearing the varifocals more frequently it was worth paying more to have a pair I felt good in.

The Reception Desk haven't had any specs handed in so I retrace my footsteps of the last couple of hours, going in and out of shops and finally to the bank. I check my backpack again, several times. They've gone. I feel anxious. Will I manage without them?

## 30th December

## Four day Trek Shivapuri Nagarjun N. P.

### Day 1

Early this morning I'm meeting Ram Kumar Agar who will be my guide for the next four days on a trek through Shivapuri National Park. The trek is exactly what I'd hoped for and more perfect because Ram is a friend of Sanjay's and I feel confident that I can trust him.

I've packed my small rucksack with essentials and Sanjay tells me I can leave my big pack with my laptop in it, in his office. I have some trepidation about this, his office is ground level and the front door is left open, but he assures me it'll be fine.

The first task Ram and I have is to negotiate a price for a taxi to take us to the start of the walk. As well as a shortage of gas there's also a shortage of petrol causing taxi costs to escalate. Ram seems satisfied when we negotiate with a driver who settles on a fare of 1200 rupees, about £8.

Half an hour later, we're in a tiny village with a few dwellings and the start of our walk. The early morning weather is cold, but sunny. Ram is nice, he's seems gentle and courteous and his English is quite good, he tells me that he's learned to speak my language from tourists and I think he wants me to talk English with him to help him improve.

We haven't walked very far along the path when we come to a small shack with some chairs outside and Ram says we can stop here for coffee. When it comes, the coffee is ridiculously sweet. Ram buys some sweet biscuits for the journey. My pack is already stocked with protein bars, nuts and dried fruit and I think it's likely I'll be sharing these along the way.

We walk to the gates of Shivapuri National Park where I pay for permission to enter. As we start trekking, the sunshine warms us and I feel super happy reflecting on my good fortune that I have Ram to guide me. The path is small, dusty and stony and takes us mostly uphill. We pass by little villages and I feel sad noticing tumble down dwellings destroyed by the devastating earthquake in April 2015 that claimed 9,000 lives. Ram shares his personal experience of the time the earthquake struck and it gives me an insight into how shocking it must have been. I'm fascinated to see villagers washing their hair, clothes, kitchen utensils outside their homes along the path. They're using water pipes and hoses that hitch together from a communal one that runs down the hillside.

Rows of colourful prayer flags flapping in the breeze indicate that we've come to the monastery at Nagi Gumba. It looks strange to me, quite modern and not how I would expect. It's occupied by nuns and as we pass they seem totally disinterested in us. Ram's walking pace is rather slow and when we stop for a rest and something to eat I'm not tired at all, but I'm happy to look out over the valley. The sun feels hot now so I shed layers until I'm only in my T shirt and jeans.

We arrive at our first homestay around 12.30 pm and I'm disappointed to learn that this is as far as we're walking today. I'm feeling anxious that we're here so early in the day and I have nothing to do. No book, notepad, laptop, nothing.

We sit on picnic benches outside with a lunch of noodle soup and I notice a Nepalese man walk along the lane leading a herd of goats. He's dressed in simple traditional clothes and I laugh when he reaches into a pocket and answers his mobile phone.

Ram and I take a stroll down to a large water filter system and small reservoir that he tells me serves Kathmandu. Ram tells me that a treaty between India and Nepal some years ago means that Nepal's rivers provide water for India, who now sell the water back to them for a high price, I'm not sure I understood the story correctly, but it's clear that Ram feels angry with India's treatment of Nepal.

Exploring the homestay accommodation, I realise it's suffered from earthquake damage and the rooms at the back are destroyed, just two bedrooms remain at the front and Ram and I occupy these. My room is next to the kitchen and has a horrible smell of cooking fuel. It's also noisy with only one flimsy door separating two rooms, I can hear a woman clearing her throat in the loud, guttural manner so common with Nepalese people. There isn't a bathroom, only an outside water tap and a toilet a short walk up some stone steps, shared with several other dwellings. I do no more than clean my teeth and wash my hands and pray I won't need the toilet in the night.

As darkness falls I'm grateful that a small fire is made outside and Ram and I, along with a couple of family members sit around it. Although I can't join in the conversation because they're speaking Nepalese, I'm content to lie back on the wooden bench and star gaze, I've never before seen such an incredible night sky, it seems there are more stars than sky. Supper is dal bhat which is rice and lentil soup and the temperature outside is now so cold I ask if we can stay by the fire to eat, which we do, although without lights it's difficult to see the food on the plate.

Back in my room and away from the fire, I'm freezing. The bedding is heavy, but has little warmth, so I curl up wearing all my clothes including hat and mittens.

## 31st December

### Day 2

We leave early to trek onwards to Mulkharka, walking mostly along a stony track, sometimes up, sometimes down, surrounded by trees and the occasional amazing view. The sun stays with us and again I'm shedding layers as we walk. We reach Mulkharka early in the afternoon and in front of us is an extraordinary sight. Several tall, modern buildings have been tilted askew by the earthquake, they're leaning at alarming degrees and look in danger of toppling over. The properties here have been abandoned.

At the first opportunity for accommodation Ram asks for a room, but there are none available. There are no available rooms at the next place either, so we walk on. The afternoon is getting late as we come to the last chance for accommodation and I find myself agreeing that a bed in a tin hut on the top of a very cold ridge will be perfectly fine!

The dwellings in this village were destroyed by the earthquake and the few villagers who are left, live in make-shift corrugated tin huts. I'm puzzled that they don't seem to have put any effort into insulating them at all, there are huge gaps between the sides and the roof and around the openings for windows, so the freezing wind blows inside.

Today is the last day of 2015 and it's turning out to be quite an experience. The owner whose accommodation we're using, allows Ram and I to sit inside her make-shift kitchen where she's cooking over an open fire. It's dark and smoky inside but at least it's warm. She invites me to drink home-brewed millet wine and although it tastes pretty horrible, I drink it anyway. Then other people start coming in to stand around the fire and with her kitchen becoming cluttered she shoos us all out into the cold, so Ram and I go for a stroll.

Not far up the road we come to what was a small meeting house, now destroyed by the earthquake. Looking inside I can see colourful life-size statues of gods, toppled over and surrounded by fallen bricks. Some have lost their heads which have rolled onto the floor lying among the bricks, their brightly painted faces and eyes have a look of shock on them. It's a bizarre and chilling sight.

Walking along the road in the other direction we

meet a woman who invites us inside another tin dwelling. I'm amazed to see a skinny old man sitting right next to a smoking fire. There's no chimney and I don't know how his eyes aren't streaming from the smoke. The lady tells us he is 83 years old and he lives here on his own. I ask if it will be okay for me to give him some money, which I do.

Not far from our shelter I meet a mother of two, she's just twenty-one years old, very pretty, with a smiley face and Ram and I are invited inside her tin shelter. She also has an open fire and she's boiling a large kettle over it. Her little boy is clinging to her legs gazing up at me. He's called Rojan. He pees in his pants, the urine trickling onto the earth floor and with her sandaled foot she scuffs the dirt to cover it. I wonder how she's able to wash him and his clothes, there's no bathroom and the temperature is wintery cold. I've already discovered that, like the previous village, there are communal outside toilets. The young mother hands me a cup of hot black tea which Rams tells me is made from black pepper.

Outside again, the evening is becoming freezing and I don't have enough clothes to keep warm. I ask Ram if we can make a fire outside, there's rubbish everywhere so there will be plenty to burn. He's oddly reluctant, I'm not sure why, but with my encouragement we gather enough material to get a fire started. When the flames get going a few men come and join us. Someone produces more millet wine which is passed around. It amuses me to realise that tonight is New Year's Eve and I'm standing in the remains of a mountain village in Nepal, hugging a make-shift fire and sharing millet wine with strangers.

Eventually the smoke from the fire makes my eyes sore and I'm tired enough to go to bed. My tin hut is full of stuff; beds and bedding, possibly a store room for items rescued from their now destroyed property. I don't know where Ram will sleep. When he showed me the double bed earlier in the evening I wasn't sure if he was saying we'd have to share. He's left his bag in my room so I can't bolt the door in case he needs it.

This is the coldest night of my life. I'm puzzled by Nepalese bedding which they call blankets, made of thick quilted material, they're not soft like a duvet, each pocket is packed with heavy padding and the effect is something weighty but not warm. The bedding is cold and smells damp. The freezing wind is howling through the gaps around the tin walls and I would give anything right now for a hot water bottle. I've put on every item of clothing I have with me and I tell my bladder in no uncertain terms that it must behave tonight, the thought of walking down the dirt road to a stinky, cracked porcelain, hole in the ground is hideous.

Sleep seemed impossible but I must have dozed off because I'm woken in the morning by my door being thrown open, a man steps inside, retrieves his bike helmet from a shelf and leaves. He seems oblivious of me. Ram later retrieves his bag from my room and I don't ask where he spent the night.

## 1st January 2016

### Day 3

Breakfast is porridge and I'm grateful for its warmth. Today I'm determined to get a whole day of walking in, so when Ram suggests we stop at Jhule I ask where the next place is and he tells me it's *"quite far"*, I say *"that's okay, we can get there"*.

This morning's panorama is incredible, we're up high and surrounded by hills, trees and fields with the magnificent Himalayan mountain range in the distance.

Jhule is not far at all and when we come to a small, quaint eating place with wooden seats outside I'm happy that Ram tells us we will have lunch here. The daytime sun is hot again and I'm given a plate of noodle soup. Ram and I are the only customers. The place appears to be run by a mother and daughter and while I'm eating they hover close by, the mother combing her daughter's long black hair. This would be a very strange sight in an English restaurant.

Ram and I continue an amiable walk towards our next destination, the village of Nagarkot which we make by mid-afternoon. My socks have been rubbing inside my shoes making my feet sore so I'm glad we've arrived.

The first hotel Ram enquires at is full and he looks disappointed. There's another close by which is brand new and we go inside. So brand new, it isn't even finished, I don't like it at all and I tell Ram I don't want to stay there. Nagarkot must be a tourist place because there's another hotel next door called Berg Hotel. When I'm shown the room I'm happy, it's warm and boasts a veranda with far reaching views. Ram is relieved.

I'm very excited to have a hot shower, there's nothing like a few days with only cold water to make you appreciate hot water. I meet Ram in the restaurant for dinner. The menu is limited, partly because there are few vegetarian options but also because of the shortage of gas, so I have veg noodles again.

## 2nd January

### Day 4

My bed is warm and cosy and I'm reluctant to get out but the early morning light is very appealing, so I wrap myself in a blanket and sit on the balcony taking it all in.

When I arrive downstairs looking for breakfast, I'm surprised to see Ram lying on one of the benches in the restaurant area and I realise that this is where he slept all night. He's excited to tell me that he's found a private vehicle taking some Thai people back to Kathmandu and they're willing to give us a lift. This will save us having to take a bus.

Before we leave, I take a walk around the village which is located at the rim of the Kathmandu Valley within sight of the Himalayas. The road is dusty and there are dwellings and shops either side. The locals are outside washing pots and pans, or themselves, one man is cleaning his teeth. A tiny, sick puppy is staggering in the road, there's froth around its mouth. People look at it pityingly but no-one helps it. I don't know what to do, all I can think of is giving it water to drink so I get some from the hotel kitchen in a paper dish. As I approach the puppy it becomes frightened and staggers drunkenly from me and I know I can't help. When Ram emerges from the hotel I ask if there's something we can do. Ram has no idea and absurdly throws the puppy some of his sweet biscuits. I guess that, like me, he's doing the only thing he can think of.

Ram suggests we visit Pashupatinath Temple and so the car drops us off near here. This is a famous, sacred Hindu temple dedicated to the God Pashupati and built on the banks of the Bagmati River, a tributary of the

Ganges. It's a sprawling collection of temples, full of history, atmosphere and mischievous monkeys. Smoke from burning funeral pyres fills the air. From up high I watch a young boy wading in the river, stopping now and then to put his hand into the water. Ram tells me that he's probably looking for rings or jewellery that can be found on the river bed after cremations.

A small group of people are bathing the feet of a dead relative and stroking their limbs, making them ready for the cremation. I feel uncomfortable watching them and turn my attention to the monkeys who are so amusing, playing in and out of the temples and archways.

We leave the temples and Ram suggests we have lunch. He chooses a horrible cheap café which I put up with because I know he has very little money and everything he spends will be taken from the profit he makes as my guide.

To get back to Thamel we take an electric tuk-tuk minibus and I'm astonished how many people are crammed into it, there are three people in the front with the driver, five people on either side and one passenger literally hanging off the back. It was probably built to carry ten people at the most, but this one has fifteen.

We're back at Sanjay's offices, but he isn't there so I invite Ram to have coffee with me. I've come to know a lot about him and his family. During our time walking he's talked about his wife and two children and how they'd like a computer but can't afford one and how they have a TV but it only has sound, no picture. Their home is just two rooms and they share a toilet with other families. I hand Ram far more than the agreed price of the tour and I'm not sure how to read the expression on his face. Have I been too generous and made him uncomfortable or maybe I'm not generous enough, maybe he expected more?

## Thamel

Sanjay returns. He's pleased to see us and I ask him to take a picture of Ram and me. I tell Sanjay that I'm going to look for another hotel locally and he suggests that I try the Ganesh Himal not far from here. He asks me if I ride a bicycle and when I say I do, he pops to the bike shop next door and reappears with a bike for me and one for himself. He says he'll show me where the hotel is.

The next ten minutes are hilarious. Sanjay cycles off at speed, weaving around people and animals and out of the main tourist hub, round a tiny roundabout cluttered with cars and taxis and up another road. I'm pedalling like crazy trying to keep up while navigating all the hazards and the road's appalling surface. He then disappears down an alley and I discover we've arrived.

The hotel looks excellent and Sanjay negotiates a good price for me. Although a little way out of the main town, maybe that means it'll be quieter. Another manic cycle ride and we're back to his office. I'm laughing, how did I come to be pedalling along the streets of Nepal?

In the evening I find a charming restaurant called Rosemary's where I enjoy a very tasty fish dish, a welcome change from veg noodles. There's a gas fire burning, I feel wonderfully warm and sit reflecting on the amazing trek I've just experienced. I feel very lucky.

## 3rd January

Walking along the road that leads to my hotel I realise there are several opticians here, in fact the road seems to be full of opticians, I wonder I didn't notice them before. This could be a solution to my lost glasses. I'm considering getting an eye test, when I have a brainwave. I can contact my opticians back home, they'll still have my prescription, I can choose frames online, get them made up and sent to my friend Fliss who's coming to southern India in a few weeks to meet me. She can bring them with her. I'm excited by this solution and have no doubt it will work.

I pop into one of the opticians and ask about reading glasses. They have some neat fold-up magnifying specs and for the modest price of around £3.00 I buy a pair that will be perfect for me to use in the meantime.

I've been thinking about Ben, in fact he's in my mind often and I decide that it would be okay to send him a Happy New Year email, so back at my hotel I spend time composing it. I send it off to his sister, aware that it could be several days before she can to give it to him.

## 4th January

About a mile out of Thamel is an area called Durbar Square where several ancient temples were built. The square was hit badly by the 2015 earthquake and several temples collapsed, but I thought it worth exploring so set off walking. Fortunately, the route is pretty straightforward and I enjoy the walk, passing small businesses and shops. The street becomes busy with a crowd of local people and I realise they're queuing for gas. Some of the now much-coveted gas bottles have arrived and people are desperate to get hold of them.

Durbar Square is fascinating, but oh so sad to see the fallen-down temples, some of them had been around for thousands of years before the recent earthquake, now they look like piles of stones. It must have been devastating for local people to experience this damage. This is a UNESCO Heritage site, so maybe Nepal will get help restoring them. Some temples and towers are still standing but are now propped up, supported by massive wooden poles. Even so, I love the colours, the bustle and atmosphere of the area.

Thamel has numerous eating places and I've a new favourite called OR2K. It's quirky, with funky lighting and most of the seating is on cushions on the floor. The menu is restricted at the moment because of the lack of gas but it still boasts an excellent selection of vegetarian fare. I sit myself in a corner, plug my phone into a nearby charging point and check my emails.

Two people come in and ask if they can join my table. An older guy who introduces himself as John from the US and Ali, a much younger, pretty, outdoorsy girl, who tells me she's from Lincoln in England. They're both on a 'high', having just finished the three-day Annapurna trek and I enjoy hearing about their adventure. John clearly found it extremely challenging and had to resort to riding a horse for some of the way. Ali takes my email address and says she'll email me, she's also travelling alone. I love how easy it is to get acquainted with fellow travellers, a shame it feels so uncomfortable in the 'real' world.

Leaving the restaurant, a handwritten advert on the noticeboard by the door catches my eye. It's asking for volunteers at the Children's Innovation Centre, a home for orphaned children. I make a note of the email address, I think I'll contact them.

## 5th January

A few brief email conversations with Sujan from the Children's Innovation Centre are enough for me decide

I'd like to work there as a volunteer and today's the day.

Checking out of the Ganesh Himal, I ask the receptionist if he'll take a photo of me with my backpack, front pack and ukulele, which he cheerfully does. I'm also carrying a bag of reading books, colouring books and crayons that I've purchased from a bookseller in Thamel, to take to the children.

Feeling rather weighed down, I walk slowly until I reached the main road where I'm immediately spotted by a cycle rickshaw. I tell him that I don't need a rickshaw yet as I want to get my shoes cleaned first, but he insists on waiting for me. I come to the shoe cleaner I'd seen a couple of days before and he does an amazing job polishing my leather walking boots until they look very loved. I feel sad that a split in the leather means they're no longer waterproof. I ask him how much payment he wants and he says 500 rupees which is way too much, but I pay it anyway.

I load my bags onto the patiently waiting rickshaw and show the driver a piece of paper where I'd previously written the name of the bus stop, he nods in recognition and we're off, weaving our way in and out of the people and traffic.

## Children's Home, Narayanthan, Nepal

It takes about 15 minutes to get to the area where the buses come in and I love the ride. I've written the place name 'Narayanthan' on the other side of my piece of paper so I can show it to the buses going by and with luck, the right one will stop for me. The area is chaotic. They have a crazy system where a guy on the bus leans out of the door or window, then yells out the names of all the places they will stop at. The problem for me is they yell the names so fast I can't catch what they're saying. A young man, also waiting for a bus, recognises the place I'm going to and he tells me he's going there too so I happily follow him.

When our bus comes, it's small and very crowded and squeezing myself plus my bags on board requires some athletic skill. I manoeuvre myself to a seat at the back and buried under my bags I pray that the two people I'm hemming in on either side don't want to get off before me, because I doubt I can move.

The ride takes about half an hour. Lots of bodies in a small bus makes for a very hot journey, but nevertheless the experience is highly entertaining. Passengers are happy and animated and chat to each other. A lady with a small boy gets on, and with nowhere to sit she hands the child to an already seated passenger, who seems quite happy to look after him.

Arriving in Narayanthan, I manage to extricate myself and my clobber and alight onto a dirt road. There's the usual array of tiny shops, shacks and stalls, but I have no way of finding the 'orphanage' which doesn't have signage, so I look for somewhere to buy a drink and work out how to contact Sujan.

The only place nearby where I might get something looks seedy, but I go in and order a Lassi. I instantly regret this, realising the drink is made with cold milk and I probably can't trust the hygiene. Too late to change my mind, it comes and I drink it anyway. It's not pleasant and tastes as though it has black pepper in it.

I show the guy in the 'café' Sujan's mobile number and using sign language ask if he can call him for me and he does. I'm relieved that Sujan answers and says he'll come and meet me. To my surprise, he turns up in a taxi as he's come from the airport where he collected another volunteer. I'm introduced to Denisse who's arrived from Costa Rica and is going to be at the orphanage for a month. Sujan is a handsome twenty-two year old with a charming smile and a gentle manner and I feel comfortable with him.

The Innovation Centre is only a couple of roads away. We walk down a rock-strewn side street, a small alley and across, what seems to be a school playground, to a couple of stone steps and the entrance.

Up some stairs, along a corridor, we come to an outside patio area with a kitchen and two bedrooms off. There's an iron spiral staircase that leads to another floor with more rooms. It all looks rather temporary. There's rubbish and broken bits of furniture strewn around the patio and a broken concrete floor.

The children are at school, but I meet Mommie, Sujan's mother, and Usha, Sujan's younger sister. I'm told that Sujan's grandpa is upstairs. Denisse and I chat and I'm delighted we'll be volunteers together. My bedroom is off the patio and looks okay. It's clearly a young female's bedroom and I wonder if Usha has had to move out so I can move in. On the upper floor, Sujan proudly shows us a newly created bathroom and it is very nice but doesn't boast hot water.

When the children come back from school there are hugs all around, they're delightful and call me 'sister'. Bimala, one of the oldest at 13yrs, is very helpful and writes down the children's names in order of their ages. I hand out the colouring books and crayons I've brought with me and sit on the concrete patio with the children while they colour in. I notice how kind they are to each other, sharing crayons and concentrating on their pictures.

Mommie asks me if I'll go with some of the children to fetch water. I've no idea what she means but say *"yes"*. She gives me a bucket and the kids excitedly jump down from the wall that surrounds the patio to the ground below, then dash off across the field. I struggle to keep up. They run to a muddy part of the field, announce that there isn't any water and run back again. I'm breathless and bewildered. Surely they don't really get their water from here?

Sujan tells Denisse and I that there's decorating to be done and we're keen to get stuck in right away, but he's reluctant and suggests instead that the three of us go for a walk. The dirt roads are dusty and dry and the concrete slabs that serve as footpaths are broken and irregular. In the middle of the village we come to a rectangular pond. There's a large painted figure of one of their gods lying in the centre of the pool on a concrete slab and it looks odd to me. Sujan tells us it's a place for worship.

We stroll to a tiny café where we sit outside at a plastic table and Sujan orders coffees. This is a good opportunity to get to know him better. Currently half way through a four-year engineering course, he's very entrepreneurial and has some innovative business ideas. Sujan tells us that his father is in the army and wanting to make amends for past deeds, he decided to take in orphaned children. This is how the Innovation Centre came about. However, although his father initially funded and set up the venture, the responsibility of looking after the children and the rest of the family has now fallen onto Sujan's shoulders. He shows no resentment about this at all.

We walk on to a small monastery which looks more like a village hall and Sujan invites us to step inside where there are two monks chanting and praying. A few other visitors are kneeling and standing around. After a few minutes, a gong sounds and some curtains open, it looks like there's going to be a theatrical performance.

As the curtains part, they reveal an amazingly bright, jewelled 'alter' with colourful painted statues. More people come in and start chanting and swaying back and forth. A monk moves among us and we're invited to take food from a plate. I accept the offered food but keep it in my hand until we leave, when I discreetly discard it.

We had started our walk in the late afternoon when the weather was still warm, but now the sun has gone, the temperature has really dropped and we're very cold walking back.

It gets dark early here and the evening feels long. I take out my uke and sing some children's songs I'd learned especially. To my surprise, the children are already familiar with them and sing with me, adding 'London Bridge is Burning Down' to our repertoire.

Meals are eaten outside on the concrete patio with everyone sitting on large pieces of cardboard. Mommie brings supper of dal bhat out just as the electricity cuts off and we're plunged into darkness. A couple of candles are lit and I fetch my torch. The children and Mommie eat their food with their fingers so I'm glad I'm given a spoon and a fork. I'm incredulous at the massive pot of rice the children consume.

After dinner I sit on Sujan's bed in his room and he explains some of the business and charity ideas he has and the Facebook pages he's working on to promote them. I'm genuinely impressed, he's a remarkable young man.

## 6th January

I'm up by 7.30 am guessing most others are up too because of the noise but only Mommie is about and I stand around for a while in the cold morning air.

Mommie is in the kitchen and doesn't speak much English. I show her that I'd like to help and she indicates that I can peel potatoes. She hands me a knife that is more like a machete, it's enormous and blunt and there are a zillion small potatoes to peel. Mommie also hands me a cup of shockingly sweet tea and five plain biscuits, I think she's trying to fatten me up.

Breakfast is more dal bhat, but I don't mind, I'm hungry and it tastes good. Denisse and I are keen to start working, but with no sign of Sujan we stroll into the town instead, to buy some drinking water.

By mid-afternoon the children are back from school. They're a happy bunch and very affectionate. I read stories with them and show them how to play some chords on my uke. Sujan appears and asks me if I'd like to go into town with him to get some shopping.

He wanders in and out of the shops, stopping to buy a toilet brush and some flower holders for the plastic flowers that he loves. He's keen to make the home a nice place. We go into another shop where he orders ten of the heavy cloth 'blankets' the Nepalese use. He's going to give these away to other children in need. I'm baffled by his generosity because it seems that his own family are struggling with the cost of looking after so many children. Sujan asks me if I like cake and takes me across the wide main road to a cake shop where he buys us one each and we eat them on the spot. We go into another little shack where meat on skewers is being seared over a roaring fire and he buys a rod and eats it straight away. He tells me that he really likes western food.

The next place we visit is a total surprise. Just off the main road, we walk into the beautiful grounds of the Village Park Hotel. This hotel belongs to the same company that owns the Kathmandu Guest House and

I'm bewildered how it comes to be located here, in the middle of this small town. Sujan tells me he has learned how to make hammocks and he wants to sell some to the hotel. He says he likes having a blonde European lady with him because it gives him more credibility. We go to the reception desk and ask if the Manager will see us. An arrangement is made for us to return for an interview tomorrow.

## 7th January

Denisse and I have agreed to run together this morning. I'm slightly daunted because of the altitude which is around 1200 metres and I haven't run for a long time. With assurance from Denisse that she's also a slow runner, we set off gently, paying great attention to the road under our feet because there are so many hazards around.

I enjoy the early morning run, I like the scenery and the sun rising through a misty haze. Getting warm from running has the added benefit of giving me courage to brave putting my head into the cold shower to wash my hair. I feel I owe it to Sujan to look my best for his hotel interview.

The interview has been arranged for 11 am, but Sujan is in no hurry and with Denisse accompanying us as well, we set off at twenty minutes past eleven for the Village Park Resort Hotel, Sujan cradling his demo hammock.

We're in the garden and I'm highly amused when no less than nine staff emerge from the hotel to see the hammock, each with varying suggestions where to place it. Eventually agreement is reached and it's tied between two trees. I'm concerned that there's a concrete path underneath it. Sujan wants me to demonstrate the hammock, so I gently lower myself in, fervently praying that I won't tip out, and relax back to show the comfort and pleasure of the experience. With all nine hotel staff standing around and watching me, I'm careful to get out as gracefully as I can and without cracking my head on the concrete underneath. The result is an order for four hammocks which Sujan promises to deliver in two days.

Sujan tells us that he now needs to buy fabric to make the hammocks and alarm bells ring. They haven't been made yet and he said he'll deliver in two days! The three of us take a bus into Thamel, which I enjoy as much as my previous journey.

Apparently in no hurry, we visit the Garden of Dreams, a pretty park and a haven of tranquillity, even though it's right next to the busy ring road around Thamel. It has a coffee shop and I buy us all a coffee. Sujan looks uncomfortable and I realise he's put salt in his coffee instead of sugar. The coffee here is expensive and he's embarrassed. He doesn't allow me to buy him another coffee.

Being in Thamel with these two is fun. Denisse wants to photograph everything. Eventually we make it through the tiny and busy alleyways to the fabric shop where we choose four different fabrics for the new hammocks. Next stop is a rope shop where Sujan gets exactly what he needs for 10 rupees a metre.

Getting hungry, we stop for lunch in a Nepalese fast food place, super busy and full of red plastic tables and chairs and a great selection of fresh cooked food.

From here we walk to the back of Durbar Square and by entering through a restaurant we avoid the 1000 rupee charge that tourists have to pay. From the top of the restaurant we're able to look down on the square and I see again the earthquake damage. It's still an appealing sight though, with colourful flags, stall holders and people milling about.

As we make our way out of Durbar Square, Denisse sees a trader selling hats and gloves and she stops to look at them. Sujan suddenly grabs me and pointing towards the ground says *"look, here is the world's smallest man"*. I look towards a small boy standing nearby, then realise from his mature face that he is indeed a man. Sujan wants to take a photo of the tiny man with me and I'm really embarrassed when a man standing next to the little fellow suddenly picks him up and pops him into my arms. The little guy doesn't look happy and I don't know what to say. He appears to be perfectly proportioned and weighs nothing in my arms. I wonder if this can be true, is he the smallest man in the world? Sujan recognised him because he's seen him on the TV and says he's in the 'Guinness Book of Records'.

We make our way through the crowded streets to the bus stop, but by this time it's rush hour and it becomes clear that the three of us won't get on a bus together, so we take a taxi back to Narayanthan.

The power has gone off again and we all sit as usual on mats on the patio and eat dal bhat by the light from my torch and one candle. After clearing up, Mommie gets out her treadle sewing machine and in the candlelight, starts sewing hammocks from the material we've bought. I go to bed early again, it's cold and dark and there's not much else to do.

## 8th January

I'm running again, on my own this time, it feels good to be outside in the early morning. I walk up the hill on the edge of the town, taking in all the sights, sounds, smells and I capture some photos of the sunrise.

When I return, Mommie hands me another cup of the ultra-sweet tea and a pile of biscuits. She's a kind, hardworking lady and I want to help her, so I offer to wash up the large mess of pots and plates in the kitchen. It's a hideous task. The sink is bunged up with yesterday's rice and food and the washing up 'cloth' is a filthy rag. The water is cold and the pans are greasy. I am not happy.

Today Denisse and I are painting the 'library', a makeshift room made from poorly fitting plywood. The blue paint is so thin it soaks straight into the wood and even after two coats it doesn't look as though we've painted it at all. I'm beginning to wonder why Denisse and I are here, we're not asked to help with the kids and Sujan seems reluctant to give us work to do.

I'm becoming fond of the children, especially Mandip who always asks if he can play my ukulele. He practices over and over the three chords I've shown him. It would be such a joy to buy him a uke, but it wouldn't last five minutes in a household of eleven boisterous kids.

In between all her other work Mommie is making the hammocks. I'm surprised that Sujan doesn't help and although Usha is very good at knotting the rope she quickly loses interest. Denisse and I offer to help and slowly master the art of knotting, enough to be of some use. We work on until late in the evening and I want to go to bed. Usha and Sujan have already disappeared and since they're not helping I don't feel inclined to continue working, so I go back to my room.

## 9th January

Waking this morning, I learn that Mommie has been up all night and has finished all four hammocks. I feel mean now that I didn't stay to help her for longer. I accompany Sujan back to the hotel with the newly made hammocks and notice that he's quite nervous. He's very endearing and I want to give him a hug, but of course I don't. In the hotel garden, he ties the hammocks to various trees along a walkway and they look really good. He wants me to take photos of himself with the hammocks so he can post them onto Facebook. Eventually the Manager and his entourage comes along and he's delighted with them.

I discover later that the hotel has posted pictures of the hammocks on their website including pictures of me in the demonstration one!

## 10th January

Sujan asks me to come out with him and we walk down some narrow pathways that I haven't been on before. He says we're going to the house his family rented previously. They didn't leave it in good condition and have to pay money for repairs and redecorating. Sujan tells me the children didn't know how to use the western toilet so they kept standing on the toilet seat and broke it. This is a much better house than the one they have now and I wonder why they had to leave it.

When Sujan has done what he came to do, he says we're going to visit the house where his aunt, cousins and grandmother live. They welcome me and bless me by placing a bindy on my forehead and handing me some marigold petals, some money and something to eat, which I have to pop into my mouth and I really don't want to because I've watched 'Aunty' finger it several times.

Everyone disappears leaving Sujan and I in the living room. It's well furnished with a few pieces of old fashioned furniture, a very floral sofa and net curtains at the big windows. There are vases of colourful artificial flowers. Aunty reappears with two trays of food for Sujan and I. The trays each hold several small dishes of dal bhat, rice, vegetables and sauces. I don't want to eat but of course I tuck in with enthusiasm because they're watching to see how much I like their food. I'm desperately thirsty and the food is spicy. I can't ask for water because I can't drink their tap water. My mouth is on fire. I manage to eat enough to be polite and thank them warmly for their hospitality.

On the way home, we walk past some very big homes and I realise that Narayanthan has a wealthy area. Sujan is good company, he's interesting to talk to and we talk at length about wealth. I appreciate his enthusiastic, entrepreneurial spirit.

We pass some men playing table tennis by the side of the path. The table is a very small wooden one with stones laid across the middle instead of a net. I love how these people use their imagination and improvise; yesterday I watched the children playing badminton with two bats and tangerine peel for a shuttlecock.

Dinner is more dal bhat with rice and spinach. I'm getting pretty fed up with it and I don't think my body likes it much either. There's another power cut again and there's not much to do but go to bed, it's only 8.30 pm.

## 11th January

Sujan has gone mad. He's ordered floor tiles to be laid on the rough concrete patio which would be great if this wasn't a holiday and the children are off school for a week. The patio has to be crossed to access all the rooms. This is a family of four adults, eleven children, two volunteers and two dogs, one being a puppy. How are the three builders who've just arrived, going to lay cement and tiles? I suggest to Sujan that we take the children out for the day and to my delight he agrees.

Denisse comes too and we gather everyone together and walk to some woods on the side of the hill which Sujan calls 'the jungle'. We take skipping ropes, a hoop and some balls with us and on the way we stop at a little kiosk to buy food and water. The area we come to is high up with amazing views. The children are excited and it's a joy to watch them running and playing. Sujan sees this as a marketing opportunity for the home and he takes lots of photos with his mobile.

We've settled ourselves at a suitable picnic area and Sujan points out a large monkey watching us from a nearby tree. Suddenly, really fast and taking us by complete surprise, the monkey leaps down from the tree, runs to the bags of food, grabs one and makes off with it. Our reactions are too slow to intervene and Sujan is frustrated that the monkey now has half our picnic. He says they are dangerous and can give you a nasty bite. The monkey sits not far away, examining his booty. I tell the children we need to scare the monkey away and that on the count of three we're all going to shout very loudly. I count, one, two, three and everyone yells and roars and the monkey takes absolutely no notice. Defeated, we move to a different area and hope he doesn't follow us.

The children are a delight, they play hide and seek and love the freedom to explore. We eat the remaining picnic food and walk back 'home' at the end of the afternoon. I know they've had fun on their day out and I'm sure the builders were relieved that we weren't under their feet.

I'm not sure I can face rice again this evening, so

I'm delighted when Sujan suggests the three of us go to a restaurant in town to eat momo's. The evenings here are always cold and this is an outdoor restaurant but I'm getting used to eating meals wearing a coat and gloves and I'm grateful to have a change from rice. Back at home Sujan entertains the children, Denisse and I in his room with a Bollywood movie, YouTube clips and the TV programme 'Britain's Got Talent', all on his laptop.

## 12th January

Denisse and I run again this morning and we have a discussion about head lice. She's concerned because the children are all clearly riddled with lice and she doesn't want to cuddle them in case she gets them too. She wears a cotton scarf around her head for protection. It's making her rethink how long she will stay as a volunteer at the home. I can't deny I'm puzzled what made Denisse come here, she's barely shown any interest in the children.

Sujan still isn't good at giving Denisse and I anything useful to do. He asks me to go back to Thamel with him to buy more cloth and rope and while we're there we have a really good meal at Northfield Café. It's dark when we leave Thamel in a taxi and he asks the driver to stop at a shop en route so he can pick up the ten heavy 'blankets' he's ordered. They're massive and Sujan, the shopkeeper and the taxi driver pile them one on top of each other on the roof of the taxi. It's so funny, like piling ten mattresses on top of each other on a car and I'm amazed they're all still there when we arrive back at the home.

# 13th January

I'm a mixture of emotions because I'm leaving the home today. Part of me is glad to leave the chaos, the cold, the lack of hot water and electricity, but I've become fond of the children and this affectionate family and especially Sujan.

Sujan is up early to deliver the blankets to the charity and won't be back to see me depart. We say a hasty goodbye and I give him some money, I think we both feel uncomfortable. I find it hard saying goodbye to the children, so I don't make a big deal of it. I'm sad to realise that Mommie has gone out and I can't tell her I'm leaving. I write a note expressing my admiration for her and her lovely family and thank her for her warm hospitality. Usha is upset, she had thought I was staying longer. My heart goes out to Usha, she's so young and pretty and she doesn't like studying, I think she will tie herself to her mother and the kitchen. I give Denisse a big hug goodbye and she tells me she doesn't want to stay at the home now I'm leaving, she's booked herself into a hostel and will go on Saturday.

I walk away, down the rock-strewn path onto the dirt road with my back pack, front pack and uke and wait for my bus to Thamel. I reflect on my time with Sujan, his children and family. I've glimpsed a slice of life totally different from any life I would normally experience. I'm very happy that I suggested the outing with the children because they really did have fun and I hope that Sujan has felt encouraged and supported by my enthusiasm for his entrepreneurial endeavours. I'll keep in touch with his progress, I have a feeling he will do something special with his life.

\*\*\*\*\*\*

Back in Thamel I book myself into Ganesh Himal Hotel for three days and stand for ages under a hot shower.

Before I left England, I started an online 'Teaching English as a Foreign Language' course and I need to complete some assignments. This hotel has good Wi-Fi, so it's the perfect opportunity. There's a very attractive balcony one floor down from my room, with a cushioned bench and a table. The sun is perfectly positioned to warm the balcony and I'm very content working there.

Another huge benefit for me is the small electric fire in my bedroom which helps fend off the night time cold. It feels strange being in a place where the daytime temperature can be hot and mornings and night times extremely cold. I can't keep the fire on all night though and I'm never warm enough in bed, even though I've got a second duvet from the other single bed in my room, the cold keeps me awake.

## 14th January

I wake early to the sound of noisy construction work happening next to the hotel and I realise one should abandon all hope of finding anywhere quiet here, there's no such place.

A generous breakfast is provided by the hotel offering eggs and porridge and coffee. I've been curious to notice that Nepali people eat and drink extremely noisily. I think it's intentional as they bend over their tea and slurp it into their mouths. Noticing this at breakfast this morning makes me want to giggle. A Nepali man sitting at the next table strikes up a conversation, he's keen to talk when he learns that I'm English. He tells me he studied for a while at a university in London. He then picks up his cup and slurps the drink noisily and I wonder if he did this in London.

## 15th January

Strolling from my hotel to Himalayan Java to treat myself to some good coffee, I feel a wonderful happiness bubbling inside me. I love walking along the now familiar, poorly kept roads, passing the fruit sellers and stalls with tourist tat, noticing the dust and the smell of incense and the noise of dogs and horns and chatter. How easily I've come to embrace the apparent chaos. I like passing the shops with their offerings of tiny candles, incense sticks and marigold petals placed on the street outside their door. It amuses me that my backpack and blonde hair attracts the attention of taxis, rickshaws and street peddlers and I'm constantly saying *'namaste'* and *'no, thank you'* when they call out to me.

# Darjeeling, West Bengal

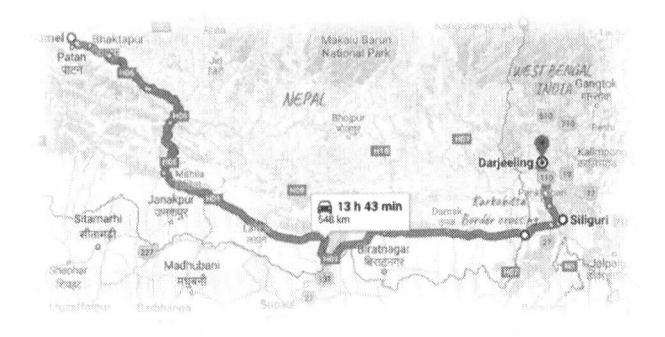

## 16th January

### Bus to Karkarbhitta, 15hrs (460 kms)

I'm going to Darjeeling, the land of tea. The kind and helpful Sanjay not only books a bus for me but has offered to take me to the bus station on his motorbike. We strap the backpack on the bike, Sanjay wears the front pack and I hang on to my uke case. He skilfully whizzes in and out of the clutter and traffic on the streets and we arrive at a mad, busy area with people and buses everywhere. I'm massively grateful that I have Sanjay with me because he talks on his mobile phone to the driver of the bus who keeps us updated where he is and when he'll arrive. I can't imagine I would ever have found the right bus without Sanjay.

The buses are all in terrible condition, some of them have lost their front windscreens and have temporary replacements, plywood with a hole cut out for the driver to see, sometimes semi-transparent polythene. I'm told this is a result of skirmishes at the border. I'm curious to see what my bus will be like, I'm going to be on it for seventeen hours so my fingers are crossed that it will be roadworthy. It arrives and it's okay, luckily it has a windscreen.

Sanjay's father lives in a small rural village devastated by the earthquake and they're still trying to rebuild their homes. I want to help and I've taken cash from the ATM to give to Sanjay and I ask him to take it to his father's village. I don't word my offering well and he refuses to accept the money. He won't be persuaded to take it and says I'm embarrassing him. I give Sanjay a big hug and climb onto the bus. Such a shame. I can't spend Nepalese money outside of Nepal so it's no use to me.

I'm sitting on the front seat next to a pretty young lady who has excellent English. Although I like the space and looking out of the front window, it's draughty and there's a TV screen right in front blaring out Bollywood movies. The bus comes to a halt and as everyone piles out the lady next to me says *"it's a comfort break"*. It isn't at all comfortable; when I get to the 'toilet' it's a rank, dark hole in the ground.

This journey feels exceptionally long being mostly in the dark. I'm very cold and slightly regretting offering to share my fleece blanket with my fellow passenger as I would love to wrap it around me and snuggle into it. I doze on and off which is a blessing because the Bollywood film in front of me is hideously violent. A girl approaches the driver and the bus comes to another stop, she calls to the passengers that this is an 'open' toilet which I take to mean there is no actual toilet. It's cold and dark outside and I decide to wait.

## 17<sup>th</sup> January

Fifteen hours have passed and when the bus comes to another stop I'm told to get off. I'm again glad the lady next to me speaks English, she explains that I'll need to change to another bus. I hadn't expected this, but with much pointing and gesticulating from my bus driver I find the next bus and within ten minutes I'm en route for Karkarbhitta and the border back into India.

Karkarbhitta is another busy, sprawling mass of small shops, kiosks, stalls and sellers of every kind along with the usual tuk-tuks, motorbikes and people. I'm about to leave Nepal and I still have the 3,000 npr in my purse. There's nothing I want to buy but I look around for something I might do with the money. Unusually I don't see anyone begging which is a pity. All I can think of spending some money on is chocolate. I've been surprised by the popularity of Cadbury's chocolate in India and Nepal, I've seen it sold in many of the little provision shops I've passed and wondered how it doesn't melt in the heat. When I ask the shop keeper for five bars of chocolate his face is a picture. Maybe I can post the remaining Nepalese notes to Sujan.

Walking slowly in the heat I head to the Immigration Office and the border. My passport is stamped and I join a throng of other people walking across a very long bridge. The scenes on either side look magical with dry, golden fields shimmering in the hazy sunshine, another scene from a story book.

Three cheeky young men are grinning at me and giggling with each other and ask if they can take photos of themselves with me. I'm amused and happily oblige, I'm getting used to this request now and I ask if they'll also take a photo of me with my mobile.

At the Immigration office I answer all the necessary questions and I'm delighted to be allowed back into India.

Luckily there's a bus to Siliguri leaving straight away and although the journey is further than I'd expected, it's uneventful. I'm not sure where to get off so alight when I seem to be in a busy part of town.

I need to get up to Darjeeling from here and previous research suggested I should be able to get a shared taxi. I'm immediately hassled by three men who ask where I'm going and when I say Darjeeling they want me to get in their jeep. I don't like the look of them and say 'no', but now they want to know why I won't go with them. They follow me, talking all the while as I walk away from them. A rickshaw driver wants to help and tells me to get into his rickshaw but I don't want to go anywhere with any of these people and when more people get involved, all talking at me and gesticulating, I feel overwhelmed.

Turning my back on them all I walk over to a nearby hotel for advice. I had thought Siliguri was close to Darjeeling, so I'm surprised when the hotel receptionist tells me it's a two-hour drive. I sit for a few minutes to calm my nerves, then armed with fresh information I go outside again. The three men with the jeep are waiting for me and again tell me I should ride with them. I'm very firm in my answer and walk on. I want to get a taxi that has other passengers, I'm not travelling alone.

Crossing the main road, I'm relieved to find a taxi that I can share with a couple of other people also going to Darjeeling. The taxi has a driver and a man touting for customers and collecting the money. He wants to put my back pack onto the roof and I'm very unhappy about this. He says he'll have to charge me for two seats if I want to keep it with me. Reluctantly, I agree to put it up there, but only if I can strap it on myself, so I climb up and tie it down so I can feel confident it will stay put.

The drive is incredibly long on small winding roads and we climb up and up. We stop every now and then to pick up more passengers and I understand now why I wasn't allowed to keep my backpack with me. The guy I'm sitting next to is told to get out and sit on top of the vehicle, along with other passengers and eventually our 'taxi' is stuffed with people clinging on top and bottom. I can't believe how far we continue driving upwards.

I'm squeezed in, clutching my front pack and uke and motion sickness kicks in. Although I'm sorry to miss seeing the phenomenal views, I'm grateful that I doze on and off which helps me cope with the journey. Nearing the end of the drive, I'm just waking up from another doze and I can feel that someone has their arm around me. It's the taxi guy who insisted I put my backpack on the roof. As I stir he removes his arm, I don't know what to make of this so, I ignore it. Three hours have passed since leaving Siliguri and I'm now in Darjeeling, West Bengal.

I'm hot, tired and still feel nauseous, so I hope I'll reach my accommodation, the Ivy Castle Hotel easily. I don't. It takes a lot of walking uphill and several attempts to find the right path and I start feeling sorry for myself. I haven't found a way to make the backpack fit comfortably and it pulls on my shoulders and I'm already disappointed with the look of Darjeeling. It's funny how you can have an image of a place in your mind. I'd been expecting green tea fields and a quaint village but first impression shows a place as chaotic and manic as the rest of India.

Just off the Chauk Bazaar, I see a sign directing me to Hotel Ivy Castle down a narrow alley. It's very small and dark inside. There's a young lad at the reception desk and he doesn't speak English. He shows me my room which has a door onto the path and the street outside. I'm not thrilled about the security of this. My room is small, shabby and not very clean, but it does have windows with a view. The price is cheap and will do for now.

There's no Internet here, so after a rest I go back to Chauk Bazaar in search of an Internet Café, I want to let Sanjay know I've arrived safely.

## 18th January

I've had an email from Ben! It's a long, funny email and signed 'lots of love'. I'm very happy!

I'm exploring my surroundings today and walk around Darjeeling, up and down the narrow streets. The weather is cold and damp and the roads are wet and mucky with rubbish. I'm on a mission to locate the train station and book the famous Toy Train back to Siliguri when I'm ready to leave Darjeeling. I find the station and to my delight there are seats available and I can make a booking. I also want to book a trek and having done some research on the Internet, I come across a tour company called Ashmita Tours and book a two-day trek. They tell me that a German may join the same trek, they're waiting to hear back from him. My fingers are crossed that he does join so I won't trek alone.

## 19th January

I'm not happy in Darjeeling and I don't know why, but I want to make the best of it so I take a long walk to the cable car that boasts incredible views across the tea fields. A sign tells me it's 'closed for maintenance'.

Looking at my guide map there's a popular tourist place called the 'Happy Valley Tea Factory' so I walk there instead. I approach it along a narrow footpath across a field and as I arrive a lady comes out of a small dwelling to greet me. She tells me the factory is empty, there's no work at the moment, something about it being pruning time. She invites me into her house for a cup of tea. I feel comfortable with her and happy to go inside.

She has an interesting tale to tell, having worked at the factory herself for many years and she has an extensive knowledge of the different kinds of tea. There are dainty dishes attractively laid out on a small round table, each containing different dried tea leaves. She hands me a cup of No.1 Darjeeling tea which, she tells me, is only sold in Harrods. I enjoy listening to her. When I get up to leave I thank her and give her some money.

It's a long walk back to the town, made even longer as I take a detour to the train station to book more train tickets. I've discovered that it's impossible for me to book train tickets online because the Indian railway website doesn't accept credit cards that are not Indian. I want to book a train from Siliguri to Kolkata. There aren't any $2^{nd}$ or $3^{rd}$ class seats available so I book sleeper seats. The ticket price to travel for twelve hours is 175 rupees, about £1.75. I wonder what the carriage will be like.

# 20th January

## Two day Trek in Singalila National Park

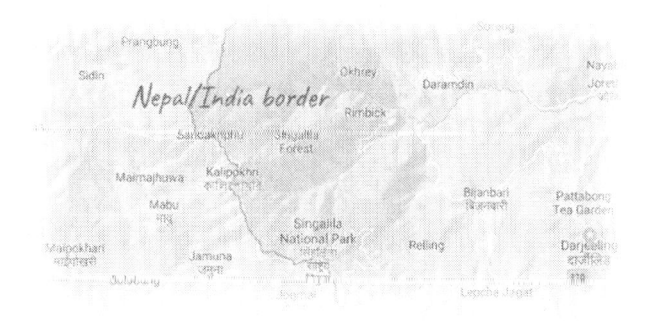

## Day 1

Today I'm beginning my trek in the Singalila National Park with a guide called Rajen. There are no other trekkers, only me, and I don't have the same reassurance that I did in Nepal of knowing who my guide is. I have to trust that all will be well. I arrive just before 8 am as instructed and the office is closed. I'm feeling nervous. I start worrying if my guide will show up and after just a few minutes, he does.

As we start walking to his vehicle I realise I need a toilet and ask Rajen if there might be a hotel I can pop into. He points down an alley and I see a sign saying 'public toilets' and there's a requirement to pay. Entering, a lady is squatting and I assume she's the attendant and hand her money. To my horror I realise these are 'open' toilets, there are no doors and I walk past other people making use of a hole in the ground! I find it difficult to 'perform' feeling very public. Then it dawns on me that the lady I just handed money to is not the attendant at all, simply another person who came in to use the toilet and remembering how quickly her hand shot out to take my money, it strikes me as very funny.

Rajen drives for an hour and before we begin the trek we go into a typical general store-cum-tea room with a couple of tables inside. At one of the tables a man is having his face shaved and his hair cut, all with a razor blade. It feels odd drinking tea in the same room as the barber and his customer.

Starting the trek, the weather is misty so although we're high up, there's not much in the way of landscapes. I'm aware of my disappointment but thinking about it as I walk it occurs to me that the reason I'm travelling is to have experiences, I'm not just travelling to have a nice time. I like this thought because it means I don't have to mind about the weather, or anything, because everything is an experience. I'm just experiencing having a trek in the mist. This thought makes me happier.

We walk at a fair pace, climbing up higher and following the Nepalese/Indian border. My guide is pleasant, his English isn't great but I don't mind, I'm content to walk without chatting. After a couple of hours, we come to a Sherpa Stall, basically a wooden hut selling snacks and food and a corrugated tin shed next to it with plastic tables and chairs outside. We're stopping here for lunch. Two other people arrive, another guide and a trekker. It turns out that the trekker is the same German who may have come on my trek, whose name is Stefan. We're all walking to Tumling and after lunch we walk together. I have a trekking companion after all! He's a friendly young guy and good company.

The landscape coming into Tumling is amazing, we're now at 2,900 metres high, there's some snow on the ground, the mist has gone and we can see snowy mountains in the distance.

Our homestay for the night is called Shikhara Lodge, it's single storey, brick built and looks clean. Rajen shows me my bedroom in an outside block, it looks basic, clean and freezing cold!

Stefan and I are delighted that a fire has been made up for us in the lodge and we settle in cosily and share travelling adventures while we wait for dinner. A very smiley Nepalese lady brings us several dishes of very tasty food. We're both loathe to leave the warmth of the fire to go to bed.

## 21st January

### Day 2

Waking in a panic, I look at my phone, what time is it? The phone has 'died' in the night so the alarm hasn't gone off. I want to see the sunrise so I dress super fast and rush outside. There are clouds but some clear sky too and I love being out in the early morning, even though the temperature is very cold. No-one else is about. Rajen had pointed out Mt Kanchenjunga to me the day before, the third highest mountain in the world and I take a great photo of it. I walk a short way from the homestay and watch the sunrise over the hill.

We're treated to a generous breakfast of porridge, boiled egg, spicy roasted potatoes, doughnuts and a mug of hot coffee. Stefan tells me his guide had said it was too cloudy to see the sunrise so he'd stayed in bed. I think it's a shame he missed it.

They are walking further than us today and I'm sorry we won't be trekking with Stefan. I learn that my trek ends here and we're walking back today, mostly the same way we've come which feels disappointing. I'm beginning to realise that two or three-day treks don't mean two or three days of walking, something worth remembering for the future.

The walk back seems short and the promise of sunshine from the early morning doesn't materialise. Rajen tells me he has a family wedding to attend and he's arranged for a driver to take me back to Darjeeling. I have a suspicion this is why today's trek ended so abruptly but there's nothing I can do to change things. I'd like to see Tiger Hill, mentioned in the guide books as a famous hill where tourists watch the sunrise and Mt Kanchenjunga, so I ask the driver if he'll take me there and he does, for an extra fee.

Tiger Hill is a surprise. It may be a hill, but it's ugly, there's lot of concrete; concrete walls, concrete paths and a concrete viewing tower and several communication masts and aerials. I guess if you arrive in the dark to see the sun come up and the magnificent view, it doesn't matter too much, but I'm glad I didn't get up at 4 am and pay for the experience, which I had considered doing.

Back in my grimy bedroom I feel quite low. I consider moving to better accommodation, but on my first night here I'd asked for a heater and was given a one-bar electric fire. I covet this and doubt I'd get my own heater if I changed accommodation. I make the mistake of looking underneath my bed trying to locate a missing sock and really wish I hadn't. The filth and dust suggest that a brush hasn't been here for a long time and I see what looks horribly like dry dog poo. I withdraw hastily and try to put it out of my mind.

For comfort, I pay a visit to the excellent coffee place I've found called Glenary's where I can connect with the Internet. I order a pot of Darjeeling tea and settle in for a while.

Returning to my room, I'm walking slowly behind a

boy with odd legs and an uncomfortable looking walk. We go the same way down the damp, smelly, narrow alley where the street sellers sit cross legged on top of their rough wooden counters, selling cooked food and vegetables. I'm struck by how ugly life can be, it hits me that life here is not pretty, it's difficult and dirty, there's filth everywhere, nothing is shiny and bright and it feels like a big contrast to "my" world. I think that maybe the reason I'm feeling so low, the reality of other people's lives is seeping into me and I don't like the contrast.

Twice now I've walked passed an old beggar who sits on the pavement and I haven't given him any money, reasoning that I can't give to every beggar. I've already given money to an old man struggling to walk up a hill, carrying a heavy load of bamboo on his back. Today I see the same beggar hobbling along with the aid of a long pole, he has only one leg. As I pass him I feel ashamed and mean. He sits on the cold pavement all day begging, he has only one leg. I have so much and he has so little. If I see him tomorrow I'll give him some money.

## 22nd January

He's in his usual place today begging and I gave him a big smile, say *'namaste'* and hand him 100 rupees. He smiles back.

The sun is out and I'm walking again to the cable car which they call the rope way. The Chief Minister for West Bengal is visiting the town today and there's wall to wall traffic, police cars and people everywhere.

I'm relieved that the rope way is working, and after paying 150 rupees I climb into a car with two girls and two boys. The landscapes from the cable car are lovely and I enjoy the ride. I hadn't planned to get out the other end, I thought I could do a round trip but it appears to be compulsory, so I spend a strange half an hour with nothing to do but watch with amusement as the other occupants from the cable cars take dozens of photos of themselves and each other. Some men arrive dressed in army uniform and they ask if they can take photos of themselves with me, so funny.

Craving more comfort at Glenary's, I go back there and order a coffee. A man about my age sits down at a nearby table, he sighs several times, quite loudly. I'm curious, are they sighs of contentment or despair? I watch him for a few minutes, I'd like to talk to him so I think of something to say and approach him. He's willing to talk and we chat for a while, I learn that he's a New Yorker and he spent ten years in the marines. He came to visit Darjeeling and loved the place so much that he sold up everything to come and live here. He tells me that he goes to 'Joey's Pub' every evening if I feel like popping along later. I'm about to say I'm unlikely to come when he mentions gin and tonic; this changes my thinking and I'll probably seek out 'Joey's Pub'.

I wash my hair and put on makeup which I haven't worn in a long time and it feels good. It takes about ten minutes to walk to the area I think the pub should be then I stop and ask a local if he knows Joey's place. When I find it, the door seems to be locked. I'm a bit puzzled but fortunately someone comes to the door. I ask if the pub is open and he doesn't look sure but holds the door open for me to come in, all rather strange. The inside is tiny and dark and the only person in there is Dennis, my new friend from Glenary's. He looks pleased to see me and embraces me.

Dennis introduces me to Parva, the man who opened

the door, he and his wife run the pub. I think this is Dennis's 'second home', he and Parva are clearly very good friends. They are both mad keen on '60's music and especially The Beatles, he's met John Lennon and George Harrison. Parva plays guitar and I mention that I'm learning to play the ukulele, being taught by Sam Brown, daughter of the famous '60s singer Joe Brown. Dennis is beside himself with excitement, wanting to know if I've met Joe Brown and I'm very chuffed that I can show him a photo on my mobile phone of Joe with his arm around me, taken a few months earlier. My association with Joe Brown makes me an instant hit with the two of them and during the remainder of the evening we enjoy several gin and tonics and they are not pub sizes!

Wobbling back towards my hotel along the cold, dark streets I reflect on how entertaining life can be if you're a bit bold. A conversation with a stranger in a coffee shop turned into two new friends and a fun evening.

23rd January

# Darjeeling Himalayan Railway to Siliguri (7½ hrs)

Today I'm happy that I'm leaving Darjeeling and my grubby room. Loaded with my stuff, I start the twenty minute walk towards the train station and Darjeeling Himalayan Railway, affectionately known as the Toy Train. The beggar with his long pole is standing in the square talking to someone, he notices me and gives me a nod of recognition and a smile.

At the train station the guy in the ticket office confirms that the train is running today and I'm excited. This 2ft narrow gauge railway was built between 1979 and 1981 and is listed as a UNESCO World Heritage Site. An announcement comes over the tannoy that there's a delay and I wait another hour before the train arrives, but at least it has come eventually. I was feeling anxious that it could be cancelled.

Darjeeling is over 2,200 metres high and the scenery from the train is amazing. The sky is blue and I can see the snowy peaks of the Himalayan mountain range in the distance. The narrow tracks run by the side of the road and they travel through small villages, sometimes so close to the traders that I could put my hand out of a carriage and grab their produce. Occasionally we go around a bend on the road and there are steep drops on one side. For the first couple of hours I'm happy.

There's nothing to see now, it's been dark for the past few hours and I've been on the train for seven hours. The novelty wore off some time ago and my body is aching from sitting on a wooden seat. I hadn't expected the journey to be this long and I feel anxious about my next train. Will I get to the station in time? The train to Kolkata is due at 8 pm and if I miss it I'll probably have to spend the night at the station. As the tension mounts up inside me I remember that *"everything is always alright in the end, and if it isn't alright, it isn't the end"*. Everything always works out for me and I let go of my fear and trust that all will be well.

The train finally comes into Siliguri and I'm asked at which station do I want to get off? I didn't know there are two and I don't know which one I need. Fortunately, a young Indian couple come to my rescue, I show them my ticket and happily they're going to the same station as me and they offer to show me the way. I say a silent 'thank you' to God and the Universe for again sending someone to my rescue.

The young couple seek help from a station master and together we find the relevant platform. It feels later in the evening than it actually is and unusually for an Indian train station there aren't many people about, so I'm especially grateful to have their company. The man reassures me that he will put me on the correct train and that I have no need to be concerned. Alone I would have been very anxious because the train is late and we wait for an hour and a half. This gives me the opportunity to get to know the couple better. They're married, she's expecting their first baby and she's beautifully dressed in a traditional sari. His English is excellent. We're joined in conversation by another Indian gentleman who also speaks some English. They're not easily able to converse in their own languages because my new friend speaks Hindi and the stranger comes from the south and I think he's speaking Tamil. They take photos of me and I do the same of them and I agree we can connect on Facebook.

I have no idea how they know when our train comes in, there are no overhead signs and the name on the train means nothing to me, but my new Indian friend assures me this is the correct train and I climb on.

## Train to Kolkata (580 kms)

My seat is No.36 but the only possible space for me to sit is squashed in the middle of a family, still clutching my front pack and uke. There's not much room for my back pack so I stow it as best I can under the seat opposite. Lying right across the seat is a tiny old lady curled up, she's covered herself with a sheet and her wrinkled face peers out occasionally and she stares at me. I'm reminded of a tortoise poking its head from its shell. There are two other larger family members sitting either side of me and two youngsters who pop in and out from time to time. They've been eating curry, there's evidence from the packaging on the floor and the strong smell pervading the carriage. I feel very uncomfortable. I really want to go to bed but this is impossible until everyone else does. I also want to go to the toilet but don't like the idea of leaving my stuff, so I wait.

There's a lot going on, passengers coming and

going, vendors walking up and down shouting to advertise their chai and food. The carriage is grey, dull, smelly and noisy. After a while the man next to me indicates that we can put up the seat to make the middle bunk bed and he indicates to me that I should get on it. My 'bed' is actually the one below which I would prefer, but I decide not to argue assuming that the old lady will require the bottom bunk. I'm relieved I can now climb up and out of the way of the family.

Leaving my stuff on my bunk bed I find the toilet and this time I choose the western style one. I wash my hands, clean my teeth hastily and scurry back to my bunk.

There's more coming and going in my carriage, the lights have been turned off and I realise that the family have vacated and the space is now occupied by three very large Indian men, one below me and two opposite. The night feels very long. My backpack had felt relatively safe surrounded by the 'family' but I don't feel confident about the three men and now wish I'd locked it to something. Every time the train stops I feel compelled to lean over the bunk to check my bag is still there and be sure no-one tries to take it off the train. There's not much chance of sleep anyway, all three men are snoring loudly and one of them adds frequent fits of coughing and general guttural sounds for good measure.

I put some music in my ears from my iPod to drown out the noise but the battery drains quickly and I'm back to the snoring. The bed is hard and narrow and I can't move much and I've got my front pack, ukulele and walking boots in bed with me. I'm also very cold; an unpleasant draught is blowing across me from a vent in the ceiling and the thin blanket provided does nothing to warm me. I have to remind myself that this is just another experience.

# Kolkata (Calcutta), India

## 24th January

My station is Sealdah in Kolkata and being the last on the line at least I know when to alight. I'm not feeling very well and allow the first yellow taxi driver that approaches me to take me to the hotel I'd previously booked online, called the Heera International.

Kolkata is a mass of traffic, we drive along several cluttered streets and then the taxi stops. Apparently, we've arrived. I carry my bags into reception and realise he's brought me to the wrong hotel, this is the Heera Holiday Inn. I shoot back out the door and fortunately the driver hasn't left, so I get back into the taxi and this time he takes me to the correct hotel.

The hotel receptionist doesn't offer a warm greeting but I'm very glad he'll let me have my room early. I feel exhausted and I'm content to 'hole' up for the day, sleeping on and off. I order tea and toast for lunch and later toast for supper. I sleep surprisingly well most of the night as well and wake up feeling much better.

## 25th January

Looking out of my window in the early morning I see a magnificent reflection of a big red sun on the window of an ugly, empty building opposite and I decide that tomorrow I'll go out early and see the sunrise properly.

I'm excited, I'm in Calcutta, now called Kolkata. Who'd have thought I'd ever come here, the place of history and story books. I venture out of the hotel and saunter up and down the nearby streets taking in my area of Kolkata. It has some of the sights of a big city, some wide roads and larger hotels, but there's still a lot of 'life' happening on the streets with food being cooked and sold, people washing dishes and themselves, sitting and standing about and the usual rubbish and stray dogs. As I pass by, people call 'hello' to me and a group of giggling children ask me to take their photo. They're funny and affectionate with each other and I take many pictures while they giggle hilariously and choose different poses.

I have coffee and a sandwich in a corner café and watch a man on the street with a monkey that's tied to him with a collar around his neck. The man uses a stick to make the monkey perform tricks, doing a somersault or bowing and he asks people for money.

## 26th January

I leap out of bed early enough to catch the beautiful red

sun I'd seen yesterday and wander up and down the street but I'm thwarted, I can't see it anywhere. It's interesting seeing Kolkata waking up. One sight makes me very sad. A man on a bicycle with maybe twenty chickens tied by their feet to his handlebars. They're upside down and I'm distressed to realise they're still alive because every now and then their wings flap in attempted feeble protest. I give up looking for the elusive sun, but when I get back to my room, what a tease, the sun is there again, reflected in my window, huge and red!

I'm changing hotels today, moving to Sudder Street which seems to be where most backpackers stay. I leave Hotel Heera walking, but something's wrong, I'm not going the way I should be. I ask for directions and get directed right back past my hotel going the other way. Two roads further along I ask for directions again when a friendly (aren't they all) cyclo insists he'll take me to Sudder Street for 50 rupees (about 60p) and this time I'm willing. I'm already hot and realise I have no idea where I'm going.

My cyclo driver looks old and thin and he's pedalling hard. I tell him to go slower, I'm in no hurry, but he doesn't understand me. I've now said several times that I want Stuart Lane which is off Sudder Street but he pedals the length of Sudder Street and I realise he doesn't know where Stuart Lane is. Eventually he asks for directions and we finally reach Hostel Galaxy. I give him double his fee.

The area I'm in now is full-on busy, with narrow streets, people, noise and colour. I step inside Hostel Galaxy which looks old and small but quaint with a veranda and some green plants outside. The receptionist tells me that he doesn't have a booking for me and appears totally disinterested. I explain that I spoke in person to someone yesterday but he shrugs and says there aren't any rooms. I'm not very good at walking far with my backpack, so I hope I'll find alternative accommodation easily.

A friend of a friend on Facebook had mentioned that they'd been on a tour of the Sundarbans while staying in Kolkata and I made a note of it thinking I might like to do the same. Whilst looking for Hostel Galaxy I'd noticed a sign for the 'Sunderban Tour Company' nearby, so I decide to pop along there before looking for another hotel.

I'm introduced to Ragesh, one of the brothers that runs the company, and he's very helpful so I choose and book a tour. Ragesh says I can leave my big bag in his office while I look for accommodation and he suggests I try the Hotel Sham International just across the road.

If the name Sham International conjures up an image of something large and luxurious, this Sham International is the complete opposite. Indeed I wouldn't have recognised it as a hotel at all if it didn't have the name outside. It's a rickety old wooden building (I use the term 'building' lightly) and I walk up a wooden staircase, stepping on the treads carefully because I'm not convinced they won't give way. The reception is at the top and I'm told a room will cost 1200 rupees. For such a dump this seems too much so I make to leave. The price is reduced to 1,000 and in the interest of not having to look further, I agree. On the 'up' side they have Wi-Fi and I'm told there is hot water.

Back at the tour office, Ragesh expresses an interest in my ukulele and asks me to play it, so I play a couple of tunes, badly, but he doesn't seem to mind. His young brother is in the office and I hand him the uke so he can play with it. Ragesh clearly loves music. He shows me some brilliant Indian musicians on YouTube and we spend an amiable twenty minutes or so listening together. Two more children have arrived now and they take turns to strum my uke.

I think people back home were surprised by my decision to travel with a ukulele but, so far, I'm very happy to have it with me. It's been a constant conversation starter, everyone wants to know what's in the instrument case.

Outside again in the daytime heat and dusty streets I explore the area around Sudder Street and New Market, getting money from the ATM and buying bottled water. An obvious tourist target, I'm again continually saying *'no thank you'* to traders.

Trip Advisor suggests that backpackers love the Blue Sky Café located just off Sudder Street and I go inside. It has the look of a canteen, with long tables, but it looks clean and busy and the menu is very inviting. I've been craving salads but have been generally doubtful if I should eat them. However a conversation with another backpacker in the café suggests they're fine to eat here as they are all washed in bottled water. When my salad comes it looks and tastes delicious.

Sleep at Sham's seems unlikely. My small room is on a corner with a curtained window onto a rough wooden balcony where a group of teenagers have congregated, chattering, laughing and playing music so loud they may as well be in my room. It seems as though no-one sleeps in this area; the noise of traffic and dogs continues all night.

# 27th January

## Three Day Sundarbans Tour

### Day 1

Today I'm going to have another adventure courtesy of the Sundarbans Tour Company. The Sundarbans are located in the Bay of Bengal in Bangladesh. They are a World Heritage Site and boasts the largest mangrove forest of any coastal environment.

Joining a group of other tourists, we're taken on a bus for a long drive, travelling across roads that are unmade, making it a very bumpy ride. After three hours driving, we pile off the bus and follow our guide who weaves in and out of people and market stalls down to the water and a boat.

Clambering on board the wooden boat I realise there are no seats, some people sit along the edge of the boat and the others stand. More people carrying boxes, bags and luggage pile in until it becomes very crowded and reminds me of pictures I've seen of 'boat people' fleeing their war-torn country. I wonder what 'health and safety' departments in England would make of this arrangement. We putt-putt out across the water and it's not as hard to stay standing as I was expecting.

Arriving at the other side, there are old motorised cyclos waiting for us. A glance at the exposed motor underneath the cyclo I can see the parts are tied together with string and wire and I wonder how it keeps going. We bump along at surprising speed down unmade paths through green countryside and, sitting on seats of wooden slats, it makes an uncomfortable but hilarious ride.

Arriving beside more water, another wooden boat takes us to our accommodation. This boat is colourful and characterful and has seats. I introduce myself to my travelling companions; three friends from Canada, two young women with their elderly mother from Delhi, and a twenty-five year old student called Rishul, from Bangalore.

Our charming accommodation is in an eco-village near Gosaba. We each have a small wooden straw covered hut and mine has a double bed with a mosquito net and a tiny bathroom. It's rustic and basic but clean and I feel very happy. The area we're in is very secluded, there's only us and some staff.

In the evening, we're invited to go out again on the boat. The air is still and cool and it's peacefully quiet as we join a large expanse of water with mangrove forests either side. I think we're on the Gomdi River. I find it very relaxing. Our guide shows us different birds as we pass but I get the most pleasure from watching the sky and water change colour as the sun goes down.

## 28th January

### Day 2

We have an early start this morning so we can have a full day out on the boat. We'll be exploring the shore lines and hoping to glimpse the famous Bengal Tiger. Our boat is painted green, a bigger one than yesterday, and I love it, I'm sitting right on the bow, close to the water.

The scenery doesn't change much, there's a vast expanse of river with muddy mangroves either side. Our guide is called Om and he points out sightings of various birds, a kingfisher, some deer and a small croc but I feel a creeping anxiety that this day could be very boring. We've been motoring along quietly and slowly for about three hours now and it's still only 9 am. And then I have something of a breakthrough. I sort of 'give in' to it, I let go and stop minding that nothing's happening and after a while I realise I'm completely content.

As an aside, I'm reading the book 'Eat, Sleep, Pray' and the author Elizabeth Gilbert talks of a charming expression in the Italian language *"bel far niente"* which means *'the beauty of doing nothing'*. I like that.

I encourage Rishul to come and sit at the front of the boat with me. He's easy company, well-educated and his English is excellent. We chat sometimes but we're comfortably quiet sometimes too. I don't think I've ever been so long awake without food, so I'm very happy when a meal materialises and I don't even mind that its Dhal Bat with rice.

We have the chance for a leg stretch when the boat moors up and Om takes us for a short walk in the forest where we're entertained by some small monkeys in a tree. Sadly, no tigers though and Om makes us all jealous showing a video on his mobile phone of an elegant Bengal tiger he saw recently while out with another tour group.

The Canadians leave the tour this evening but the rest of us have booked another night. There's not much to do while we wait for dinner, so I bring out my ukulele and strum a tune or two. Rishul, I discover, is a brilliant guitarist and happily we find a guitar for him to play. Although it's missing a string he can play pretty much anything and knows every artist I can think of mentioning. He's a big fan of Guns 'n Roses. A couple of the staff want to play my uke and I'm happy to let them, I like how it brings people together, music is great for that. It would have been the perfect evening to have some wine, a shame there isn't any.

## 29th January

### Day 3

I'm awake and up early to catch the morning light and delighted to see Rishul is also about, so we take a walk together. It's misty but warm and we stroll and chat. A woman is fishing, she whirls around and throws a net out in the water then gently brings it in again and we watch her for a while. The morning light is soft and makes the grass look pretty. The area is rural and quiet and a huge contrast to the noise and chaos I've been experiencing in the towns of India and Nepal.

It's a long wait for breakfast of curry and chapati bread and a slab of sweet semolina. I realise we had rice three times yesterday, I'm not sure how much more rice my tummy can take. With time to relax before our journey home, I take my uke up to a wooden roof 'terrace' to practice but I'm not alone for long, one of the staff joins me and wants to have a go. Then Rishul joins us and I'm again asked to play something. I need to increase my repertoire if I'm not to keep feeling humiliated by my lack of ability.

The journey back to Kolkata is very long, a road sign tells me we have 106 kilometres to travel and traffic in

Kolkata is stuffed. We crawl along for the last hour.

Rishul wants to help me find alternative accommodation and together we start looking at different hotels. Both wearing backpacks we're soon hassled by touts advising us to stay at this hotel or that hotel and he expresses sympathy for me, saying he now understands how it feels to be a tourist in India. We don't have success, so I suggest letting it go and we have a farewell drink at Blue Sky Café. Rishul is very kind and says if I need to book any trains he'll do it for me, I can pay the money back into his account. This is a generous offer and may prove invaluable for me.

## 30th January

I want to volunteer to work at the Mother Theresa Missionaries of Mercy and they're located here in Kolkata, so I set off today to find the place. I walk to the end of Sudder Street onto a road full of market traders. Beyond this, the area becomes more like a city.

A.J.C. Bose Road is the road I'm looking for, it should be somewhere nearby. I've come to a wide, busy road that seems to be walled off from pedestrians and wonder how I'm supposed to get across. There isn't an underpass, although there is a massive over-pass road. I tag onto a group of Indians who also want to cross, they expertly weave in and out of the traffic and I follow them.

On the other side, in a nearby park there's a game of cricket going on. I stand for a while watching the game, then to my amusement I notice a herdsman walking along the massive main road with a huge herd of goats, he seems oblivious of the buses, motorbikes and traffic, it's a very strange sight.

I can't locate the Mother Theresa 'House' and my

inability to map read frustrates me. My task is made harder by the change of street names. When Calcutta became Kolkata, road names were changed too, sometimes the original name is referred to, sometimes the new name. As a bonus though, in my search, I come across the famous Flury's Tea Shop which looks very inviting and I decide I'll have to come back to it.

I also come across the luxurious Park Hotel and it crosses my mind to go in and see if they have a hairdresser. My hair needs recolouring which is a problem in India because everyone has black hair. I haven't found blonde hair dye in any of the shops. The hotel does boast a hair salon and yes, they can colour my hair right now. I'm given three colours to choose from and I pick one called 'ash' which I hope will make my hair a bit darker because I've gone extra blonde in the sun. The young male hairdresser does a great job trimming my hair and he 'tut tuts' at its dryness and adds a conditioner.

While I'm waiting for the colour to do its work, I'm persuaded to have my first ever manicure and pedicure. The result of my hair treatment is soft, beautifully conditioned, bleached blonde hair, even lighter than it was before. Oh well, at least there aren't any grey roots showing now. This entire pampering session has cost a lot of money by Indian standards, the U.K. equivalent of £75.00 but still far less than I'd pay at home and I'm probably in the best hotel in Kolkata.

## 31st January

I've been a frequent visitor to the Blue Sky Café, their Wi-Fi is excellent and so is their food. I'm here for breakfast and the South African man I'd seen yesterday is in the café again and keen to chat. I don't enjoy his company, he wants to share his misery with me, he's not happy and has decided to curtail his holiday here and go home. He tells me his wife of forty years has recently died and then he shows me a horrible chest scar. He says that after she died his heart exploded. I don't want this kind of conversation with a stranger. He recommends the hotel he's staying in and says that it costs just 1,000 rupees a night. I'm interested and ask the name of it, but he can't remember and offers to show it to me after we've finished breakfast.

We walk down Sudder Street together and as usual I'm approached by street peddlers and tuk-tuk drivers wanting to sell me something. As always, I smile and say *"no thank you"*. The South African exclaims *"you're nice to these people!"* as though this is odd behaviour. At the hotel he shows me his room and I'm shocked. It's tiny and windowless and his bed is unmade, there are clothes strewn on the floor. There is nothing I like about it and I find it strange that he's shown me his room.

As we're leaving, he tells me there's a place behind the hotel that does laundry and he suggests I go with him to see it. He has some trainers to collect that he's asked to have cleaned in readiness for travelling home. On enquiring, the young Indian woman tells him they're not ready, they're still wet. The South African explodes in anger, they've had his trainers for two days and he feels there's no excuse for them not being ready. The old lady who does the laundry looks terrified. The gentle Indian lady he's yelling at says *"why are you shouting, don't shout, there are people sleeping"* and indeed there are bodies lying about the place. I have to admit this strikes me as slightly funny because in my experience everyone's always very noisy, but I am horrified and upset by the behaviour of the South

African. Still fuming with anger, he leaves and so do I, feeling very uncomfortable to have witnessed this scene.

## Paul Liu

This afternoon I'm meeting Paul Liu. I'm excited and nervous. Paul came into my life a few years ago. While I was working on my computer at home, a message came up from Microsoft saying there was something wrong. I then received a phone call from a person claiming to be from Microsoft and telling me they need to fix my computer. I absurdly gave control of my computer over to the complete stranger calling me from India. To this day I have no idea why I did that.

For the next two hours I watched the cursor whizzing about my screen checking or changing this and that. I thought it entirely likely that my computer was being hijacked and I was resigned to the fact that it would be rendered useless. But it wasn't. When he'd finished, the 'cold caller' and I spoke again. I learned his name was Paul Liu and I found him really engaging. To shorten a long story, we kept in touch. I sent him a gift of a box of English biscuits and on one occasion I spoke on the phone with his mother, who is a school teacher. I told him that if I ever came to India I would look him up. And this is how we come to be meeting today.

Paul arrives at the appointed time and he's with his fiancée Bobby. This makes me feel more comfortable than meeting him on my own. He suggests we all visit the Victoria Memorial, a short walk away. Paul wants to pay for my admission ticket, but I'm embarrassed because the cost for locals to visit is 10 rupees and for foreign visitors the price is 150 rupees!

We have fun. They're an endearing couple and I'm very happy to be with them. In the grounds of the palace, a family I've never met ask if they can take my photo and Bobby and Paul are highly amused. Outside, we sample street food and later take tea at Flury's; this time I have the chance to pay. We wander around Hogg Market and have dinner out. Paul seems very happy entertaining me and says he wants us to go out again next Sunday.

## 1st February

I have a mental shopping list and I'm amused by its simplicity. Water, a packet of tissues and some nuts. Different from my shopping lists at home. While I'm out, I look at some beautiful cotton fabrics thinking it would feel nice to have my own clean bed sheet but I give up the idea when I think about the added weight to my backpack.

I've decided the best way to find Mother Theresa's 'House', known here as the Mother House, is by transport. I agree a price of 50 rupees with a man who pulls a rickshaw. It's very hot and he starts to run so I call to him *"there's no need to run, there's no hurry"*. It takes around twenty minutes for him to pull the rickshaw up to the house and I'm glad I now know the location. When I offer him the 50 rupees he demands more money, so I argue with him saying *"no, we agreed on 50 rupees"*. I'm amused when an English-speaking schoolgirl standing nearby hears us argue and asks what the problem is. She's clearly willing to help.

Walking into the Mother House I'm amazed to see there are several volunteers like myself and it takes quite a time to get us all registered. There are six different charitable locations in Kolkata and we can choose which one we want. Some of them are a bus ride away, so I decide on Prem Dan because it's within walking distance. The nun tells me I can start tomorrow and if I'd like to join mass in the morning then I should arrive by 6 am. They provide breakfast of bread, banana and chai. I think I'll skip mass. My duties will be from 8 am until 12 pm daily.

Two elderly ladies, also registering as volunteers, Judy and Sheila from the United States, chat with me. It turns out that they are also staying in Sudder Street so we walk back together. Their accommodation is the very enviable and famous Fairlawn Hotel situated right in the heart of bustling Sudder Street and they invite me in to join them for tea.

Entering the gates, Fairlawn is an oasis of tranquillity. The furniture and woodwork are painted a peaceful green, there are lush green plants and ferns everywhere and old-style cane furniture. The effect is charmingly 'colonial English' looking. The walls are adorned with photos of famous people who have stayed here in the past, I recognise Princess Diana and Prince Charles, Felicity Kendal, Julie Christie, Michael Palin and Sting.

The pot of tea comes with chocolate cake and I'm told there's no need to pay because tea is free for residents. I think I'm in heaven. Judy and Sheila have been friends for years and they're entertaining company. They tell me that arriving in India they joined a rally of 30,000 people to hear the Dalai Lama speak and afterwards he gave a special 'audience' to the few westerners attending, because he appreciated they'd come a long way to see him. Imagine that!

Reluctantly, I leave the delightful 'Fairlawns' and go in search of some items I may need for volunteering tomorrow. I think that rubber gloves would be a good idea, extra food because I can't imagine surviving all morning on bread and banana, and flip flops because we're not allowed to wear our outside shoes inside the compound.

## 2nd February

## Mother Teresa Missionaries of Charity

## Day 1

My mobile wakes me and with time to spare I take the easy fifteen minute walk straight down Marquis Street.

The early morning walk is interesting; Indians are sleeping on the pavement, stretched out underneath their blanket, some are still asleep in their rickshaws. In front of me I'm upset to see more chickens hanging upside down alive from the handlebars of a bicycle. I reach the part of the street where there's a communal rubbish dump and cows are grazing in the rubbish. Next to the spire of a mosque, and right in front of me, is a pale orange sun looking very atmospheric in the early morning haze. I turn right onto A.J.C.Bose Road and in another five minutes reach the Mother House in time for breakfast.

The breakfast hall is packed with volunteers, I'm amazed how many we are. I queue up for chai, bread and banana and chat with people. A nun invites us to join in a prayer and a song. Eventually we disperse into small groups and I link up with a group of about six heading for Prem Dan.

We cross over two main roads and into an area which looks very poor. It's busy and full of people, street sellers, beggars, children and dogs. There are small, rickety dwellings, presumably homes, with low doorways and openings that I take to be windows. We cross over a railway line and past Park Circus train station. This is a colourful scene with Indian ladies dressed in their elegant, colourful saris and people walking along the railway lines, just like I've seen on the TV. The whole area is bustling and lively. The people look at us as we pass by and some giggling children try to grab the carrier bag I'm holding to look inside. I'm not sure I'd like to do this walk alone.

Thirty minutes later we arrive at the gate to Prem Dam. A security guard opens the gate onto an area with wide concrete paths and several concrete buildings all exuding quiet, orderliness and calm.

A couple of the volunteers have been here a while and they show me what to do. I put on my flip flops and choose an apron, then join a group of people who are doing the laundry.

There's masses of laundry, clothes and bedding, and vast pots of soap suds as well as a whole row of large sinks. Everyone seems cheerful and friendly and I join a girl at a sink rinsing clothes. I like getting physical and in the heat it's a pleasure working in cold water. Washed and rinsed, the clothes are taken up a couple of flights of stairs to a roof top where they're hung on dozens of lines to dry. The sight of all the colourful sheets, tablecloths and clothes waving in the breeze is wonderful to me and there are fantastic scenes of the tangled, messy city all around.

With many volunteers, the mass of laundry is soon finished and we go across the compound to an area where the resident women are sitting. The area is mostly open with a low surrounding wall and a tin roof. Some ladies are sitting on chairs at tables and a few are sitting on the ground or on the wall. I'm told that we should pamper them, massage their hands or feet with lotion, give them manicures or comb their hair and I feel really uncomfortable at the thought of this.

Walking among the ladies I see that most of them are elderly. They're not talking to each other, in fact they seem disinterested. I notice with horror a lady who is hideously disfigured. She has no face. I think she must have been burned, all that's left are two holes where her nose was and an opening for a mouth. I feel shocked.

A volunteer hands me some massage cream and I know I have to get close to these women. With some reluctance I approach a skinny, bent, old lady and offer to massage her hands but she points at her legs so I presume she wants me to oil her legs and feet. I steel myself and take her rough, gnarled feet in my hands. She's so tiny with old fragile skin that I immediately have overwhelming tender feelings towards her. Even though she doesn't know what I'm saying I chat and smile. Her face doesn't change and there's no smile in return.

This place is a sanctuary for ladies that have suffered terrible physical or mental abuse. They don't have families or anyone willing to take care of them. I'm told that relatives will sometimes put an unwanted sick family member onto a train and at Sealdah Railway Station, the end of the line, they're evicted from the train onto the platform where they're abandoned. The nuns find them and bring them to Prem Dan.

Another volunteer asks me go with her and we walk into a bare concrete room where I'm confronted by the largest pile of potatoes I've ever seen. They're tiny and they stink. Our job is to separate out the ones that are okay to eat. There are a few of us and we sit on upturned boxes to tackle the job. I enjoy chatting to the other volunteers, all from different countries, Spain, Italy and Germany. The work makes my back ache and I'm glad when a nun tells us that tea is ready. Ooh, we get a tea break!

The tin mug of chai and plain biscuits are most welcome and I chat with a volunteer from Germany called Barbara. I'm surprised to learn that she has come here every year for many years and she tells me this isn't unusual, many volunteers come back time and time again. She's familiar with the residents because many of them have been here for years.

The arrival of large pots of rice suggest that lunch is ready and the volunteers gather at the tables to take plates of dal bhat to the ladies, still sitting where they've been all morning. Some of them need help to feed and spoons are available, but most use their hands and feed themselves.

As soon as they've finished eating, the ladies go back to their dormitory and beds for a nap. It's a pitiful sight to see their progress out of the dining area across a few yards of concrete and then up some stone steps. Some can walk unaided, some shuffle across the floor on their bottoms, others are put into old fashioned wheel chairs and wheeled to the steps where they haul themselves up as best they can.

I hold the arm of a tiny blind lady, she's muttering all the while. Her brown face is very wrinkled and she has large ears with floppy lobes. One of the staff hauls another blind lady to her feet and she holds onto the shoulders of my blind lady, then another lady joins the second one so, like children playing choo-choo trains, I guide them along slowly together. The thought pops into my mind that it just goes to show 'the blind *can* lead the blind'.

It's a struggle to get my lady up the stone steps but I manage and we make it into the dormitory. I'm horrified when she gathers her dress up around her waist and crouches down to the floor as if to pee. A nun hastily grabs her and shoves her into a nearby room with a stone floor and I realise this is where they go to the toilet. The floor is hosed down when they've finished. I feel a bit shocked.

My first morning as a volunteer is over. Barbara, the volunteer I met at the tea break, suggests we walk back to the Mother House together, I'm very relieved, I would never find my way back along the lanes on my own, nor do I want to.

The walk back feels long and hot. It must be the end of the school day because dozens of boisterous boys spill onto the street, some of them call to Barbara and I saying *"hello"* and *"how are you?"* in their best English. I reply back and there's lots of giggling.

Forty-five minutes later I'm back in the now familiar Sudder Street and I decide to pop into the Hostel Galaxy and see if any beds have become available. A bed in a shared dorm will be free tomorrow, oh joy! I'm very happy to tell Agar, who runs Shams, that I'll be checking out tomorrow.

3rd February

Day 2

Leaving my room at Sham's at 6.30 am I notice again that there are two Indians asleep on the floor of the corridor. I'd seen them yesterday and thought perhaps they were guests desperate for a bed for the night. It now dawns on me that they're staff, hotel staff. They lie sleeping on a single blanket on the tiled floor.

My walk to the Mother House is now familiar and I like walking along the streets feeling confident. After breakfast of bread, banana and the sweet chai, I link up with Barbara again and together we make the thirty-minute walk to Prem Dan.

The Prem Dan Unit is run by Nuns with the help of

paid staff. They are referred to as Muzzies, short for Muslims. I don't know if this is a disrespectful term or not. Volunteers don't come in on Thursdays which gives the staff a day without us and I wonder if the staff resent volunteers because we're taking their work. The thought comes to my mind that the Missionary is in fact doing the volunteers a favour, giving us the 'feel good' factor, rather than the other way around. This thought unsettles me, I want to feel that I'm being useful.

My routine is similar to yesterday. I love doing the washing and I especially love hanging it out on the roof top.

At lunch I sit with a very old, sad looking lady; she has a brown, wrinkled face that reminds me of an African warrior and there's something about her that makes my heart ache. In the centre of the seating area there's a fixed carousel, oddly like one you'd see in a playground and she's strapped onto one of the hard seats so she won't fall out. I stroke her forehead and her face very lightly and after a while she touches my hand and looks up at me. I want to weep, her thin body looks uncomfortable and I wonder how long she's been sitting on that hard seat, her feet dangling above the ground.

Back in Sudder Street in the afternoon, I install myself at Hostel Galaxy. I have some initial anxiety when the receptionist again declares that I'm not booked in, but since it was he that had shown me the bed only yesterday, he rather ungraciously hands me a key.

The place is basic, rickety and quirky, but seems clean and there are other travellers here. There's a kettle I can use and I even have a lockable drawer for valuables. My dorm sleeps six people but it has two partitions so doesn't feel too crowded. Off the corridor is a small balcony with a table and two chairs and a washing line holding up brightly coloured travellers' clothes. I like the feel of the place and I'm happy to be here.

Wi-Fi at Hostel Galaxy is good and I have a very cosy evening on the warm balcony checking messages and using social media. Facebook has been brilliant for me and is definitely one of the reasons I haven't felt lonely. It's fun 'posting' photos and I get some encouraging and generous comments back from folk which feels very heart warming.

## 4th February

The Spanish lady in the bed next to mine has a cold, she's a smoker and snores loudly. Oh the joys of communal living. At least I don't have to get up early, today is Thursday and I have a free day. There's nothing I have to do and I'm struck by how wonderful this is. My life is now so simple; make sure I have drinking water, wash a few clothes and decide where I'm going to have my next meal. I'm the proud owner of a new mug, bought yesterday, and I make a packet cappuccino and settle myself back onto the veranda. I can hear birds, distant music from a TV or radio, cars hooting, a cart rattling along the street and there's a light breeze. Looking over the balcony I can see a young boy in the yard below with a plastic bowl full of water, diligently washing shirts.

My challenge this evening is to try some "authentic Bengali cuisine". The restaurant I choose is tiny and looks quite new. There's nothing I can understand on the menu and the waiter doesn't speak English. I say "vegetarian" a word that is usually understood in restaurants and he 'gets' it. He points to something on the menu and I nod having no idea what I've ordered. The waiter brings my dish which I discover is an aubergine dal and I quite like it, but the bright orange sauce is terrifying and very fiery.

Back at the Galaxy, I open the door to my dorm and I'm hit by a hideous chemical smell, it's shockingly pervasive. I look enquiringly at the Spanish girl who shows me her arm and leg, both covered in bites. She thinks there may be bed bugs and the hostel is obliged to spray everything with chemicals including our mattresses. I don't want to breathe it in, but not breathing all night isn't an option.

## 5th February

### Day 3

Today at Prem Dan I sit with an elderly lady who has no teeth and I'm very surprised when she speaks to me in English. I ask her questions; her name is Simani and I learn that she studied at a university in London for two years and became a maths teacher. I'm amazed. She tells me that her family disowned her because she didn't get married. I can't make out how she has come to be here. I ask her if she can read English and she says yes. I ask one of the Nuns if she's aware that Simani can speak and read English and she seems oddly disinterested. I want to know if there any books and I'm told no, there are none. No books! They don't have any books!!

Prior to working for the Mission, at the volunteers' orientation meeting, we're told not bring any gifts or items for the residents and I understood that there was a reason for this. People may have favourites, it could be deemed unfair. But now, thinking about all the interesting things volunteers would be willing to bring, I'm puzzled. Surely gifts could be put in a central place and brought out for the residents to use. There is nothing for the residents to do here that I can see, no stimulation, nothing to look at. They don't even have their own clothes, everything is shared, there's nothing that they own, nothing personal. I feel upset. Everyone needs some identity, something that belongs to them. The sisters and staff didn't know that Simani can read.

I go to the Sister in charge and ask if I can bring some books in tomorrow and to my delight she says this will be okay.

After lunch I help with the washing up which makes me late leaving, Barbara has already gone, and for the first time I have to walk back alone.

I guess it may be because of my mood but on my long walk back to Sudder Street I feel surrounded by unpleasant sights. One road I walk down I've nicknamed Smelly Alley, it's where the raw meat and the fish is sold, laid out in the hot sun, the smell is awful. There's a dozen or so crows sitting on the pile of meat. A few yards on, some people are watching a little dog. He's dying, convulsing, lying in the wet and filth of the road. Small chickens are packed into a cage in the sun, possibly the same chickens I saw this morning hanging upside down alive from the bicycle, the chopping board used to slaughter them sits on top of the cage. I make it back to my room and overwhelmed with emotion I give in to tears.

## 6th February

I've taken the day off from volunteering so I can meet up with Paul and Bobbie again. Paul comes over to Sudder Street and we take an AC bus to the north of Kolkata where they both live. I'm struck by how kind he is, coming all the way over to my location and taking me back to his home.

The journey takes nearly an hour because there's so much traffic. I don't need to worry about paying; Paul explains that he'll give the conductor a few rupees for his personal pocket, it costs him less than the bus price and he considers this fair; a 'win-win' because he gets a cheap ride and the conductor makes more money.

As our bus journey progresses, Kolkata begins to change and looks more like the kind of city I'm familiar with. The shops and restaurants are bigger, there are office buildings and the roads become wider. This is a side of Kolkata I haven't yet experienced.

Leaving the bus, Paul hails a tuk-tuk and we whizz down a few narrow lanes to a residential area and Bobby's home. She lives with her sister and brother-in-law, not far from the airport.

Bobby, with her beautiful smile, is waiting at the door to greet me and I'm welcomed inside the house into a room with a large high bed which fills most of the space. The room has a TV and a couple of pieces of furniture and the floor is wooden with a line of red paint giving it some decoration. The room has a homely feel.

I'm introduced to Bobby's older, married sister. Unlike Bobby, she's traditionally dressed in a beautiful sari, she's smiley and shy and doesn't speak English. I'm invited to sit on the bed and Paul tells me the women have been preparing a meal for me.

They're very excited to bring me a large tray of dal bhat which is placed in front of me on the bed. Oddly, the bed is also the dining table and the chairs, as there are no chairs in the room. No-one else is eating. They stand around and watch me with anticipation. I'm sitting cross-legged on a large bed with a tray of food, eating with my fingers and doing my best to get the food to my mouth and not drop it on the bed. There are several dishes, with different sauces, vegetables and rice and they're very tasty. Just one dish is a challenge for me, it's fish with lots of tiny bones. Fortunately, my fingers can feel for the little bones and although my tummy is knotted with anxiety, I'm able to finish it. I tell them how delicious the food is and they beam with pleasure. I'm very touched by the obvious care they've taken to provide lovely food for me.

Paul turns on the TV, joins me on the bed and suggests I have a rest. The kitchen work done, Bobby joins us and the three of us take a stroll out along the main road and into a very modern shopping mall. It's huge and beautiful and a massive contrast to anything I've seen in Kolkata before. Paul wants to take more photos, one of me, me with Bobby, me and himself, then all three of us. We come to a small shop selling gifts and ornaments and I'm puzzled when Paul asks the shopkeeper to take yet more photos of the three of us. Bobby chooses a coffee mug to buy and passes it to the shopkeeper.

Half an hour later we're back in the shop. Excitedly, Paul hands me the coffee mug which now has a photo of the three of us on it. Their gift is very kind and thoughtful. I wonder how I'm going to carry the mug in my backpack which is already full to bursting.

## 7th February

### Day 1

I've bought some colourful and visually beautiful books about Indian festivals and gods and I'm excited to show these to the ladies at Prem Dan. After doing the laundry I can't wait to show Simani the book. She looks at it slowly and carefully and gives me a big smile as she points to the words and starts reading them. She tells me her eyes don't see well, so I'll bring her the magnifying spectacles I bought in Nepal. It occurs to me that none of the residents are wearing glasses which, given their age, seems strange. I give the other books to my fellow volunteers and they sit with the ladies showing them the pictures. I'm very happy, they're interested to look at them. One lady said to me "beautiful", referring to the book and I realise that she too has some English words. She recognises the festivals and looks at me nodding and smiling.

Barbara has invited me to join her and some friends at a musical event this evening. It's called 'World Peace Music Festival' and is a metro ride away at Rabindra Sadan.

I'm waiting to meet her at the entrance to the tube station but being a tourist it's a mistake to stand still and a middle-aged Indian man, wearing a neat white shirt, starts talking to me. We have an amusing conversation. He asks me questions and tells me a bit about himself then he says *"we're friends now, aren't we?"* and I say *"no, we're not friends yet because I've only just met you"*. He thinks about this and says *"Oh, so when will we become friends?"* and I say *"well, we'd need to meet more than once to be considered friends"* and he says *"Oh, so if I see you again tomorrow will we be friends then?"* I find this very funny, although I'm aware I may be getting myself into trouble, so I'm glad when Barbara shows up and I have an excuse to move on.

The Kolkata metro is modern, it was opened in 2010. We travel a couple of stops then take a short walk to Chandra Road. The theatre is inside a large modern building. The event is free so I'm surprised to see there are empty seats. The first artists perform Sufi music which is designed to lift the spirits and couldn't be timed better for me. Artists from around the world are performing and oddly, the second act is called 'Jennie

Grove' from Scotland. I love their music which is fast and folky, but I don't think the Indian audience appreciate it so much, they are far less animated while this act is performing.

## 8th February

### Day 5

I'm up ridiculously early to attend mass at the Mother House because I feel I'd like to experience this at least once, if only to hear the nuns sing. It takes place in an upstairs room, already full with people sitting on the floor. The building is next to a main road and even this early in the morning there's constant noise from the traffic outside, but the people inside sing their hearts out and I find it very uplifting.

At Prem Dan, Barbara asks me to help her clean beds instead of doing the laundry. The dormitory is filled with about fifty single, iron framed beds with a thin plastic covered mattress on each. Our job is to wash down both sides of the plastic mattress, then cover each bed with a small sheet, a pillow and a folded sheet at the foot of the bed. All the residents are in the common area, so the dorm is peaceful. Buckets of soapy water are thrown onto the floor and mopped up and when we finish the place looks perfectly organised with every bed covered in a purple coloured, gingham check sheet. I wonder if attention here has become so focussed on cleanliness and organisation they've forgotten to take care of the people.

During the morning I see a car pull up and a sick lady is carried out of the back and taken into the dormitory. I'm told she's another 'victim' found on the station platform.

## 9th February

## Day 6

A sleepless night, it's raining heavily and very noisy in the hostel dorm because our roof is corrugated. The lovely Welsh Emily disturbs me again, she gets up at 4.30 am to attend the Mother Teresa mass, though only the Lord knows why she gets up so early!

I'm glad the rain has stopped when I leave for my walk to Prem Dan. Along the route I'm amused at how many times I have to respond to people who call out to me as I pass them by. Today I have my camera in my hand and along the railway line young children want me to take their picture, which of course I do until there are too many of them and I have to wave them away.

It's a good day. I work with Barbara, cleaning mattresses and beds, then putting on the sheets, I miss doing the laundry which is more fun, but all the volunteers want to do the laundry.

When the work is done I again take the books to the women. There's a beautiful young woman here who is called Rita. She looks very vacant and seldom moves. I sit beside her and hold the book up to her. I'm astonished when she points at the words with her finger and her lips start moving, she speaks very softly and I struggle to hear her words. It seems as though she might be reading but the words are written in English. She's holding it now and looking at it with great intensity. I leave the book with her and I'm excited to see one of the nuns sit with her and talk to her, I haven't seen Rita interact with anyone before.

I've brought my ukulele with me today and brushing aside my inhibitions, I play my repertoire of three songs, moving among the ladies. They don't show much interest but I keep going, singing and smiling and occasionally I'm rewarded with a smile back or a nod. At the far end of the room there are some ladies sitting on the floor and I wander over to them strumming "Keep on the Sunny Side". To my absolute delight one lady stands up and she begins to sway and gently dance to my strumming. Barbara notices and comes over and starts clapping to give the lady encouragement. Another lady gets up and others start clapping. I play the same tune over and over, loathe to stop and interrupt this delightful scene. When I finish, the lady who started dancing stoops in front of me and touches my feet. I want to cry.

The lady who was brought into the unit yesterday is lying in a bed in the dormitory today, she's crying out in pain. My heart feels heavy for her, will she spend the rest of her days here?

At the end of our work I walk back with Barbara and we marvel how it's possible for cows to graze on rubbish, eat plastic and still look healthy.

## 10th February

### Day 7

I've been increasingly upset at the lack of attention and stimulation the residents of the mission receive and I've been puzzled that other volunteers don't express the same concern. I wonder if it's me being arrogant and really what right do I have to criticize anything that's going on here, so today I've decided that I'm going to stop thinking negatively. This is a fantastic sanctuary and the women who are here are safe and cared for.

I've brought colouring pencils and a drawing pad today and while I play my uke I suggest Barbara might like to take them to Rita. By the time lunch arrives Rita has covered the blank page with hundreds of different colour squiggles, neither I nor the nuns know if this is writing, apparently Rita speaks Bengali which the nuns don't understand.

I read to my 'African' lady again, she doesn't react much but she does hold on to the book and I think she likes me being with her. I want to scoop her thin body up and place it somewhere soft, I can't bear seeing her on this same hard seat every day.

Later in the afternoon I walk back to the Mother House to listen to a talk by Jan Petrie, a lady who has worked with Mother Teresa for 30 years, she made a documentary 10 years ago. I'm glad to have listened to Jan who clearly reveres Mother Theresa. My thoughts about the charity are confused and I'm at odds with myself about it.

I've visited the "authentic Bengali cuisine" restaurant three times now to experience different dishes and I've exhausted their vegetarian menu, so this evening I opt for street food. I watch them stir fry veg noodles which are piping hot, they're very cheap and very delicious.

## 11th February

There's no work today because it's Thursday. I sit for a long time on the veranda chatting with two other guests, Cecelia from China (that's her English name) and an older lady from Japan. Cecelia brings out Chinese tea which she made in a tiny pot and shares with us.

In the afternoon heat I walk along the famous Park Street, lined with shops. I'm looking for a gift for Paul, he has a birthday in a few days, on the 22nd February. Barbara has told me of a good book shop called 'Oxford' which has an excellent tea shop on the top floor.

As I enter the store I'm asked to hand over my backpack to the security guard, something I always hate doing but it happens in all the larger stores. I love the store, it could easily have been in Oxford and the air-conditioned tea room at the top is a welcome relief from the heat outside. Back downstairs there's a selection of beautiful pens and I choose a Parker pen for Paul. I pay at the counter then go to retrieve my backpack. Before I'm allowed to leave, the security guard asks to see the receipt for the pen he just watched me purchase.

## 12th February

### Day 8

I learned today that the lady I saw brought into the unit has died and I wonder why she wasn't taken to hospital. I feel upset and confused

## 13th February

### Day 9

Today is my last day as a volunteer. I had intended to stay longer but I've been wrestling with my emotions and I don't feel right about the Mother Theresa Mission. I want to believe I'm being of use or making a difference to the ladies, but it doesn't feel like it. I'm confused because I think the charity's intentions are good, the sisters are good people, everyone has been kind, but something feels wrong. The residents remind me of 'birds in a gilded cage', it isn't enough to keep people safe, they need to *feel* alive.

The day a volunteer is leaving, it's customary for everyone to sing a song to them at breakfast. The tune is sweet with simple words "we miss you, we miss you…." As they sing I look around the room and there are many now familiar faces. Barbara is smiling and acknowledging me and it makes me want to cry. I've been lucky to meet Barbara, she's been a good companion for me at the charity.

My last day is a good one. I clean and make beds and play my uke to everyone, I get more smiles now they've become used to me. One dear lady strokes my face and holds my uke next to her cheek, she strums the strings and starts singing softly, she looks deep into my eyes with such love that my eyes well up with tears, as do hers. It's enough to make carrying my ukulele with me this far worthwhile.

I wave and call out to Rita and I'm rewarded with a big smile, she even claps her hands a bit when I play my uke for her. I think it a tragedy there appears to be no-one working with this sweet soul to bring her back to life. I give Rita the book written in Bengali that I'd purchased from the Oxford book shop.

## 14th February

My phone is on silent but I feel it 'buzz' in the early hours of the morning. I've had a text message from Ben. It's Valentine's Day and he's sent me a message signed "with much love and xxx" I'm thrilled and write a text straight back, but it won't send. Oh, the frustration. My phone has no signal. I desperately want to reply but I can't. I have to focus on being excited that I've received a message, not at being upset that I can't send one!

There are two things that I'd still like to see in Kolkata, so today, my last day in the city, I've booked a short motorbike tour, recommended by an Italian traveller staying at the Galaxy. Aquil is going to take me out on his old British 'bike to see the Hoogli River and the flower market.

We approach the river from the Babu Ghats, a very popular area. There are people wading into the river known as the Ganga, they consider it sacred because it's a distributary of the Ganges. Under the arches of a bridge people are lying prostrate on blankets being given massages. Aquil asks me if I'd like a massage and although I believe them to be good, I politely decline. From where we stand we can see the spectacular Howrah suspension bridge, built by the British in 1943.

I love being on the back of Aquil's motorbike, weaving in and out of the traffic. Along the way he points out various historic buildings. The flower market isn't far.

The market is a large maze of wholesale flower sellers with stalls in narrow, wet and muddy paths. But oh, the flowers. I've never seen anything like this. Beautiful, brightly coloured flowers are threaded into long garlands or braided, they're hanging everywhere. There are large bags of petals and stunning bouquets, beautiful colours and sweet perfume, all gorgeous. I'm so glad I've come to see this.

Aquila takes me back to Sudder Street and before I leave he talks with pride about his old British motorbike. I've thoroughly enjoyed the morning.

Paul wants to see me again before I leave Kolkata, we both have birthdays in February and because today is Valentine's Day he's keen to celebrate, so I'm seeing him and Bobby this afternoon.

We go to a Chinese restaurant and they give me a beautiful red rose, so sweet. We spend the afternoon pottering about in and out of shops and, to my amusement, we finish the day at a Pizza Express. I give Paul the pen I've bought for him and I'm not sure what to make of his reaction. He doesn't open my wrapped gift and I'm worried I've embarrassed him.

## 15th February

I'm leaving the Galaxy Hostel and Kolkata and I have mixed emotions. I realise I've developed a fondness for the place. I hail a yellow Ambassador taxi to take me to the airport. Driving out of the city I notice there are chicken 'wholesalers' by the side of the road, wide round wicker paniers stuffed with little fluffy chickens. I watch as a man reaches into the basket, grabs a chicken and swiftly ties its feet together holding it upside down. This is probably the start of the chicken's journey onto the bike and then the slaughter table. It feels like Kolkata is throwing me a last parting shot.

## *Sri Lanka*

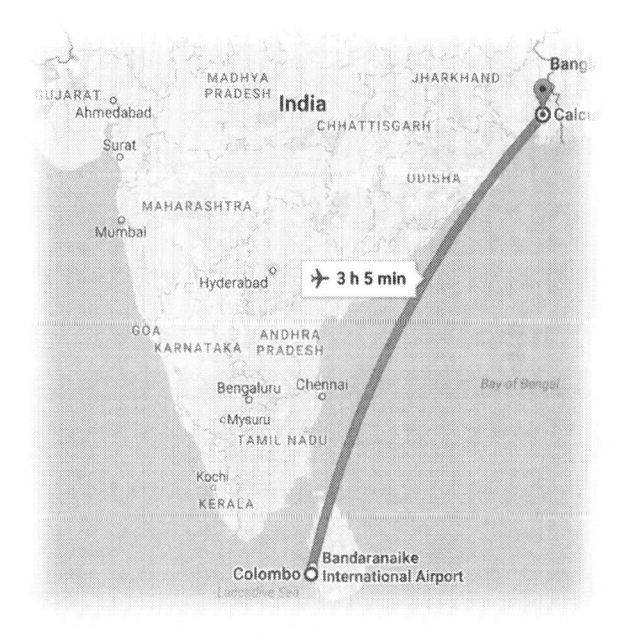

The flight to Sri Lanka takes three hours and I'm thinking about my Mum. We had a holiday booked to come here together in 2004 but she died three weeks before our trip. I wonder what she would have thought about me travelling alone for a year.

The pilot announces before landing, that the temperature in Columbo is 31 degrees, it's mid-afternoon.

A taxi driver approaches me as soon as I leave the airport and although my hostel isn't far I don't know where to go, so I agree to go with him. I think he charges me too much money and have an argument with him. I must remember in future not to take the first taxi that approaches me.

The hostel is surprisingly nice, newly decorated and clean but located on a dull looking main road and I kick myself for booking accommodation near the airport and not having the courage to take a bus directly to Columbo.

I need food, so walk out along the main road, it doesn't seem likely there will be anywhere decent to eat, but I hope at least to buy some fruit. Then, looking through some trees, I see a stunningly beautiful orange sun. I look for a gap between buildings that I can walk through to get a closer look and I come to a restaurant called 'The Mermaid'. At the back is a patio overlooking a lagoon with this magnificent sun setting over the water. I can't believe my good luck. I order a fruit juice and a dish of mixed vegetables and take in the fabulous scene.

## 16th February

## Bus to Colombo and train to Galle (160 kms)

Something has eaten me. I wake up to discover a massive area of my leg is covered in raised red bites, they don't seem to itch. I hope it isn't anything to worry about.

I leave the hostel in a tuk-tuk and ask for the bus station because I want a bus that will take me to Colombo and the train station. I've been told there are good fast buses and there are local slow buses, the distance to Colombo is about 20 kms and I'm keen to get a fast bus. The area is confusing, buses are everywhere, they all look similarly old, they all claim to be a fast bus and they all want my custom. I pick one and climb on board, but if this is a fast bus, I'd hate to be on a slow one. More than an hour later I arrive in Colombo and thankfully, the bus stop is next to the train station where I buy a ticket for Galle.

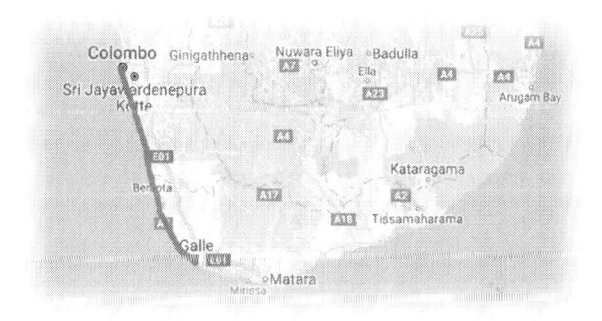

It's an enjoyable and pretty two-and-a-half-hour coastal train ride to Galle. When I arrive, I hop into a tuk-tuk to my hostel and find I'm in a disappointing location, quite a long way outside Galle, in an area which looks very uninteresting.

I've been suffering from a nasty sore throat the past few days and I feel rather glum walking about looking for somewhere to eat. There are no restaurants here, so I buy some crackers, cheese, yoghurt and milk from a teeny-weeny store and a melon from a road seller and take them back to the hostel.

## 17th February

Evelyn from Germany is staying at the hostel and also wants to go to Galle, so we share a tuk-tuk. The old part of the town near the Fort is quaint and peaceful sitting right by the Indian Ocean. It's quite touristy but the small shops and restaurants are very inviting. I walk into the main town which is less attractive. I want a post office because I've decided to post the mug given to me by Paul, back to the U.K. The cost of sending my parcel to England is just £7.00.

I buy a few things to eat and finding a spot along the beach I sit on the sand with my picnic. I'm immediately joined by a young fisherman who starts chatting. At first, I feel a bit irritated, I'm content being alone, but there's something sweet about him and I engage in conversation. He's very young and extremely slender. He tells me the men are hauling the fishing nets in and I should stay and watch. I can see the net is vast, it stretches far out across the water. He tells me about the area and how it was devastated when the tsunami came and he points out that there used to be buildings along the side of the road by the sea, now all gone. Looking out at the sea I imagine how it might feel to see a huge wall of water coming toward you. It must have been terrifying.

I follow the young fisherman over to his friends. They're standing one behind another hauling a massive rope and every now and then the one at the back moves round to the front, I guess the hardest work is done by the lead hauler. They are all very good natured and seem happy with their work. The hauling goes on for about two hours and I'm encouraged to join in. I have a go pulling the rope with them but it's not long before I'm hot and exhausted.

Eventually, the massive net is brought onto the beach and they empty out a huge pile of sardines. Customers are already waiting and there's a lot of weighing and exchanging of money. Hundreds of tiny fish are caught in the net that don't get used or eaten, they just die. I feel sad to think this happens day in, day out.

I say goodbye to the fishermen and walk back into the old town with its attractive quaint streets. The posh looking Galle Fort Hotel looks very inviting and I treat myself to the Fort Grey tea which comes with a custard tart, chocolate ice cream and raspberry coulis.

## 18th February

### Bus to Weligama (35 kms)

Today I'm taking a scenic bus ride to Weligama, along the coast. I'd made a note of the location of my homestay from the Internet so when I arrive I easily spot Raja's Villa down a small sandy lane, a few yards from the beach. It's small, mostly painted wood and very quaint. I'm given a coffee and I sit in the sun and talk with Raja. He wants to know what's in my instrument case, then asks me to play my uke for him. I explain that I'm not very good yet, I'm still learning and he replies *"lady everybody learning, 'aint nobody perfect"*.

I like it here. I retrieve my swimming costume from the bottom of my backpack and walk along the gorgeous beach. It's perfect. The sand is a pale beige and soft. The waves are perfect too, big enough to be fun, but not so big that they're scary and the water is very inviting. I approach a couple sunbathing and ask if I can leave my backpack near them so I can take a dip in the sea.

There are belly boards for hire on the beach and learning that the cost is only £1 for an hour, I hire one. While I'm in the sea the clouds come over and it rains heavily, I feel excited, like a kid. The clouds pass and I stay on the beach until the sun goes down creating a gorgeous golden light. When the best of it has gone I return to my hostel Rajas' to try out his home cooking.

Dinner is amazing, Raja loves to cook and he produces some tasty dishes. This time I don't mind the rice, which is flavoured and delicious. I share the dinner table with five other travellers, four from Germany and Greg from the US. We swap travelling stories and I'm particularly interested when Greg tells me that he has a friend called Troji who welcomes volunteers to come to his flower farm in Malaysia. He gives me his contact details.

After dinner Raja is keen to help me plan the next stage of my journey. He's very excited that I want to go into the central lands to see the forests, hills and tea plantations, he says he's frustrated that so many tourists only want to go to the beach. He's clearly very proud of his country.

## 19th February

I'm up early to go whale watching and a tuk-tuk arrives, an hour later than it's supposed to, to take me to the boat moored in another small town called Marissa. The day is gorgeous and hot and the Indian Ocean is an amazing colour, a dark, inky blue. After ten minutes of lurching up, over and down the massive waves I remember that I'm not a good sailor and I feel sea sick.

This does nothing for my enjoyment of the trip. There are three whale sightings and I struggle to be interested, but one whale kindly appears on my side of the boat so I see him clearly, including the dramatic rise and fall of his tail and I'm grateful for his appearance. We're out for about four hours and I doubt there was anyone happier than me when the boat arrives back at the quay.

My bedroom at Raja's is clean and pleasant and I have my own little bathroom. It's nice to know I can comfortably get up in the night to use the loo but this time I wish I haven't; turning on the bathroom light reveals a white wall covered with many large black cockroaches. I make a hasty retreat and remember that sometimes it isn't a good idea to turn on the light, sometimes it's just better not to know what's there.

## 20th February

## Buses to Deniyaya (70 kms)

I've had an enjoyable time in Welligama at Raja's Guest House, his meals are exceptional and I'm sorry to be moving on. After another delicious breakfast of banana pancakes and seriously strong Sri Lankan coffee, I follow Raja's advice and take a bus to Akuressa, then change to a bus for Deniyaya. I don't know when to get off because Deniyaya is a small place but asking my fellow passengers they tell me when I've arrived.

Thank heavens for tuk-tuks, they make life so much easier, I wish we had them in England. I don't know how to get to Deniyaya Guest House and neither does my tuk-tuk driver so I give him the owner's phone number and he gets directions.

It isn't a guest house so much as a homestay, there

are two rooms and Gihal, the owner, lives here with his wife and small son who are currently out. He's an excellent host, he makes me noodles for lunch then invites me to walk with him to a water fall and a place where we can swim in the rocks. I hesitate. I don't know this man, I haven't met his wife or child and he's suggesting I walk into the unknown with him. I don't hesitate for long and grab my swimming stuff and camera.

Talk about everything always works out for me. We stroll down the lane and we're surrounded by lush green grass, low mountains and rice fields where workers are harvesting the rice. There are white heron birds standing in the water and tall green trees everywhere. I see the largest squirrel ever and a pineapple growing by the side of the path, everything looks gorgeous.

We walk for about fifteen minutes until we come to a place where water rushes down over rocks and there are several rockpools. Gihal whips off his shirt and jumps right into a pool. The water looks very inviting and he waves, beckoning me to join him. The water is cool but not freezing. Gihal tells me to stand on a rock in the water, he says that I will feel fish come and nibble the dead skin on my feet. And they do! There's a tickling sensation on my feet, it's a funny feeling. He says that people pay a lot of money in expensive beauty parlours to have this treatment and I recall hearing about this.

After strolling back to the homestay Gihal takes me into town on the back of his motorbike so I can buy more credit for my phone. When we return his wife and young son are at home. She's made me rice and dal for supper and I again experience the embarrassment of eating alone while they watch, keen to know if I appreciate their food. It's been a lovely day and I finish it off by playing a couple of tunes on my ukulele for them.

## 21st February
## Bus to Embilipitya, Somewhere Else and Ella (150 kms)

I love this place so much I ask if I can stay another night, but my room is booked by another so I have to move on. My next plan is to get to Ella, recommended to me by fellow travellers. Gihal has given me guidance how to get there and I take a bus going to Empilibitya, where I expect to change for a bus to Ella.

The journey on a local bus is long and hot. At Empilibitya I change buses to one I'm assured will reach Ella but I'm having doubts. I've been on the bus a very long time now, the mountains have disappeared and the land is now flat, which doesn't seem right. The journey ends at a bus station in Tunanialwar and I have no idea where I am. I'm directed to another bus apparently bound for Ella, which seems to go back the way I've just come. I'm hot, hungry and frustrated but there's nothing I can do about it. After another hour we stop at a bus station and I learn that it's lunchtime and the bus won't leave again for a while. I've been travelling for a few hours by this time, probably going around in circles.

I find a toilet, the second most disgusting one I've used in my travels and I even have to pay 20 rupees for the privilege. Outside, a big Express Bus pulls up, with the destination Ella on the front of it. A couple of backpackers also wanting to go to Ella climb on, and I decide to change to this one, I have more confidence this bus will take me where I want to go. I grab my uke and large backpack from my previous bus and climb on. Another hour later I finally arrive in Ella.

Directions from the Internet suggest it should be a short walk to Mr Sonny's Guest House called Grand Peak and before long a sign on the dirt road directs me there. The cost is a little pricier than a hostel but it looks worth it, I have a decent room and a bathroom of my own. I ask Mr Sonny if I can stay for two nights.

I've come to Ella because I've heard the surrounding scenery is beautiful. Ella is a village inland in the south of Sri Lanka, at an elevation just above 1,000 ft. There's a scenic train journey from Ella to Kandy and that's how I plan to leave here. I walk along the main street which is lined with tourist accommodation, small shops and places to eat, this is clearly a popular place. It's quirky and I like the atmosphere. I find the little rural train station and walking out onto the platform I can see a single track winding off around a bend, surrounded by green grass and trees and mountains in the distance. I'm amused to see cows walking along the tracks.

There's a scenic view point from Little Adam's Peak, 1141m high and I walk there, hoping to see the sun set. The walk is long and it's been a tiring day but the surrounding vistas of hills and mountains are worth it. I'm disappointed that the setting sun disappears behind a large hill without any drama, so I determine to come back early in the morning and catch the sunrise instead.

I've at last been able to send a text message to Ben and he messages right back. His text says *"I was beginning to think the earth is flat and you had disappeared over the edge"*. This is a long text by Ben's standards and I'm like a kid, all bubbly and excited to hear from him.

After an evening meal of vegetables and roti, a sort

of flatbread, I go back to my room. I'm looking forward to a shower. Divested of my clothes I step into the shower cubicle and turning around I see giant ants are pouring in through a high grill in the wall. Against the white tiles they look like something out of a horror movie. I try to shower them away but it seems to make it worse, they charge through in their hundreds and then all the light goes out and it's pitch black. No! I'm in the bathroom, in the dark with a huge army of ants, I'm out of here!

## 22nd February

In my enthusiasm to catch the sunrise on Adams Peak I'm up at 5.30 am. I'm not sure this is the smartest thing to do, it's still night time dark and walking along the road I feel nervous about the roaming dogs. The public notice telling me to "take care, there are robbers and thieves about" doesn't add to my confidence. I reach the narrow footpath that takes me into the hills and realise someone is walking behind me, I'm uncomfortable and stop so he has to pass by. After a few yards he seems to have disappeared, so now I can't see where he's gone and I'm more nervous that he might be hiding in the bushes ready to leap out.

My heart's pounding, but I won't be put off and resolutely keep walking. With some relief I notice the sky is becoming less dark and I make it to the top of Adams Peak. My efforts are rewarded, the light from the sun rising over the hills is gorgeous and I spend a happy time taking in the atmosphere and the scenery. About an hour later I start the walk down and meet other people walking up, I feel sorry for them that they've missed the gorgeous sunrise, but also slightly smug – hey, you snooze, you lose!

After scrumptious coconut and honey pancakes for breakfast at my guesthouse, I walk to Ella train station to buy a train ticket for Kandy tomorrow. I'm told the train is fully booked, there aren't any tickets available. All is not lost though, I'm advised that if I turn up early tomorrow I may be able to get a 'general' ticket, whatever that may be.

I can't leave Ella without paying a visit to the amazing looking Ella Rock which according to the guide books boasts stunning views. The walk starts along the track from the train station. As I start out I meet a young couple, Emil and his very pregnant wife, May, from Denmark. They invite me to walk with them and I'm massively grateful for their guidance. We have to walk on the tracks some of the way, there isn't much of a path at the side and I pray that, like on the films, the tracks will vibrate in good time to let us know if a train is coming. The scenery all around is lush green and very pretty and there are waterfalls in the distance.

We've been walking for a couple of hours and feeling lost, unsure of the last part of the route up to the Rock, when a Sri Lankan guide approaches us and offers to show us the way. He's come out of nowhere, there's nothing here but rice fields. He takes us round and up and through woods and I wonder if we're really taking the best route to the top. Although May is pregnant she copes well with the walk and the climb and we do eventually make it out onto the open summit.

The vast landscape is spectacular, jaw dropping wonderful. Emil and May sit one behind the other, May with her arms around Emil's neck and they look out across the vista. They make a sweet picture. By the time we get down from the walk we've been trekking in the heat for over four hours and I marvel at May's stamina. We offer our guide some money but he says it isn't enough, he expects more. Emil and I both agree that we're offering a fair amount, he invited himself to be our guide and no fee was agreed, so we refuse to pay more and walk on, which makes the guide get angry and shout abusively at us.

## 23rd February

### Train from Ella to Kandy (120 kms)

Checking out of my accommodation, with my rucksacks, uke and faith that things always work out for me, I'm at the train station early to get a ticket. I'm in luck and for the first time in my life I purchase a first-class ticket which is my only option. A smart looking blue train arrives. The journey is wondrous with such beautiful scenery that I don't want to sit down. I stand by the open doorway of the carriage and with the cool air rushing by I love every minute of what, must surely be, the prettiest train ride in the world. We pass through hills and forests, by waterfalls and tea plantations, all simply stunning. I'm amused to think I have a first-class seat yet I've been standing the entire journey, but when I later notice the number of people getting out of the standard fare carriages I realise I've been very lucky, they're packed in like sardines.

I've arrived in the city of Kandy in central Sri Lanka. Described as being 'set on a plateau 500 metres high and surrounded by mountains', my first impression is it sounds nicer than it looks. It's searingly hot and the walk to my hostel along a busy, traffic filled road is longer than I'd expected.

Hostel Kandy is basic cheap accommodation in a shared dorm. I've just met my dorm mates, Beca from Germany and Jasmin from Holland. Beca is keen to do a hike to The Knuckles and is organising a guide for tomorrow and Jasmin and I want to join her.

24th February

Our guide, Praba, picks the three of us up from the hostel early and drives us to the start of the walk. It's magnificent. We walk for hours with stunning landscapes of hills, fertile fields, forests, rivers, all wonderfully lush and green. I'm on gorgeousness overload.

We stop at a waterfall and a series of rockpools where Praba tells us we can have a swim. I don't have any swimwear with me and Beca offers to let me use her pyjamas. I'm intrigued why someone would go on a trek with pyjamas in their rucksack but I'm happy to accept her kind offer. The only way into the water is to jump, and I'm scared, but I'm not going to miss out, so I jump anyway. It's cold but feels good and the three of us have a lovely time swimming in and out of the waterfall. There's a dilemma though, having jumped in, how do we get out? Jasmin finds a way across some alarmingly slippery rocks and I gingerly follow her, fortunately Praba is there with an outstretched hand to help us to safety.

Our walk finishes when we emerge through some woods onto a high plateau with spectacular views all around. This is one of the most perfect days I've ever had; our guide, my two lovely trekking companions and the beautiful walk. I'm tired but 'off the scale' happy.

## 25th February

I haven't arranged to do anything today so I think I'll stay at the hostel and plan where to go next and catch up on admin. Frustratingly, there's a power cut which means I can't work on my laptop. Instead I walk out to locate the bus station, I need a bus for Badulla where I'll change for a bus to my destination, Sigiriya. I'm glad I check, because confusingly, there are two bus stations and I now know which is the one I need.

## 26th February

### Buses to Sigiriya (100 kms)

My bus to Badulla is a good, air conditioned one and I settle back in comfort for the next three hours. I'm on my way to Sigiriya to visit the famous Sigiriya Rock Fortress, another UNESCO site. At Badulla I have a long wait for my next bus, but I'm glad for the opportunity to find a toilet, always a challenge when travelling.

Getting close to Sigiriya I show the bus conductor where I'm staying, the Wipula Homestay, and he tells me when I need to get off. The stop is very rural and I can't see any buildings. I wonder what I've booked for myself this time. Fortunately, even here, a tuk-tuk appears, he knows the Wipula Homestay and drives me down a dirt track stopping outside a small, single storey property.

A young lad of 17 years introduces himself as Tharindu, he tells me this is his homestay and he'll look after me, and indeed he does. He brings me a cup of coffee and explains about the meal he'll prepare for me later.

With plenty of daylight left, I take a walk down the country path to find Lion Rock. Rounding a bend in the path, I'm astonished to come across an enormous white Buddha statue, he's surrounded by many life size statues of worshippers. It's an extraordinary sight, seemingly in the middle of nowhere.

The walk to the Rock is delightful and not too far from my homestay. The area becomes more commercialised with market style stalls at the side of the paths. There are monkeys scampering about, in and out of the trees. I'm amused to pass a large public notice declaring that *"It's dangerous to walk after 6 pm, elephants may be roaming"*.

When I see 'The Rock' appear in the distance, I'm excited. It's mind-blowingly huge. The area around is grassy, green and peaceful and as I approach I see a large moat surrounds the rock. There's still enough daylight left for me to make the expensive (rs 4320) and long climb to the top. I feel very lucky that I've come this late in the day, there are very few people here, yet the guide books warn of huge crowds.

Over 2,000 steps to reach the top, the panorama is truly incredible. I can see for miles in all directions, all forests and jungle and I wonder how many elephants are wandering there among the densely packed trees down below.

I spend a long time happily pottering about on the top, then slowly make my way back down and explore the grounds around the rock. I see several large reptiles that look like miniature dinosaurs. I realise how relaxed and happy I feel and how I'm at ease being alone and able to please myself.

Arriving back at the homestay I hear the tune of Fur Elise coming from a tuk-tuk and remembering the mobile bakers in Weligama, I rush out to see if this one is also a baker. He is, and I buy some vegetable bread and a sugary doughnut and I'm pleased that I have some food for a picnic tomorrow.

My homestay host, Tharindu, makes me a tasty vegetable and rice dish for supper and I wonder at the responsibility he has at the age of 17 years. Then the electricity goes off and plunged into darkness I retire to bed early.

## 27th February

Today is my birthday. I'm sixty-three and according to the U.K. Government, officially a 'pensioner'.

My day starts with an unusual breakfast of roti and dal with a fried egg and coffee, which I have at a table outside my room, in the warm sunshine.

I'm going to visit Pidurangala Rock Temple today, it's smaller than Lion Rock and a couple of kilometres away. I meander back down the same lane I walked on yesterday, until I reach the moat that surrounds Lion Rock. I feel explosively happy, everything looks perfect to me. The monkeys scampering along the path are funny and I take lots of photos of them. There's a pretty, small lake with beautiful lilies and I sit by it for a while taking in its gorgeousness.

There are more people around this morning and several passing tuk-tuks all looking for a passenger, but I want to walk. I follow the moat around to the left in what I think is the correct route to Pidurangala Rock but with my sense of direction I can never be sure.

Along the path there are wild flowers and more butterflies than I've ever seen in my life before, there are swarms of them. I have a fun time photographing the butterflies, waiting to get an even better picture than the one before. If I'd taken a tuk-tuk ride I would have missed this wonderful display.

The entrance to Pidurangala is through the remains of an ancient temple and walking through the arch I notice a large bell. I ask the attendant if it would be okay if I ring the bell, I childishly want to ring it for my birthday. It makes a loud, rich clang and I ring it again.

The walk to the top of the rock is mostly paved with old stones and it's shaded with trees. Climbing higher, the rocks become much larger and harder to navigate until I'm not sure how to reach the summit. There has to be a way, so I keep clambering up and over the boulders until I can see the top. It's a stretch for my short legs and I wish my arms had more strength, but I make it out onto the top of the rock. I'm exhilarated. I feel as though I'm standing on top of the world, the green trees below reaching far into the distance. There's an incredible view across to the Lion Rock that I was on yesterday and with only a few other people here I stay for a long time soaking it all in.

Getting down from the rock is harder than getting up, the boulders are massive, but I make it back onto the path and down safely. Outside the temple there's a quirky, tiny, shop with a small table and some rickety chairs occupied by a couple of tourists, so I go inside to see if they serve coffee. I'm delighted to learn that they do.

Looking around, I'm curious that the 'shop' is so empty. There are very few items on the shelves, just the usual packets of crisps, but no food that looks inviting. A wooden chair is brought outside for me to sit on and another wooden chair is provided to become the table. When my coffee arrives, it's served in a tea pot, the milk comes separately in a coffee mug and I'm given a tea cup for the coffee. I wonder how these people make money. I take my time drinking the entire tea pot of strong coffee and muse on the business potential of the place.

I'm on a caffeine high and have a hot but delightful butterfly-filled walk back. I spot a kingfisher by the moat and reflect on how wonderful life is when you have time to be leisurely. This is a glorious way to spend my birthday and while I don't feel lonely, it does make me think of my family and friends. I take my phone out and record a short video to put onto Facebook. It's meant a lot to me that so many kind and interested people comment on my Facebook posts and I want to use the opportunity to say 'thank you' for their support.

## 28th February

### Buses to Maskeliya (200 kms)

Another early start today to catch the bus back to Kandy and I'm relieved that the tuk-tuk driver arrives on time to take me to the bus junction.

It's a two-and-a-half-hour journey on a very packed bus and many passengers are standing, so I'm grateful I have a seat. My final destination today is Maskeliya which requires another two bus rides, Kandy to Hatton, two and a half hours, then Hatton to Maskeliya which should only take an hour. The total distance is about 200 kms and I don't mind the journeys at all, the scenery along mountain roads, is beautiful. I reach my homestay called Madhusha Rest by mid-afternoon.

I can tell that this is a really attractive place and before it gets dark I take a walk to see where I am. There are tea plantations and hills all around. The sky becomes very black so I don't stay out too long and I need to spend some time this evening on the Internet researching the next part of my journey. Frustratingly when I reach the homestay the Wi-Fi has been switched off because of the impending storm.

## 29th February

I've come to Maskeliya because it's home to the famous Adams Peak. It's a conical mountain 2,243 m tall and in Buddhist tradition is held to be the sacred footprint of Buddha, in Hindu tradition that of Shiva, and in Islamic and Christian tradition that of Adam, so lots of people make a pilgrimage to Adams Peak especially at sunrise.

My homestay host is used to travellers coming for the purpose of seeing Adams Peak and is able to arrange for a tuk-tuk to meet me at the unsociable time of 1.45 in the morning to take me to the start of the climb.

I'm wondering what the hell I'm doing, waiting outside in the night-time dark, when the tuk-tuk arrives with a bearded driver wearing a hoodie. This is a surreal experience, we speed off into the darkness along lanes for half an hour, I have no idea where I'm going or if this is safe. I'm relieved when the tuk-tuk comes to a standstill and I can see signs indicating I've arrived at the site of Adams Peak. My driver points to a concrete path with many steps and I assume this is the start of the walk.

The night is still black and my hand torch chooses this moment to stop working. There are other people about and they create enough light for me to see the steps and since the only way is up at least I know I won't get lost. The steps are sometimes concrete, sometimes rock and never an even height which makes the climb tiring. To my relief lighting is provided alongside the path so the lack of a torch isn't an issue.

The steps climb up and up endlessly, occasionally there are refreshment stalls by the side of the path where people stop to rest. I keep going but there is nothing about this that I'm enjoying. I've been climbing for hours and have no idea how much further there is to go, there is a continuous unpleasant smell, and the further up I climb the more crowded the path becomes. After about three hours of this I feel as though I must be nearing the top, I can see the string of lights up ahead reaching the probable peak and then I join a people jam.

The light in the sky is beginning to change and I'm not sure I'll make it to the summit for the sunrise. The queue takes one step then pauses, takes another, then pauses, it's really slow progress and I'm tired and bored. An hour of this slow-moving traffic and I'm losing the will to live. Suddenly I can see what I believe to be the summit and it is, it's a temple. The dawn breaks and it's magnificent. The sky changes to pinks and oranges sadly difficult for me to see in its true splendour because I'm a 'short-ass' hemmed in by a mass of people and a railing all around.

I'm grateful that I don't suffer from claustrophobia because leaving the temple is tricky, more and more people are trying to reach the top which hinders people trying to get out and there's only one path up and down. I feel miserable at the thought of the long walk back down the steps, and my mood isn't improved by the daylight, which exposes the disgusting filth and rubbish that lines the path. I regret wearing my heavy leather walking boots instead of my running shoes which are much lighter. The sun makes me hot and sweaty and I'm feeling very grumpy.

Finally, finally, with weary legs I reach the bottom of the steps and I'm desperate for a toilet. Seeing a sign for one I follow its direction away from the path. It's a typical hole in the ground but my need is urgent and I don't care.

I think I've picked up the path again but having arrived in the dark there's nothing here that I recognise. As I continue walking I grow more concerned that I've taken a different path and wonder where I'm going to end up. Eventually after a long walk I arrive in a little place called Dalousie and oh joy, there are buses and one is labelled Maskeliya on the front, so with great relief I jump aboard.

1st March

Bus back to Colombo (150 kms)

I'm on my way back to Colombo, it's another five-hour bus ride and I've booked a night's accommodation at the City Rest Fort, before going to the airport tomorrow. I need some time to research a few things on the Internet and this is an ideal opportunity. Colombo seems to be a fairly typical, busy city and it doesn't hold much interest for me. I take a walk out to locate the bus station, something I like to do because I still get nervous about arriving at airports on time and, as I've previously found, there's more than one bus station. From my research I know there's a large purple air-conditioned fast bus that goes to the airport and I know the name of the bus station it departs from, so armed with this information I feel confident about my journey tomorrow.

## 2ⁿᵈ March

The hotel orders a tuk-tuk for me and I ask the receptionist to explain to the driver exactly where I want to go. I'm very specific, I don't want the slow, local bus, I want the fast airport transfer one. To my exasperation the tuk-tuk driver takes me to the wrong bus station, exactly where I don't want to be. I try and explain but he shakes his head so I tell him to drive back to the hotel where I again ask the receptionist to explain what I want. There's an animated discussion between the two of them and the receptionist tells me that the driver had taken me to the correct bus station. I'm completely bewildered, this doesn't fit with the information I have, but what can I do? They must be right. I get back into the tuk-tuk and we go back through the busy city to the bus station. I feel bad that I've caused such a kerfuffle so give the driver extra money, then go in search of my bus. There's no sign of the purple one and I'm persuaded to get on another bus which I'm assured is the fast transfer to the airport.

It isn't the fast transfer. The bus meanders here and there stopping to pick people up and the journey is unbelievably slow. Finally, finally, we reach the airport. The conductor hasn't asked me for any money so before I get off I offer to pay. He demands an absurd amount of money and I say *"you have to be joking"!* I intentionally have very little Sri Lankan money left in my purse and tell him *"I can't pay that, I don't have that much money"*. I honestly think he plucked a figure out of the air to see if I'd pay it. I give him what I have which is half what he's asking for and it leaves me with nothing, not even enough money for a cup of coffee.

# *Back into India -Palolem (Goa) and Mumbai*

The authorities let me back into India and I notice that I have mixed feelings about returning. I've arrived at Cochin International Airport near Kerala in the south and it doesn't take long to realise that this is very different from the India I've previously experienced. The atmosphere is different, it's quieter and cleaner. I've chosen a modest hotel not far from the airport because I'm coming back here tomorrow to meet my good friend Fliss. She's coming to join me for ten days and I can't wait to see her.

3rd March

Fort Cochin, Kerala with a Friend

I'm at the airport early to meet Fliss, quickly scanning each arrival and enjoying watching the reunion scenarios as people wave, kiss and greet each other.

And there she is, on time, smiling and looking fantastic.

My lovely friend has booked us into a beautiful hotel in Kochi and I'm going to love every minute of living in luxury for a while.

After freshening up at my hotel, I check out, we've extravagantly hired a taxi to drive us the 40 kms to Fort Cochin. Ten minutes into our drive I realise I've left the silver necklace that Ben had given me on the dressing table in my hotel room. I've worn the necklace every day of my travels. The driver offers to take me back, but I remember that luckily, I'll be returning to the same hotel, so I can pick it up then. We phone the receptionist and he promises to keep my necklace safe.

Getting into Fort Cochin requires a crossing on the Ernakulam Ferry and Fliss and I walk on board while our driver stays with the taxi. I'm already having fun sharing India with Fliss and it feels great to have her company.

The hotel is as good as we hoped, everything about it is tasteful, with an 'old Colonial' feel. Our bedroom is spacious and airy with large beds and white linen. Getting changed after our travels, Fliss notices that my skin is dotted with insect bites and alarmingly suggests they may be bed bugs. I don't think they are, but the image of me contaminating this fabulous hotel (and Fliss's stuff) with bed bugs is hideous and I give up a silent prayer to the universe that she's mistaken.

Outside, the hotel has well-kept gardens, a dining area and a gorgeous aqua blue swimming pool which we're looking forward to trying after we've ordered some coffee. Bed bugs forgotten, we have a relaxing time in and out of the pool.

We're keen to take a look around Fort Cochin which a Telegraph report describes as "the oldest European settlement in India, a melting pot of diverse cultures…".

It's now late afternoon and we wander along the waterfront. It's messy here, but nothing like as filthy as other cities in India, although Fliss having just arrived is quite shocked. Along the water's edge are the amazing Chinese net and bamboo fishing contraptions I've seen in the tourist books. Some of the little stalls by the path are selling fish, presumably caught today.

Fliss has done some research and suggests we eat at the nearby Malabar Hotel and with a vision of cold Sauvignon Blanc in my mind, I'm more than happy to agree. We're not disappointed, it's very elegant and I take my first glass of white wine for ages and I don't think I've enjoyed one so much before.

### 4th March

After an excellent breakfast, Fliss and I wander into the town. It's seriously hot and we meander slowly, curious about the interesting old character buildings lining the road, many of which appear derelict. We come to an open shop where the owner is sitting at the front totally surrounded by books, really old, tatty books that look as though they've been there for years. I wonder why he keeps them there and decide that maybe it's to show that he's very well read.

Fliss has heard there's a spice market here but we haven't found it yet, so when a tuk-tuk passes and asks if we need a ride we ask him to take us there. It's a short distance and he stops outside a large spice 'barn'. Inside are two ladies sifting ginger with a large sieve that they each hold and shake from side to side. They're very friendly and willing to let me have a go so I take one end and shake the sieve watching the small pieces fall through, the aroma from the ginger is amazing. I wonder if these ladies do this task all day.

Fliss has another gem of a place in mind for dinner this evening, a 300-year-old hotel and restaurant called Old Harbour, it's built in the Dutch style and packed with character, our meal is excellent and so is the red wine. Oh, life is good!

## 5th March

We've booked a day out on the Kerala backwaters and along with a group of other tourists a bus takes us to the waterways. We start out in punts, our pilot wielding a long pole and gently guiding us through pretty, narrow waterways surrounded by lush green trees and vegetation. It's a hot day and it feels good to be on the water. We pass the occasional dwelling and see a lady washing clothes in the river, beating the garments on a stone, I always marvel how the garments aren't reduced to shreds doing this.

Just as I'm wondering how much longer my empty tummy will last, our boats moor up on a small, green island and we're told that it's lunchtime. We dine in a rickety old sort of caged gazebo, with plastic chairs and tables. Our dinner plates are large palm leaves and we're served the usual rice and dal with bananas and fruit. The food is good and I'm full again.

In the afternoon, we move onto a bigger wooden boat with a thatched roof which takes us to some larger waterways and gives us hard-working tourists a chance to relax and take a nap.

Later we have another short excursion onto land to watch a lady making rope from the fibres of coconuts. She walks continuously up and down a few yards, gradually teasing fibres into a length of twine. I again wonder if this is a job she does all day, every day and I'm curious about her hands and ask if I can see them.

She laughs and opens her hands out. Not unexpectedly, the skin on her hands feels like leather.

Fliss has found us yet another fabulous place for our evening meal. This time we've come to the History Restaurant at Brunton Boatyard, a hotel lovingly restored and rebuilt to maintain the original character and with views of the Periyar River and Chinese fishing nets. Our food doesn't disappoint, neither does the red wine and I wonder how I'll go back to dorms in hostels and 'do it yourself' meals when my time with Fliss comes to an end.

### 6th March

We're having a relaxed "pottering about" day. We've hired bikes and are cycling along the sea front when Fliss spots what she thinks is a dolphin, so we park our bikes and to our delight realise there's a pod of dolphins and we watch them launching up and out of the water. A group of young Indians are watching too but their attention is diverted towards us and they ask if they can take their photos with us. I still find this very amusing.

We have fun pedalling around and stopping when we feel like it. We come to a quaint place called 'The Teapot' and stop for refreshment, ordering banana pancakes and pineapple lassi. I've been hoping to buy some hippy style trousers and I find a little shop that has exactly what I want, although they're too long in the leg. The shopkeeper tells me he can shorten them in an hour and suggests I return later when they'll be ready.

As we cycle a bit further down a main road the area becomes much more 'town' like and busy with traffic. I'm nervous about getting lost and Fliss seems nervous because it's much more crowded, so we cycle back. Reaching the shop with my trousers I'm frustrated to discover that it's closed. I'll have to return tomorrow.

Kerala is famous for Ayurvedic treatments and there are plenty of small businesses around to tempt tourists in. Fliss and I picked one this morning and made appointments for this afternoon so after a quick swim in our hotel pool, we grab the bikes again and cycle back to the beauty parlour to be pampered. Still suffering from a sore throat and, what I now refer to as my 'India cough', I've booked a face massage and nasal clear out.

The 'clinic' is tiny and over-staffed with one person on reception, two young females hovering and a lady who comes out to discuss the treatments. I've no idea if the massage is good or not and it feels odd being massaged by a lady with rough hands. I can imagine that when she's not giving Ayurvedic treatments she's busy scrubbing, cooking and cleaning. At the end of the treatment I'm told I should come back again for the next two days which annoys me, partly because I won't be able to since we're leaving tomorrow, and partly because I think they just want to get more business from me.

7th March

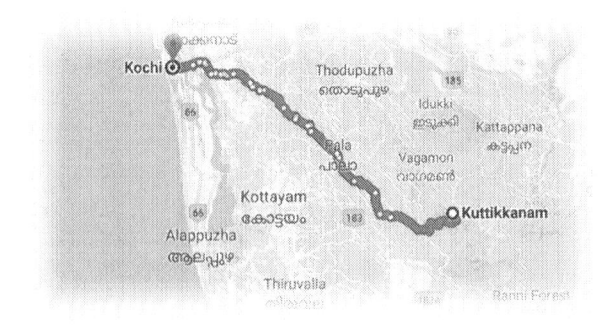

## Mundax Yoga Retreat, Kuttikkanam Village

We're leaving this comfortable hotel today and I'm a mixture of 'sad to go' and excited at the prospect of our new adventure - five days in a yoga retreat.

Fliss and I are enjoying an excellent breakfast and chatting. I lament how I miss my watch which I ruined when I left them in my trouser pocket as I vigorously washed Kolkata's dirt out. An American lady at a near table apologises for over-hearing our conversation and says she has a watch she no longer wants and if I'd like it she'll happily give it to me. It's a large, yellow watch and I wonder at the chances of someone having a spare watch to give away! I thank her profusely and ask her name and it's Wendy. The watch is christened the 'Wendy Watch'.

Before our taxi arrives I quickly pop to the tailor and collect and pay for my newly shortened trousers.

The drive to the Mundax yoga retreat in Kuttikkanam Village takes almost four hours. We drive up high into the hills, which look more like mountains to me, and finally stop outside some big gates in a small village. We'll spend the next five days here, just Fliss and I with our hosts Agi and Mathew.

They introduce themselves and welcome us to their beautiful home. It looks recently built and it's light, clean and spacious. Mathew asks us if we'd like to do two hours of yoga today and we would, so after some refreshments and time to relax, we seek out the yoga room.

It's exactly how it ought to be, white walls, red tiled floor, spacious and light and three yoga mats and yoga stools. We're invited to sit in front of Mathew and he starts our session by talking to us. This puts me in panic mode, his voice is quiet and soft and with his strong Indian accent I can barely hear what he's saying. I explain that my hearing isn't good and although he turns the volume up for a few sentences his voice soon drops back down. I can feel my neck craning forward and I've just about had enough of straining to listen when he suggests we do some stretches.

For dinner in the evening we all sit together at a large dining table and Agi brings out different dishes of rice and dal with various sauces. They have a cook who has been working all day preparing the meal. The food is excellent but conversation doesn't flow. Fliss does a sterling effort of asking questions and engaging Agi, but Mathew doesn't join in and I get the impression he'd prefer not to talk over dinner.

## 8th March

I wake early and creep out of our bedroom to watch the sunrise. The morning air is very still and there are a few bird calls. As the sun comes up it turns the sky into delicate shades of pink and orange.

We start the day with two hours of yoga but my body would've preferred breakfast. I'm rewarded with a morning feast of dal, omelette, toast and coffee, which Fliss and I eat without the company of Agi and Mathew.

Afterwards we go for a walk to explore the area and we're surprised by how hot it is, at 1400m high we thought it might be cooler here. There isn't much to see in the village so we walk into the tea plantations and catch views of the surrounding mountains.

Another two hours of yoga this afternoon. This has to be good for my concentration! Four hours of yoga in one day, including two twenty-minute meditations.

Dinner again in the evening is delicious but again slightly uncomfortable. It's a good job Fliss is willing to make an effort with conversation as on my own I think I would stay quiet.

## 9th March

Another lovely sunrise this morning and another two hours of yoga followed by an excellent breakfast. I can't yet see me doing this at home, my tummy would rather have breakfast first. Two more hours of yoga in the afternoon. I'm still struggling to hear Mathew when he delivers his talks to us. It isn't a problem at dinner though because this evening he suggests we eat in silence. I was right, I had a feeling they don't usually talk. It feels weird. I don't know where to put my eyes and the odd gestures from Agi inviting me to try another dish or have some more to eat seem frankly, daft. I do understand that it's a good idea to focus on and appreciate your food, but with company it feels strange and uncomfortable.

## 10th March

Fliss and I are excited. There's an authentic and well known Ayurvedic Hospital near the village and at our request, Agi has booked appointments for us to see a doctor there. A tuk-tuk drives us to the hospital which appears to be several low brick buildings.

We both have a consultation with the impeccable English-speaking Dr Halesh Babu. I explain about the cough I've carried with me since Kolkata and he writes out two prescriptions which I can hand into the on-site dispensary. He also recommends an Ayurvedic massage and I'm delivered into the care of a smiling Indian woman.

My Indian lady gestures to me to take off all my clothes and she gives me a small strip of paper cloth with ties to go around my waist, the cloth hangs down between my legs and is brought up the back and tucked into the tie at the back; a cross between a paper G string and a paper nappy. Lying on a couch I'm given a hot oil massage. It feels wonderful; very loving and gentle, all over front and back and I feel like a child again being taken care of.

After the massage, my Indian lady shows me into a small bathroom and still wearing nothing but my paper loin cloth, I sit on a plastic stool and with hot soapy water she washes me all over. I'm glad I'm not a bashful person because this is very intimate, but I'm willing to relax into it and love the pampering which continues with a muddy body scrub all over, followed by hot water to rinse me down. Finally, I'm handed a large cotton tea towel which I use to dry myself.

Pampering over, I meet up with Fliss who was also given a massage and we swap notes, both agreeing that it was an unusual but lovely experience. We have a long sociable chat with Dr Halesh who rather endearingly asks us an English grammar question which we have fun trying to explain; the difference between 'have been' and 'had been'.

Back at Mundax I'm eager to try my Ayurvedic prescriptions. I have nasal drops for sinuses and a sticky treacly stuff to swallow which tastes utterly vile - anything tasting this bad must surely be good for me.

## 11th March

I'm up at 6 am and outside in the garden to catch another sunrise. It rained last night and the air smells fresh. The sky becomes a rich orange then fades into a pure, soft light diffused by the mist. The mist starts rising and suddenly I see the tip of a large orange ball. It's the sun and it's huge. The birds are singing and one in particular makes me giggle. It sounds like an old man trying to whistle to make himself happy, but his tune isn't jolly, then he stops and a few moments later has another go. I walk towards the lake and almost walk into a huge shiny spider's web strung across the path at exactly the same height as my face. It's an abandoned web, not quite perfect but still very eye-catching with the morning dew shining on it.

## 12th March

It's our last yoga session with Mathew, the routine is the same every time and today he waits for us to work out which exercise follows another. I'm amazed after all these sessions I still don't remember the routine, but I have written it down for future reference. Mathew tells us that if we continue this daily for three months then it will flow and become part of our lives. We both have good intentions of continuing.

Another excellent breakfast, we've been fed here extremely well, and then it's time for us to leave. Biju, Mathew's taxi driver neighbour, will take us to the airport. Saying goodbye to Mathew and Agi feels awkward, there's something uncomfortable about it. They come across as very nice people and they appear loving with each other but I haven't felt any warmth from them, the kind that makes you want to give someone a hug. It just isn't there, so I shake hands with them instead.

Fliss and I are in the taxi chatting and she comments that she's disappointed to leave India without seeing an elephant. Biju says *"I think I can show you one"* and to our astonishment, within ten minutes he stops the car and points to some trees near the side of the road. Standing among the trees is a very large elephant. We get out of the car and see two Indians nearby. Their job is to take care of him because he's a logging elephant used in the village for the heavy work. The elephant's trunk goes out and up and he lets out a roar which suggests he's not happy and we're advised not to go too close. I have to laugh, what are the chances of saying *"I'd like to see an elephant"* and one appears within ten minutes!

Back in the taxi and only a few minutes later, we come across some loggers in the road. I can't believe the sight in front of our taxi; a colourfully painted truck has been loaded with logs and it's leaning precariously to one side looking as though it may topple over any moment. A crane is trying to add yet another huge log which will surely be one log too many. Men are working with ropes and one is standing next to the truck and it's leaning his way. My heart is in my mouth, it's such a dangerous situation. We're stationary, watching, then our driver sees an opportunity to drive past and Fliss yells *"go, go, go"*, we don't want to be underneath the truck when it topples! I wonder how the rest of the drama played out.

Fliss and I have a final meal together at the Flora Hotel by the airport. I'm sad to wave her off as I'm going to miss her company. A tuk-tuk takes me back to the Sapphire Inn and as soon as I walk in the door the receptionist opens a drawer and proudly hands me an envelope with my silver necklace inside.

## 13th March

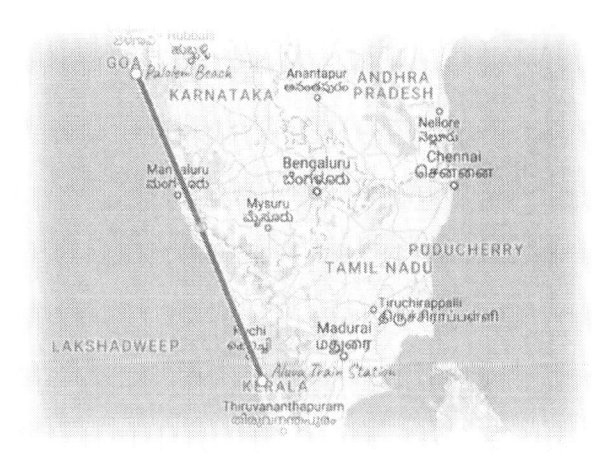

### Train to Palolem (700 kms)

I'm on the platform at Aluva train station, far too early as usual and feeling nervous. My train is the overnight Nevrathi Express, kindly booked for me by my new Indian friend Rishul, and I hope I'm waiting at the correct platform. As trains arrive I look for clues to tell me the train name or destination but nothing seems obvious. As always I ask for, and receive, help and happily the Nevrathi Express arrives at 3 pm, only half an hour late. I have no idea how I'll know when to get off but for the moment I can relax. This is a long journey of some 700 kms and it's likely to take about 15 hours.

On the train, an educated Indian called Anand takes an interest in me and we chat for a while. When I tell him I'm getting off at Madgaon because I'm going to Palolem Beach, he suggests it would be better to alight at the station before Madgaon. I'm a bit uncertain now, but what Anand says makes sense, and then to my amazement he offers to contact my hostel accommodation and ask them to provide a taxi to meet me at the station. He uses his mobile phone and after a brief conversation tells me that everything is sorted, he'll let me know when we arrive at the station and the hostel will have someone there to meet me. As I'll be arriving in the dark at 4.30 am I pray that this will all happen as he's arranged.

## 14th March

Feeling anxious hasn't stopped me sleeping and I waken when Anand comes into my carriage at 4 am to tell me the next stop will be mine. I'm truly grateful to this very kind man. I grab my stuff and get off onto an empty platform in the dark, in what feels like the middle of nowhere, and cross my fingers that someone is here to meet me. A young Indian man approaches me and asks if I'm Hazel. His name is Jay and he's booked an auto-rickshaw to take me to the hostel and will escort me on his motorbike. I laugh with relief and amazement; how wonderful it is that everything always works out.

The auto-rickshaw drives off into the darkness. There are no street lights and no house lights. After about 15 minutes we turn off the lane into some trees. Oh help, where am I being taken? The rickshaw stops and Jay tells me to follow him on foot. Apparently, I've arrived. I can't see it, but beyond the trees is the beach and Jay shows me my own wooden beach hut. It's all ready for me with the bed made up. As it's still dark, and with relief that I've survived my train adventure, I go to bed.

The morning light reveals a totally different scene. I've come to a beautiful place. My colourfully painted beach hut is just thirty metres from the sea, which I can hear but can't see because it's hidden by trees. Outside my hut are two large hogs snuffling about.

The beach is by the Arabian Sea and unexpectedly, it isn't at all crowded. Everywhere looks clean and very pretty with colourful huts, umbrellas, small restaurants and bars and painted boats. The sand is custard coloured and soft underfoot. There's a café with Internet and good coffee nearby and I sit for ages watching the waves. I'm very happy.

I have no reason to go anywhere other than here and I savour the deliciousness of having nothing to do but relax. I have some internal wrestling about whether it's okay for me to be having such a decadent time while other people work. Is this alright? How can I be so lucky? The sea water is warm and I dip in and out, but mostly I wander along the beach or just sit. The sun sets in front of me over the Arabian Sea. It's an idyllic scene and I watch other tourists, like me, walking along the water's edge taking photos.

With my tummy rumbling I find a little restaurant and order veg noodles. A couple of older men nearby chat with me, one is English, the other French. They've been here for some weeks and I enjoy their company, I think it's a shame the Englishman is leaving tomorrow.

I think I must have some insect bites on my bottom, I can feel unpleasant stinging sensations. Back in my beach hut I try investigating but without a bathroom mirror this is tricky, so I put my mobile behind me and take a snapshot. What the picture reveals is alarming, there are a couple of angry red-looking patches on my buttocks. I can't imagine what has caused it. Snake bite, spider bite, ants?

I get under the cold shower and wash myself thoroughly. An hour later and I'm feeling anxious, the skin is now blistering and becoming increasingly more painful. I remember an incident this morning when I sat on a wooden block near some boats. I became aware I might be sitting on what could be oil, so went into the sea to wash it off and I forgot about it. Now, looking at my swimsuit it reveals a dark stain, exactly the same shape as the red patch on my backside. I think I must have sat on something caustic and it's now painfully destroying the skin on my bum! I lather my backside with the aloe vera gelly that I always carry with me and lie on my tummy for the night.

## 15th March

Investigations this morning reveal that the damage to my bum is considerably worse, even though I washed the area thoroughly, it seems the acid is still eating through my skin and my flesh is raw.

With so much pain in my backside it's difficult to know what I can do, I can't sit down. For a while I lie on my tummy on Palolem Beach, reading. It's an enlightening book called 'Conversations with God' and out of one of the pages comes a 'lightbulb' moment. The damage to my bottom makes it impossible for me to sit comfortably, which means I can't relax. Given yesterday's guilt about having nothing to do and wondering if it's okay for me to enjoy doing nothing, today I'm *unable* able to sit. I have to laugh, it feels like this is a self-inflicted injury, a sort of personal sabotage, so I don't have to feel guilty about having so much pleasure. With this in mind I determine to have as much pleasure as possible today and go in search of a large ice-cream.

16th March

## Bus to Margao (40 kms)

I have a tasty breakfast at a beach bar and a last stroll along the water's edge, then take the local bus to Margao (Madgaon). I'm trying not to let my injury cause me concern, the location of the wound makes it difficult to manage and painful to sit down, but I'm coping.

Margao is an average looking town. I've booked a room to myself in a passably nice hotel so I can nurse my sore backside.

Hunger sends me in search of food and I'm excited to learn that the famous old restaurant called Longuinhos is right across the street. It has quite a history having opened in 1950, so I'm excited to check it out.

I step inside and approach the counter asking *"do you have Wi-Fi?"*, I'm told *"no"*. I ask *"do you serve milk coffee?"* and I'm told *"only black coffee"*. A waiter looks at me and says quite gruffly *"sit down, we do coffee"*. So I say, *"yes, but do you have white coffee?"*, he again says *"sit down"*. I sit down and another waiter brings a menu. The first waiter returns with a black coffee. I ask *"can I have some milk?"* The waiter looks annoyed, so I explain, *"I want a milk coffee"*. The waiter talks to someone else then says I have to have a pot of coffee. I say *"okay"*. He takes away my black coffee. I ask if I can also have a lemon tart. The waiter brings me a white coffee in a cup, not a pot. He doesn't bring the lemon tart.

I'm not sure Longuinhos have heard of customer service.

## 17th March

### Train to Mumbai (580 kms)

Today I'm taking the Mandovi Express further up the west coast of India to Mumbai, 580 kms and 13 hr trip, it's a journey recommended by 'The Guardian' newspaper for it's amazing scenery. I'm not quite so nervous this time, although when the train comes in half an hour early I'm a bit thrown, Indian trains are known for being late, not early! I have a 2nd class ticket. The beds are two tier and I have a window seat with great views. I'm thankful the train isn't too crowded because I won't be sitting down much.

As with all the train journeys, I'm amused by the continuous stream of 'vendors' selling all manner of food and beverages. They walk up and down shouting out their wares, you'd never go hungry on an Indian train. I have three cups of coffee, a veggie burger and a cup of tomato soup. One vendor is selling chicken lollipops and I feel outraged to think that's how a poor chicken ends up – as a lollipop! I don't have to worry about where to get off because thankfully Mumbai is at the end of the line, but I am slightly nervous about arriving in the city in the middle of the night.

I've booked a single room in a modest hotel close to the train station and emailed the hotel for exact directions how to locate them. Alighting from the train I'm amazed to see a young man holding up a card with my name on it, the hotel has sent someone to meet me. Now that is good service.

### 18th March

The wound on my rear is really bad, it doesn't seem to be healing and I'm anxious that it may become infected. I probably should stay in my room but by mid afternoon I feel stir-crazy and venture out. I start by going back to the Chatrapati Shivaji Terminus where I arrived last night. It's Mumbai's iconic railway station, huge, ornate and very busy.

Mumbai has the feel of a big city with wide roads and big buildings, masses of traffic and numerous old black and yellow taxis, some of which don't look roadworthy. Like Kolkata, there's plenty of activity on the pavements; stall holders, fast food sellers, people sitting on blankets. I even pass a man with two cows who are lying contentedly on the pavement. I like the feel of the place.

### 19th March

Yesterday I booked a tour with a company called 'Reality Tours' who will take me to the Dharavi slums. I'm inspired to visit them because I've been reading a book called 'Beyond the Beautiful Forevers', a true story about the Mumbai slums right next to the airport. I meet up with the group at Churchgate Train Station and we start our tour by boarding a modern train to Dharavi, crowded with students and business people.

A walk over a high bridge gives us our first sighting of the slum area below, home to over a million people in an area of just over 2.1 square kilometres. I take a photo here because we've been asked not to take pictures while we're in the slums.

Our guide leads us in and out of the numerous tiny lanes that make up the slum area, some of them are only a single person wide. The ground is mostly wet and mucky underfoot and we pass by scarily unsafe looking wires and cables hanging in and out of the dwellings. I'm fascinated by everything around me. It seems chaotic but there's order here and our guide introduces us to some of the many small-scale businesses. The pocket-size industries here turn over millions of dollars annually. Recycling is big business and we see plastics and metals being sorted by hand. I watch in awe as a man stands, without any protection at all, in front of a massive open fire pit stirring aluminium to melt it. The heat must be incredible.

We're shown a pastry making business in a large, semi-dark room, almost below the ground. A man is rolling out massive pastry on a vast surface, then he folds it and hands it to another man who lays it out on cloths. The pastry looks like folded bed sheets. The pastry made here is distributed around Mumbai. We see freshly made chapattis, the size of dinner plates, being laid onto the sides of wicker baskets to dry out. The baskets line a dusty dirt road and these are also distributed around Mumbai.

It's obvious the people here work exceptionally hard. We're told that some work twelve-hour days, seven days a week and I can't imagine living their life day in, day out, but there is an enviable sense of community here and I definitely don't feel they need to be pitied. It's a fascinating place and it has really brought to life for me the story of Anund and his recycling business from the 'Beautiful Forevers' book.

The tour has ended and our guide indicates a taxi that will take us back to the train station. We are eight people, but that doesn't faze the guide, he shoves us in piling one on top of another and I'm glad it's a short ride.

Back in Mumbai, I ask the group if anyone is interested in meeting later at the famous Taj Mahal Palace Hotel. I'd like to have a cocktail there and would love to have company. A young guy called Uri from Israel is up for it and we arrange to meet in front of the Gateway of India monument at six o'clock.

It's about a twenty-five-minute walk from my hotel to the 'Gateway of India', an 85 feet high arch monument. Waiting for Uri to arrive I have time to read a plaque which tells me the foundation stone was laid on 31$^{st}$ March 1911 and the arch, made of basalt was erected to commemorate the visit to India of King George V and Queen Mary in 1911. The construction was completed in 1924. It's located on the water front in South Mumbai and overlooks the Arabian Sea which, from where I'm standing, looks disgusting; it smells and looks filthy but is nevertheless dotted with colourful boats.

Uri arrives on time and we walk across the road to the iconic and very elegant Taj Mahal Palace Hotel. Built in 1903, this is where the rich and famous choose to stay and apparently where Ravi Shankar taught George Harrison to play the sitar. I ask Uri if he'd mind coming up to the top floor to see if we can see some views over the Arabian Sea, so we take a ride in the lift as far as we can. Along the corridor is a conference room where tables are being laid and the staff allow me to go in and peek out of the windows over the rooftops of south Mumbai.

The Harbour Bar looks inviting and I order the Taj's signature cocktail intriguingly named 'From the Harbour Since 1933'.

A waiter brings a large wine glass filled with sliced fruits and gin and flamboyantly adds some freshly squeezed fruit juice mixed with ice. In another glass poised at an angle over a tea-light is Chartreuse and our waiter sets light to it creating blue flames and pours it, still flaming, into the cocktail glass, it's very spectacular. All the while he's telling us in a theatrical manner the story of how the cocktail got its name.

*In 1933 an American docked his yacht at Bombay harbour and learned that Prohibition, which meant no alcohol since 1920, had ended in America. You can imagine he wanted to celebrate with a drink and sought one in the Taj Mahal Palace Hotel. He asked the bartender to make a drink that would "quench his thirst from the last thirteen years" and the bartender produced a cocktail so good the American wanted to know what it was called but it had no name, so the bartender invited the American to give it one. He raised his glass and shouted out "from the Harbour since 1933".*

Uri is excellent company and we chat happily about education, world travel, life plans and with our second drink, conversation turns to love and relationships. Uri is 31 years old, younger than my children, yet I don't feel at all uncomfortable talking with this Israeli student in the poshest hotel in Mumbai. Such is the common bond of fellow travellers I think.

Leaving the Taj, Uri suggests going to a popular bar called 'Leopolds', he's keen to see the cricket match currently being played between India and Pakistan. I stay for a while but it doesn't hold my interest so I decide to walk back to my hotel. I don't mind walking in the city at night, but after going up and down a couple of roads I realise I have no idea which direction to take and since the hotel is some distance away I think it wise to hail a taxi.

## 20th March

This is my last day in India and to my surprise I feel sad and the thought of leaving makes me well up with tears. I've had something of a love-hate relationship with India and I'm glad I came back again after Sri Lanka and got to know it better. I still have time to explore, so I set off to find the Marine Parade and the sea on the other side of Mumbai. I think I'm following the map but a detour leads me to walk across the Mumbai Oval cricket ground. It's fantastic, there are cricket games going on everywhere and in their coloured cricket shirts the cricketers look quite a sight.

Eventually I come to the sea front and Marine Parade which is disappointingly unattractive. There are massive concrete three angled slabs keeping the sea at bay and the lapping waves throw out a disgusting smell. What fascinates me are the courting couples sitting along the sea wall, seemingly impervious to the stink.

I'm very lost now, I've been walking for hours and I'm hot and tired. Down a side street I come across some youngers playing street cricket and I stop to rest and watch the game. They're very friendly and like having an audience. I enjoy seeing the way they interact; Indian boys are easily affectionate and tactile with each other. One of them, a youngster called Raj comes to chat with me and I ask him for directions to

The India Gate knowing I'll be able to find my way 'home' from there.

21st March

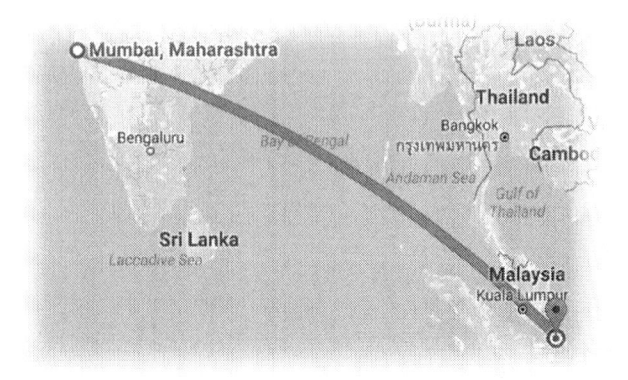

Aeroplane to Singapore (6hrs)

Mumbai airport is surprisingly architecturally attractive. It's modern and light with geometric white pillars that splay out and hold up the roof, possibly the nicest airport I've seen. As my plane takes off for Singapore I look out of the window and realise we're flying over the Annawardi slums, the ones I read about in 'Beautiful Forevers', I thought they had been demolished. There's a massive contrast between the beautiful Mumbai airport one side of the fence and the Mumbai slums the other.

# *Singapore*

Singapore is two hours ahead of India and it's 6 pm when I arrive after an uncomfortable six-hour flight. I'm encouraged that my injured backside is at last healing but enforced sitting is still painful. I take a taxi to my hostel at 89 Geylang Road. It's small but seems nice and I'm given a pleasant welcome and shown to my six-bed female dorm room.

I need food, so step outside into the humid evening air. There are several 'eateries' nearby, all with large photos of their food in the window. I'm not sure why but I find this off-putting. One has a picture of what seems to have become my staple diet, veg noodles, and I go inside. My noodles arrive swimming in a pool of gravy and I'm given chopsticks. I hold the bowl close to my face and try scooping everything into my mouth with small success until the waiter comes over with a spoon and apologises for forgetting to bring it sooner.

## 22$^{nd}$ March

Breakfast at the hostel is a 'do it yourself' buffet with bread, bananas and yoghurt and I'm joined by a family of adults, teenagers and small children. I'm not feeling very sociable but one of the youngsters is friendly and starts to chat. He has a lovely smile and not wanting to be mean, I have a conversation with him. His family are from the Philippines, they're in Singapore on holiday.

Back in my dorm room twenty minutes later, there's a knock at the door, the same young man from breakfast is standing there, he puts out his hand and says, *"I'm sorry, I forgot to introduce myself this morning, I'm James David"*. I'm completely disarmed by this engaging teenager of seventeen years, the same age as my granddaughter, and we talk some more. James tells me of his aspirations, he has exciting plans for his future and I'm impressed by his self-confidence. I give him my card saying we can connect on Facebook if he'd like to.

This is a new country to explore and with a few ideas of the places I should see in Singapore, I walk in the direction of the train station which I know is very close. Singapore has an extensive rail network called the MRT (mass rapid transit) which, according to the guide books, makes getting around very easy. The ultra-modern station is quiet, I get help purchasing a three-day ticket from the ticket booth person and within a few minutes a train arrives.

I've seen pictures of a stunning looking hotel called Marina Sands Bay and it has its own train stop, so this will be my first destination. Leaving the train, I arrive inside somewhere, but I can't make out where I am, there doesn't seem to be an 'outside'. I follow signs and realise that I've arrived *in* the hotel, except that it doesn't feel like a hotel, it feels like a vast shopping mall with restaurants and conference rooms.

I'd like to go to the top but the stairs and escalators require security passes. I've seen pictures of a beautiful infinity pool at the top of the hotel and I'd love to see it but getting to it is impossible. After about half an hour of walking up and down, I feel as though I'm in a nightmare, I want to get out but every doorway leads me to more 'indoors'. I haven't previously suffered from claustrophobia, but I think I'm feeling it now.

At last some glass doors lead to fresh air. Now I'm on the outside but there's nothing but main roads, a multi-storey car park and high-rise buildings. There's nothing to see. Signage with an arrow directs me to the Observation Deck. At last, I'm getting somewhere.

Inside more glass doors there's a ticket office and I'm told that it costs $24 to go to the observation deck and if it rains, which is likely, it won't be very pleasant and I won't get my money back. I'm not sold on the idea and give up on the Marina Bay Sands Hotel.

I have to go back inside and make my way back to the MRT. I'm now feeling unhappy, stressed and I want to cry. Singapore is a massive contrast to India, it's big, super-modern, clean and impersonal and I feel like a fish out of water.

My next stop is Chinatown which is very 'touristy', so after an odd lunch of an onion omelette, the only meal available without meat, I use my map to walk to Boat Quay.

It's a long walk in the heat, but I like the area, set around a small harbour with attractive restaurants and bars and city buildings behind. On the outside of some restaurants are large fish tanks with live crabs and lobsters, presumably so customers can choose their meal. I don't recall ever really looking at lobsters and I'm struck by how amazingly complex and beautiful they are. I can't bear to think of them trapped behind the glass with the cooking pot as their end fate, it feels all wrong to me.

I'm going to treat myself to a 'Singapore Sling', the gin-based cocktail made famous over a hundred years ago, at the hotel known as 'Raffles'. It's another long, hot walk along empty paths and roads. I don't think Singaporian dwellers walk much and I feel very alone. It takes me a while to locate Raffles and I'm looking forward to a rest and a drink. I find the famous 'Long Bar' and order myself an outrageously expensive Singapore Sling, at $32 it may be the most expensive single drink I've ever bought, but at least it comes with a free cloth sack full of peanuts which I unashamedly tuck into. I sit back, relax and 'people watch'.

Hot and weary from so much walking I'm finally back at the hostel and realise I've had a message from a friend of my nephew's, called Adam, saying he can see me this evening. I give him a call and he tells me he's just leaving his office and can meet me at Boat Quay in half an hour. I don't even have time to wash and change so I clean my teeth and walk back to the MRT. Although I'm exhausted from today I do want to link up with Adam and this is the only opportunity.

We meet at 'The Penny Black', an English pub in Singapore and laugh at the irony of it. We could move on but Adam has bought a bottle of my favourite wine, Oyster Bay Sauvignon Blanc and I know we're going to get along very well. He's from Australia and I love hearing stories of his travels in Oz, his passion enthuses me and I get good info on where to visit when I get there.

We've finished the bottle and getting down from my high stool at the bar it's clear the wine has gone to my head. Finding my way back to the hostel might prove a challenge. I thank Adam for being willing to give up his time to meet me and totter off to the MRT. Boat Quay looks very pretty at night with its coloured lights, I'm glad to be out in the evening and very grateful to Adam. Meeting him has made Singapore much more fun.

## 23rd March

I'm told the Botanical Gardens in Singapore are worth seeing, so I'm back on the MRT again. The guide books are right, the MRT makes this a very easy place to explore. The gardens are beautiful and I find a cafeteria where I can have lunch. The menu offers an aloe vera salad, something I've never seen on a menu before. It's delicious, not because of the aloe which doesn't have much taste, but it comes with a tasty lemon dressing. After lunch, I sit in a quiet spot in the garden and attempt a fifteen-minute meditation.

By late afternoon I've had enough of Singapore. I'm not happy here, I'm going back to the hostel to pack ready for my next adventure – Vietnam tomorrow!

## Vietnam

24ᵗʰ March

Changi airport, like Singapore, is very efficient and I transition through the system with ease and again I have no problem carrying my ukulele as well as my hand luggage onto the plane.

Arriving at Nội Bài Airport in Hanoi I *do* have a problem. A visa is required, which I knew in advance and I have a valid visa, but what I don't have is cash. I have to pay the official behind the desk to stamp my visa and they don't accept credit cards, I must pay in Vietnamese Dong or US dollars, neither of which I have. I'm not the only one in this predicament, a young woman is also expecting to pay with a credit card. I think this situation must arise frequently, there has to be a solution. We're both told to sit down and wait, I don't know what we're waiting for.

After about fifteen minutes, the official behind the desk calls out my name. He gestures to me that I should give him my stuff, so I hand over my front pack and uke. Another official points to the exit doors. He says *"ATM"* and it dawns on me that I'm going to be allowed out of the area to get cash from the ATM. He accompanies me and shows me the cash machine. I'm really nervous and pray that the machine doesn't swallow my card, I punch in my pin numbers and hear the reassuring "dikadikadika" sound of money being spewed out.

Carrying an alarmingly massive wad of money tightly in my hand I scurry back to retrieve my luggage. I'm now concerned about my back pack abandoned on the airport carousel. I've been such a long time I hope no-one has taken it. The baggage carousel is empty and I feel panicked, it's not there. Then I see it, a lonely backpack left on the floor. I laugh at myself, calm down, everything is always alright.

The airport has a 'help desk' and they show me where I can get a shuttle bus which will take me to Hostel Ga in Hanoi. I discover that it's in a very hectic part of 'old' Hanoi, down an alley and although it's an odd little hostel I rather like the feel of it.

Intrigued to see Hanoi, I step outside, taking mental note of my surroundings so I'll know my way back. It's raining here. I'm in a historic part of Hanoi and the roads are small and packed with motorcycles, I've never seen so many, they're everywhere. The riders wear round helmets that remind me of German soldiers and because it's raining many of them are wearing coloured plastic capes, the effect looks rather comical and I amuse myself taking photos.

I've noticed several small open-fronted cafes in the

area, furnished with tiny plastic chairs and low plastic tables, like the ones you see in infant schools in the U.K. I pop into one and ask for a white coffee, clarifying by saying *"a milk one"* and I look to see if the young guy serving me has understood. He nods and returns with a black coffee in a Pyrex mug. I say again *"milk"?* He nods and points to my cup and when I stir it I realise it has thick condensed milk at the bottom. The coffee is probably the strongest I've ever tasted and it's absolutely delicious.

A short walk brings me out of the small roads into a wider area and a large lake with a wooden, red painted bridge across the middle. As I stand leisurely taking in my surroundings a shoe cleaner starts cleaning my leather boots. I ask him how much he charges but he won't tell me so I say *"you must stop cleaning my shoes, I won't pay you"*, but he keeps on. I'd quite like to have my shoes cleaned, but I want to know the cost up front, so I again tell him to stop. I say very firmly *"I am not going to pay you"*. He continues cleaning both boots. When he's finished he hands me a piece of paper with 600,000 scrawled on it. I am shocked, is this the price? This is a ridiculous amount to ask for, I can't believe it, this is the equivalent of nearly £20! I look at the paper again and shake my head, there's no way I'm going to pay this. I argue with him but he's insistent. I tell him I don't have that much money. He indicates the ATM over the street. I walk towards it as though I'm going to use it but instead I dive into a nearby hotel and ask the receptionist if she speaks English. She does, so I tell her about the shoe cleaner and ask if 600,000 for cleaning shoes could possibly be fair. She shakes her head and very kindly comes out and talks to the shoe cleaner who has followed me and is waiting outside the hotel. I don't know what she says to him and he's still demanding 600,000 from me. I hold out a 100,000 note and say *"this is all I will give, take it or leave it"*, he shouts *"this is nothing!"*. I'm genuinely puzzled, but stick to my guns, even though he's now yelling abuse at me and passers-by are staring. Eventually he takes the 100,000 note and walks away angrily. The incident leaves me feeling shaken but also empowered, I liked standing up for myself. This has been another learning experience.

Back at Ga Hostel I calm myself with some yoga exercises, which I confess to only doing sporadically since the yoga retreat, and I reflect that I rather like the range of emotions I've experienced today. After all I have just changed countries and it wasn't an easy transition.

## 25th March

There's a free walking tour of Hanoi available, provided by students, so after an early breakfast courtesy of the hostel, I'm ready at 8 am to join it. When the students turn up they tell me the tour is all day which takes me by surprise, but having no other agenda, this isn't an issue. Three other girls from the hostel join me, Nicola, Shalaker and Vidia and we're accompanied by three female students.

They're very passionate about Vietnam and keen to share its history with us. I notice that they never say *"Vietnam"* but always *"my country"*.

We walk first to Hỏa Lò Prison built by the French and now largely demolished, but the site has been made into a museum. French colonists used it for political prisoners and later the North Vietnamese used it to house U.S. prisoners during the Vietnam War. The U.S. soldiers nicknamed it the 'Hanoi Hilton'. Our student guides are careful to tell us and show us how badly the French treated the Vietnamese and how well the Vietnamese later treated the American soldiers, I have my doubts that all they said is true. The models, photos and memorabilia make it quite a chilling place.

I'm really enjoying my companions and their conversation. We take a long walk to Ho Chi Minh's mausoleum and museum which, to the dismay of our student guides, is closed today. This is good news for me, I've already been given so much information my saturation levels are challenged.

Our students suggest we stop and have street food for lunch and I mention that I'm vegetarian which causes them concern. After an animated conversation, one of them takes me to a take-away restaurant and orders a meal especially for me. Being vegetarian in Vietnam may not be as simple as I'd expected. We then join the others at a street food stall and sitting on tiny bright red plastic chairs, a variety of dishes are brought out.

More walking, and passing by shops and eateries I'm sad to notice that many have little song birds in cages hanging outside. It occurs to me how strange this is; I've been shown prison bars and how terrible it is to put a man in a 'cage' but it's okay to do the same to a song bird.

Our day finishes at a bustling coffee house full of character and called The Giang Café where we're going to try 'egg coffee', popular throughout Hanoi. Our students tell us that the owner of this café was the first to introduce the recipe back in the 1950s. There's a menu with a selection to choose from but I decide to go for the original egg coffee, I want to know what it's like. The coffee is brought to us in glass beakers and it's rich, creamy and delicious.

## 26th March

There's excellent Wi-Fi at my hostel and I have time to make plans for my stay in Vietnam. I've been given some good information by a helpful English-speaking waiter at a restaurant where I had dinner and based on this I've decided what to do.

Just a couple of roads away from Hostel Ga is an 'ethical' tour operator I like the look of, so I pay them a visit. The lady behind the desk speaks good English and together we plan my trip to Halong Bay for two days, return train ticket, then a three-day trek in Sapa. The price is very good, especially taking into account that I won't need accommodation for seven days because I'll be sleeping on trains and boats and I won't need meals for five days because they're provided. It feels good to have forward plans made with relative ease.

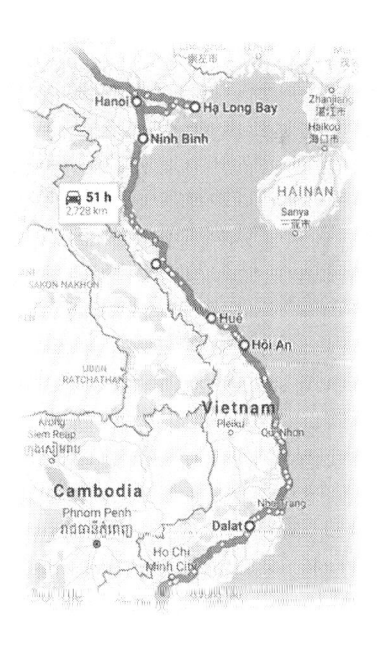

## 27th March

## Halong Bay Tour

I'm being picked up from my hostel to start the tour to Halong Bay on the west coast in Quảng Ninh Province. It's a three-hour ride and the time passes pleasantly chatting with Irish Michael who's sitting next to me.

We arrive at the harbour, an area busy with tourists and boats. Our guide called Linda amuses me, she always starts her instructions with *"excuse me people...."*. We get into small boats which take us to the larger boat where we'll be staying on board and Linda puts us into pairs and gives each pair a key to their room. I'm rather taken aback when I realise that I'm expected to share my cabin with a very large Korean man. He seems embarrassed too.

The cabin is small but neatly fitted out with a comfy bed and a tiny private bathroom. It has large picture windows and a good view of the emerald coloured water. I decide not to worry about my bedroom companion, I only hope he doesn't snore.

Halong Bay is in the South China Sea and is very extraordinary because there are about two thousand tall, yet small, dark green islands growing up from the water.

We sail a short way then lunch is provided, a vegetarian one for me and it's excellent. I sit with a guy from Hungary called Akos, he's interesting and we chat for a while. This afternoon our boat stops and we're taken onto small boats then onto a bus to explore a large cave. We're told that Vietnamese soldiers lived in these caves for a long time during the war. Caves don't interest me much, I'd rather be back on the boat, but we're not out for long and when we get back I'm excited to learn that we have an option to go kayaking.

Akos suggests I partner him and we take a kayak out, Akos in front and me paddling at the rear. I like the physical activity and being close to the water. Akos paddles out further than I'd like to and I ask if he thinks this is okay. He's seems quite happy so we continue on. Neither of us have a watch and I'm getting anxious about the time. He suggests we paddle around the next island then head back to the docks, but as we paddle around, it becomes clear the island is larger on the other side than we'd thought. I'm massively out of my comfort zone now, we're far from our starting point and it feels late. I'm uncomfortable because I have no control over this situation. We paddle hard and I ask Akos if he knows which of the many wooden kayak docks is ours and he has no idea, neither do I. We search for a sign showing which is the right one and eventually, with great relief, I see our guide waving to us. I apologise to the rest of our group that they've had to wait for us but although we're late, we're not the last in.

In the evening we're given 'welcome' drinks and dinner, then a karaoke machine is set up. The group on the boat are friendly and fun and the karaoke is hilarious, I love that so many people are willing to 'have a go'. My Korean room-mate starts singing The Beatles 'Hey Jude' and I join in and sing it with him.

## 28th March

I sleep well and when I wake I realise the Korean hasn't slept in the bed next to me. I ask him at breakfast what happened and he tells me he slept with his two friends in their cabin. Bless him, it must have been very cosy in their room, they're all big men and the cabin is tiny.

It's disappointing that the boat doesn't move all

morning, we don't go anywhere, so I chat with Akos and get to know him better. After lunch the boat chugs back to the harbour and we take the bus back to Hanoi, it's been a short day and I feel a bit cheated.

I'm going to catch the Chapa Express train this evening, but first have to go back to the hostel to collect my big rucksack which they've been looking after for me. I find a local restaurant for my evening meal and a friendly English couple, here on holiday, invite me to join them. They're interested to hear about my travels when they learn I'm travelling alone. They're called Lynne and Bernie and I'm glad to have their company as I have a long wait before I catch my train.

## Chapa Express train to Lao Cai (300 kms)

It's too far to walk with my backpack so I take a taxi to the station and oh joy, the Chapa Express is in early and I can get on board. It's an elegant train and the cabin which sleeps four looks comfy. Because I'm here early I have time to 'play' and I feel excited like a kid. I open the free biscuits and bottle of fizzy water and get my stuff organised on my second-tier bunk. Three friendly German girls, holidaying together, join me in the cabin.

## 29th March

## Three Day Sapa Trek

### Day 1

The train arrives at Lao Cai station at 6 am, we've travelled 300 kms and I've slept through most of it. I'm happy to see a man is holding up my name and he's here with his car to greet me, and several others, presumably also doing the trek. We drive for about an hour along windy roads until we reach the Sapa O'Chau tour office.

For a while there's confusion. It seems I'll be leaving my big back pack here at the offices. I have to carry everything with me that I'll need for the next couple of days so I restrict myself to the vitals and then stuff everything else into the big pack, quite a challenge, especially as it has to house my laptop. I try not to think too much about the agony of leaving my laptop in an unlocked backpack in a large well-used baggage room.

It turns out that there are just three of us on the trek. My two trekking buddies are Suzannah and Carl, friends who've known each other for years, both from the U.S.A. They're friendly and make entertaining companions. Our guide is a youngster called Khai, he tells us that he lives in Sapa with his parents and siblings.

The weather turns out to be perfect for walking. It's cool, but not cold and the early mist has lifted so we're able to see the awesome scenery around us, although the tops of the tall mountains in the distance are in cloud.

We walk along narrow, muddy paths, in and around rice terraces which, for the most part, aren't planted. We're followed by four cheerful local ladies in colourful traditional dress. We're puzzled that they're with us and we ask Khai why. He tells us they want to sell to us but they won't ask for our business right away, they'll walk with us for a while, they want to create rapport before selling to us. I think this is nice. Carl asks Khai if he can send them away, he won't want to buy from them and doesn't want them to walk for miles. Khai explains that this would be very rude, so they continue the trek with us.

When we stop for lunch the ladies show us some of their handmade products. There's nothing I want, but I pay for an embroidered purse anyway and the lady I buy from gives me a gift of a heart shape made from grass.

They're very sweet and friendly and I wish Carl and Suzannah would also buy something, but they don't.

We think we've walked about 12 kms when we reach our first homestay around 3 pm. It's getting cold and I decide to have a shower because I didn't have the chance to have one yesterday. The showers are very basic, in a concrete block. I turn the water on and let it run but it doesn't come even warm. I emerge freezing cold. Fortunately, I have the chance to warm up later when the homestay owner lights some charcoal in a small tin bowl and we sit around it.

Dinner is served at a dining table in the large communal living room and the tin bowl, still hot with charcoal, is placed under the table to keep our feet warm.

At dinner the host produces alcohol which he pours into shot glasses and we all have some. Then he refills the glasses and we drink again. This ritual doesn't stop, each time our glasses are empty he refills them so he might as well have poured out a tumblerful in the first place. The taste is okay but I don't want a hangover so I don't accept the fourth one. Khai and Carl keep going along with the host and I wonder if they'll feel alright tomorrow.

The sleeping arrangement is unusual. There are beds in the same room as the dining table, colourful blankets hang down from the ceiling and provide some privacy. Carl, Suzannah and I are all side by side and the children in the family, along with their parents will occupy the beds on the other side of the large room.

When we retire to bed, the family and Khai remain at the dinner table chatting and pouring shots. Now this feels very odd, the three of us are only a few feet from the dinner table behind a blanket and we can't help giggling. It's very funny and I can't imagine sleeping while they chatter.

## 30th March

### Day 2

Amazingly, I've slept well and I've woken up by the sound of a cockerel. I take a look outside to see if I might catch a sunrise but I don't see one, instead I take the opportunity to do some yoga practice.

Breakfast is crepes with honey and bananas, and strong coffee with condensed milk. We set off walking around 9 am.

The weather is again ideal for trekking and the terrain similar to yesterday. I'm very happy, this is as good as I'd hoped it would be. I love the walk and I like the people I'm with. The paths disappear for a while and Khai guides us around the edges of rice terraces. It's muddy but rather fun and we make it to our next homestay around 3 pm.

This homestay is quite different from yesterday's. It's warmer here, maybe because we're not so high up. I'm fascinated by the inside of the house. There's a huge room with a massive open fire and a huge cook pot, containing something like soup. Hanging above the fire are blackened legs of animals, complete with hoofs which look bizarre. We sit together on tiny plastic stools with a plastic table and we're given another good meal.

Our beds are upstairs this time. They're mattresses on the floor but fairly comfortable. The toilet is in a building outside and not that close to the house and I give my bladder instructions to hold on until morning.

## 31st March

### Day 3

We're given crepes for breakfast with good coffee, then set off on another walk. This one is shorter than I'd expected and I feel disappointed. After a lunch of noodles in a small village, a car comes to pick us up and take us back to Sapa, where I'm reunited with my backpack.

Another car takes the three of us to the station and, with time to spare, Suzannah, Carl and I find a modern restaurant and have a meal together before catching the Chapa Express back to Hanoi. This train is as charming as before, but not so my sleeping companions, who are all snoring men.

## 1st April

### Bus to Ninh Binh (95 kms)

Back in Hanoi at the unsociable hour of 6 am, I find a taxi and show the driver the name of the bus station I want. A ticket tout gets to me the instant my feet step out of the taxi and shows me to a shabby small bus bound for Ninh Binh. The ride is cheap, 85,000 dong, less than £3, to travel almost 100 kms.

The bus driver shows me where to get off in an area of town with several large roads at a crossroad section. It's raining. I attempt to follow the mobile app called 'mapsme' to find my hotel. I don't know if it's me or the app but I walk around in circles and by the time I arrive at Than Thuiy, I'm wet, tired and grumpy.

I book a motorbike tour for tomorrow then retire to my room. As I have a room to myself with a decent bathroom I'm going to make use of the hair colour Fliss brought out from England for me.

## 2ⁿᵈ April

I'm on a motorbike again, hanging on for dear life, as we weave our way through traffic to Tam Coc on the Ngo Dong River. I'm going to take a little boat on the river and my driver tells me where to get a ticket and says he'll wait for me.

At the water's edge, a lady rowing a shallow boat and wearing traditional dress and a coolie hat, invites me to get in. The air is damp, there's a layer of mist and the threat of rain, it adds to the atmosphere on the river.

The water is shallow and calm and around us are rice fields, large grey rocks and vast limestone islands, covered in trees, with narrow waterways in between them. It's very tranquil. It's also comical as my lady rower isn't using her hands to pull the oars, she's using her feet. This is clearly a great idea because when her mobile phone rings she's able to answer it without stopping rowing.

Back on dry land I fend off the photographer who's taken my picture and now wants to sell it to me and look for my motorbike driver.

He takes me to see Thai Vi Temple and Bich Dong Pagoda, a cluster of cave temples. My guide leaves me to explore on my own and there are only a handful of other tourists about so it feels very quiet. Then we continue to our last stop, the Mua Cave where I unexpectedly come upon stone steps that climb up high.

I start the climb enjoying seeing the surrounding countryside and I really like that it's still misty and damp which adds to the surreal ambience of the place. There are 450 steps to reach the top and I push aside the horrible memory of Adams Peak as I keep going. I don't think I'll ever lose the excitement I feel at being on high viewpoints.

My rider takes me back to the hotel safely and I reflect on the wonderful things I've seen today and this time I wish I could have shared the day with someone.

## 3rd April

Ninh Binh is an uninspiring town. I borrow the hotel bike and have a go at cycling around but the roads are big and busy, the traffic is manic and I decide walking is safer. I'm feeling lonely and flat and decide to munch on the bread roll I've popped in my bag, left over from breakfast. There's nowhere to sit, no benches and no grass, so I sit on a stone step outside a shuttered shop. A middle-age man on a scooter pull up, he nods acknowledgement of me and I wonder if I'm sitting on his shop forecourt. From a small bag he's carrying he takes out a banana and hands it to me. He then goes inside a door next to the shop and few minutes later he comes out and hands me a glass of 'tea'. I am very touched by his gestures, we don't exchange any words, he simply nods. It reminds me that we're never really alone.

I miss being with people, so I've decided to leave Ninh Binh and go to Phong Nha-Ke National Park. I recall someone recommended a backpackers hostel there called Easy Tiger, it'll be a good place to meet travellers. My hotel books the overnight bus for me which leaves at 9 pm this evening.

## Bus to Phong Nha-Ke Bang (400 kms)

The bus arrives half an hour late and it's not like any kind I've been on before. I have to take my shoes off and I'm given a black bag to put them in, then I find an empty sleeping 'pod' which I slide into in a prone position. There's not much room by the time I've put my front pack, uke and shoes in and for once I'm glad I'm small, goodness knows how larger people cope. It's difficult to sleep, we stop frequently and people are coming and going all night.

### 4th April

The bus arrives at Phong Nha in Quang Binh Province at the ungodly hour of 4 am. Fortunately, my hostel Easy Tiger is right by the bus stop and it's open, there's a few of us from the bus going in, but there's no staff around, so I curl up on a comfy chair and wait. Eventually someone appears and happily there's a sort of cafeteria opening so I can have coffee and breakfast. The place is livening up, it's definitely a youngsters' backpackers hostel but I like the vibe and it has an inviting swimming pool too. I finally get the key to my dorm room at midday, the bunk beds are large and clean and we have locking lockers. I'm not feeling too good so decide to pop myself into bed and I fall instantly asleep.

### 5th April

I've slept for nearly 24 hours! I love the hostel, I love the pool and they sell great food for backpackers. I'm excited they have muesli, fruit and yoghurt on the breakfast menu. They organise some great trips from here too and I've booked a motorbike trip for tomorrow that sounds like fun, joining a couple of girls called Natasha and Eleanor.

### 6th April

Our motorbike riders have come to meet us and they

take us first to the six-kilometre-long Dark Cave. We were briefed yesterday what to expect, so we change into swimwear and join a group of people where we're individually hooked onto a very high and long zipwire that whizzes us across some water. It's the only way to reach the entrance to the cave.

From here, we swim a short way to the entrance, then follow a guide across some shingle and onto rock. The route is challenging, the passages are narrow with jagged rocks, sometimes slippery, and very uncomfortable for bare feet.

Now it's become muddy and I mean seriously muddy. There's mud everywhere and it's hard to stay upright. We slither and slide in the dark until we come out into a huge mud pool. I've never experienced anything like this.

The mud is like thick liquid chocolate and it comes up to my chest. We have fun trying to move around in it and I discover that if I relax back it holds me up and I feel weightless. I can sit in it and lie in it. It's not warm though, the cave is cold, the mud is cold and our guide is nowhere to be seen. We look at each other with some concern. We've been here a while, why has he left us?

We're relieved when he finally reappears and we have a hilarious and exhausting walk slipping and sliding to return to the entrance, covered from head to toe in mud. Back in the water, we wash the mud off and we're given kayaks to paddle back and reclaim our clothes.

Our motorbike riders are waiting for us and I again love the ride. I love being on open and relatively empty roads, though I do still need to hang on tight. We're taken to another cave, this one is Paradise Cave. Before we can go in, there's a long hot walk to reach the entrance.

It's cathedral-like inside and at seven kilometres long it's the largest dry cave in the world. Tourists are only allowed to explore the first kilometre. The inside is tastefully lit with soft coloured lights that show off the natural rock sculptures and the cavernous vastness of the place.

It's a fabulous ride back to the hostel through stunning scenery. I've absolutely loved the day and Natasha and Eleanor have been highly amusing and excellent company.

In the evening, I meet up with Rachael who's sharing my dorm. It's 'Happy Hour' so we both have a gin and tonic. I've forgotten how good they taste and we have a second one which is possibly not wise, I don't think they're English pub measures.

## 7th April

The hostel has bicycles to lend out and today I'm going to take advantage of this. I've heard about a bar called 'The Pub with Cold Beer' owned by a farming family and located *"up a dirt track in the middle of nowhere, but well signposted"* and I think it could be fun cycling there as my map suggests it's within my capability. A friendly young couple from Germany are borrowing bikes at the same time, they're going to Phong Nha Homestay and they ask if I'd like to go with them.

We set off on a good tarmac road but not for long. We turn off along a dry mud track with lush green fields either side. I'm glad I'm with the German couple because it feels as though we're on a farm track and if I was on my own I'd probably have turned back thinking I'd mistaken the road. They're confident in their directions and after another half hour cycling we come to Phong Nha Homestay. It's a charming place, quite 'up-market', with stunning views across rice fields. They have a pretty swimming pool which they allow us to use and great coffee.

My friends from Germany decide to cycle back after our swim, but I want to continue on through the Bong Lai Valley to the 'The Pub with Cold Beer' which still doesn't look far on my map. I'm wrong, it's very far. I've been cycling for ages on these dirt lanes that are seldom flat. I cycle up, then down and up and down, I'm tired and it's searingly hot. There's nothing and no-one about and I wonder if I should turn back, but I've come a long way. Then with relief I see a make-shift wooden sign by the side of the lane saying the pub is 3 kms ahead.

With renewed enthusiasm I set off again but on these rough lanes three kilometres seems a lot further. Then I see another sign like the last one and I hope it tells me I've arrived but this also says the pub is 3 kms ahead. What!! I can't turn back now so I continue cycling. The next sign I come to also tells me the pub is 3 kms away but this time it points off the lane and I cycle across a long metal bridge over a river.

I'm hot, tired, hungry, thirsty and grumpy and then I fall off my bike. The front wheel hits a stone and I land on the path tangled up in my bike. A young boy runs out from a nearby dwelling to see if I'm alive and my response is less than gracious, feeling that I don't need an audience right now, and wondering how I've managed to make a spectacle of myself right by the only property I've seen in miles.

I'm actually a bit shaken, there's a nasty cut on my foot and my knee feels bruised, but nothing's broken and the bike's fine. I walk the bike a short way and there up ahead I can see 'The Pub with No Beer'.

I have to laugh, there's really not much here, a barn-cum-shack with some trestle tables and presumably beer, which ironically, I don't drink. I ask for a menu and it's short, but they do have spring rolls and I order some. When I bite into the spring rolls I suspect they're made with meat, I've forgotten that spring rolls aren't always vegetarian and although I'm hungry I'm put off eating them.

It's a relief to see a road sign near the pub suggesting I can get back to Phong Nha using the Ho Chi Minh road. It may be busy with traffic but I haven't the energy to cycle back the way I've come. The path takes me through wonderful scenery of green fields and rice paddies with mountains in the distance and then I come across a wide river with a boat and fisherman and cows in the foreground. It's unbelievably idyllic. With some relief, I come to the excellent, tarmacked Ho Chi Minh road and although there is traffic, it's not scary and after cycling a few more kilometres I make it back to Easy Tiger.

I've booked a trek for tomorrow but I'm feeling anxious. It's a 12 km jungle trek and I'll be with a group of 'twenty somethings' and I'm concerned I won't keep up with them. The guide who'll lead the trek is called Li, he's twenty-five years old and the only Vietnamese I've seen with bleached blonde hair. While I'm eating my dinner of pizza he comes to talk with me and reassure me that I'll be fine to come on the trek. I learn that Li has never tasted pizza and offer him a slice of mine which he accepts, but doesn't finish eating, I don't think he's sold on pizza.

8th April

Already worried that I may not be fit enough for a 12 km trek through a hot jungle, I've woken to find my knee is swollen and the wound on my foot is nasty. I tape it as best I can and put on my walking boots but it's too painful, so I switch my footwear to trainers.

We're a group of seven trekkers plus our guide Li and two helpers who carry supplies. As we walk through the dense undergrowth of the jungle, which seems to go only upwards, Li tells us about his childhood. He's says that growing up he was always hungry and his family used the jungle for life's necessities, in those days it wasn't a National Park. He's very familiar with the area having spent a lot of time here with his father. Now his family are no longer allowed to use the area for food or firewood, but he makes good money as a guide.

The trek is arduous and hot, even though we're shaded by bushes and trees. Eventually Li beats a path that starts to go down and we clamber across boulders and rocks until we come to a stream. I start to take off my trainers and Li says *"don't remove your shoes, there will be many streams"*, so we wade through with our shoes on. I'm glad I chose not to wear my leather boots. Li is not wrong, there are many streams to walk across and then one of the streams opens out and we see in front of us a massive cave with a blue pool in front. Li tells us this is the rear entrance to Dark Cave, the other end of the one I went into two days ago. We take a break here and the assistant guides hand out bananas and chocolate biscuits, then Li gives us all head torches and we go inside the cave.

We clamber, scramble and cling to jagged rocks as Li leads us further and deeper into the cave. He seems casual about the expedition, but I have no doubt that a slip or fall would cause serious physical damage and I'm pretty nervous. We come out into a massive cavern and it feels other worldly. One of our party suggests we turn off our head torches which we do. It's very eerie not being able to see, only hearing the strange sounds of the vast cave.

Miraculously we make it back out of the cave without injury and continue trekking until we reach an open sandy area by a stream which feeds into a pretty aqua blue pool. Swarms of butterflies settle in groups on the ground nearby. Around us are lush green bushes and trees. I'm happy to learn that we'll have lunch here and an amazing picnic of rice, tofu, meat and vegetables is laid out for us on palm leaves. It's a relief to take off my shoes and lie back for a while. Li notices the wound on my foot and fetches some iodine which he puts on to help it heal.

After a rest, Li gives us life jackets and head torches, we're going to swim into the cave. The water is cold and Li swims out fast with the rest of the group following at competitive speed. I'm not able to keep up and I'm now in a very dark cave unable to see more than a few feet in front of me. I don't know whether to try and follow or swim back because I can still just about make out the circle of light that is the opening to the cave. I swim on and to my relief I reach the group who are treading water. Again, we all turn off our head lights and I experience bobbing about in cold water in total darkness surrounded by the strange sounds of a watery cave.

With the picnic all packed up and our lifejackets and head torches put away, we continue the trek. This really is the jungle, there's no obvious path and Li cuts the bushes back with his machete. We progress slowly up a long climb and come out high on a rocky outcrop with incredible views of the mountains around. No-one is talking, it's awesome. Eventually Li leads us back onto the road and I see the vehicle that brought us here.

We're handed cold cans of drink by the driver and everyone collapses onto the tarmac. I'm not the only one who's exhausted, but I'm very happy. Today has been amazing, I've been out of my comfort zone and I kept up with the group. I feel good.

## 9th April

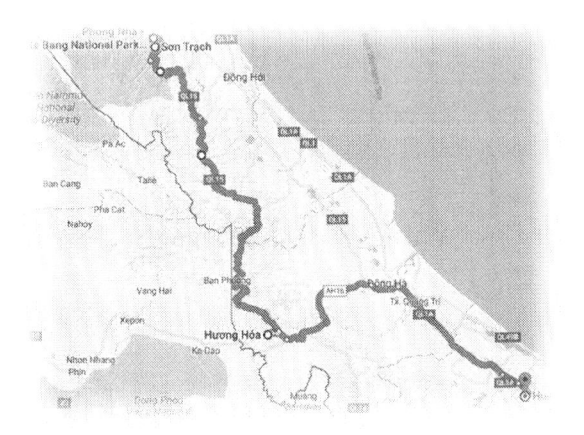

## Two Day Motorbike Ride to Hue (220 kms)

Please tell me this isn't happening. I'm about to spend the next two days on a motorbike and I've woken up with diarrhoea. My tummy feels weird and I can't eat breakfast. My driver, called Rin will be arriving in half an hour. I take two anti-diarrhoea tablets that I'm carrying with me and ask the Universe to please make me alright.

Rin is very friendly and kind. He straps my backpack complete with laptop inside, onto the back of his large, old (really old), motorbike, then straps on my front pack and ukulele. He's going to take me to Hue which will take two days, mostly down the Ho Chi Minh trail. He hands me a cycle helmet several sizes too large and I ask if he has a smaller one. He doesn't and he makes a play at adjusting the straps which don't make a scrap of difference. I climb on the bike behind Rin and with a high five and a fist in the air we set off, me praying that the diarrhoea tablets will work. The helmet bounces around my head and swivels around until I can see nothing, the only way to prevent this is by holding it in place with my hand, leaving only one hand to hang onto the speeding bike.

We've been riding for a couple of hours and I feel weak and drowsy and I'm in danger of falling asleep on the back of the bike which doesn't seem like a good idea. During the ride we've passed nothing, no grass verges, nowhere to rest up and no shade, but up ahead I spot a couple of large trees and I ask Rin if he'll stop the bike here. I don't want to sleep on the ground and there's a large low branch that I think I can rest on. Poor Rin is bewildered and I try to explain that I'm not well and I need a nap, I tell him I'll climb into the tree and he watches anxiously saying *"slowly, slowly"*. Lying along the branch and with my back against the trunk of the tree I doze off.

I feel much better and ready to set off again. Rin is happy that I'm happy and I notice he's started calling me Mom. It's an incredible ride. The trail is quiet and the scenery is amazing. We have another stop later at a roadside eatery, it's an open wooden barn with a corrugated roof and the usual array of little plastic chairs and tables. Rin kindly fetches an old sunbed for me to lie on and still not able to eat, I have a much-needed sleep. When I wake I notice Rin is stretched out asleep on the back of his motorbike.

We continue on our way down the trail, me still hanging onto my helmet with one hand and the back of the bike with the other. Arriving at a small village a gaggle of young children come running out when they hear the bike. Rin gives me sweet rice cakes to hand out to them and I realise they know to expect this. I'm invited to go into the village and look at the basic wooden houses which are all built on stilts and completely open at the front, but while I'm content to look around I'm embarrassed to go into the houses. I talk to the little children and smile a greeting to the older folk. There are cows and chickens scattered around, it's like a scene from a story book.

The trail is about 1000 kms long and my bottom feels as though it's travelled the whole of it, I'm looking forward to arriving at our hotel. It seems that we've arrived somewhere, but to my dismay we're at some sort of war museum and a guide is going to show me around. After ten minutes of listening to him talk at length about the American war in the area, I can tell that this will go on a very long time and I can no longer feign interest. It's 4.30 pm and I've been on the back of a motorbike for about 7 hours, I'm not well, I haven't eaten and I'm tired. I stop him in mid-flow and say *"I'm sorry, I'm not well, can we just look at the exhibits?"* He looks crest-fallen and I feel mean.

Rin looks surprised by how quickly I've emerged from the museum and I ask *"can we go to the hotel now please?"*. We make the final stop at a two-star hotel called Khanh Phuong Hotel in Hoa. I still don't want to eat and with an empty tummy I collapse exhausted into bed.

## 10th April

I'm feeling better and eat some breakfast. My backside knows it's been on a bike. The ride today is very different, we're driving along Highway One and it's not pretty, but there's plenty to look at. We stop for a while at The Hien Luong Bridge which crosses the Ben Hai river and where the north and south borders of Vietnam meet, it's an area that's seen continuous conflict over the years.

Another 13 kms and we come to the famous Vin Moc Tunnels made and used by the civilian population to protect themselves from the American bombing. They cover several kilometres on the north shore of the Ben Hai River in Vinh Moc village in the Quang Tri province.

I spend some time exploring the tunnels then meet up with Rin again to have a drink and some freshly sliced mango. A very old woman is sitting nearby under the shade of a tree, she asks me to buy her wares, fresh 'tea' leaves. I smile and say *'no thank you'* and offer her a slice of mango. We laugh because she tries to pick it up with her fingers but it's slippery and she struggles to get hold of it. She has a lovely smile and I ask her if I can take her photo. She doesn't mind, but I don't get her smile because she sticks a cigar in her mouth for the picture.

We've arrived in Hue, it's a city and mad with traffic. Rin takes me right to the hostel, the Hue Citadel Backpackers Homestay which seems very central. There's a query with my booking which was arranged by Seamus from 'Easy Tiger' so the receptionist gives him a call. He says *"the older lady has arrived..."* and I'm grateful he didn't refer to me as "the *old* lady". I give Rin an affectionate goodbye hug and a large tip, he's looked after me well for two days, he says *"goodbye Mom"*.

According to Trip Advisor there's an award winning vegetarian restaurant along the road from the hostel and I'm ravenous, so without stopping to shower or change, I walk to it.

I sit at a small table near to a massive table surrounded by about twenty beautifully dressed ladies, at the end nearest to me is a young girl. She looks at me and gives me the most delightful, sunny smile and waves, so I smile and wave back. When the group get up to leave she waves goodbye to me and then a moment later she comes back with her mum and rather shyly comes up to me. Her mum is holding an iPad and I realise they want a photo. I put my arm around the young girl and smile for the camera. When they've left I realise with embarrassment that they were both exquisitely dressed and I'm unwashed, wearing two-day old clothes having been on a motorbike.

## 11th April

I'm out in the city to explore and today I'm going to practice map reading. The roads here are wide and busy and approaching a large roundabout with five major roads spurring off, I'm fascinated to realise there are no road markings, no white lines, no give way signs. This makes everyone drive slowly and carefully as they weave their way around and it seems to work fine.

Hue is on the charmingly named Perfume River and there's an old Imperial City on the other side, so I'm finding my way there. I'm making a passable attempt at map reading but holding a map in my hand is attracting kind folk who want to help me and for the third time in ten minutes I'm asked *"where are you going"?*

Another UNESCO World Heritage Site, Thai Hoa Palace, known as the Imperial Palace was built in the 1800s inside a walled city for Emperor Gia Long of the Nguyen Dynasty. The palace and city have been extensively damaged over the ensuing years but some of it remains and some has been restored. The area and gardens around the Imperial Palace are quiet and peaceful and there's a gentle breeze which makes the heat bearable.

I have a happy time wandering around and exploring and it occurs to me that I haven't seen any beautiful man-made structures in a long time. I've seen natural beauty in scenery, but not in buildings, the properties in Vietnam tend to be very plain, so seeing these sumptuously decorated buildings is a feast for my eyes.

Leaving the Imperial Palace, I strike up a conversation with a Canadian couple and they tell me they've come to Hue from Dalat, a town in the mountains. They say it's cooler there and I like their enthusiasm for the place, I think I'll go there next.

The night market in Hue is something of a 'must see', so I wander in search of it in the evening. It's by the river and looks pretty with rows of coloured lights and plenty of stalls selling unusual hand-crafted wares. Travelling with a back pack means I can't buy anything which makes walking around local markets less fun and a shame when there are so many different and interesting things at incredibly cheap prices.

I'm back at yesterday's vegetarian restaurant again this evening and choose vegetable soup, mostly because I'm getting fed up with tofu that seems to come in vegetarian meals as the alternative to meat. When it comes it's a bowl of almost clear liquid with chunks of tofu swimming in it.

## 12th April

## Bus to Hội An (130 kms)

Vietnam is a long skinny country and I'm working my way down it. Many of the travellers I meet have started in Saigon at the bottom and are working their way up but I guess it doesn't matter which way we travel.

The bus for Hội An leaves at 8 am, it's a 130 km journey and my ticket cost me $5 (about £3.50), I'll change buses at Da Nang. We drive five minutes along the road then the bus stops and it's another 40 minutes before we move off again. Half an hour later we stop again, this time for a twenty-minute break and everyone piles off the bus.

I'm sitting next to a chatty young lady called Margot, who's French and 25 years old. She tells me she's lived in China for three years and then spent three years in Hong Kong working in the wine industry. She asks me lots of questions and is keen to have my advice about money issues, I'm amused by this because although I'm more than twice her age she's far more 'worldly' and accomplished than me.

The bus arrives in Hội An just after mid-day and as arranged, I call my accommodation, the Hội An Life Homestay and let them know I've arrived. They send a driver to collect me from the bus stop; amazing service.

The homestay is large and modern. I have a room and bathroom to myself so I take a shower then sleep for an hour until my rumbling tummy tells me to go out and get food.

Li is working on the reception desk, he's very friendly and gives me information, a map and a bicycle. Armed with the knowledge that Hội An is a small place and I can't get lost, I set off to explore.

Situated by the Thu Bon River that feeds into the East Vietnam Sea, the old part of Hội An has a long and colourful history as an important trading port, dating from the 15$^{th}$ century. The varied architecture shows Chinese, Portuguese, Japanese and Dutch styles and the area is now a UNESCO World Heritage site. Coloured lanterns are strung across the streets outside the attractive shops and restaurants, giving the area a picturesque and quaint feel. I know I'm going to have a happy time here.

Making good use of my bike, I cycle away from the old town, through the busy streets in search of the beach. I think I know the direction to take but I've been cycling a long time now along a long road and I feel less sure. I can see someone sitting on a buffalo some distance away in a field near the road, and I use the excuse to take a rest from my bike and grab a snapshot. As I photograph him, the man waves and beckons to me to come over to him. He invites me to climb onto the buffalo. It's enormous and I look at the man quizzically, like how? He kneels down in the old fashioned 'marriage proposal' position so I can use his knee to stand on and I have my first experience of sitting on a buffalo. I see now that the man is very young, probably a teenager. He takes the coolie hat from his head and pops it on mine and offers to take my picture. He doesn't ask, but I give him some money, I think he's done this before.

The long straight road continues and I finally arrive in a small place that has a beach feel to it with stalls selling swim-wear. Cycling up and down a couple of lanes I come across a river but no beach. I'm getting worried that it will get dark soon and I've quite a long way to cycle back without lights, so give up my search for the sea and determine to try again tomorrow.

## 13th April

I've woken up in very good spirits, I really like being here. I have breakfast outside in the sunshine and I'm joined but an attractive young couple from the U.S.A. They tell me they're newly married and they're spending four months travelling together. The new wife tells me that she's known her husband since high school but she's learned more about him since travelling and recommends all newly-weds should do this. I wonder if it might be better to do it *before* marrying, just in case.

Borrowing the bike once more, I set off again in search of the beach. It's blisteringly hot. I've been given a recommendation by Seamus at Easy Tiger to go to Paddy's Beach Bar which I've now discovered is on the way, so having checked the map again and with renewed confidence in my navigational skills, I cycle back down the same long road. It's about 7 kms to Paddy's place, a modern hostel with a bar and a swimming pool which they allow me to use.

At Paddy's they tell me how to get to the beach and it's not far. There's a shop nearby selling swimwear and having damaged my swimsuit with the chemical solution in Palolem, I think I'll buy a bikini to replace it. They're very cheap and there are plenty of them, so I pick out a couple I like the look of and ask if I can try them on. To my amusement I'm directed to the nearby public loo and the shop keeper carries a long mirror over for me, placing it in the toilet cubicle. I've chosen a turquoise blue one, it's not brilliant, but it'll do and it hasn't emptied my purse.

The beach is very narrow, there's not much sand and the water doesn't look inviting. I don't think I've come to the main Hội An beach yet. I carry on cycling along the coast road but although at one crossroads I see a signpost 'to the beach' somehow I miss it *(how can I miss a beach?)*. A few more kilometres and I'm back on a familiar road in Hội An and heading for 'home'.

A restaurant, recommended to me by the American couple, is in the guide book as having *"the best Vietnamese Bánh mì sandwich in the world"*, quite a claim, and I'm looking forward to trying it. Bánh mì is Vietnamese for bread or baguette. When I find the place, it's packed with people and is a simple sandwich shop with some small tables to eat at . I order a salad filled baguette and it's delicious and filling.

14th April

I'm on a mission today to take photos in the early morning light and avoid the crowds so I take the bike early and pedal back into the old town. I have to laugh, it's rubbish collection day and the streets are full of boxes and bags of rubbish, which doesn't look good in photos. The morning light across the water is very pretty though and I take some pictures here then cycle back in time for breakfast.

I'd like to stay out for an evening meal but it's too far to walk from the hostel and I wonder about using the bike at night. I ask the hostel owner if I can keep the bike until after dark and does it have lights. She looks at me as though I'm being odd and replies yes, of course it's okay and no, they don't have lights. It doesn't seem to be an issue.

A restaurant by the river has a blackboard at the entrance telling me they serve Oyster Bay white wine. It's a quick decision and I sit on an upstairs balcony with a large glass of chilled wine and an entertaining view of the street below, with its coloured lanterns, people and the boats on the river.

The meal I've ordered turns out to be an unusual combination of mushroom, pineapple and tomatoes with rice, the flavours are very intense and tasty. Cycling back in the dark without lights isn't fun, but I'm glad I've experienced the old town at night.

Probably because I've been out on my own and had wine, but I'm thinking about Ben and wish I could talk to him. I haven't had a response to my last email. I email his sister asking her to let me know he's okay.

## 15th April

I'm checking out today from Hội An Homestay. At $15 a night it was more than I usually pay, but it was worth it. I've loved having my own space, free use of a bike and excellent free breakfasts, not to mention free pick-ups to and from the bus stop.

Ben's sister has replied to my email! All is well, he's just busy. I spend time carefully writing a postcard to him. I feel excited to think of him receiving it and reading it. My homestay host has promised to post it for me, I do hope it will reach Ben.

## Bus to Dalat via Nha Trang (635 kms)

I'm taking the overnight bus from Hội An which will take me to Nha Trang where I'll change buses for my ultimate destination, Dalat. I'm still working my way down the coast of Vietnam.

This bus has the same style sleeping 'pods' I experienced last time. A young Australian couple are on the bus with a small baby. The man is incredibly tall, well over 6ft and I wonder how on earth he will fit into the tiny sleeping pod. The baby cries on and off throughout the night which is a shame and I feel immense sympathy for the parents, travelling with a little one can't be easy.

After twelve hours in the bus and not much sleep, we've arrived at Nha Trang. I had considered staying here a night but made the decision to continue to Dalat, aware that I have to leave Vietnam when my thirty-day visa runs out.

With an hour and a half before the next bus comes, I walk to the beach a couple of roads away. It's fascinating, this early in the morning there are a surprising number of people on the beach exercising, doing yoga, tai chi and running. The sun has just risen and makes a pretty picture over the water.

## 16th April

The bus to Dalat is a modern one and it makes a change to be travelling in the daytime so I can see the amazing scenery. Located 1,500 m above sea level on the Langbian Plateau, Dalat is inland, in the Central Highlands Region. Known as the "City of Eternal Spring" the guide books tell me '*it has a temperate climate all year, it's centered around a lake and surrounded by hills, pine forests, lakes and waterfalls*'. Sounds like my kind of place.

I'm walking from the bus stop to my hostel which has the oddly old-English name of Dalat Cozy Nook, but after ten minutes it's clear I have no idea even which direction to walk, so I hail a taxi. I'm glad I did, the walk would have been very long.

Situated down a side alley off a main road, my first impressions of my new 'home' are good. I'll be sharing a mixed dorm and there are ten beds in the room and only one shower, but I've received a charming welcome from the owners, Diem and Tham, and everything looks very clean.

After stowing my backpack and uke under my bed I walk into town to find food. There's a small eating place nearby and I tuck into the best spring rolls I've tasted so far. As I've been led to expect, the temperature is definitely cooler and it's also a bit rainy.

This is turning out to be a wonderful hostel. The family provide a cooked meal in the evenings for guests, for the small price of $3. There are about twenty-five of us sitting around a long table with a generous variety of food dishes laid out, including several vegetarian options. The food is delicious and we sit chatting and swapping travelling tales.

The young girl next to me comments on my yellow watch, she says *"I like your watch",* I thank her for the compliment and tell her the story of how I came to own the 'Wendy' watch. It occurs to me that with such a divide in my age and hers, she's not sure how to talk to me, but wanting to be friendly she starts with a compliment. I frequently forget that I'm way older than most of the travellers I meet.

## 17th April

Rather than spend the day in the town which holds little interest for me, I'm taking a taxi 3 kms to the cable car at Robin Hill. The ride costs 70,000 VDN (about £2.30) and I can take the cable car there and back although I'm not sure where 'there' is.

The ride is 2.3 kms with views across tea fields, trees, green hills and a lake. At the top is a signpost pointing the way to the Truc Lam Monastery and pagoda. The area feels very tranquil, the sun is shining and the temperature perfect. Strolling down the path I see a European lady also on her own, she looks a similar age to me and I start a conversation with her. Her name's Christiana, originally from Switzerland but now living in Exeter, U.K. She's pleasant company and we continue walking together.

There are beautiful flowers planted around and one vine particularly attracts our attention, hanging from the stems are unusual bright turquoise coloured flowers. They don't look real and neither of us can remember seeing natural flowers that colour in England. Christiana is a keen gardener and wants to take a cutting home, so with the small penknife attached to my day pack I cut through a woody stem and hand the cutting to her. I'm feeling very uncomfortable doing this to the vine and I'm interested to recognise the thought in my head that I wouldn't do this in England in case security cameras were watching me.

We walk to the immaculate pagoda with its golden roof and the small monastery, then we return on the cable car.

Christiana is hoping to take a steam train ride on the Da Lat–Thap Cham Railway, so with nothing else to do, I walk along with her. It's a long way and we arrive on the platform just in time to see the train in the station, but all the seats are taken so we can't board the train. We watch in amusement as two brides come on to the platform to have their photos taken with the train, this 'stage managed' kind of photography for weddings still seems bizarre to me. One beautiful lady dressed in traditional bridal white also has a tiny white fluffy dog with her and I wonder if the dog is really hers or only a 'prop' for the photos.

Christiana and I part company in the late afternoon and I give her my card, she's also travelling on to Ho Chi Min City so maybe our paths will cross again.

## 18th April

I've found a one-day trek that will take me to the summit of Langbian, Dalat's highest mountain and an Australian girl called Lydia, also staying at the hostel, is keen to come along. We have a young guide named Thuan and he drives us the short distance to the start of the walk.

The weather is dull and not too hot, which I'm grateful for because we start with an arduous climb through a pine forest. My previous experience of Australians is they tend to be very fit, but this doesn't seem to be so with Lydia. She's a big, strong looking girl but she's already struggling with the climb and thinks the altitude may be affecting her. I'm not sure she will keep going.

To her credit, Lydia doesn't give up and with frequent stops we make it to the top, her legs are like jelly and she's exhausted. We've left the pine forest behind and come into a green jungle and the landscape is now stunning. Thuan has been carrying a picnic with him and when we reach a plateau he lays it out on the ground and we tuck into cucumber, tomatoes, mangoes and pineapple with bread.

The sky has changed and we notice ominous, grey clouds in the distance, the wind is picking up and it looks likely that a storm is coming our way. The scene in front of us is spectacular in its drama, with the green tree covered hills and the foreboding dark sky as the backdrop.

We start heading back down and sure enough the rain comes. It makes the downhill trek tricky and we slip and slide much of the way. Lydia is not happy, she didn't like going up and she doesn't like going down. The walk finishes sooner than I'd expected. I don't believe we covered all the areas originally planned and I think Thuan must have decided to shorten the walk, either because of the rain or because of Lydia's complaints.

## 19th April

I recall Adam in Singapore telling me about the Dalat Palace Hotel, and I've decided to take a break from researching on my computer to see if I can get a cup of tea, it feels like ages since I've had a cuppa.

Dalat has a large lake in the centre which helps me with navigating and I easily find the hotel. It's luxurious, and for a very small price I sit outside on a veranda with tea and cake and take in the view across the lawns to the lake and mountain beyond.

I've shared another delicious dinner at the hostel and the youngsters have all gone out to a bar, I turned down their generous invitation for me to join them. From upstairs in my dorm I hear Diem playing the piano, it sounds lovely and I come downstairs to listen to her. She's a truly delightful person and I think her husband Tham is very special too. Diem tells me she'd like to play the piano more but her time is limited, she has a young daughter and running a hostel is a 24/7 job. I can't imagine how she fits everything into her day.

## 20th April

### Aeroplane to Ho Chi Min City (40 mins)

Time is running out for me in Vietnam as my visa will end on the 22nd of this month, so I've decided to save some time and fly to Ho Chi Min City, originally called Saigon. The flight is excellent and only takes forty minutes.

I've gained confidence in my travelling and take the public bus from Tan Son Nhat airport to Ben Thanh Market, which I believe to be near to the hostel I've pre-booked. The bus ride costs 20,000 VND (61p). Alighting from the bus and loaded with my stuff, I can tell I'm back in the heat of a city. My hostel is in a road called Tôn Thất Tùng (try saying that in a hurry), it's about 1 km away and happily, I locate it easily.

The hostel seems nice and Anna the manager gives me a map of the city, so after a short nap, I walk onto the streets, with songs from the musical 'Miss Saigon' going around in my head.

Following the map, I walk a fair distance and come to the Government-run War Museum. Outside the building is a 'Huey' helicopter, several fighter planes, a tank and various other large pieces of war equipment. It makes a dramatic scene. I go inside, but not for long, the pictures and graphic photos are harrowing. There are poster size photographs on a large wall depicting demonstrations from around the world against the American involvement in the Vietnam war. One picture in black and white shows demonstrators holding up banners and carries the headline *"People in London (United Kingdom) demonstrated to request the U.S. withdraw its troops from Vietnam, March 17$^{th}$ 1968"*.

From the museum, I make my way to the Bitexco Financial Tower which, at 262.5 metres (861 ft), is the tallest building in the city. The tower has an observation deck giving incredibly clear 360-degree views of the city and Saigon River, and I again experience the thrill of being up so high. On the 50$^{th}$ floor there's a restaurant and looking at the menu I can't resist ordering a tuna sandwich and chips. When it arrives I devour every morsel with pure pleasure.

I stay in the tower watching the light change as the

sun goes down, then start walking back home. I'm amused to notice that no matter where I'm staying I always call my hostel or hotel 'home' in my mind, I never think in terms of going back to my 'hostel'. Along the way I'm asked by twelve different motorbike taxis if I'd like a ride, it's not easy to keep smiling and being polite.

## 21st April

It's my last day in Vietnam and I can't leave without a visit to the Mekong Delta so I've booked a tour which goes there and back in a day. It's not ideal, I wish I could have been out on the Mekong Delta in the early morning, but it's all I can do. The bus ride is a long two and a half hours but as always, I'm happy looking out of the window at the passing scenery.

Arriving at The Delta a group of us pile onto a boat and we're taken out to see the sights of the river. I can imagine it crammed with boats selling their wares in the early morning, but it's late morning now and most of them have left. We pull up alongside a boat selling fruit and vegetables. I haven't tasted jack fruit yet, so I buy some that has been sliced and prepared ready to eat. The lady 'seller' puts my fruit into a polystyrene box with a plastic fork, both of which are placed inside a polythene bag and tied with a wire clip. I'm really dismayed, here I am on the Mekong Delta in Vietnam buying fruit from a little boat and they're using all this packaging!

Our tour guide takes us to a quaint place by the river where we have a simple rice lunch on trestle tables under an awning. Afterwards there's an opportunity to borrow a bike and explore the area. Cycling along the sandy lanes by the river is tricky and I don't get far. In the afternoon our guide takes us by boat to an area by the water where small food industries operate. We meet a bee keeper and a tiny confectionary producing place where I stand fascinated watching a man wrap small boiled sweets individually by hand.

Cambodia next!

# Cambodia

## 22ⁿᵈ April

### Aeroplane to Phnom Penh (45mins)

The lovely Anna, who runs Saigon Charming Hostel, hands me a large jack fruit as a parting gift and we hug goodbye. It's a fifteen-minute walk to the bus station and the bus is already waiting to take me back to Tan Son Nhat airport.

Going through security at the airport, the scanner highlights my penknife attached to my rucksack and it's taken from me. I'm annoyed with myself for forgetting to check, it's been in my possession for many years, a shame to lose it.

For a ticket costing £74 and less than an hour in the air, I arrive in Phnom Penh, Cambodia. How amazing life is, one minute I'm in Vietnam, the next I'm in Cambodia and it's all so easy. I'm relieved that there's no problem with my visa which I had bought and paid for on the Internet.

Outside the airport there are the now familiar tuk-tuks and I pick one and show the driver on a map where my hostel called 'One Stop' is located. It's about 11 kms away and we agree a fee of $6 to take me there. I check in, but don't hang about because it's now gone 5 pm and I'd like to do a river cruise on the Mekong and take in the sunset.

The quay is just across the road from my hostel and as I stand checking the blackboard for boat times, an English couple arrive. They're very friendly and we board the boat together. The vessel takes us a short way out and we watch the sky change colour to a dark orange. Multi-coloured lights come on all along the shore line, it makes a very pretty scene.

It's dark now and departing from the boat, the English couple invite me to join them for a drink at the famous FCC Club, the Foreign Correspondents Club, along the sea front.

The FCC has plenty of character and we sit on the third floor with a good view of the river and street below. I have a delicious pinacolada to drink, entertaining company to share the evening with and to top it all a massive moon like a big orange ball, adorns the night sky. Walking 'home' late in the evening I feel relaxed and in spite of the warnings about pickpockets and the dangers of Pnom Phen city, nothing in me feels afraid.

## 23rd April

The Killing Fields are a number of sites where more than a million people were killed and buried during the 1975-79 Khmer Rouge regime and they're located 17 kms south of Phnom Penh. Like most visitors who come here I want to visit the area and get in touch with that horrific part of history that took place during my lifetime, something I'd learned about from the news but didn't touch my personal life.

The hostel staff are able to arrange a tour and along with three fellow travellers, we go with the guide who's arrived with his tuk-tuk. We drive to the site of a former high school which was turned into a Security Prison, known as Tuol Sleng S-21 by the Khmer Rouge regime. This is only one of at least 150 execution centres. Tuol Sleng is now a museum and chronicles the Cambodian genocide. In this prison all but seven of the twenty thousand prisoners were executed, it's hard to get my head around such a massive number of executions.

As we enter the area, a large signboard is in front of us stating "The Security of Regulation" on which there are written ten chilling commandments. The 6th commandment horrifically states *"while getting lashes or electrification you must not cry at all"*.

Strangely, every prisoner that was brought here was photographed and their portraits are now displayed in monochrome on boards throughout the rooms of the building. Looking at hundreds of these faces makes me feel very emotional, I can't bear to imagine what thoughts must have gone through their minds as their photographs were taken, some of them are very young and vulnerable looking.

We're a quieter and more thoughtful group now as our guide takes us to another location, the site known as The Killing Fields.

It's not how I'd expected it to be, I think I thought I would see fields, this is a smaller grassy area that has been well trodden from many visitors. Footpaths take us past places where mass graves were found. There's a tree with a wide trunk, it's called the Killing Tree because this is where prisoners were beaten to death. Touchingly the trunk is now decorated with hundreds of coloured bracelets and hair bands placed there by visitors. Reading some of the horrific stories on the plaques along the way, I feel totally bewildered by the ability of humans to inflict such pain on their fellow men. Overwhelmed, my tears flow and right now, the vast contrast of the lives of people who lived through this and my own joyful existence is difficult to reconcile.

At the end of the walk we come to a tall monument of stone and glass where hundreds of skulls are stacked in the windows. Each one has been carefully documented. It's crowded with tourists inside and I don't stay long.

Our tour is over and we're taken back into Phnom Penh. Ruben, one of the group, is from Spain and we have lunch together. Sitting outside a simple restaurant in the sunshine, I'm glad to have his company.

## 24th April

## Bus to Saen Monouram, Cambodia (365 kms)

I'm moving on today and very excited because a while ago, after considerable searching, I found an ethical and genuine Elephant Project where I can volunteer. There are many animal welfare projects, especially in Sri Lanka, but from articles I've read it's likely most of them have been set up to make money from tourists and they don't genuinely have the welfare of animals at their core.

It's a five-hour bus ride ahead, so I get up early to take advantage of breakfast, but the young woman who prepares the food isn't about. Just as she appears so does the motorbike taxi that has come to take me to the bus, he's fifteen minutes early and I miss breakfast.

Because I don't like an empty tummy I habitually carry food in my uke case, it's become my larder, the small pocket is always stuffed with 'goodies', usually nuts, dried fruit and muesli bars, so even though I didn't make breakfast, I won't go hungry.

It's a long wait for the tourist bus that will take me to Saen Monouram, but when it comes I'm pleased that it's a decent one. The bus drives off scarily fast, at this speed I can't believe it will take five hours to drive the 370 kms.

It does take five hours. The bus stops in Saen Monouram and I get off on a wide, dusty road. This place has a different feel from any other I've been to, it makes me think of the small towns I've seen in old cowboy films.

I'm not sure which way to walk, but I've plenty of time, so I just start walking. My guest house is called 'Sokchcav' and I know it isn't far from the centre. Across the road I can see a sign for 'Heffalump Café' and I'm very pleased to see it because this is where I have to come tomorrow to meet the project leaders of my volunteer work. I go inside, have a delicious iced coffee and contact my guesthouse. The owner kindly comes to meet me, his home is only a short walk away.

The guesthouse is large and seems out of place, I think the owners have more wealth than most of the people around here. I love having a room to myself again with my own bathroom but I don't stay in it long, there's some exploring to do and I'm in need of food.

I take a walk about the small town. Reminiscent of India, there's rubbish strewn around and it seems a fairly poor, simple place. I've come to a large road with a big expanse of nothing beyond it but a large sun, so I sit on a bench to watch the sun go down.

A group of small children come up to me playfully and say *"hello"*, the young boy wants to shake hands which we do, several times, then we do 'high fives'. I take a photo of the children and give the boy my pen, to which he says *"thank you"* very sweetly.

When the sun has almost disappeared, I look about for somewhere to eat but I don't see any restaurants. This isn't a tourist place, so I buy some roasted sweetcorn from a street vendor and some fruit to take back to my room.

## 25th April

## Elephant Valley Project

### Day 1

The guesthouse owners are willing to let me leave my big backpack and uke with them while I spend a few days away as a volunteer.

With only the basics in my small pack I walk to Hefalump Café to meet up with folk from the Elephant Valley Project. Another couple are there, also joining the project, Sebastian and Mariana. The group leader arrives and takes us in a jeep to the location of the project where he gives us an introductory talk. I'm very impressed with the organisation so far, I have a good feeling about it.

There are five elephants in the full-time care of the project, other elephants, also looked after by them, live with their owners in the village. Elephants are still widely used here for labour, but their owners are generally poor and paying for health care for the 'ellies' is often beyond them. To pay off debts many villagers have sold off their land to large corporations, land that is now used to grow trees for palm oil. This results in a lack of jungle and vegetation, which in turn means that food and natural habitat for the elephants is scarce.

And now we're walking through some jungle and we're going to meet two elephants. We sit and wait for a while then hear the sounds of them approaching. As the first one emerges through the trees I watch spellbound. She's walking towards us and another one is close behind, they're very near, I feel as though I've stopped breathing, there's something magical about this moment.

The elephants stop in front of us and casually reach out with their trunks and strip leaves off branches to put into their mouths. Each elephant has a 'mahout', someone who looks after them full time. I take dozens of photos, I'm in awe of these two amazing mammals standing so close. The project leader tells us that the ellies are allowed to roam where they want during the day, the mahouts walk along with them and make sure they don't come to harm.

When the elephants move off, we all follow a short distance behind. Listening to the project leader, a lady called Dee, it's clear that she's totally passionate about the ellies in her care.

We come to a shallow, running river and here the elephants walk into the water. We sit on boulders on the bank, watching their mahouts give them a scrub with long brooms. One of the elephants sucks up river water into her trunk then blows it out, soaking the mahout, and making us laugh. I wonder if she did it on purpose.

At midday, we walk back to the lodge, where lunch is provided. There are about six other friendly volunteers already there, and together we pass through a kitchen area where we're served rice and dal which we eat at trestle tables. I love the lodge. It's made from timber, comfortably furnished and set up high surrounded by jungle. I had no idea it would all be so wonderful and I feel immensely lucky.

It's swelteringly hot now and I'm grateful to learn that we have time for a siesta before we go out again, so I settle myself onto a huge bean bag on the veranda and feast my eyes on the treetops and skyline.

It's mid-afternoon and we walk with Dee back to the jungle to find the other elephants. After just a short while we know they are coming, yet they're surprisingly quiet. Just like this morning, we follow them as they saunter through the undergrowth, chomping as they go, they appear to amble slowly yet they cover a lot of ground. It's a truly remarkable experience observing them so closely.

Ahead is another elephant and we're told this is the 'old lady', she's called Maelot. She doesn't have any teeth, so she's given banana tree leaves to eat, they're spread out on the ground. She stands under the shade of a tree surrounded by the huge rolled up leaves and we sit for ages watching her eat. This elephant definitely has a twinkle in her eye and she's clearly enjoying herself. She sifts through the leaves with the end of her trunk choosing the ones she wants, then she curls her trunk around them and brings them to her mouth. I'm sure I can see her grinning.

Around 5 pm we take a slow stroll back to the lodge and I spend a fabulous half hour watching a stunning sunset from the balcony, before we're served another excellent meal.

The other volunteers are a nice bunch; Tiana, Cara, Brendon, and Dom. Seb and Mariana who arrived with me were only here for the day. After eating, we lounge around, reading or dozing. I love the quiet, the only sounds are a few insect noises. The lodge has electricity from 6 pm until 9 pm so I'm told that it's wise to be ready to hop into bed by nine when the lights will all go out.

My room is a small timber hut and would be cute but there's an uncomfortably large spider on the floor. I look at him for a while contemplating how best to deal with him. I decide that I'm the intruder here, this is more his jungle than mine and I suspect that if I looked, I'd find others like him in the room, so I let him be and pop into bed.

I'm just drifting off to sleep when I hear the strangest noise, it sounds like a dog's squeaky toy and it's shockingly loud. There it is again and it sounds as though it's in my room. I can't do anything about it and I don't want to put my torch on and see what other creatures are sharing my bedroom, so I close my eyes and eventually drift off to sleep.

26th April

Day 2

Stepping outside, the early morning light is lovely and this is the perfect place to practice some yoga. Breakfast at 7 am hits the spot; pancakes with banana, eggy bread and coffee. I mention the 'squeaky toy' noise I heard in my room last night and learn that it's a lizard making the sound.

This morning there are some D.I.Y. jobs to be done and I volunteer to work with one of the staff called Clare, sawing wood and making a frame for posters. It's enjoyable work and I like the physical activity although the heat saps my energy.

I have a fun task this afternoon; Dee, Tiana and I go in search of Maelot to give her a health check. When we find her, she's about to have a dip in the river so we watch and wait until she goes back to the tree where she knows she'll find the banana leaves.

She needs to be measured and I stand next to her side and throw one end of a tape measure over Maelot's back to Tiana, who then passes it underneath Maelot's belly for me to grab hold of, now we can take the measurement. More checks are done and then we sit back and relax, watching her eat. I'm fascinated by her dexterity, using her trunk to pick out the juicy inner leaves and discarding the ones she doesn't want.

Back at the lodge I go to the shower block, there's only cold water, but in this heat it doesn't matter at all. Before using the toilet, I lift the seat and underneath, sitting at the back of the toilet rim is a massive black spider. I shudder to think I might have sat on it if I hadn't lifted the seat and vow that I will always remember to check under toilet seats in future.

At dinner time I meet two new volunteers from Baltimore, Tanner and Andrew. The evening is spent quietly reading and some of the group play monopoly. I'm in bed by 9 pm for 'lights out' but not tired enough to sleep I put on my head torch to read. Bad idea. This attracts a million small flies, so I give up and listen instead to the 'squeaky' lizard which I've yet to meet.

## 27th April

### Day 3

It's my last day here and I wish I was staying longer. After a strange breakfast of veg noodles, omelette and fruit, I go with Clare, Tanner and Andrew to the area they call the garden.

Together we create four steps in a sloping path, using small tree trunks and carved pegs to hold them in. We cover the trunks with wire mesh to provide some grip, then fill the gaps in between with small stones. That task finished, the others work hard clearing weeds from an overgrown patch of land, and in this heat, I don't envy them. I'm grateful that my job is far less physical and involves repairing holes in the nylon mesh that surrounds the baby trees.

An excellent lunch of spaghetti with mixed vegetables and avocado, followed by a siesta and we're off again to see the elephants.

We're led by two long-stay volunteers, Tuon and Tyler and head down to the river to meet up with ellies 'Easy Rider' and 'Gee Nowl'. They come with their mahouts and bathe in the river and as before, we follow them while they wander through the jungle.

I'm sorry when the day comes to an end and it's time for me to walk up the hill and meet the van that will take me back to Saen Monourom.

## 28th April

### Bus to Kracheh, Cambodia (204 kms)

When I knew I wanted to come to the Elephant Valley Project, I looked at a map to determine a possible route to Siem Reap, which will be my last Cambodian destination. I found a place called Kratie (pronounced Krachie) which is on a bus route from Saen Monourom and famous for pink dolphins. I've been able to book a bus to take me there.

I'm told the bus will come to the Green Café at 7.45 am so I walk there early and have breakfast of coffee and carrot cake. I still get nervous waiting for transport and I'm relieved when it arrives, half an hour late at 8.15 am. The bus then drives around the block and parks five yards from the guesthouse I left an hour ago and sits there for forty-five minutes with the engine running. There's no explanation. This is a local bus, not a tourist one, and there are plenty of stops along the route to Kratie, so it's a miracle to me that it still arrives at one o'clock, as expected.

I have only one day here in Kratie, so waste no time in locating where I can book my bus for Siem Reap tomorrow, then I get a tuk-tuk to take me to the river boats.

It's a fascinating and very bumpy 10 km ride and sitting opposite me is my driver's young son who looks about five years old. He stares at me the whole way. I smile at him but he turns his head away shyly, I wonder if he's ever seen blonde hair before.

The road we're driving down is brownish-red dirt and the traffic is mostly motorbikes, bicycles and tuk-tuks. There's a variety of stand-alone buildings lining the road, some businesses and some dwellings. Many are timber and built on stilts which suggests the road sometimes floods.

At the riverside there's a small wooden boat waiting to go out, so I hop in. It seems I'm to be the only passenger. The boat ride is superb, I'm on the Mekong River again and the water sparkles gloriously with reflections from the late afternoon sun. The temperature is swelteringly hot and looking at the bright water makes my eyes feel on fire, even behind sunglasses.

I'm lucky to get several sightings of the rare freshwater dolphins known as Irawaddy dolphins. They don't leap out of the water in the way that regular dolphins do and they're smaller. There's something joyful about waiting and watching to catch a glimpse of one of nature's wonders.

The tuk-tuk has waited for me and under the watchful gaze of the driver's young son, I'm taken back to Kratie and Le Tonle guesthouse.

## 29th April

### Bus to Siem Reap (332 kms)

I miss breakfast. My bus for Siem Reap leaves at 7 am before the kitchen is open. The ride is about seven hours but I don't mind because it's a good way to see more of the country and my time in Cambodia is short. The scenery doesn't change much, the land looks very dry even though there was a massive downpour of rain last night. The villages we drive through look much alike, ramshackle dwellings, shops and timber homes on stilts.

On the bus, I meet a guy called Mac, he's a retired English professor and tells me he's visited Siem Reap many times, bringing students here. He says that if I want a guide to show me around Angkor Wat he can recommend someone. He has a sweet story about a young Cambodian man called Sopeara. They met a few years back and Mac employed him as a guide for his student group. He liked the youngster so much he decided to help him, both financially and with his education. They've become good friends and Mac is now godfather to Sopeara's baby daughter.

I arrive in Siem Reap around 2 pm and take a tuk-tuk to my pre-booked hostel OneDerz. The hostel looks spacious and new, I'm impressed by how good some of the hostels are and wonder if I may be getting better at choosing my accommodation.

Before I go out exploring I need to organise a tour to Angkor Wat for tomorrow, so I call Sopeara on my mobile. His price as a tour guide is high, I can take a general tour for considerably less money, but I like recommendations and decide to go with him.

A fellow traveller at the hostel recommended a restaurant called 'Sister Sley' and her enthusiasm for the food makes me determine to go there for dinner. I set off walking using an 'app' on my mobile for directions, but before I've got very far the battery dies.

Siem Reap is a busy place with an especially popular road called Pub Street, well known as the place where backpackers converge. It's packed with pubs, restaurants and tourists and not my sort of street at all.

I think I'm walking in the right direction so keep going, but after a good half an hour it's clear I've gone wrong. Going back the way I came, I walk in the other direction and eventually, foot weary, I see a sign saying *'SISTER SLEY' CLOSED ON MONDAYS*. It's Monday.

I'm tired and frustrated but I remember that Mac had recommended a Café called Genevieve which I'd noticed earlier, so I walk back there. I'm told that they're full at the moment but if I wait a table might come free. I'm not going anywhere else so I wait and luckily not for too long.

There's a story written on the menu about Genevieve, whom the café is named after. She was the much-loved wife of the owner and she died in 2009 *"after a brief and courageous battle with cancer"*. Her husband came to visit Siem Reap with his daughter and stayed to teach English, eventually opening the café.

I'm slightly ashamed to admit that I ordered fish and chips and a glass of Sauvignon Blanc. When I finish my meal, the owner and husband of Genevieve comes to my table and we talk for a while. The evening has turned into a very pleasant experience.

## 30th April

Sopeara is going to be my guide today, taking me around three temples, Ta Prohm, the temple that featured in an Indiana Jones movie, Angkor Thom and Angkor Wat. Sopeara is a joy, his English is excellent and he's playful, he makes me laugh.

Each temple is built from dark grey rocks and surrounded by the brown-red dirt I've come to associate with Cambodia. Although they've been preserved to some extent, they retain an ancient, ruined feel to them and as we explore them, Sopeara tells me interesting stories.

Angkor Wat is the largest religious monument in the world and it's truly spectacular. The slabs of stone that have created it are huge and many of the stones lie haphazardly on the ground outside the monument. There are very few tourists about and I'm grateful, not for the first time, that I again seem to be travelling outside high season.

At the end of the afternoon, we walk up a hill where tourists like to watch the sun set over Angkor Wat. Sopeara makes me giggle when he addresses me as 'my Queen'. We have a long wait and I don't mind at all because I ask Sopeara to tell me about himself and he talks about his life.

His parents were very poor and during the time of the 'killing fields' they lived in a village bombed by the Americans. They moved to Siem Reap when Sopeara was 13 years old but he didn't want to leave the village so remained and worked as a cow herd. Age 15yrs he had to join his family in the city, his father didn't find work and although Sopeara wanted to study, his parents needed him to work and support them financially. He said his life was so hard that he would often cry. He studied English because he knew it was important and then Mac found him (the guy I met on the bus) and invited Sopeara to be his tour guide when he brought students. Sopeara is married and has a daughter of two years and a baby on the way, he said he's concerned how he will be able to support another baby. He told me he has a brother and two sisters and he gives them money too.

Sopeara is 30 years old and seems to be responsible for taking care of everyone.

The clouds have covered the sky and we don't see the sun set but I don't mind at all, listening to Sopeara talking about his life is a privilege. Just before we get back to the tuk-tuk he reveals that the man who's been driving us around all day is his father. I ask him why he didn't say so before and he says he was embarrassed. I know I'm gullible and maybe Sopeara tells all the tourists how hard his life is in order to secure a decent tip, but he has my heart and I give both him and his father a generous amount.

# 1st May

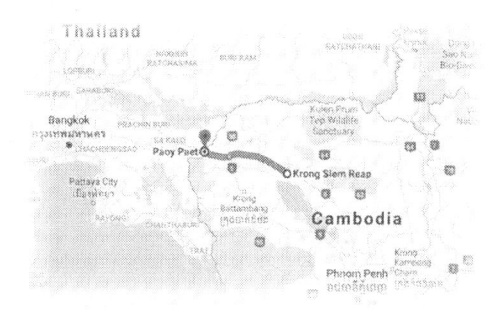

## Bus to Poipet, Border with Thailand (160 kms)

Today I'm changing countries again, leaving Cambodia and entering Thailand. I had to make the decision how to travel to Thailand and decided to take a bus to Poipet to cross the border, then take a train to Bangkok. I'm now regretting my decision because my fellow travellers are all staying on the bus all the way to Bangkok, much easier and quicker. I'm tempted to ask if I can stay on the bus, but then I remind myself that I'm here for experiences, not just an easy life.

The timing is tight for me to get to my train but I'm reasonably comfortable it will work out, until we reach about 9 kms from the border and our bus stops for a lunch break. This is unexpected, we're only 9 kms from the border and we stop for half an hour!

I'm not panicking yet, leaving Cambodia is relatively easy, the queues are short and I meet a friendly guy from Chile called Miguel. He's very relaxed and chatting with him eases my stress. It's a hot, sweaty rush through crowds of people to get to the next part of the crossing. Carrying my stuff, I'm struggling to keep up with Miguel but totally grateful for his guidance.

This side of the border there are long queues and I'm feeling stressed now but again Miguel's conversation helps keep my mind from the clock. I run different scenarios through my mind what to do if I don't make the 13:55 train from Aranyaprathet to Bangkok.

Finally, it's my turn at the passport control desk and they let me in to Thailand. Knowing I don't have any Thai money and no time to get any, Miguel has very kindly given me 60 bhat so I can pay for a tuk-tuk to take me to the station. He's still at the counter, so I yell a hasty goodbye and hurry outside.

I can't see any tuk-tuks or taxis. I'm feeling panicked. I walk a few yards then wave at what could be a taxi. It is, and I ask the driver if he'll take me to the station and show him the 60 bhat Miguel gave me. He tells me this isn't enough money. I don't have any more. I offer the driver U.S. dollars but he shakes his head. I'm almost begging now, I have only ten minutes to get the train. I don't know what makes him change his mind, but he takes the dollars and drives me to the station.

I show my ticket at the kiosk; the train will depart in 5 minutes.

# *Thailand*

## *Train from Aranyaprathet to Bangkok (276kms)*

My ticket for this train cost 48 baht, less than one pound in English money and this is a journey of six hours! The taxi ride to get here cost considerably more.

I'd expected to find an ATM before boarding the train but I didn't have time, so I still don't have any Thai money, and I can't buy food or water. Knowing that, makes me feel immediately hungry and thirsty. Teasingly, vendors walk up and down the corridors calling out their wares. There's a young girl sitting on the seat opposite me munching on some prepacked food. She doesn't finish the food and when she leaves the train she puts the package under her seat along with a half-finished bottle of drink. I'm tempted to…

Arriving in the dark I spill out of the station into the chaos of huge traffic-filled roads in a confusing mess of road works. I've booked a hostel very close to the station, but I can't make out which way to go and give in to the bombardment of tuk-tuks that urgently want my custom. I know this is likely to be tricky from a money point of view, because the station ATM paid out 1,000 notes and the cost of the tuk-tuk is 60 bhat.

I show the driver the name of my hostel, then feel like an idiot when the tuk-tuk drives around the roundabout and stops a few yards away. I'm annoyed with myself for not persevering to locate it, but it's been a long day. I persuade the hostel receptionist to pay the tuk-tuk driver for me and add the cost to my bill.

This hostel is weird. The inside feels like a warehouse, the plumbing and heating pipes are exposed in trendy, city style. It's newly decorated in battleship grey, with brightly coloured lockers and oddly boasts a swimming pool. I'm ravenously hungry so I don't hang about, I dump my stuff by my bed and go back outside

The area feels like a business district and it's now 9 pm, there's nothing open and very few people about. I keep walking and eventually spot a tiny, cheap looking eatery and enter inside. I think they're about to close, there aren't any other customers, but when I ask if they have veg noodles they seem happy to serve me.

Back at the hostel I don't see a soul, it feels as though I'm the only one here and it's quite eerie. I have a swim in the pool then flop exhausted into bed.

## 2nd May
## Bangkok

I have the day to explore Bangkok and I recall my nephew suggesting that if I come here I should visit the big golden Buddha. I hop into a passing tuk-tuk and ask the driver to take me to Wat Pho which houses the Temple of the Reclining Buddha.

Entering through the ticket kiosk I've come to an extraordinary world of gold and sumptuously decorated temples, monuments and statues. There are complex, decoratively tiled roofs and glorious mosaics made from mirrors and coloured stones that look like jewels. Everything is 'over the top' richly adorned and I love it.

Locating the structure that houses the Reclining Buddha, I find him lying prostrate, a massive 46 metres long (think of a swimming pool length) and covered in gold leaf. He's so vast I can't see all of him at once, I have to walk along his length. He has a kind face with a hint of a smile and he's very, very beautiful.

I'm happy to stay here for a while, pottering about in the sunshine and revelling in the beauty of it all. Inside a small temple, there's a luxurious red carpet on the floor and a sitting Buddha, spectacularly bejewelled. This looks a good place to do a meditation and I sit on the sumptuous carpet with my legs crossed and focus on my breathing. A few minutes into my meditation a guide comes in and asks me to move. I'm puzzled, am I doing something wrong? Then she comes back in with a gaggle of tourists, she just wanted my space, cheeky woman.

Eventually it feels like time to leave and I decide to walk to the Grand Palace which I think is quite near. As I walk I meet a guy from Vietnam going the same way and we chat. He tells me he did a Masters Degree in Southampton.

When I reach the Grand Palace, it's heaving with people and my enthusiasm to go inside wanes and I turn around to leave.

On the path back out, I notice a guy advertising boat rides on the canal. A friend from back home had mentioned that this would be a fun thing to do while in Bangkok, so I talk to the boatman to negotiate a better price. He tells me he needs more passengers, so I look for some other Europeans among the crowd and ask a young couple if they'd be willing to join me on a boat. Amazingly they agree and we share the cost.

We have a five-minute walk from the crowded palace to reach the Chao Praya river which feeds into the canals. The area is bustling with people and we climb onto a long narrow, curved, sampan style boat that has a motor and a long pole out the back.

We start our ride on a large expanse of water but quickly turn off under a bridge and into the narrow canals. The boat is brilliant, we whiz around the canals, passing other sampans and the properties that are built along the sides. The youngsters I'd encouraged to come along with me are clearly enjoying it too and I marvel again at how well things have worked out.

I had to check out of my hostel this morning but the staff were willing to look after my backpack for me, so I go back to retrieve it. I have an overnight train booked for 7.30 pm to take me onto the next part of my journey.

## Overnight Train from Bangkok to Chumphon (9 hours)

My train is already on the platform even though, as usual, I've arrived early. On board I meet my fellow passenger who will have the bunk bed opposite. He's called Keenan, from Seattle and he's fun to talk with. My destination is Chumphon and from there I'm going to take a bus and a ferry to Koh Tao Island.

## 3rd May

We arrive in Chumphon in the darkness of 4.30 am. There's not much here, it's a station with a toilet and a kiosk selling some food and beverages. I'm not alone, there are other people on the platform, presumably also going to Koh Tao. The bus, we're told, isn't due to arrive until 7 am. Waiting on this dark station platform for two and a half hours could prove tedious.

There aren't any seats, so I sit on the ground, leaning against my rucksack and take out my electronic reader. The time passes and, as promised, a bus turns up to take us to the quay for the ferry.

## Koh Tao Island

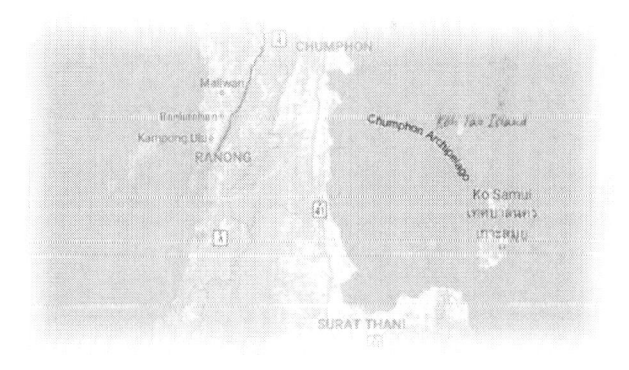

I have another long wait for the ferry boat, but in the sunshine this time and there's plenty going on to keep me interested.

The ferry is a catamaran, it speeds across the water

and the ride to Koh Tao takes just over two hours. Landing on the island, the area is manic with taxis. They're called taxis, but they're all pick-up trucks, I've no idea why. I share one with another guy who's going to the same area and we climb into the back of the truck with our stuff. It's a five-minute ride to Sairee Beach and my hostel called 'In Touch'.

This is a fabulous location. My accommodation is one of several small huts, close to the beach. I have the room to myself and although there's no aircon it does have a fan, which annoyingly refuses to swivel. There's a small outdoor restaurant and bar area a few yards down the path, with wooden decking and big comfy looking cushions. I suffered from doubt and indecision before coming to Koh Tao, not knowing if it was the right thing to do, but now I'm here I feel very happy. With a beach of clean, white sand, aqua blue sea, not too many people and no traffic, this place is idyllic.

I'm feeling unsettled and decide to hire a snorkel for 50 bht, about £1 in U.K. money.

Walking down to the sea's edge I'm feeling oddly nervous, I haven't snorkelled before. I peer into the water. I am absolutely blown away by what I can see; it's a stunning, amazing, undersea world, full of fish, corals, plants, rocks, it's beautiful. I've never seen this before. I swim out and there are hundreds of fish, all shapes, colours and sizes. I don't want to ever come out of the water. I amuse myself for hours, chasing fish to photograph them with my waterproof camera. Trying to grab a picture of fast moving fish while bobbing around in the current is hilarious. I feel like a shrivelled prune I've been in the water so long.

Now I've had a taste of snorkelling I can't wait to do more, so I book a tour group that's going out tomorrow to different islands. I'm excited.

Sairee beach is perfectly positioned for the setting sun and I sit on the wooden decking of the restaurant and order my dinner. Watching the sun turn the sea and sky into a stunning gold is totally glorious.

Back in my room I'm in pain and I feel like an idiot. It didn't occur to me that the sun would burn through the water while I was snorkelling and I now feel my back, shoulders and legs are raw from sunburn.

### 4th May

A pick-up truck taxi takes me and four others to the pier, where we join a larger group for the snorkelling tour. We go out on a fair-size boat which takes us out across the calm, blue sea. The boat stops now and then so we can jump off the side and snorkel and sometimes we stop at a different island and beach. I've remembered to wear a T shirt in the water this time to protect my, now very red, back. I'm having a wonderful time.

We've landed at a larger island and our guide tells us we have time to explore here. There's a viewing point at the top of the hill so of course I take advantage of this opportunity and walk up. This high up, the seascape is stunning, like a picture from a travel brochure and I stay for a while taking it all in.

Walking back in the direction of the boat I start feeling anxious because I can't see any familiar people and, as I so often do, worry that I've missed it or gone to the wrong place. As always, all is well and, with relief, I catch up with my group.

Back at Sairee Beach, the sunset this evening is the best I've ever, ever seen. The sun is like liquid gold and it literally appears to pour itself into the sea, while the skyline is an explosion of fierce orange with grey clouds creating a dramatic backdrop. This fabulous display goes on for about an hour, truly a stunning show. I have dinner alone in the most perfect place to have dinner; on a beautiful beach, looking across the sea with the sound of the waves and pretty lights and at this moment I really wish I was with a friend. Five minutes later a man called Walter from Germany comes and asks if I'd mind if he sits at my table and we have an amiable conversation.

## 5th May

I'm leaving this paradise island today, back the way I came, ferry boat, bus and train.

My train isn't due to leave until 10.45 pm and I have five hours to wait in the small town of Chumphon, which at first glance, doesn't look very interesting. Happily, I discover on the train station a lady willing to look after luggage for a small fee. I'm glad I don't have to carry my large backpack with me for five hours, my sunburned back and shoulders are still raw and carrying it is painful.

I explore the nearby streets and as daylight fades, roadside stalls open up and the place becomes lively. There are many food sellers and I'm fascinated to see all the different and interesting 'fast food' on sale. The offerings are mostly meat or fish, but I find some cooked water chestnuts and a corn on the cob to buy. Out of curiosity I buy some colourful sweet looking things which turn out to be like crispy doughnuts with a green custard.

The evening is still warm and there are some tables and chairs near the station to sit outside where I can eat my food. A guitarist nearby is strumming and I'm his only audience, so when he stops playing I clap and smile at him. The guitarist comes over to me, he looks similar to my age, he's wearing round sunglasses which must be a fashion thing because it's now dark. We chat and he tells me his name is Tuen. He speaks reasonable English, he lived in Bangkok for thirty years and has come to Chumphon recently and now owns a restaurant. He's entertaining company and he's helped me pass another hour.

# Malaysia

6th May

Overnight Train to Padang Besar and Butterworth (14 hrs)

The train comes on time. It's going to take me to the border into Malaysia in the morning. I have a top bunk and the air conditioning is cold so I don't sleep much. When we arrive at the border we all pile out of the train and through 'Departure' then through 'Arrivals'. They let me into Malaysia, hooray! I don't have too long to wait for another train which will take me to Butterworth.

On the Butterworth train a man dressed in a uniform comes up to me and says something I don't understand. I think he's asking for money or payment for something and because we're at the border I wonder if I have to pay for a visa entry. I go into my purse and bring out some Thai money, looking at him questioningly. He takes the money then hands me back some Malaysian currency. Then I laugh, because I now realise he's a money changer, I didn't have to give him money at all. I wonder what rate of exchange I've been given. Oh well, at least I don't have to arrive without local currency this time. The train reaches Butterworth station around midday.

## Bus to Kampung Raja (350 kms)

I walk in search of a bus station and a bus that will take me to the small town of Kampung Raja on the other side of Malaysia. I'm relieved to learn that there is a bus due and it should leave at 2 pm. The bus ride is about five hours and the driver lets me know that I've arrived.

Alighting from transport in a new place in a new country is always interesting, if a little scary. I look about to see where I am. I wouldn't even have known this was a bus stop. I walk a short way towards some buildings and notice a small open 'eatery' so I head over to it.

I'm here on the recommendation of Riley, the American I met in Sri Lanka. I've been in touch with his friend Troji who has a hostel here, and his family own a flower farm where I can work as a volunteer. I'm able to phone Troji and he says he'll come and meet me in a few minutes. While I'm waiting a young woman comes out of the restaurant and ask me if I'm okay, do I need any help. It's so nice when you're alone, to discover how kind people are.

Minutes later, a very handsome young man with dark hair swept back in a ponytail, arrives on a scooter and stops next to me. He has a disarming smile and asks *"are you Hazel?"*.

# Flower Farm, Westwood Highland, Malaysia

Ten minutes later I'm in Troji's hostel called Westwood Highland. I think the journey to this place has been my longest yet, I left Koh Tao yesterday at 2 pm and I've arrived at 6 pm today; twenty-eight hours, that's epic! I'm very happy to be here, although I don't actually know where here is yet.

The hostel is beautiful. Troji has travelled in Europe as a backpacker and worked in London and he decided to build a hostel incorporating all the things he would like as a traveller. The result is a clean, airy place with excellent facilities and attractive rooms. Troji is adorable, I'm in love with him already, he has the sweetest smile and an endearing, gentle way of talking. His parents live close by and the hostel is next to their flower farm, so we're surrounded by gaily coloured gerbera flowers underneath polythene tunnels.

A group of youngsters appear with armfuls of cooking ingredients. They're also staying at the hostel, having a couple of days break from their busy working lives in Kuala Lumpur. They prepare and cook their food, Chinese style, over a flame in a big pot on the outside picnic table and they invite me to join them. I'm massively grateful because I have nothing to eat, it's now dark and I don't think the town is within walking distance.

## 7th May

Having volunteered to help on the Flower Farm, I ask Troji what I can do. He tells me they don't work on Saturdays so I have the day free. He says I can get into the village using a shortcut and points out a way through the polytunnels and past a construction site, so I give it a go.

It's easier said than done. This is a very precarious route, not a path at all, but a balancing act on a foot-wide ledge that skirts around a concrete wall. I negotiate the narrow, muddy edge of a field with a drop one side into a brook below, then swing under some construction poles to reach terra firma. I make a mental note of the place so I can find my way back.

Walking around the village there's not a lot to it. A couple of small shops, like grocery stores but they don't sell fresh fruit, mostly biscuits, crisps and sweets and I wonder again how these people stay so skinny. I buy eggs, a tomato, four potatoes, mayonnaise that comes in a sachet, and a tin of sweetcorn so I can make an omelette for my supper with potato salad. The morning weather started out dull and now it's raining, my route back to the hostel will get trickier.

I've made it safely back, but now realise I've lost my cap. It's a baseball cap that I've had for years, the one I wear when I'm running. I'm very upset. My 'upsetness' is out of proportion to the loss. It's just a cap. But it isn't just a cap. It's been with me for years, I've worn it through three marathon races, it fits me, it's comfortable. I probably took it off when the rain came and I put on my mac, maybe it fell out of my rucksack.

I decide to risk the treacherous path back to the village in the hope of finding it, retracing my steps and asking in the shops I had visited but without success. My cap has gone.

## 8th May

Today I start work. Out in the yard, near the hostel, I

meet Troji's mother and father. They don't speak much English but they're very friendly. Troji's brother is there too, they look alike, and there are two paid workers. The yard is full of the brightly coloured gerberas, buckets full of them. We sit on little plastic stools or upturned buckets and slide a plastic cone up the stem of each gerbera to protect the delicate bloom, which is like a large daisy. This for me is a slow process and I watch admiringly the dexterity of the others as they work. I like the work and I can feel the love and friendship between these delightful people.

The job is soon done and the flowers are loaded onto a truck and taken to Troji's parents' house down the road. I hop in the truck for the ride. Troji's parents have a modern, brick-built home and I'm invited into their large kitchen where his mum wants to feed me and I'm given a generous plateful of food.

## 9th May

More flower packing this morning and more food in Troji's mum's kitchen. I'm invited to take a ride with the family in the afternoon. Troji says they can drop me off at the start of a walk that will take me through tea fields and they'll pick me up again later. He assures me I can't get lost, so this sounds like a good plan.

The path they leave me on heads up and into the hills. It's a hot, sunny day and the landscape is stunning. I keep walking for about an hour, all the while enjoying views far into the distance across tea plantations and hills.

There's no traffic here and no-one about, until I hear a motorbike, and a man with a small child on the bike rides past, waving acknowledgement. It feels like the right time for me to turn around and head back down and as I walk, the man on the motorbike passes me again, also going back the other way. I keep walking and see he's parked his motorbike, the small child is still on it and he's standing in some trees. I assume he's stopped to pee, so discreetly turn my head away. The motorbike passes me again. Ten minutes later as I come around a bend in the road he's again standing among some trees. This feels odd. When I look in his direction I realise he's 'exposed' himself and he calls out to me "come here".

There's nothing I can do but keep walking. I quicken my pace. I had this experience as a teenager, we called these men 'flashers' and I remember learning that they're generally harmless and the thought makes me feel less afraid. The motorbike passes me once more and my heart is pounding. About fifteen minutes later, he's standing in some trees again. I walk swiftly past. I feel concerned for the young girl on the bike, is she his daughter? I'm walking fast and I hear his bike behind me, but I can see signs that I'm getting close to town and I don't feel so anxious this time. As he goes by I take a of photo of his bike with my camera and capture the number plate.

Troji and his parents pick me up as they said they would and I relate a shortened version of the incident to Troji. I wonder if I should report it. Troji seems oddly disinterested, it feels like he doesn't want to admit anything can be wrong. With visions of spending hours in a local police station looming into my mind I decide to let the incident go.

Back at the hostel, new guests have arrived. There's a couple called Louis and Josephine from France and I like them straight away, and also a young Russian man called Alex, who maybe harder to get to know. Troji drives us all into town to experience the night market and we have fun tasting local food. I feel upset when I see a man purchase a live chicken, he stuffs it into a plastic bag and carries it along with the rest of his shopping.

We go to an outdoor restaurant and Troji orders meals for us, buying extra to take home to his parents. I love being here with these wonderful people. Troji won't let us pay for our dinner, he's very generous. We call at his parents' home on the way back to give them the food and we're invited to stay and take tea.

## 10th May

I'm up early ready for flower packing around 8 am. I like putting the colourful gerberas into their protective cones and wonder where they will end up.

I had thought I'd spend the rest of the day 'at home' studying, but Josephine and Louis invite me to join them on a trek and I can't resist. Alex is coming too. He's an unusual man, very confident in himself and quite serious. He's used to hitch-hiking and suggests that we hitch a lift to the town where the walk starts, which we do. For me this is great fun, never having hitched a lift before. I'm told this is not unusual in Malaysia, people are used to stopping and giving lifts and we don't have to wait many minutes before a lady in a car pulls up.

Alex has a sixth sense about the start of our walk, how he finds it I have no idea, but I'm very glad we have him with us. We're in the jungle-cum-forest and the climb is immediately up. It's steep and very challenging, over massive tangles of tree roots and I'm grateful for shade from the trees. Alex is wearing knee length cotton khaki trousers and a coolie hat, nothing else. No shirt, no shoes and I marvel at him doing this strenuous climb in bare feet.

I hope all the while that we'll see some amazing views but although we've now climbed upwards for over an hour and must be very high, the trees surround us. I'm beginning to wonder if we'll ever reach the top. The trees start to thin out and I get a glimpse of a view in the distance and feel encouraged.

It's been two hours of uphill clambering and we're finally emerging out of the jungle and onto a path. I can't quite believe what I'm seeing, we come out on the top, right next to a communications mast and a small tarmac road. A signboard tells me we've climbed up Ringian mountain, 2032 metres and don't my legs know it.

The mast has a look-out tower so we all climb the steps and here is my reward. The panorama is stunning, we can see far out across the tops of trees 360 degrees.

After a while it feels the right time to leave, Alex elects to stay longer, saying he'll make his own way, and Josephine, Louis and I walk along the narrow road down. It takes us another two hours walking to get to a main road where we can hitch a lift. A pick-up truck stops for us and we pile into the back and sit on the floor. It's a bumpy, bruising ride back to Kampung Raja. I've had a brilliant and memorable day.

## 11th May

It seems 'staying in' is not going to happen. I had decided to study, but I'm invited to go with Troji and the others to visit a pineapple farm and I don't want to miss out. After finishing the flower packing in the morning, we all get into Troji's car. The drive is long but pleasant and we stop on the way at a small town and an eatery for food.

Troji is having trouble finding the pineapple farm and he drives off the main road, along some narrow tracks into a very rural area, with gorgeous tall grasses and a stream. Indigenous people live here in small dwellings and we stop and say 'hi' to some excited young children. The atmosphere is charming. I've no idea why Troji is looking for a pineapple farm, but it doesn't materialise and it doesn't matter a scrap to me, I'm thoroughly enjoying where we are.

We drive on a few more kilometres to a tea plantation where we take a tiny road up very high, it has a scarily long drop down on one side. Troji parks the car perilously close to the long drop to allow other cars to pass by and we get out and take in the gorgeous landscape of tea fields.

On the way home, we stop at some market stalls to buy fruit and we go into a shop selling clothes and hats. I buy a cap to replace the one I lost. It's not very stylish but it will keep the sun from my head.

## 12th May

Josephine and Louis are moving on this morning and I'm sad to say goodbye to them, they're genuinely lovely people. This afternoon I stay at the hostel and I complete an online test as part of my teaching qualification, with a result of 80%. I'm disappointed not to have achieved more, but it's good enough for a pass.

I'm very touched that Troji's parents have invited Alex and I for supper this evening. Alex appears rudely ungrateful to receive the invitation and says he may not come. Troji is always very kind to Alex who seems not to appreciate it, I've never met anyone from Russia before so I can't work out if it's Alex or his 'Russianness'.

I've been craving fresh salad and fresh vegetables so when we arrive and sit at the dinner table I'm excited to see a crisp, green, whole lettuce. Fui Shon puts a big cooking pot in the middle of the table containing boiling liquid, to which she adds tofu, mushrooms and root vegetables and NO, she's tearing up the lettuce and putting it in the boiling water! All that crisp, crunchy lettuce gone. The resulting meal doesn't taste nice to my palette, but I do appreciate having home-cooked food.

After we've eaten, a young couple join us who are friends of the family. I'm sitting next to the man and he tells me he's visited Europe, he has photos on his iPad to show me. He's very enthusiastic and I do my best to be interested. He hasn't edited the photos and there are many very similar, a picture of him by the fountain, his friend by the fountain, both of them by the fountain, both of them doing a silly pose by the fountain. After about an hour of this, thinking I may expire from boredom I say *"thank you so much for showing me these, I'm quite tired now, I think I've seen enough"*. To say he looks crestfallen is an understatement, I feel mean, but relieved to have ended my ordeal.

It's raining and Troji takes me back to the hostel on his scooter. Tonight is my last at Westwood Highland and I feel sad that I'm leaving. I ask Troji to let me know what I owe for my accommodation and he's reluctant to charge me so that I have to be quite firm with him. I pay more than he asks for, which is still only £45 for a seven-night stay.

## Kuala Lumpur, Malaysia

13th May

Bus from Kampung Raja to Kuala Lumpur (450 kms)

Troji takes me on his scooter to the bus stop outside a tiny general store in Kampung Raja and I give him a hug goodbye. He hands me a package, a gift from his parents, it's a pack of Cameron Highland Tea bags. I hope I'll see him again one day, I could happily adopt him he's so adorable.

Standing waiting, I realise I need the toilet and knowing a long bus ride is ahead I pop into the shop and ask if I can use theirs and they kindly allow me to. It's an experience.

The bus arrives on time and the cost for the journey of some 450 kms is 35 ringee, about £6. It's a good bus and an excellent ride and I arrive in Kuala Lumpur five hours later.

I've pre-booked a hostel called Paper Plane and I

don't know where it is in relation to the bus station. As so often happens, there's more than one bus station and I couldn't work out which one I'd arrive at. A man carrying a suitcase approaches me and asks if he can help. I thank him and say *"it's okay I'm going to get a taxi"* but he then explains to me that I should get the train, even though I'll need to change to a second train, because it's cheaper. He fetches a map from his pocket and shows me where we are, then hands me the map to keep. I'm again struck by how kind people are to a stranger.

The train explanation is too complicated for me with all my stuff but I don't want the kind man to see I'm ignoring his advice, so I take the escalator into the station and walk across to the other side. And just across the road are taxis. I pick one and before I get in, as a safety precaution, I take a photo of the number plate with my mobile phone, a good trick I learned from a travelling blog. If the driver sees you take his number he's less likely to misbehave.

The driver has me spooked. It is hot in KL, but he's sweating profusely and behaving weirdly. He keeps touching things repeatedly, his hand goes to his phone then to his face and back to his phone again, like he's really nervous. I've given him the address of the hostel, but he can't find the road and I'm aware we've been driving around the same route more than once. I give him the hostel phone number and suggests he call them for directions, which he does.

I'm very glad to get out of the taxi and into Paper Plane hostel which looks rather unique. It's run by a man who introduces himself as Andrew, he's endearingly camp and very kind

I've come to KL to meet up with Barney who I'd previously met on my first tour in India, he lives in KL.

We'd agreed to meet at The Pavilion shopping centre at two o'clock and I'm running out of time. Andrew kindly walks me to the nearby train station and even helps me buy a ticket. I have only two stops and a five-minute walk to the shopping centre where Barney is already waiting for me. I'm happy to see him again.

Barney is very comfortable here in KL and knows it well. When I express a desire to eat he knows exactly where we should go. Nearby, there's a large market-style place with individual stalls selling different food, they all have the now familiar pictures of plates of food posted around their counters. To Barney's surprise, we have difficulty finding anything vegetarian and Barney asks if I've ever had to 'give in' while travelling and eat meat. I told him no, I don't think so. We persevere until I come to a stall selling the usual veg noodles which at least fills my empty tummy.

After eating, I ask if there are any tall buildings where we can get a glass of wine and take in a view and again Barney knows exactly the place. It's quite a walk but I don't mind at all, it's a good way to see more of KL. The building he chooses is ideal, with panoramic windows overlooking the city and the famous twin Petronas towers and I settle into a comfy chair, with a large glass of cold white wine.

Instead of taking the train, Barney knows the way back to my hostel on foot. He tells me there's a brilliant coffee shop close by and after all this city walking I'm ready to sit down. I order cappuccino coffee and Barney recommends the cake, a wedge of banana cake topped with peanut butter and called 'The King', apparently a favourite of Elvis Presley, hence the name.

## 14th May

How wonderful, to wake up knowing there's nothing you have to do. I love this hostel, it's very comfortable and there's only one other traveller in my dorm. I think I'll have a day shopping, it's the thing to do in Kuala Lumpur and the elegant, modern shopping centre I saw yesterday looks amazing. There are four things on my list to buy, a bra, pants, a watch and ear-rings.

Getting the train and the five-minute walk to the shopping mall is easy and when I arrive I can't resist starting with coffee and cake in Starbucks. Sitting here 'people watching' I'm overwhelmed with happiness and gratitude. I feel incredibly lucky. Here I am in KL, I can buy anything I want, I can stay out shopping all day and all evening if I want to. I have so much freedom it blows my mind.

Wandering in and out of the shops, I find exactly the right underwear and some pretty ear rings. No luck with the watch yet.

I don't continue to love the day. I've made my way over to the Petronas Towers using the air-conditioned walkways that allow you to move around the city without going into the heat outside. I've come to try and get a ticket for a concert this evening because the KL Philharmonic Orchestra plays here. I'm inside the towers which is packed with people everywhere. There's a maze of turns and corridors and different levels; the inside of this building is vast.

I have no idea which way to go and ask for directions several times but just keep going around in circles and I'm feeling tense and sweaty. I've been walking for ages along crowded corridors and feel anxious, the way I did in Singapore in the Marina Sands Bay Hotel. I have to get out into fresh air. The nightmare continues, it's as hard to locate the exit, as it's been to find the booking reception and I come across the theatre reception first. There's an Elgar concert this evening, but I feel so miserable in this building I can't see myself coming back and don't book a ticket.

Exiting at the first available opportunity, I've no idea where I am, but at least I'm outside. I nearly give in and take a taxi but instead keep walking and eventually come to the shopping Pavilion and now know the way back to the train station.

Going up the escalator to the platform I realise that I've only found three of the four things on my shopping list, I haven't found a watch. Looking down, there's a street market on the ground below. I'm tired and my body is yelling "go home", but I go back on the 'down' escalator and at one of the stalls I find the perfect watch for less than £6. The stall holder even puts a new battery in it for me. Success.

# *Bali, Indonesia*

## 15th May

### Aeroplane to Bali (3hrs)

Andrew has booked a taxi to take me to the airport and I give him a hug goodbye. He insists on taking a 'selfie' photo of us together.

It's a smooth transition through the airport and the flight to Bali takes around three hours so I arrive early in the afternoon. I've met a guy from Germany on the plane and he's also going to Kuta so I suggest sharing a taxi if we both emerge through customs around the same time. Visa control is easy, I find an ATM, get local currency, meet up with the German and we go in search of a cab.

I wish I hadn't suggested it. The two of us wanting to share causes a kerfuffle because the taxi driver will only go to one destination, not two. But our stuff is in the boot of the vehicle so then the driver changes his mind, he says he'll take us, but we each have to pay. There's a bonus in this for me, because we go to the

German's accommodation first which turns out to be quite far from mine and I get a tour around the very popular beach resort of Kuta.

I'm so glad I haven't booked to stay in Kuta centre, the place is heaving with tourists and beach shops and it's so stuffed with traffic we mostly drive at walking pace. Eventually we emerge out of the chaos and into a more rural area. Although he'd previously said he knew it, my taxi driver can't locate the address and he's getting annoyed. I suggest he phones for directions which he does, but he still doesn't find the location and gets even more annoyed. He phones again and this time, after driving around the same area a couple of times, we drive down a quiet residential road and arrive.

It's an attractive guesthouse, clean, light and airy but it does seem to be rather 'out of the way'. I'm given directions to a supermarket and to my surprise, after a short walk along a country lane, there's an excellent one along a main road and I'm able to stock up on bread, salad and vegetables. Back in my room, I sit on the balcony on a beanbag, eat the fresh salad and watch the sky change colour as the sun sets.

Before retiring to bed, I think to recharge my mobile and I realise I can't. The electrical sockets here are not what I thought they'd be and the part of my adaptor that I need here, broke some time ago. I can't think how to resolve this situation but decide not to let it spoil my night's sleep. There will probably be a solution when I reach my next destination, Ubud.

A solution comes sooner than I expect. I mention my mobile charging problem to the guy running the guesthouse and he reaches into a drawer and brings out the perfect adaptor. I can't believe my good luck, he happens to have a spare British adaptor!

The reason I've come to Bali is to visit Green

Village. Some months ago, I saw, online, an interesting presentation by a woman called Lenora Hardy about bamboo architecture. I was very enamoured with her talk and showed it to Ben. Lenora has built some stunningly attractive houses using only bamboo and after watching it I thought it would be fun to come to Bali and see the houses. The guesthouse manager has found a taxi driver to take me to Green Village tomorrow and I negotiated a priced on the phone with him, he asked 400,000 IDR and we agreed on 300,000 (about £17.00).

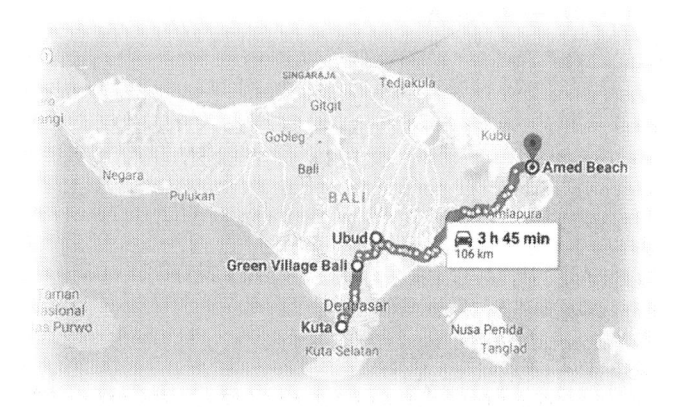

16th May

Green Village

The taxi arrives on time, my driver is called Nusa and he seems nice. The traffic is very congested so the 22 kms journey is slow, but I'm not concerned, I've allowed plenty of time. There are two tours daily to see 'Green Village' and I've booked the afternoon one. I'm grateful Nusa has been here before and knows where to go. When I arrive I'm very early and the morning tour is about to begin, so it's suggested that I join this one, which is perfect for me. In spite of my protestations, Nusa says he'll wait for me until I'm ready to move on.

With a few other people, I follow our guide who takes us to a beautiful and surprisingly large bamboo house. It's elegantly built on two floors. Everything inside and outside is made from bamboo including the furniture and it has a beautiful, huge, egg-shaped door that pivots open and closed. After this we're shown a completely different but equally beautiful bamboo house. The craftsmanship is amazing, just looking at the work in the staircase and the floors with such attention to detail is awesome. Having watched the talk about it I'm excited that I'm actually seeing the houses.

After the tour we're shown where we can have lunch and a swim in a pretty freshwater pool. I have plenty of time before the late tour of the factory which is in a different location, so I have a lovely cooling swim in the spring water pool. When I finish lunch the afternoon group is going to see the houses and I ask if I can come along again, so I get to see them a second time.

I'm massively grateful that Nusa had chosen to wait for me because I need him. I hadn't realised there isn't any transport to the bamboo factory and I would have been stuck.

I'm not enjoying the factory tour, they don't give out much information and the temperature is searingly hot. I'm carrying my computer with me because I don't want to leave it in Nusa's car and I'm concerned that this high temperature will cause it harm. I'm relieved when the tour finishes. Nusa is still waiting for me, he'll take me to my next destination, the town of Ubud.

## Ubud

It doesn't take long to drive the 15 kms to Ubud and it's an interesting route, but when we arrive, just like Kuta, the place is blocked with traffic and we inch our way along Monkey Forest Road, looking out for my hostel called 'Jukung'. Although the address gives it a number, none of the properties along the road are numbered, so this doesn't help. Fortunately, Nusa is very patient, unlike some of my other taxi drivers, and we eventually find it. When I get out of the car and gather my bags, I'm bemused when Nusa gives me an embrace and a kiss on both cheeks.

The hostel is very quirky, it feels a bit like being in an old 'shipwreck', the rooms are built using old wood and there's a nautical theme to the furnishings and décor. I'm not pleased to have been given a very high, top bunk in the dorm having asked on my booking form for a lower bunk. The wooden ladder only has one handle and it's difficult for me to hold on while climbing on and off the bed.

I've met an amazing woman called Janneke, also staying at the hostel. She's from the Netherlands and in our conversation she revealed that she's cycling around the world. She's just cycled across Australia on her own! She was delightfully modest about her achievement too.

## 17th May

Monkey Forest Road and the area of Ubud around my hostel is something of a shock, it's way more touristy and busy than I had expected. The road gets its name from the Monkey Forest Sanctuary located at the bottom of the hill which sounds like a fun place to visit.

I've read that the monkeys can be very naughty, jumping on tourists and pinching stuff from their rucksacks, so before I purchase a ticket and go into the forest, I stand across the road by some market stalls and check my bag for food. In one of the pockets I discover a muesli bar so I pull it out and unwrap it to eat. Taking me totally by surprise, a monkey swings from somewhere above my head, grabs the muesli bar and leaps away. Now that's not fair, I'm not even inside the forest yet!

The forest is a welcome surprise. I've stepped off a busy road and now I'm in a completely different world. There are monkeys everywhere and they're highly entertaining. Obviously used to people, they're very bold and don't mind you getting close to take a photo. There are trees all around, it's a large forest and a path meanders through them. There aren't too many people either so the place has a relaxing feel. I come to a pond with the branches of a tree hanging over and I spend ages watching the monkeys play in and around the water, climbing along the branch and doing acrobatics before jumping in. I like it so much here that when I've done the complete circuit I do it all over again.

## 18th May

I'm floundering in Bali, trying to decide where to go next and not able to come to a conclusion. There isn't much in the way of public transport. I've tried booking a bus but they won't accept a single booking, they can only tell me the bus will go when it has enough people, which makes it impossible to plan ahead. A friend from England recommended a trip to the Gili Islands, or I could go to Amed, a fishing village on the east coast, which sounds good for snorkelling. I'm a mass of indecision.

My day is spent in and out of the tiny shops around Monkey Forest Road. I haven't been able to buy anything on my travels so far because I can't carry anything, but there are tempting things for sale here and I have fun choosing gifts for my daughter and granddaughter with the idea of posting them back to England.

On the way back to my hostel I stop off at a tour kiosk and book a 'sunrise climb to the top of Mt Batur' for the morning. I'm feeling happier now.

Or at least I was feeling happier. I've fallen off the ladder from the top bunk bed. I lost my balance, my body swung away from the rail and I couldn't hold on with one hand and I've landed heavily on the tiled floor. My ribs feel sore and bruised but I'm grateful I don't think I've have done too much damage to myself.

## 19th May

I'm up and ready at 2 am for the vehicle that comes to pick me up, as well as five other girls from the hostel. It's still dark and quite cold. We stop along the way for pancakes and coffee. I think we've been driving for an hour. It's still very black when we reach the start of the trek where there's a parking area full of vehicles and people milling about. I have a head torch and a hand torch that works this time, and from here we start the walk to the top of Mount Batur.

It's a tough climb. We're walking on loose stones and scree and I hadn't considered how painful it would be walking with sore ribs. The exertion of the climb is making my breathing hard and it's uncomfortable.

We've walked for about two and a half hours and the timing for the sunrise is perfect. We arrive at the top and watch the sun appear over the distant mountains. In front of us we can see Mount Ajung and Mount Rinjani on Lombok. As the sun rises, it changes the colour of the black lake below to a very pretty blue. There's a party atmosphere, it's fun being with a crowd of people all enjoying themselves. I'm amused that our tour guide gives us breakfast here at the top of the mountain of warm banana sandwich and a boiled egg, an unusual combination.

Climbing down is as challenging as going up, especially the first part which feels quite treacherous on the scree and now we can see how high up we are. Although I'm exhausted and in pain from my bruised ribs, I appreciate the effort it takes and the feeling of achievement. Back in the car, the drive in daylight is beautiful but I'm struggling to keep my eyes open.

One of the girls on this morning's trek recommended a restaurant in Ubud called Yellow Flower Café and I step out in search of it. It's quite a long walk in an obscure location away from main roads, and I'm pleased with myself because walking up some steps and along a narrow path, I've found it. It's charmingly set in a pretty location. The area has an 'arty' and relaxed feel to it. The menu at the café makes my mouth water and after considerable thought, I choose some organic veggie tapas. I sit here for ages and feel at peace, something I haven't felt so far since coming to Bali.

When it seems rude to stay any longer without ordering more food, I leave and walk along the maze of small paths, passing pretty rice paddies and quaint properties. There are several yoga and healing places here. A young boy is selling jewellery and items from a wooden table and although I don't want anything, I buy some earrings anyway.

I still have two more days in Ubud and I can't shake

off this feeling of confusion. I feel unsettled and unsure of myself, which is a shame because this is a nice place, I'm enjoying the heat and I'm happy with the hostel. I'd like to go water rafting but my bruised/cracked rib is still sore and this doesn't seem wise.

I spend the rest of the afternoon pottering about the small roads and many shops and find a post office where I can package up the gifts I've bought for my family and send them to England.

In the evening, I do the tourist thing and buy a ticket to watch a traditional dance performance. I don't know why I'm here, these performances rarely interest me. The costumes are colourful and elaborate, but the continuous chanting and monotonous music aren't pleasing to my ears, the 'actors' are wearing masks and I've no idea what the movements mean. I'm bored and not at all sorry when the performance is finished.

## 20th May

The decision is made. I'm going to Amed on the northeast coast. Frustratingly, I can't take a bus because I'm a solo traveller, there's an odd booking system that requires more than one person to book tickets. I decide to get in touch with Nusa my taxi driver but I don't have a Bali SIM so can't use my mobile. I ask the receptionist boy at my hostel if I can use the hostel phone and he says they don't have one. With a little pleading on my part, the boy agrees to send Nusa a text message on his own phone and Nusa calls back. He says he'll come and pick me up in the morning and take me to Amed.

I spend more time at the Yellow Flower Café where I'm happy chatting with another customer, a young man, possibly in his twenties, who tells me he's looking for somewhere in the area to rent. Originally from the U.K. he now lives here in Ubud working in a bar. He's very content and I'm intrigued by this guy who's chosen to live such a tranquil life, in a hot climate, doing casual work.

## 21st May

Nusa arrives at Jukung hostel on time, he's pleased to see me. I've had breakfast of cold banana pancake and fruit, so I'm good to go.

I ask Nusa if we can take the coast road, I've read that there's a Water Palace along that route called Ujung. We come to it and stop so I can explore. It's a pretty area. There's an attractive red tiled dwelling in a lake, with an old stone bridge to cross the water. I learn that it was built by the King of Karangasem and completed in 1921. With several ponds and water features surrounded by green gardens, trees and mountains in the distance, the whole scene is enchanting.

When I get back to the car Nusa is happily chatting with another taxi driver. He's becoming very 'familiar' in his language with me and I'm feeling a little concerned. He asks me if I have a husband and when I tell him I don't he says *"you sleep alone, you should sleep with me"*. I'm rather taken aback, apart from the fact that he's married he shouldn't say things like that and I tell him he's out of order. I'm less comfortable now about being in the car with him and there's still a long way to drive.

I'm wrong, Amed, it turns out, isn't a long way at all. Balinese have 'small island' mentality, it doesn't matter where you want to go they always say *"oh, that's very far"*, even if where you're going is just down the road. I'd been led to believe that Amed is far too, but it really isn't. We've pulled up outside my guesthouse called Bali D'Sawah which looks newly built. I pay Nusa for the last time, I won't be using him again.

## Amed

I'm given a spacious room with a modern bathroom. I'm aquiver with excitement, the landscape from the large glazed sliding doors in my room is fabulous; vibrant green fields with a massive backdrop of green mountains. I can't believe my good fortune. I sit with a cup of coffee and talk to the owner of the guesthouse. It's a recent project for him and his wife and they've taken a big risk. They have a large mortgage and his wife still works at a nearby restaurant. The owner and his daughter Mena work at the guesthouse, which is also a restaurant.

A poster on the wall says I can rent a scooter here, something I've been wanting to do. I'm nervous about the idea but this looks like a quiet place to have a go. I explain that I'll need a lesson first because I haven't ridden a scooter before. Mena says she can show me now, before she finishes working at 3 pm which feels rather sudden for me, but I don't want to let the opportunity go.

The scooter is parked on the forecourt of the guesthouse which is on the only road in and out of Amed, a small, dusty road with only just room for two vehicles. Exactly opposite the guesthouse some workmen are digging a trench so the road becomes narrower here.

The workmen are not helpful. They clearly find me very entertaining. Mena explains how to start and stop the scooter and I climb on.

Fortunately, the road is straight and I kangaroo slow then fast, then slow again down the road. I don't go far because I want to practice stopping, then I realise I don't know how to turn the thing around. At this moment I'm surrounded by three young boys on cycles, I'm worried about running one of them down and wave my hands to explain that they need to move, but they happily stand close by to watch. I wait for Mena to come running up to me and she shows me that you 'walk' the scooter in a U turn. I really wish I don't have an audience, my palms are sweating and my heart's racing. I have another go, wobbling embarrassingly, but this time I'm able to turn the bike around and ride back and I start feeling a bit more confident. Returning the scooter to the forecourt I thank Mena and tell her I'd like to rent it tomorrow and now can I borrow a bicycle instead?

Punishment for not being braver and taking the scooter, this bicycle is the most uncomfortable I've ever sat on. Even so I'm glad to have it, cycling to the beach takes just ten minutes straight down the road. This beach is very different, the sand is black and I think I'm the only tourist. There's nothing commercial here, just fishing boats and some farm animals in wooden pens, a goat, a cow and a pig. There are a couple of men sitting on a rickety wooden structure, they're watching me so I nod and say *"Hi"*.

A fishing boat is coming in and people are coming across the beach to meet it. The colourfully painted boat is lifted and pulled across the sand and they haul out the net which holds their catch of mackerel. I'm very entertained watching as weighing scales are brought out and people buy the fish straight from the boat.

I've heard that Jemeluk is also on the beach, just beyond Amed and excellent for snorkelling, so I cycle in the direction of it. I pass warungs (restaurants), beach accommodation and tiny tourist shops, but happily nothing like Ubud, these are quaint and inviting. There are signs advertising diving lessons, they're clearly popular here. Diving isn't something I'm yearning to do, but it will be very cheap to learn here and I wonder if I'd be silly to miss the opportunity. I pop into a diving 'shop' and have a chat with a French diving instructor. I'll have a think about the idea.

I think I've probably cycled through Jemeluk without realising it, so I turn back. I'm hungry and head for 'home'.

After a very tasty meal of home-made bruschetta at the guest house, I take the bike again to the beach to watch the sunset. It looks very pretty, there's a pale pink sky and the coloured fishing boats make an attractive scene. As I cycle back I'm bewildered to see a massive mountain in the distance right in front of me, I'm sure it wasn't there earlier in the day! I couldn't have missed it! I can only assume it was covered with cloud earlier and I realise it must be Mount Ajung. I think I'm going to like it here. By the time I reach 'home' a perfect and very beautiful full moon is hanging in the sky.

## 22$^{nd}$ May

I've rented the scooter today. The tiny shop down the road sells fuel and they fill up the tank for me, the cost is 4p a litre, wow, if only it cost so little back home. I'm very nervous and don't feel in control, but I can start slowly. There's only one road so at least I won't get lost, it goes over a bridge then up and down along the coast. But the road is narrow and everything is unpredictable, children, animals, other road users. I find a patch of land where I can practice turning around and stopping which gives me more confidence.

Setting off again, I've ridden through a couple of villages and ahead of me is a very steep hill. I don't want to go up this hill but I can't stop, there's a vehicle behind me. There's a steep drop on my side and I pray I can stay on the road. I wonder how I'll manage going down and what the bends will be like. I concentrate hard and believe I'll be fine. My heart is pounding.

It's okay, I've made it and when I get the chance, I stop the bike and pull over to breathe. My palms are sweaty and this is a problem because one hand has to control the accelerator. The view out across the sparkling blue water is spectacular and I start feeling pleased with my achievement.

I stop several times during the day for a break; pineapple milk shake, coffee, then lunch. I'm excited riding the scooter but I'm still very tense. I call in to see the French diving instructor I spoke to yesterday and book myself in for a dive lesson at 5.0'clock this afternoon, he tells me I'll need some tuition and equipment instruction before going into the water.

The instructor is called Jean and he's ready for me. He starts pouring out a volume of information about breathing and diving depths and drawing diagrams on his white board and I suddenly know that I absolutely don't want do go through with this. Everything in my body is telling me that I don't want to dive, there's no point continuing this lesson. I explain to Jean as gently as I can that I realise this isn't for me, I tell him that it's nothing he's done, I just know I don't want to do a dive. He looks bemused, but also very kindly tells me I don't need to pay for the lesson.

On the way back, I again stop off at Amed beach as the sun is going down. I spend time watching the fishermen setting out to sea in their boats. Some girls are playing in the waves, they want me to take their photo. I chat with a Balinese boy sitting on the rickety wooden structure, his English is good. I feel privileged being here, watching local people on a Sunday evening on a beach in Bali.

Back at d'Sawa I have a glass of white wine called Aga. It's Balinese wine and not bad at all and I check my phone. I've had a long, affectionate message from Ben in response to mine. He's received my postcard. I go to bed happy.

## 23rd May

It makes more sense to take the bicycle today to Jemeluk Beach for more snorkelling, there's not much point having the scooter because I'm unlikely to go anywhere else.

The homestay owner has lent me a snorkel and there's a stall on the beach hiring out flippers so I get some. Outside a warung is a sunbed where I can leave my stuff if I buy a drink. Being on my own it's tricky leaving my belongings on the beach, so for security I've developed a system of tying everything together. If someone tries to take my rucksack they'll discover that it's attached, not only to the sunbed, but to my shoes and my clothes as well.

Putting on flippers at the water's edge then walking into the sea is a challenge and I laugh at how ungainly I must look, especially with the mask and snorkel too.

I'm beyond excited. The sea life here is incredible, many varieties of fish and coloured corals, all right off the shore, totally awesome. I stay in the water for hours, taking photos until my camera runs out of battery. This has been the best fun so far, the thrill of seeing a big fish and then a bigger one, or a whole school of fish, spotting the different colours and all the beautiful corals, trying to make each photo better than the last, absolutely fantastic.

On my way back 'home' I notice the Amed Bali Tour operators are still open and I book a boat to take me to the Gili Islands in two days time. Finally, I've made the decision that I'll go there next.

## 24th May

I'm out early to catch the sunrise, but not early enough, the sky is already light. Walking to the beach the morning light is pretty and I stroll along the shore appreciating the quiet. I can see the trails in the sand where the fishing boats have gone out and I count twelve of them. Each one of them has left an offering to their gods on the sand; a small circle of leaves and flowers, some have lighted incense sticks.

I've asked to rent the scooter again today and for reasons unknown I'm given a different one which seems a bit heavier. It does nothing for my confidence when I learn that there is no insurance on the scooter. The locals know I'm a 'beginner' and as I set off I hear the chant of *"slowly, slowly"*. I can't resist going back to Jemeluk beach to snorkel some more. I'm super excited when I see a huge blue star fish resting on the sea bed but realise at the same time that I've exhausted the battery on my camera and I can't take a snapshot.

## 25th May

Today I'm going to be very brave. I've rented the scooter and I'm going to drive down the long road in the opposite direction to the beach. I want to visit the Water Palace at Tirtaganga and I know the scenery along the way will be lovely because I experienced it when I first came into Amed with Nusa. I haven't previously had a bike helmet, but now I'm driving further afield I ask for one.

The ride is exhilarating and very scary. The road goes up and up around the hills, very high. Vehicles overtake me on the bends and some of them are large trucks so I have to hug each bend and my lack of driving skill makes it quite alarming. I concentrate, give myself positive self-talk and keep calm. At the top of the hill the panorama is stunning and I stop at the side of the road to take photos. I'm so nervous my legs feel like jelly.

I've come to Tirtaganga but I can't see the Water Palace, so keep driving, assuming I'll find it on the other side of the village. Still no sign of it. I stop several times to ask people for directions but can't make myself understood. I must have passed it, so turn around and this time I find it. There's no signage, nothing to announce that it's there until you walk inside an archway.

I'm glad I've come. This is a pretty place, similar in style to the Water Palace at Ujung, and although it was constructed later, in 1948, it looks older. The architect was the last Raja (King) of Karangasem who not only designed it but got 'down and dirty' to help build it. There's an attractive restaurant here overlooking the water gardens and I decadently enjoy a decent cup of coffee and chocolate cake.

On the way out of the gardens I stop to buy some bananas for my lunch, then get back on the bike to ride home. It's another scary ride down and round the bends but this time I've gained some confidence and I make it safely back.

I want to make use of my last chance to snorkel on Jemeluk beach, so head back into the water again. I'm looking for the blue starfish I'd seen yesterday and spend ages swimming around hoping to spot him. Just as I'm about to give up, I find him, or one similar, this time only two of his 'arms' are protruding from the coral, but at least I can take a photo as a memento.

# Gili Islands, Indonesia

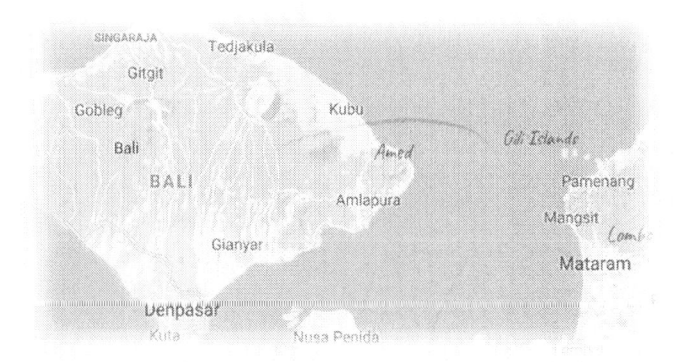

## 26th May

### Boat to the Gili Islands

I'm up early one last time to watch the sunrise over Amed beach, then head back for my usual breakfast of coffee, fried egg on bread and fruit. The food all comes to the table at the same time, I've tried asking for the fruit first, then the egg so I can eat the egg hot, but they haven't understood my request, so I've given up.

A car comes from the tour office to take me to the beach where I'll board a boat to the island called Gili Air. There's a fun atmosphere here with tourists milling about, all wonderfully relaxed. There are three 'bag drops' on the beach with a signpost on a stick designated for each of the three islands; Gili Trawangan, Gili Meno and Gili Air.

While waiting, I watch a salesman walking with a huge bag of sunglasses, approaching each person he enquires *"sunglasses?"*, he comes to me and changes the glasses in his hand to reading specs saying *"reading glasses?"*. This does nothing for my ego.

The boat, when it comes, is large and comfortable and I'm relieved that I don't feel sea sick at all. In a little over an hour I land on another island paradise.

A few yards from where I've arrived, a hand painted sign saying Melbao Homestay points down an alleyway and it's a short walk to my accommodation. I'm greeted by a cheeky looking boy wearing a bright red baseball cap the wrong way around and he shows me my room.

The homestay seems to be a row of rooms in a single storey brick building. It's very basic but painted a sunny yellow and has a nice vibe. My room has a bathroom at the back with shower, toilet and basin but no roof, sort of outdoor. Outside my room is a wooden table and chairs.

The homestay also has bikes to rent, so I don't waste any time hiring one to explore. I take the narrow coast path and soon discover that cycling is impossible, the small lanes have turned into sandy tracks and I have to get off and walk.

The island doesn't have any roads and there aren't any cars here, only horse-drawn carts. The area where the boats come in is colourful and busy with tourists, bars and accommodation, but as I walk and cycle further it becomes quieter and more rural. In complete contrast to Amed, the sand is white and the beaches narrow. The heat is intense and coming to a deserted strip of beach I stop to take a swim.

The water is a pretty aqua blue and very inviting but so warm it doesn't cool me down at all. Looking beneath the surface I don't see any sea life to get excited about.

Continuing along the coast path, it takes me about forty-five minutes to walk and cycle a complete circuit of the island. There's plenty of time left, so I continue exploring, turning inland this time.

The paths and lanes that crisscross the island are easier to cycle but I'm not sure which are public paths and which paths lead to someone's property. No-one seems to mind when I mistakenly end up on their land though, I just wave and turn around again. I get very lost but it doesn't matter, the island is so small I know I'll come to the coast path at some point and can find my way from there.

It's getting late, I've been cycling a long time now, so I stop at an inviting warung with comfy sunbeds, order food and settle back to watch the sun set. The scene in front of me is stunning, like something out of a movie. The sea has receded and there are a handful of locals paddling about collecting something, shells maybe. As the sun goes down the sky becomes a palette of rich oranges giving everything a warm glow, including me.

## 27th May

The Melbao Homestay serves a massive breakfast which is placed on the small table and chairs outside my room; an omelette that must contain at least four eggs, fruit, papaya juice and coffee. I'm not going to go hungry here.

I've booked a snorkelling tour for today to see the pink coral I've heard about off the island of Gili Meno. My tour boat is at the quay and I join a group of about thirty other tourists. The boat has a glass bottom intended to show the water underneath, but the combination of scratched glass and sandy water means we don't see much. It doesn't matter, the boat stops frequently and we can jump off and snorkel.

I'm relieved that I don't feel sea sick, something of a

miracle given the movement of the boat which is very up and down. I realise now how spoilt I was with the snorkelling at Jemeluk, this is nothing like as good, but I enjoy myself anyway.

Our boat stops at the island of Gili Meno for lunch and I join a couple from California, Fifi and Gary. They only met seven months ago, Fifi is white and pregnant and Gary is black and as Fifi put it, *"we're still getting to know each other",* but they want to make a 'go' of their relationship. I hope things work out for them.

Back in the water after lunch, I'm excited to spot two turtles, which makes up for the lack of pink coral.

When the boat returns to my island at the end of the day I think how nice it would be to have someone to go out with, maybe listen to some music, meet people and have dinner out. I'm walking along the coastal path and a guy on a bicycle randomly stops to talk to me. I think perhaps he's going to ask for directions but he says *"there's a reggae festival on this evening, on the west side of the island, would you like to come?"* Given the thoughts I was having only a few minutes ago I'm quite taken aback and of course I say 'yes' and ask for more details.

I'm looking forward to some fun at the Reggae Festival but the heavens have opened pouring out monsoon style rain with thunder and lightning to add to the drama. The best I can do is dash across the alley to an Italian restaurant and order a glass of red wine and a pizza.

The rain eases a little but I'm no longer keen to go to the festival, it's dark, wet and a long walk but I said I would go, so I set off.

Well I've walked and walked and it isn't fun, some of the path is completely deserted and although it looked pretty in the sunshine, at night it just looks eerie.

There are dark bushes either side and I feel nervous. Every now and then I come to some lights and a little warung and I'm encouraged to keep going, surely it can't be far now. I'm surprised I can't hear any music. I stop at a small bar to ask for directions and hear a friendly voice call out my name, Gary and Fifi are at the bar having a drink.

I'm told the place I'm after isn't much further, so I keep going and eventually I come to the bar I'm looking for. I'm completely bemused; there's no live music, only a disco. This is a typical outdoor bar with a few people meandering about, I guess the rain put people off coming. There's no sign of Derek, the guy who told me about the event. I don't want to stay here. I sit for a few minutes to gather my strength and settle my disappointment, then continue my circuit of the island to get back 'home'.

I've been walking for more than an hour in the dark and the rain by the time I reach Melbao and I can't help wondering what this evening was all about.

## 28th May

I wake early. I thought that an island without traffic would be a quiet place but there are some very noisy cockerels nearby and oddly, an early morning Muslim 'call to prayer'. I have the day free and want to spend it finishing one of my TEFL assignments, so I'm disappointed to learn that last night's storm knocked out the power and no Wi-Fi. I question my desire to work on a TEFL course when I'm on an island paradise.

## 29th May

## Boat to Padang Bai and Bus to Denpasar (45 kms)

I'm leaving today and have a ticket for a boat to Padang Bai, then I'll need a shuttle bus to Denpasar. The boat should leave at three o'clock. I check in and wait on the wooden jetty, noticing ominous looking clouds gathering. In anticipation of rain I put waterproof covers on my backpacks.

Boats to Padang Bai come and go and each time I'm told *"no, this isn't your boat"*. I continue to wait and then the rain comes. I don't think I've been in a downpour quite like this, I'm soaked through to my knickers in a nanosecond. There's a large rubbish bin near me, fortunately not full, and I stuff my backpacks inside to help them stay dry. The monsoon-style rain is unrelenting and still there's no boat. When it finally comes I'm very cold and glad to get on board.

By the time we arrive in Padang Bai it's dark and I'm still wet and cold. There's chaos, people everywhere all looking for shuttle buses, then I see a sign saying 'Denpasar' and I join a queue. I'm eventually ushered into a minibus along with a handful of other backpackers.

I don't know how long we've been driving, I've dozed off, but road signs suggest we're getting near the airport. The homestay I've booked is only a kilometre from the airport, so I ask the driver if he will take me there after dropping the others off. He says this is okay and I relax.

Traffic is rush-hour busy and after leaving the airport the driver suddenly parks up and tells me to get out. I ask him where I am and he says my homestay isn't far.

He doesn't want to go any further and I have no choice but to get out of the minibus. The bus leaves and I'm left standing on the street in the dark, with all my stuff and no idea where I am.

There are lights not too far away so I start walking in that direction. Oh joy, here's a hotel. I pop in and ask if I can connect to the Internet so I can locate my accommodation on my mobile phone. The receptionist is very helpful, they know where I need to go and give me directions. I set off down the first little lane opposite the hotel which is just wide enough to take a vehicle.

This looks like a residential area, there's an occasional light and I keep walking and talking to myself. Everything always works out for me, I don't need to worry. I notice a small warung that's open and ask if they know Kira Homestay, they point down the road, so I keep walking. And a miracle occurs, I see, right in front of me, a sign with the name Kira Homestay. I'm here and it's much closer than I had expected.

This is a large residential house and I'm shown to a decent bedroom on the first floor. The time is now 9 pm and I'm very hungry. I'm advised that there will be warungs open and shown how to reach the main street where I find a café serving food. I have a vegetable Cap Cay and the dish is really rather good.

30th May

I like the homestay. I think I'm the only guest here. In the morning they serve me breakfast of fried rice, omelette and cucumber. I'm asked *"you want coffee?"* and I say *"yes please, with milk"* and they say *"you want milk?"*, so I nod, yes. What comes is a black coffee and a tall glass of hot milk! I'm happy to have

275

some milk, even though it's diluted condensed milk, because it means I can have a cup of tea; I still have the tea bags in my backpack from the Flower Farm, and there's an electric kettle in the room. I'm childishly excited at this prospect and put a saucer over the glass so I can use the milk later.

I ask the lady of the house if she knows a hairdresser in the area, this seems like a good opportunity to get my hair cut. She very kindly offers to take me and I hop onto the back of her scooter.

We stop in front of a small house and knock on the door. Inside is the hairdresser's living room, full of furniture and customers. She's colouring a man's hair, another lady is sitting in front of a mirror and on a bed a woman is lying prostrate, presumably waiting for a treatment. The hairdresser juggles us all expertly, giving each of us attention. I ask for a wash, cut and conditioning treatment and she does all three including a relaxing head and shoulder massage for 100,000 rupiah, about £5. When she's finished, she phones the owner of my homestay, who comes back with her scooter to take me home. Amazing service.

The beach is only a short walk away from where I'm staying and in the afternoon I'm keen to explore. The beach is long, wide and almost deserted, there are only a couple of people on it. The sand is soft and I take off my sandals and walk along to an area where the beach curves around a bay.

Coming around the bay the scene changes and to my amazement I can see a row of aeroplanes and one taking off into the air. I realise this must be the airport runway and the planes are queuing to take off. It looks an odd sight because there are fishing boats on the sea in front of them and it looks as though the planes are on the water. As I watch the 'planes, a gaggle of small children come up to me, they all want me to take their photo.

The sun feels hot and I try sunbathing to fill in some of the white parts of my body but I'm soon bored. I remember passing a beautiful Japanese hotel on the way to the beach, so I pop back there and buy an expensive but very delicious smoothie and lie on one of their sun loungers watching people playing in the pool.

On my walk back 'home' some young boys are flying kites from the beach; their kites are magnificent. There are market stalls here and I say *"Hi"* to some ladies who are hand-crafting raffia decorations for a celebration. They also want me to take photos of them.

I have Cap Cay for dinner at the same café as yesterday then return to pack my bags, I'm leaving Bali in the morning and as always, I feel sad to leave and nervously excited at the thought of a new adventure.

## Singapore to Australia

### 31st May

### Aeroplane to Singapore (2½ hrs)

The homestay owner has kindly driven me to the airport at Denpasar. I'm flying to Singapore this morning and I'm excited because, John, my friend who drove me to the start of my travels, is going to meet me and from there we'll travel together to Australia.

I have a smooth flight and arrive ahead of schedule. I can't see John, surely he's here, and then I see him sauntering towards me.

He's booked us a hotel near the MRT and after checking in, we make our way to the Marina Bay Sands hotel, this time I'm determined to see the views it can offer. I get déjà vu being back on the MRT.

In the Marina Bay Sands hotel, we find the 55th floor avoiding paying the daft price of $23 to go onto the 56th floor. There are amazing vistas out across the Singapore Strait which is dotted with boats, tankers and cargo ships and below we can see the lush green 'Gardens by the Bay'.

The 'Gardens by the Bay' look inviting and so we take a walk through them. I'm surprised to notice someone who looks familiar and at the same time she notices me; she's a neighbour from my village in England and here in Singapore with her husband. We laugh at the coincidence.

John suggests we go to an area called Bugis for something to eat. This is a place with a colourful history but is now modern shops and restaurants. My meal is a very mediocre veg noodles, but it's very nice not to be eating alone. I still don't care for Singapore and I'm glad we're leaving tomorrow for Australia.

As well as being excited to see John, I'm also excited because he's brought me the 'blonde' hair dye I requested. I haven't yet seen blonde hair colour on the shelves in the shops so asking John to bring me some from England seemed a good solution.

1st June

## Aeroplane to Sydney (8hrs)

We're 'kicking our heels' a bit today because our flights aren't until this evening. Although we have separate flights for Sydney, luckily the timing isn't too different so we can meet easily at the other end. I'm not sure how I feel about going to Australia.

The flight takes eight hours and I'm very content. I like being on aeroplanes and especially love passing the time watching films, something I rarely do at home.

## 2nd June

Our flights both work out well and John and I meet up again at Sydney Airport around 7.15 am local time.

We're going to spend a few days with the family of my good friend in the U.K., her brother David, and his wife Janet. They live north of Sydney in a place called Terrey Hills.

We take a train to Pymble Station and contact Janet to come and meet us. She doesn't pick up our calls or messages and there's nothing we can do. John also plays the ukulele and has brought it with him, so we have some silly fun sitting on a wall and strumming while we wait. A short while later the messages have come through and a beautiful, beaming Janet comes to meet us and take us to her home.

Set in a residential area, their detached, single storey house is lovely. There's a swimming pool in the garden and also a chicken coop where they keep hens.

Janet is keen to show us around the area, so in the afternoon we drive out. They live on the edge of a National Park and the sea is never far away because it surrounds the land on three sides. We've arrived in Oz in their winter and the weather is cool.

On the way home, we stop to buy take-away food for supper which we share with Taylor, their son, and David when he comes in from work. After the meal David puts the TV on to relax.

I feel as though my bubble has been burst. Suddenly

I'm back in 'normal' land, no longer alone, I'm eating 'take-aways' and watching TV. I think this will be a period of adjustment for me.

## 3rd June

Janet kindly takes the time to drive John and I around again so we can see more of the area. We go for a walk which gives us a good view of the waterways and Sydney in the distance and we stop for an excellent breakfast at a waterside café. I can't help wishing the temperature is warmer. The weather doesn't improve and with a massive downpour we head back home. We all hope the rain doesn't last, David and Janet are taking us to the Blue Mountains tomorrow.

## 4th June

We're disappointed. The weather is lousy, full-on rain. We drive to the Blue Mountains anyway hoping for an improvement.

There isn't an improvement, it's a 'whiteout'. Visibility is so poor we can only see a few feet in front of us. I'm told that we're surrounded by beautiful mountains and I can't see a thing. David's brother joins us and we pass some time looking around antique shops.

The weather looks set to continue, so we carry on to the pub and our overnight accommodation which I really like. The hotel is quaint and old, with a sort of English colonial feel to it. There's a large fire alight in the lounge and we have a drink and meet the Polish man who runs the place. He's called Roman and his conversation is amazing, he speaks with such thoughtfulness and wisdom that I could have listened to him for hours.

## 5th June

We wake up to learn that the weather in and around Sydney has been even worse than here and there's been considerable flooding. The news sounds very dramatic. We have a cooked breakfast at the hotel then take a look at a small property for sale nearby. David and Janet are considering investing here. Inside a Tourist Centre I see pictures of the Blue Mountains showing me how they'd look if the weather would allow, and they are spectacular.

Our drive back reveals to some extent, how bad the storms and flooding at the weekend have been and some roads are impassable. We watch the news on the TV and it shows shocking pictures of badly damaged properties and houses near the shore that have lost their gardens, literally swept away into the sea or collapsed onto the beach.

## 6th June

John and I take a drive out with Janet to see for ourselves the devastation around Sydney. The waves along the beach are still high and dramatic and it's sad to see the damage the storm has caused to some people's homes.

The sun has come out and in the early evening when David returns home from work he takes John and I out for a spin in his 'pride and joy', a classic, shiny red, Triumph Stag and I sit in the back and watch the sun go down as we whizz around the bay.

## 7th June

We've left the comfort of Janet and David's beautiful home and we're back on the train bound for Sydney.

After checking into our basic hotel, Siesta Sydney, we walk to Sydney Harbour Bridge. John has pre-booked tickets for us to do the' bridge climb'. A walkway has been created across the bridge for people to climb up, and with my love of heights, when John suggested doing this I couldn't resist the idea. The cost of a ticket is a massive £160 which feels ridiculously extravagant, especially considering how cheap my travels have been so far.

The climb is taken very seriously and we have a safety talk before being given fleece jackets to wear and harnesses so we can be attached to the rails. The weather is kind to us and although a bit windy, there's no rain. I'm a little disappointed the climb is easier than I'd expected, reviews suggested it would be more challenging. The 360-degree panorama from the top, across the harbour and city is fabulous and we can see the iconic opera house below us.

Walking around Darling Harbour in the evening in search of a restaurant isn't fun, we don't find anywhere inspiring and can't agree where we'd like to eat. I realise that I'm struggling to adjust to the change in my circumstances. I'm now in an English-speaking country, no longer alone and the weather is cool and dull.

# *Sydney to Adelaide Road Trip*

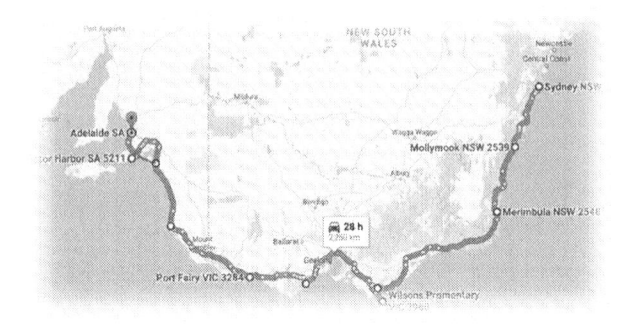

## 8ᵗʰ June

### Day 1 to Mollymook (280 kms)

Today John and I start a road trip out of Sydney. We're going to drive along the Princes Highway and the coast road to Adelaide. We've done some calculations, working out distances to be sure we arrive on the 19ᵗʰ June because we have train tickets booked.

First, we have to collect our rental car, a white Kia Cerato. The hire company call it a 'small' car but it looks big to me. Thank goodness the car has a satnav, and with John at the wheel, we carefully make our way out of Sydney.

We drive 280 kms along the Princes Highway, stopping off at Kiama, an attractive small town by the ocean and boasting a 'blow hole'. We have a delicious lunch there in the warm sunshine. We've plenty of time, so take tourist Route 9 inland and walk to see the Minnamurra Falls, which look particularly good because of all the recent rain. The scenery around us is very pretty and the green rolling hills remind me of my home county, Oxfordshire.

Our first accommodation is called 'Mollymook', it's basic but adequate and right near the ocean. We have a walk along the beach followed by dinner at the golf club opposite, then spend the rest of the evening looking on line for our next destination and accommodation.

## 9th June

### Day 2 to Merimbula (240 kms)

Breakfast at Mollymook is an excellent serve-yourself set-up. We haven't seen anyone since we arrived and the key to our room was left out for us last night.

Today we continue our drive along the Princes Highway until we come to Narooma, where we park up and take a pleasant 'board walk' by the sea.

Afterwards, the road takes us up high where we find a stunning place to have coffee, overlooking the harbour and the sea below, bathed in gorgeous sunshine.

I offer to take the wheel today and I don't feel very comfortable! The car is larger than I'm used to and an 'automatic'. I drive along Tourist Route 9, called the coastal route, but disappointingly, we only catch glimpses of the sea now and then.

We arrive early in Merimbula and find our budget accommodation; it's not amazing, but it is clean. John and I are at odds over accommodation, he wants modern motels and I'd rather choose hostels, so we're both having to compromise.

We stroll along the beach at Merimbula which is wide and long and see some pelicans on the water. As the sun goes down we go in search of kangaroos. We've been told that we'll see them in the early evening grazing and we're not disappointed, we find a whole field of them.

After a meal at a very mediocre restaurant we spend time planning the next stage of our trip. We reckon we've covered about 240 kms today and both agree the scenery has been beautiful.

## 10th June

### Day 3 to Lakes Entrance (270 kms)

I'm up at 6.30 am to catch the sunrise on the beach. It isn't spectacular because the sun comes up behind the headland, but it does make the sky a very pretty pink. The pelicans are there again and I enjoy watching them catch fish. They're standing quite near the shore, I think the tide is coming in and the waves are bringing in the fish. I feel very peaceful.

We're not inspired to dally in Merimbula, so drive straight to the next place called Eden. This is a good move because we discover a fantastic café for breakfast, right by the harbor which is bustling with boats and activity. John's young granddaughter Florrie has her birthday today and he wants to make a video for her. We're down by the harbour and John plays his ukulele and sings the 'Happy Birthday' song while I record it on his mobile. It makes us giggle.

In the town we stop for provisions and I go to an ATM to get cash. I put my card in and my PIN and a message comes up shouting *"we cannot give you any money and we cannot return your card"*! The machine has swallowed my bank card and isn't going to give it back to me. The machine isn't attached to a bank so I can't get help.

I use my mobile to call my bank and explain what's happened but the person I'm speaking to is shockingly unhelpful. She seems incapable of putting herself in my position or considering a possible solution. Her parting sentence goes like this *"the only thing we can do… well, there's nothing we can do"*. It's almost funny!

I'm not going to let this experience spoil my day, I have to find a way to 'let it go' out of my head. At least I still have another bank card from a different bank account, so all is not lost.

After a short coastal walk, we get back in the car and drive along the A1, taking a tourist detour down to Cape Conrad. There are large rocks here where we can sit and look at the sea while we eat the salad we'd bought in Eden.

Arriving at our uninspiring motel in Lakes Entrance, we're dismayed to realise they don't have Internet which poses a problem because we need to book tomorrow's accommodation. Luckily there's a hotel nearby so we have a drink and use their Wi-Fi. Finding affordable (for me) accommodation proves tricky because this is a holiday weekend and there's not much available. So far John has resisted my attempts to get him into a Youth Hostel but this time, in the light of not too much choice, he relents and I book a YHA. Now we can relax with a good meal.

## 11th June

## Day 4 (and 5) to Foster (227 kms)

We're leaving Lakes Entrance in the early morning to drive along the Princes Highway, out of New South Wales and into Victoria. The weather is cold and rainy. We stop for a break at historic Port Albert but don't leave the car for long, a squall has suddenly come up and I have trouble even opening the car door the wind is so strong. John and I share the driving and I feel more confident now.

Our next stop-over is in Foster, this is the first hostel

John has experienced and my fingers are crossed that it will be a good one. I'm delighted that we have a small unit to ourselves. We have a lounge, kitchen, bathroom with laundry and a bedroom. We also have heating and a TV, all totally brilliant. It feels like home.

Woohoo! I've had another text message from Ben. He received my postcard from Bali and sends me hugs. I've reflected before how perfect it is that he doesn't use technology, it would feel tedious to have to keep sending and replying to messages and emails. As it is, each message feels very special and wonderful.

It makes sense to me to make use of the opportunity to cook our own meal this evening, so after shopping for provisions, I prepare dinner. We've covered 227 kms today.

## 12th June

We've booked two nights in Foster so we can have a break from our road trip. Our plan is to walk up Mt Oberon on the Wilson Promontory. When we arrive in Wilson we learn that the only good view is from the top and today the mountain is covered in cloud with no visibility. It's disappointing, but instead we walk around the coast and this definitely makes up for it. There's a board walk across some water and then a climb up high where we can see across a vast stretch of sand to the sea. We walk a long way and it feels good to be out of the car. It's a shame the sun isn't shining but at least we don't get rained on.

When we get back to our accommodation we discover that we've been invaded; two girls from Germany are staying tonight in our small unit. The place is small for sharing, especially the kitchen and preparing our evening meal requires some patience.

13th June

## Day 6 to Lorne (260 kms)

I feel for John this morning, this is his first experience of shared accommodation; he wants to take a shower and there are two girls occupying the bathroom!

Today will be an interesting road trip because we're going on a ferry; our destination is Lorne. The ferry port is in Sorento and we've made good time so far, but traffic is now slow and I am feeling a bit tense, we're cutting it finer that I'd like.

All is well and we're parked up. Standing on the dock I can see it coming towards us, a typical big white ferry. On board, we sit outside in the sunshine and the wind. After a forty minute crossing we arrive in Queenscliff.

Tonight, we're staying in another motel. It gets dark early in the evening, so we don't see much of the town of Lorne, but we do find a decent Italian restaurant for dinner.

14th June

## Day 7 to Port Fairy (250 kms)

I'm up at 6.30 am again to take advantage of the perfect running beach, right across the road from our motel. I've haven't run much since I started travelling and it feels good running on the sand. The sunrise is captivating and creates an amazing display of colours.

Our drive today is going to take us to Port Fairy and we have a couple of places to stop along the way. Our road trip is never boring, there's plenty to see although I'm disappointed that we don't see the sea very often, even though we're on the 'coast' road. The roads are excellent, a real pleasure to drive on, sometimes we drive for many kilometres and see only a couple of other cars or trucks. England would be amazing if the roads were this empty.

We've taken a detour to go to Cape Otway where there's a small lighthouse. The ticket cost to go into the lighthouse is expensive and we're not interested enough to pay the price. To reach the Cape we had to drive through a eucalyptus forest and we're told that this is a great place to see koalas. I persuade John to park so we can go into the forest. John doesn't have any patience for koala watching, he's keen to get back on the road and after ten minutes we haven't spotted one and he's had enough. I love being in the forest and would like to stay longer.

Further along the Great Ocean Road we've come to the famous 'Twelve Apostles', several large limestone stacks off the shore of the Port Campbell National Park in Victoria and a popular tourist destination.

We arrive in Port Fairy and after checking into our Port Boutique accommodation we take a walk out to Griffiths Island. Tourist info tells us that Mutton birds fly back to the island at dusk. It doesn't help that we've no idea what they look like, but we see very few birds, Mutton or otherwise. I've forgotten to bring food of any kind with me to stave off hunger and I'm now ravenous.

Looking around the town for somewhere to eat the restaurants again are mostly Italian, apart from a Chinese noodle place which I really can't face. Our choice is limited and we have another Italian meal. It's a shame when 'dining out' becomes tedious.

## 15th June

### Day 8 to Robe (312 kms)

Our destination today is Robe but we're stopping off first at Cape Bridgwater to do a clifftop walk.

A small path takes us to the top of an open grassy cliff, where we can walk along looking down at the gorgeous blue sea way below. Suddenly we realise a large group of seals are playing in the water around a floating wooden structure. We sit on the grass in the sunshine and watch them, and although they're quite far away it still feels a privilege.

After a picnic on the beach we're back on the road, a very, very long, almost empty road and we make it to the seaside town and fishing port of Robe, just as the sun is setting. Our accommodation at the Guishen Bay Motel is uninspiring but comfortable.

## 16th June

### Day 9 to Victor Harbor (350 kms)

It's raining, so we're not going to hang about in Robe. We have a long drive to Victor Harbor.

It hasn't been a particularly pretty drive today but we've found a good place on the beach to stop for a picnic. The sea is dark grey with large waves and the beach is a creamy, custard colour. It isn't far from here to our hotel called 'The Anchorage'.

Granite Island is nearby, well known for the penguins that live there and we've been told that dusk is a good time to see them so we walk across to it. We're meandering along the top of the Island when we come across two large kangaroos. It's getting dark now and we haven't seen penguins. A tour guide sees us and admonishes us that we shouldn't be there without a tour ticket. We explain that we weren't aware of this and using his infrared torch he kindly shows us a group of the smallest penguins in Australia.

## 17th June

### Day 10 to Adelaide Road (122 kms)

Before starting our drive today, we take a walk along The Bluff, up high with views over Port Victor.

This is the last day of our road trip. John's done well with the planning and we'll make it to Adelaide in plenty of time. En route we detour to take a look at Ingallala Falls, not spectacular, but the area does have a tranquil feel to it.

With a little tension and some swearing at the SatNav, we locate the car drop-off point at Adelaide airport and leave the car. It's been a very comfortable vehicle and we've no complaints. Our Australian road trip from Sydney to Adelaide along the Princes Highway and the Great Ocean Road has taken us along 2,500 kms of beautiful roads.

John has given in again and allowed me to book us into a hostel, unimaginatively called Hostel 109 and a shuttle bus takes us there.

## 18th June

The hostel is decent, we have a private room and we learn we can borrow free bikes to explore. Adelaide is the capital of South Australia and the fifth most populated city in Australia. It grew up in the 1800s and has wide streets and I like the feel of it.

I'd like our first stop to be at a retail park where I hope I can buy a new electronic reader because mine has broken. It's such a brilliant device to take travelling; there's no way I could physically carry so many books.

The shopping mall has an appropriate store and I don't hesitate in purchasing a new one.

The sun is shining and we continue exploring on our bikes. We come across the famous Oval cricket ground and to my surprise we're allowed to go in and walk around, I think of all the times I must have seen this ground on the TV. Afterwards, we check out some aboriginal art in the South Australia Museum. Cycling here is easy because the city is laid out on a grid system but it means there are frequent traffic lights at all the crossroads, which makes John curse with irritation every time we have to stop and I do agree the lights are very slow changing to 'go'.

# Adelaide to Darwin

## 19th June

### The Ghan Train to Alice Springs (26hrs)

We're stepping into luxury travel today. John has pre-booked seats on the fabulous Ghan train which travels across the middle of Australia, 2,979km from Adelaide to Darwin. We'll be getting off half way in Alice Springs because we want to visit Ayers Rock. This is an expensive ride but I think it will be worth it for the experience.

We have a carriage to ourselves with bunk beds. A train stewardess with a big smile comes and introduces herself to us, her name is Rainy. I ask her how she spells it (I've found this is a good way to remember names I'm not sure of) and she tells me it's spelt like the rain. She goes on to say that she has a sister called Sunny and says *"what were my parents thinking?"* I wonder if she's become so bright and cheerful to make up for being called Rainy.

The meals and all drinks are included in our ticket price, so I don't waste any time sampling a cold Sauvignon Blanc at the bar. Meeting our travelling companions, they're mostly in their senior years. Everyone is friendly and there's a lovely air of camaraderie.

The lunch and dinner menus are very enticing and extensive, the food is delicious and I wish I had a larger appetite so I could do it more justice.

We have plenty of time to relax in the comfort of our carriage and look out at the landscape as we pass through. It's become quite barren, a vast expanse of red soil with tufts of grasses and low hills in the distance.

## 20th June

We're woken in the still dark, early morning and invited to leave the train so we can watch the sunrise. The train has stopped in the middle of 'nowhere'. I love the atmosphere, everyone is standing around, the train is behind us and a vast open land all around. The staff look after us very well, providing bacon butties, Danish pastries and hot drinks. The sunrise isn't spectacular, mostly the sky just becomes lighter, but the whole experience is memorable.

We arrive in Alice Springs in sunshine and take a bus to our accommodation, John has agreed we can stay in a hostel again.

The town of Alice is in the middle of Australia with a population around 28,000, many of the people here are Aboriginal. I can't say that I like it very much, it looks plain, and uninteresting.

I smile to acknowledge the Aborigines we pass on the sidewalk and notice they don't make eye contact, although one Aborigine exuberantly launches himself in front of John and shakes his hand vigorously, I think it likely he's high on something. John handles the jolly assault well by politely extricating himself without causing offence.

Finding a tour to take us to Ayres Rock isn't difficult, there are loads of them, but deciding how to get out of Alice Springs is proving tricky. We want to get to Darwin because it's a good launching point to start a tour of The Kimberley. John wants to fly and I want to take a bus. The bus trip will take three days and involve camping which John is uncomfortable about, but flying means staying in Alice another couple of days which I definitely don't want to do. I also feel that flying means we'll miss the scenery and experiences. Eventually, with reluctance, John agrees we can book the three-day bus tour. I know he's out of his comfort zone and this has been a hard decision for him. I pray it will work out well.

21st June

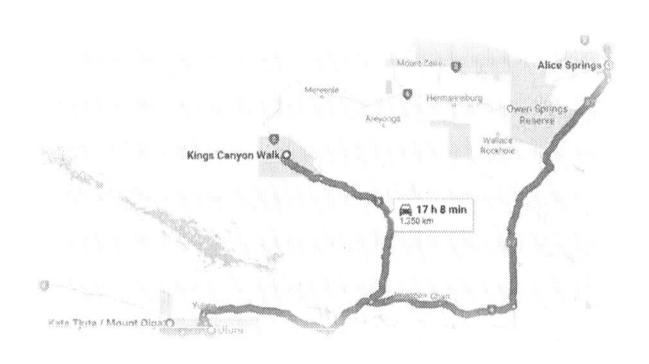

# Three Day Tour Uluru Tour

## Day 1

Tour operators here pick tourists up from their accommodation, so we're up early and waiting outside for our transport. The tour to Uluru is called 'The Emu Run' and, as always, I'm relieved when a truck arrives. Our fellow passengers are already on board. The guide is also our driver, he's called David and I think he's going to be fun.

The first stop is late morning at a 'do-it-yourself' style barbeque on a campsite and David asks us all to pitch in as he puts some food out onto a wooden picnic bench. I'm impressed that John quickly takes on the job of cooking the meat on the barbeque. Working together to create a meal is a good way to get to know each other. I really like Lucy and Tim who come from the north of England, they both clearly have a great sense of humour and I think they'll bring a lot of laughs to the group.

During the afternoon drive David points out a massive red rock in the distance, it looks like Ayres Rock. He said it's called Mount Conner and known as Fool-Uru because many tourists mistake it for Uluru. How silly would you feel if nobody told you and you missed out seeing the real Uluru?

We stop at an Aborigine art museum and have the privilege of watching and talking with some of the artists while they work. They create beautiful paintings, working freehand, dabbing dots with a paintbrush until the canvass is completely covered. The designs depict ancient stories. I love the colours which are reminiscent of the colours we're seeing in the landscape. Lucy and Tim can't resist buying one of the paintings, I settle for taking a photo.

From the art centre, a short walk takes us to Uluru, the Aboriginal name for the iconic Ayres Rock. I'm feeling excited.

The 'Rock' is vast, red and awesome. We have time to walk all around it, a total of 10 kms which gives perspective on how massive it is. I love the atmosphere of stillness here and we're lucky very few people are on the path. I keep taking photos but know that none of them will do the rock justice. The colours of the scenery around us are stunning, there are tall grasses and wild flowers and I marvel at the glorious scene nature has painted.

Back on the truck David drives us some distance away from Ayres Rock and, along with other tourist vehicles, we pull over. He puts out a trestle table and loads it with nibbles and champagne. He tells us that the sun will set behind us and we should keep looking at the rock.

Distracted from the rock, happily drinking and chatting in the warm evening sunshine, suddenly there's a shout out and a collective gasp as we see the rock change colour to a stunning bright orange. It looks exactly as though spotlights have been switched on around it. The colour lasts just long enough to take photos and then the sun moves and the bright luminescent colour goes. We're all laughing and in awe of this magical experience. When I turn around I see the sky behind us is a blaze of gold and reds.

During the day we'd collected firewood and when we reach our camp for the evening Lucy and Tim make a bonfire. I'm childishly excited because I'm going to have my first experience of sleeping in a swag, which is a heavy-duty canvas sleeping bag and inside it you put your own sleeping bag. I gather together my torch, water bottle and mobile phone and stuff them in the sleeping bag and hope I won't need the loo in the night. John elects to sleep in the tent. Four others have also chosen to sleep in swags around the fire. I feel some light rain on my face and feel disappointed that I may have to resort to the tent after all, but I pull the swag flap over the top of me for a while and the rain stops. I want to lie and watch the clouds in the dark sky and the zillions of stars, but annoyingly I'm 'out' like a light.

## 22nd June

### Day 2

Waking up in the morning, I'm puzzled to find I'm the only one left in a swag, everyone else has disappeared. Did the rain drive them into their tents? When they emerge, I learn that during the night dingoes had come around the camp scavenging and woken Tim and Lucy and so everyone had fled to their tents. I was happily oblivious to the whole episode.

We're up at up at 'silly o'clock' to watch the sunrise over Uluru. It's a short drive and then a short walk in the dark. We don't have long to wait. Again, we're rewarded with incredible views, the weather is perfect and I know we're extremely lucky. With the extraordinary Uluru rock as the backdrop, the sky paints another glorious palette of colours. We're all taking photo after photo knowing they'll never really do the gorgeous sky justice.

We continue driving to Kata Tjuta, known as 'The Olgas' and a 5.5km walk through the beautiful 'Valley of the Winds'. The sandstone domes of Kata Tjuta are believed to be about 500 million years old. I simply can't comprehend that anything can be so ancient.

Moving on, we stop to collect more firewood and pitch at a different camp in the Watarrka National Park, known as Kings Canyon. Here we're joined by Joey, also a tour guide and friend of David's. He's looking after an elderly group who have all retired to bed. Joey is a large, jovial, bearded Aussie. He's brought copious bottles of red wine to our camp and we're happy to help him drink it. He engages us all with a spoon game causing much hilarity. We're sitting around a large table under an awning. The spoons are placed in front of us and a pack of cards is dealt out. We each place a card down and when a pair of cards matches, everyone has to grab a spoon, but there's always one spoon short so each round one player is put out of the game.

This is another opportunity to sleep in the swag and having been reassured by David that dingos rarely attack people (I don't dwell on the word 'rarely') I'm willing to give it a go, especially as this evening the sky is a clear. Lying on my back in the Aussie outback and looking at the night sky is magical; the stars are out in full force and my only frustration is again the difficulty I have keeping my eyes open.

## 23rd June

### Day 3

David drives us to Kings Canyon, a semi-barren, rocky landscape and we have an amazing walk through, up and around the rim. We climb up high and standing on dark red rock we can see far across the vast land and all of us agree that this is the best experience of the trip.

During last night dingos made off with a pair of trainers belonging to one of the girls in our group and at lunchtime David drives back to the camp with her and her friend to search for the shoes, as he believes they may have been dropped somewhere nearby. The girls are very attractive and it crosses my mind that this might be an excuse for him to be alone with them as they seem to be getting along rather well. They do however return triumphant with the pair of trainers.

Our tour ends back in Alice Springs and a suggestion goes out that we meet for dinner at a restaurant called 'Uncles'. Tim, Lucy, Victoria and Sara along with John and I are the only ones to turn up. Poor Tim is struggling with a hangover from yesterday's frivolity. I'm surprised that David wants to spend another evening with us all having put up with us for three days, but maybe it's not so odd considering how dull Alice Springs appears to be. I think we've been very lucky to have him as our guide, he's been brilliant.

I doubt he made out with the Danish girls after all, turns out they're a couple!

## 24th June

We have the day to ourselves. Catching up with emails and info from the U.K. we're shocked to learn the unexpected news that Britain has voted to leave the European Union.

## Three Day Tour to Darwin (1540 kms)

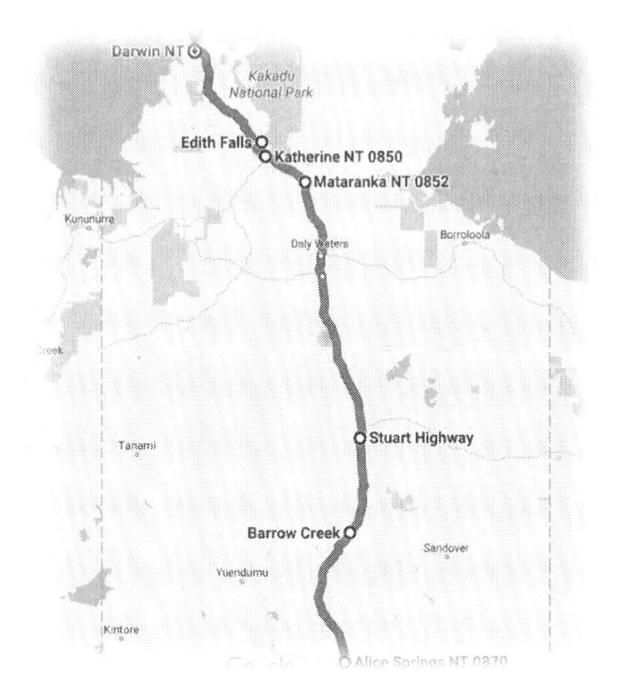

### 25th June

### Day 1

And we're off again, picked up from our hostel by our guide called Sandy in a minibus. Another three-day tour, this time we're going to Darwin. There are twelve others already on board.

We cross the Tropic of Capricorn at the equator and pile out of the bus to take photos by the marker. We're travelling with Janine and Julie (French), Lucas, Ria, Lotte, two ladies Betsy and Lyn, Merco and Asian Duca and another whose name I don't recall. I already like

Sandy, she's very easy going. I think this is going to be a fun tour.

Wauchope offers us a pit stop, then we drive on to see Karlu Karluk, known as the Devils Marbles. They're massive boulders and rocks, fabulously red and with the bright blue sky behind them they're a stunning sight. We have some silly fun taking daft photos among the rocks. The temperature is hotting up now we've crossed the line.

There's a lot of time spent in the bus as we have a long distance to cover, but I never mind. John and I are sitting at the back and we've plenty of room.

We arrive at our first camp, Barrow Creek at the perfect time to climb a high ridge and watch another stunningly beautiful sunset. Then we all chip in to help with preparing food, laying things out and collecting firewood.

We have a big fire burning and sit round it with our dinner. Lucas is travelling with his guitar and I'm keen to encourage him to bring it out, so I play *'Wooden Heart'* on the uke. Lotte loves it and I show her a couple of chords which she picks up easily. Lucas plays his guitar softly and then a young guy who works at the camp comes over and rather dominates things for the next hour. He's quite amusing and has us play a silly word game which I found rather fun but I can sense some resentment from the others at his presence.

I sleep in a swag under the stars again and I think the sky is the best yet. At breakfast I'm touched when Janine comes up to me and says *"last night you told us that you play music using your head, not your heart, well I don't think that's true because when you sang I could feel the emotion"*. I thank her for such a generous compliment and she replies *"well, I felt it was important for you to know"*. People are delightful.

26th June

Day 2

Our start this morning is 6 o'clock and we have many more hours in the bus, but I'm very happy. I love looking at the outback scenery, it doesn't change much, but the rich, red earth colours are gorgeous.

Passing the junction with Barkly Highway we're amused to see a road sign warning *'no fuel for 500 kms'*. This is one long, dry, dusty road, you'd definitely want to make sure you have fuel in your tank.

The route we're travelling along follows where the first telegraph line crossed Australia in 1872 and small towns sprang up along the route. Our lunch stop is at the famous and whacky Daly Waters pub, built in 1930. It's full of character, the walls and ceiling are completely covered in all sorts of mementos left by visitors, including hundreds of women's bras.

Mid-afternoon Sandy parks the bus so we can take a dip in the natural and very pretty Mataranka thermal pools. This is a fabulous experience, the water is warm and buoyant and I can literally lie back and float down the river.

Our overnight stop this time is in Katherine, a campsite with 'glamping' tents. They're so inviting I decide to sleep in one instead of a swag. Lotte is keen to learn to play the uke, so sitting around the camp fire I show her some more chords. She learns fast and to my delight, she's soon singing *'You are my Sunshine'* swiftly followed by *'I'm Yours'* by Jason Mraz. John and I sing *'Hotel Yorba'* together, me making a very poor job of it but fun nevertheless.

27ᵗʰ June

Day 3

We're up early again to drive to Katherine Gorge in Nitmiluk National Park where we have coffee in a pavilion that has panoramic views of the gorge. Afterwards we drive up to the top for the start of a walk. Lucas realises he's left his guitar in the car park where we started and we drive back down to look for it, but it's gone. No searching or enquiries at the pavilion reveal it. He's clearly upset but handles it well and we all feel for him.

We walk up to a lookout with incredible vistas over the gorge and Katherine River below but a bit subdued now, feeling bad for Lucas.

Back down from our walk, Lucas makes enquiries at the coffee shop again. He climbs back on the bus grinning, it's been handed in, he has his guitar back! A big cheer goes up from us all, everyone's relieved.

This is turning into an amazing day. We have a picnic lunch at Edith Waterfall, still in Nitmiluk, a beautiful area where falls cascade into a large pool and we have another opportunity to cool off with a swim. The expanse of water to swim across looks daunting and is a stretch for me to reach the waterfall so I feel exhilarated making it there and back.

Many more miles driving, but with frequent stops at cattle stations. John makes me laugh, I've noticed he seems to have acquired a desire for ice lollies and buys one at every opportunity.

We arrive in Darwin around 7.30 pm and Sandy drops us off at the Darwin YHA. We've had a fantastic three days, I loved everything and especially our entertaining group. I found Lotte very endearing and we've connected on Facebook.

## 28th June

The YHA in Darwin isn't a 'wow' hostel but the facilities are good and we're glad of the opportunity to catch up on emails and plan ahead. Being together 24/7 is taking its toll on John and I. We're on different wavelengths much of the time and making decisions is difficult.

There doesn't seem to be much to Darwin. We wander along the Esplanade. The sea is an inviting blue but we can't go near it because there are signs warning of crocodiles! We have a late lunch at a Mexican restaurant then book bicycles to hire on Thursday.

## 29th June

We're pottering about in Darwin again today; John and I are at odds with each other and it feels uncomfortable. In the evening we take a bus to the Yacht Club and I drink cider, watching the sun go down, followed by an exceptionally good value salad. I feel sad to be in this beautiful place and not in tune with my companion. I don't know how to put it right.

## 30th June

I hope today will be more fun for us. We've rented bikes and pedal along a coast path to explore the area.

We stop off to look at an aviation and motor car museum housed in the now redundant QANTAS Empire Airways Hangar, built in 1934 and part of the original Darwin Civil Aerodrome at Parap. The museum is full of fascinating old vehicles, engines and machinery.

We cycle a long way, stopping now and then to check out anything of interest like the amazing Tree of Knowledge, given the aboriginal name of Galamarrma. It's a massive Banyan tree and I do some tree hugging with the expectation that some of its knowledge will rub off on me. I don't know how far we cycled today, but my legs and backside can feel it.

We've heard that there's a night market by the beach near the Yacht Club and in the evening, we take a bus and find it. Along the beach people have gathered to watch the sun go down and we join them, there's a fun holiday atmosphere here. The market area is lively with people enjoying music and a variety of food stalls, craft stalls and aboriginal art with some especially attractive didgeridoos. I would love to have bought one.

## 1st July

It's a celebration day here in Darwin. Every year on 1st July, Northern Territorians celebrate the day they left the Commonwealth and became independent. This is also the only day the public are allowed to buy and set off fireworks. With this in mind, John and I stroll out in the evening along the sea front to see what's going on. Groups of people and families have gathered and lit bonfires along the front. A restaurant with coloured lanterns is perfectly located and we sit outside and watch the fireworks.

# The Kimberley Tour

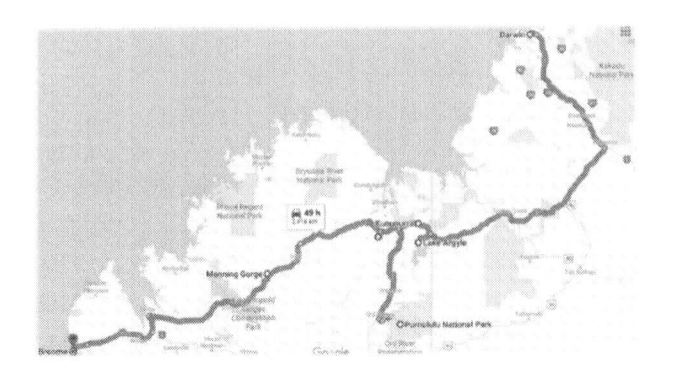

2nd July

Day 1

After considerable research, false leads and difficulty finding the ideal tour for an appropriate date, the day has arrived. Today we start a nine day 'Darwin to Broome' tour in The Kimberley and Bungle Bungles and driving down the Gibb River Road.

Located in the north of Western Australia, I want to go to The Kimberley region because of the recommendation from Adam in Singapore, his enthusiasm and description of the area made it a 'must see' place.

'Pick up' is at 6.50 am and it isn't a bus, but a huge truck. John and I choose to sit near the front behind the driver, there isn't much room and we pile our stuff around us, but I like being up high and we have a great view of the surrounding landscape out of the window.

I'm curious to see who we're going to spend the next nine days with. John and I had been slightly concerned that the tour could be pretty tough, so I'm surprised there's another John in our group who looks elderly and infirm and turns out to be 79 years old! There are others in the group a similar age to us, Sandra and Gregg and Trudie and Derek, all from Australia. Then there's 'big' John from England, Matthias from Germany, Dave also from England, Eline from Holland and Joost also from Holland, Kym and her son Josh are from Oz, so too are Cath, Helen and Camila. We're nineteen altogether including our guide Brad, a big, patient, bearded Aussie.

Our first stop is at Katherine Gorge, the same place we'd visited on our previous tour. Since the only road out of Darwin leads to Katherine we knew the beginning of this trip would duplicate the last. We again stop at Edith Falls but this time we walk to the upper falls which are very different and exceptionally beautiful. It's quite a trek over rocks to reach the waterfalls where we have a swim in the cold, clear water and we're able to swim under and behind the falls. The beauty of this experience isn't lost on me, I'm constantly filled with gratitude that I'm in these incredible places.

Our first camp site is a fixed one, we all have swags and together we set up camp, prepare our supper and clear up afterwards. Everyone is very amenable and willing to do their share, they're a great bunch of people. I love sleeping under the stars again.

3rd July

Day 2

I wake early, around 5 am, to the beginning of a fabulous sunrise and I get up to take photos. We're all up by 5.30 am anyway for an early brekkie and early start.

This is a big drive day, but we have stops along the way at various road houses and I'm never bored.

The drive ends at Lake Argyle where a boat is waiting to take us out to watch the sun set. Lake Argyle was created by damming an area of water on Packsaddle Plain to create irrigation for farming and it saddens me to think of the people who were forced to move out of the area. I can't stay sad for long because this is a magical ride. Our pilot is called Tachi, originally from India, he has a charming presence and I really take to him.

As the sun sets, the sky turns a pretty shade of pink. We're given the opportunity to swim from the boat, a delightful experience in this amazing light. Tachi tells us there are an estimated 25,000 freshwater crocs in the lake, apparently they don't bite. I hope this is true. Then we see some of the little crocs along the shore and there's a family of wallabies too. I'm sorry when the boat ride comes to an end.

It's a short ride to a large and very busy campsite and, as before we all 'muck in'. Later in the evening Tachi comes and joins us. I'm pleased to see him and hear his story. He's only been in Oz a few months. He came here because he wants more from life than India can offer him; his twenty-year marriage to his childhood sweetheart has failed and he's on his own. He has good knowledge of the stars and we spend some time looking at the clear night sky.

## 4th July

### Day 3

Another 5.30 am start to pack up and have breakfast but before leaving we take a swim in the camp's infinity pool. This has to be one of the most beautiful places to have an infinity pool, overlooking the lake, it sort of becomes a part of it. The early morning air is cool so although I love the pool I'm glad to get dry and back into the warmth of the bus.

Brad drives us to the nearby town of Kununara where he can shop for provisions. Most of us park ourselves at a good cafe and enjoy sitting in the sunshine. Because Kununara is famous for its pink diamonds I walk down the street to find a jewellery shop and see what they look like. They're gorgeous and I learn that the one I pick as my favourite pink diamond ring, can be purchased for a mere $30,000. I have to laugh because this is one 'souvenir' that *will* fit into my rucksack.

We have several hours driving to the Bungle Bungles and the passing scenery doesn't change much, but I still love it. As the sun starts setting Brad stops the truck at a high point and we all get out to watch the gorgeous colours and take photos. The red of the stone and the soil and the warm colours of the grass make a stunning scene and I feel full to bursting with the magnificence of the land around us. I'm also amused to discover that the soft, cushion-like tufts of grass I'd been seeing from the bus are in fact vicious 'blades' that scratched your legs when you walk past.

As darkness falls and the road becomes even more bumpy, one of our group realises the side hatch door has come open. Poor Brad has to turn the huge truck around on a narrow lane and drive back to rescue fallen items.

Tonight's campsite is in a very remote place and very basic, no showers, as far as I can tell there are only some 'dunnies' and a cold-water tap.

5ᵗʰ July

Day 4

I'm amused to see how we all cope in a campsite without facilities. John is not comfortable to forego his usual morning shower so he has a wash-down with a hosepipe attached to the tap. I'm reminded of India where people wash and clean their teeth in public.

After clearing up the breakfast things, we're back on the bus with a stop later for photos in Purnalulu (Bungle Bungles) at Elephant Rock. Our walk today is to Piccanny Creek, still in Purnululu National Park and Cathedral Gorge. I will be forever grateful to Adam for recommending that I come here, the scenery, the colours, the sheer vastness of the rocks and the land, the ancientness of the place, I am full up with it all.

Walking through Cathedral Gorge I feel tiny, completely overwhelmed by the magnificence of the tall rocks surrounding us.

We can pay extra for a helicopter ride over the Bungles and uncharacteristically, I choose not to go. I love helicopters and I generally don't miss any opportunities but I don't feel excited about it. John decides at the last minute that he'll take the ride and he absolutely loves it.

After another picnic lunch, we walk along the narrow paths of Echidna Chasm which has been formed over millions of years by water flowing through the open sandstone. We're dwarfed by rocks on both sides rising up to 200 metres high. Then we walk around the escarpment with rocks more than 750,000,000 years old, is this really possible?

These walks are fabulous but I really wish they were longer, I'd love to feel more challenged. The tour itinerary said we'd be walking several miles each day and that hasn't been the case and I do wonder if it's because we have 'old' John with us, he would never cope.

Brad stops the truck in the early evening so we can watch the sun go down. We take out the eski that contains our cold drinks (eski is short for Eskimo and the Aussie word for a cool box). Another perfect opportunity to drink wine while watching the sunset. I will never tire of this sight, the colours in the sky are fabulous. Night time brings a different camp site and another 'swag' slumber.

6th July

Day 5

We have another long, hot, driving day and I totally love it. The colours are fabulous, gorgeous forget-me-not blue sky, orange-red rocks and red dirt roads, eucalyptus green trees with white tree trunks and soft creamy, yellow grasses. We've left the Great Northern Highway and turned onto the famous Gibb River Road.

We stop along the way to collect firewood from scrubland by the road and Brad piles it on top of the truck. At lunchtime we have another picnic followed by a fabulous one hour walk to Emma Gorge where we arrive at a stunningly beautiful natural pool. It's surrounded by cliff high rocks and waterfalls. The water is cold enough to take your breath away but it doesn't stop us plunging in.

Back on the truck we continue driving across El Questro Wilderness Park in the East Kimberley region, which extends over 1,000,000 acres. Eventually we make it to El Questro camp passing through Warmun (Turkey Creek) and the Durack Range. By this time the sun has gone down and it's dark. There's a pretty new moon and it looks strange because the curve is at the bottom.

'Old' John is driving us all nuts, he loses everything. He lost his torch so I lent him mine, then he lost mine, then we found a torch in a shop for him to buy, he found mine and gave it back, then he lost his new torch and had to borrow mine again! That's not the only thing he's lost; water bottles, swimming trunks, the list is long. At the start of the tour everyone was very patient and considerate of him but for some of us patience is wearing thin.

## 7th July

### Day 6

In the glorious morning sunshine, we walk over rocks to Zebedee spring which is a delightful place to swim. 'Old' John comes with us looking alarmingly as though he'll fall over any moment. I admire Brad's patience with him, he lets us all go on ahead and trudges slowly alongside John. I find a strong old stick which will make a perfect walking stick and I give to John. He's hesitant to use it at first but relents and I'm glad that it will help keep him steady.

We have the afternoon off driving and can please ourselves around the campsite and it's pure joy. John and I choose to sit and snooze and read by the river. Later in the afternoon Joost suggests I join him for a walk, he's a nice guy and good company.

In the evening most of our group meet up at The Swimming Arm Bar, El Questro's pub. A guy called Chris Matthews is playing guitar and singing. I'm totally spellbound, I love his music and his skill on the guitar is incredible, I watch his fingers fly over the strings. He plays non-stop for more than two hours, I don't know how he keeps going. I'm amazed that people around us are chatting and seemingly oblivious to this guy's extraordinary talent.

## 8th July

### Day 7

Still in the Cockburn Range, we have a long drive along the Gibb River Road, some 600 kms. Brad has to drive across a wide creek filled with rocks and stones so we all pile out of the truck to take photos. I'm wearing flip flops and walking in the water across the stones I feel a sudden sharp pain in my little toe. I must have whacked it on a stone. I wait for the pain to subside, but it doesn't and I'm in agony. I don't know if it's bruised, dislocated or broken but either way, I'm pretty sure there isn't much that can be done for damaged toes. I can only pray it will heal quickly.

We're driving down a wide red dirt road and there are signs advertising tea with scones and jam. Can this be true? Following the signs, we arrive at a homestead in the middle of nowhere called 'Ellenbrae' and yes, they do serve tea with scones and jam in the garden, very unexpected. The manager of Ellenbrae comes into the garden and joins us and talks about the farm, he describes it as *"a property on 60 sq kms of dirt"*.

## 9th July

### Day 8

Today we're up early at 5.30 am and walk to a river, the rising sun makes the river look very pretty. There's a metal ferry boat, operated with a rope-pull which can carry about four people at a time, to take us to the other side. We have a couple of hours walking and my damaged little toe is painful. I find it ironic that I've been complaining that we're not walking enough and now I'm struggling to walk. We circle back and take the tiny ferry boat back to the bus.

The drive today is again spectacular. We travel further along the Gibb River Road and stop for a picnic lunch followed by a long and challenging trek. It's tricky because there are massive rocks to scramble over and around before we arrive at the gorge but, oh my goodness, the scenery is again dramatic and stunning. There's a beautiful lake to swim in, surrounded by flat rocks, massive high rocky cliffs and greenery. We have plenty of time in the hot sunshine to relax in this idyllic place.

Back in the truck and still on red dirt roads, we drive through the King Leopolds with amazing views of the Napier Ranges. Brad stops the truck to show us a rock formation ahead which looks like the profile of Queen Victoria. Our drive continues along the Fairfield-Leopold Road to Windjana Gorge.

We arrive at the campsite at dusk and some of us take a walk through the gorge to see the freshwater crocodiles. Walking in the dark feels spooky, especially when shining our torches on the water as they eerily light up lots of pairs of eyes.

Brad cooks up another excellent one pot supper and we have a jovial evening sitting around the fire. This has been another incredible day.

10th July

Day 9

In the morning we again explore the gorge which is truly magnificent with walls reaching 100 meters high, I feel I've run out of words to describe the wonder of these amazing places.

This is our last day in the truck and I determine to relish every moment. We haven't been driving long when Brad parks so we can explore Tunnel Creek National Park where there's a huge cave to walk to. Still suffering from yesterday's walking, I can't make my throbbing toe comfortable, stuffing it into my usual walking boots is now out of the question, so I settle for sandals and I manage.

After several hours driving along the Derby Highway we arrive in our final destination, Broome. The total drive according to Brad has been around 3000 kms.

Our tour ends on the wide and long Cable Beach where we carry the 'eski' and relax with some cool beer and wine and watch the sun go down over the Indian Ocean. This is a lovely place to finish our amazing Kimberley tour, chatting, drinking and paddling in the sea. But of course, it doesn't finish here.

One of our group suggests we all meet for dinner in the evening. I don't want to go, but I also don't want to be a 'party pooper'. The venue isn't exceptional, but it's an opportunity to say goodbye to everyone. They're a great bunch of people, I liked them all, but I also realise that I haven't especially 'connected' with anyone.

John and I have booked into the Broome YHA and as it turns out several of our travelling companions are also there, including 'old' John who not only survived the Kimberley tour, but along with some of the others in our group, is continuing onwards for another seven days!

# Broome to Cairns

## 11th July

From the little I've seen so far, Broome is a small, plain, tourist town but we've found an inviting place to eat called The Green Mango café. It was recommended to us and the menu offers a large selection of wholesome organic food. We treat ourselves to a large breakfast. Not far from here is a bicycle hire shop and it seems like a good idea to make use of bikes and save me from walking too much, so we book two for tomorrow.

## 12th July

We collect our hired bikes and cycle a long way on a very boring road, then in an attempt to get off the boring road we turn onto a side road. This smaller road is covered in red sand and impossible to cycle on. The only way is to continue again on the boring road. We eventually arrive at Cable Beach again where we watch rows of camels with brightly coloured blankets giving rides to tourists. And of course, we watch the sunset again over the water before pedalling back.

## 13th July

As we don't have to return the bikes until 11 am, we cycle around the streets of Broome again. I leave John while I pay a visit to a doctor's surgery that I'd noticed yesterday to get advice about my toe. They're very kind and the doctor takes a look but says that there's nothing

I can do but wait for it to heal.

Outside and pottering about on my own in the shopping area, an Aborigine passes me on the pavement and I smile at him. Unlike others, he returns my smile, then asks me the time. I feel oddly pleased that for a brief moment I have the opportunity to 'engage' with an Aborigine. It's difficult to continue a conversation with him because he has a slow, growly voice which I struggle to hear, but I learn that his name is Terry and we shake hands.

Back at the hostel, after a relaxing swim in the pool I get organised for our next adventure. We fly out of Broome tomorrow afternoon and into Cairns

## 14th July

.Aeroplanes from Broome to Perth (2½ hrs), Perth to Brisbane (5½ hrs), Brisbane to Cairns (2½ hrs)

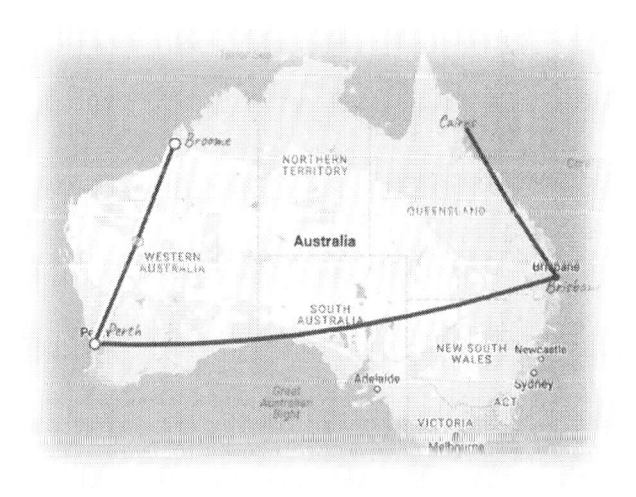

We have several hours to spare before our flight and I have a frustrating time with admin. I need to sort out bank problems and the bank's security systems are desperately frustrating, they ask for information impossible to access away from home. Wi-Fi in Australia has been tricky throughout and it's no more co-operative now. I know I'm being foolish to let technology get me down when I'm in such an enviable place, but sometimes it does makes me feel very upset.

Our destination is Cairns and absurdly we can't fly from Darwin straight there across the top of Australia, we have to go via Perth and Brisbane which means we have three flights all around Oz.

The transition and flight from Broome to Perth is very smooth and here we change to another flight to Brisbane. At Brisbane we change planes again, arriving in Cairns early in the morning. It's been a long journey with nine and a half hours spent on aeroplanes, but luckily, I've slept much of the time. A free bus takes us from the airport to our hostel in Cairns, another YHA, I think John has turned into a backpacker!

## 15th July

Cairns seems like a nice place. It's greener here and more tropical. The weather is dull and there's some light rain. Near our hostel there's a large and colourful market selling wonderfully fresh-looking fruit and veg. I wish I was a chef, I'd have a great time picking the right ingredients to buy. John is in a dull mood, like the weather, and doesn't join in with my enthusiasm for purchasing anything. I buy some vegetables for a stir fry meal and some aromatic strawberries, blueberries and an avocado.

As it happens, the hostel is offering a barbeque this evening for the irresistible price of $5. The stir fry ingredients will keep for tomorrow.

## 16th July

We have a free day and I take the opportunity to catch up on emails and banking but again the Internet is poor and the endeavour is frustrating. John is still in a low mood which is hard to be around and he's bringing me down. It feels ridiculous, we're here in Australia, tomorrow we're going to see the Great Barrier Reef, we should feel excited.

Pottering about the town we come to a small indoor craft market and I have a chat with a guy called Munganbana (Norman) Miller. He's half Aborigine and has a passion for art and aboriginal stories. He's made a book of his paintings called 'Rainforest and Reef Aboriginal Art'. If I could carry it I would buy a copy. I ask John to take a photo of me with Norman and I'll buy the book from his website when I return home.

## 17th July

Today we're going to explore the Great Barrier Reef and I'm relieved that John's black cloud has lifted. We board the 'Sea Star' along with twenty-eight other people. It's a large boat with a very professional looking crew and we're well taken care of with coffee and cake on arrival.

The boat travels about 40 kms at speed on choppy water and my tummy doesn't cope. I'm very glad when we arrive at a sandy dune where we struggle and squeeze ourselves into short wetsuits, snorkel, mask and flippers. My toe is still extremely painful and I don't want to stuff my foot inside the rubber flipper but I'm told that I can't go without wearing two flippers. I grit my teeth and try not to cry as I pull it onto my foot, then jump into the water.

The corals are spectacular in size and variety but disappointing in colour, it's probably the water not being clear that doesn't show off their colours. There's an assortment of fish weaving in and out. John has elected to do a dive (his first) so he's with another group. I thought I'd taken a photo of him and afterwards realise it was someone else – everyone looks alike in wetsuits.

The crew provide a good lunch which I struggle to eat because I still feel queasy, and the boat moves off to another area. This time the snorkelling is even more spectacular. We're out in the water for about an hour and although the experience is wonderful, the sea is cold and the outside air cool and breezy. By the time I get back on board I'm blue and shivering violently. We're given hot tea and cake which helps. During the trip I've met a charming girl called Sophie from Belgium, she's also going to Fiji in a couple of weeks so I give her my contact details.

## 18th July

A miracle has occurred. My toe is much better, the big pain has gone. I wonder if it may have been dislocated after all and shoving it inside the tight flipper yesterday has put it back where it's supposed to be. I feel very grateful.

Today we've joined a one-day tour group called 'Active Tropics Explore' to visit the Daintree area. It starts with a coastal drive to Mossman Gorge "Wurrumbu". Here we're given a 'touristy' welcome by a Kuku Yalanji tribal member who shows us the smoking ceremony, then a small bus takes us to see the gorge.

It's raining which spoils the outlook but doesn't stop some of our group taking a swim in the gorge. Rather them than me, the water is very fast flowing and there are huge rocks. It looks quite treacherous.

Back in our tour van, we drive to the Daintree River where we board a boat which takes us in search of crocs. We're not disappointed, the boatman clearly knows where their regular 'sun bathing' spots are and we see a few.

Moving on, we stop for lunch on Cape Tribulation, a wide, sandy beach with the rainforest as its backdrop. Happily, the rain has stopped and we're given lunch on picnic tables on the beach. The food is a bit reminiscent of school dinners, but this is a wonderful spot to have a picnic.

In the afternoon our guide takes us for a walk into what is billed as 'the oldest living rainforest in the world'. I'm not sure how true that statement is, I've heard other places also make this claim, but it is a World Heritage Listed Rainforest. I know they have to preserve the area and keep people safe, but the paths are so neat and prescriptive and we meander so slowly that the experience is less interesting than I'd expected.

Back in the van our guide takes us to an extraordinary ice-cream parlour at Floravilla where an entrepreneurial lady owner has created a tourist business. There's a fascinating menu of some twenty-six flavours. Her idea to create an ice cream business is more impressive when we realise that there's no running water or electricity in the area.

Our route home requires us to cross the Daintree River and our vehicle drives onto a cable ferry. The sun is just setting and by the time we drive through the town of Port Douglas it's dark.

# Cairns to Brisbane Campervan Trip

## 19th July

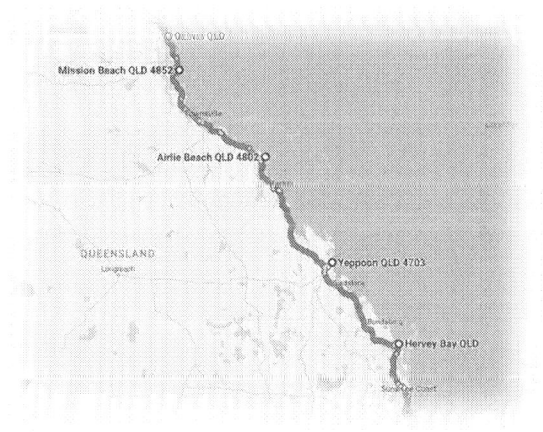

### Day 1 Cairns to Mission Beach (140 kms)

Today we're leaving Cairns to start a Campervan road trip. We take a taxi to Britz Campervan Company to collect our vehicle. I'm relieved that the campervan is quite compact because I wouldn't feel confident driving a massive one. It takes a while to check everything is okay and get our instructions and then we're off, with John driving amid some swearing as he tries to get the SatNav to cooperate. There's rain on the windscreen which doesn't help his mood.

The drive to Mission Beach is straightforward and we easily find the campsite we've pre-booked. After parking, we take a stroll along the beach as night falls and an almost full moon appears right in front of us over the sea. This evening we have our first meal in the campervan, pasta and tomatoes. I love our van, it has everything we need.

## 20th July

### Day 2 Mission Beach to Airlie Beach (510 kms)

My sleep is disturbed in the night by heavy rain. The rain has come in through our open windows and I'm wet.

We set off after an early breakfast. The drive today is long so we stop only for coffee and lunch of left-over pasta and salad. There's some rain along the way and in front of us is a stunning rainbow. It's my first experience driving the campervan and I'm nervous, but the roads are wonderfully clear and I find it's easier than I'd expected.

We have no difficulty finding our campsite called Island Gateway at Airlie Beach and waste no time taking a stroll out along to a marina, although we can't see much because it's now too dark. I cook supper again, Spanish omelette and to my amazement John decides to have a glass of wine. I'm amazed because John hasn't had any alcohol for five years! I'm worried I've driven him to it, but he assures me that it's not me, he simply wants to enjoy wine again.

## 21st July

### Day 3 Airlie Beach

We have a cooked breakfast this morning, one of my favourite things to do when camping. We've decided to stay here another night so we can visit Hamilton Island by ferry tomorrow. I'm not thrilled, because now I've seen more of Airlie Beach, I don't like it much. As it turns out we do have a nice day though. We take a bus into the town, the sunshine's back and I have a swim in the sea while John sunbathes. In the afternoon we walk on Mt Rooper in Conway National Park and climb up high where we can see out across the sea, dotted with small islands.

## 22nd July

### Day 4 Hamilton Island

We get up early to take the very expensive ($125) ferry to Hamilton Island. The island is privately owned and has been made into a resort where 'golf' cars transport people about and there are three local buses. It even has its own airport. It's very pretty, but oddly 'prescriptive' and reminds me of a TV set.

We take a bus to Hill View where we get off and find there's a coffee place. Looking out over the veranda, I think it would be difficult to find a cafe with better views; the sparkling blue ocean, dotted with green islands.

After taking the bus back down to the beach, I hire a snorkel and as I've been told I may see turtles here. The water is rather murky and I don't see much of any sea life so rather than spend too long looking, we decide to take another ferry over to Daydream Island. Luckily, we're in time to catch the 12.35 ferry so we can have a long afternoon here.

This island is also a resort and rather dated looking. We've found a beach called Love Cove which is completely covered in sharp coral, wicked on the feet. Getting into the water barefoot is a mission, either viciously scratchy and hard or really slippery. Determination takes over and I stagger and slither my way into the water. Snorkelling here turns out to be amazing. The coral is vast and plentiful and surrounded by colourful fish, all close to the shore. I don't want to come out but I've become very cold and can't stop shivering so it's time to call it a day.

After pottering further around the island, which doesn't reveal much more to see, we take the ferry back and have dinner at the Sailing Club.

## 23rd July

### Day 5 Airlie Beach to Yeppoon (500 kms)

We're driving another 500 kms to reach Yeppoon. There's hardly any traffic, sometimes we have the road all to ourselves. Along the way we come across a charming tourist information place where they give us a free cup of tea and biscuits and good info. We're able to book our campsite from here too, a relief because campsites are generally full, and in fact we get the last place available.

The drive continues to delight me, the scenery is lovely and there's a gorgeous light. It's a blue-sky day with a few white clouds, hills and mountains in the distance and grasses and trees either side, sometimes we pass large fields of cattle.

We reach our campsite called 'Ponciana' as darkness falls and it's awful. The pitch is a bit of scrubby land next to a garage and just wide enough for the vehicle. It doesn't matter much, we won't be staying another night. There isn't any Wi-Fi here either. At least I have a drinking buddy in John now so we share some wine in the campervan.

## 24ᵗʰ July

### Day 6 Yeppoon

We drive out to the Tourist Information Centre, partly for local information and partly to take advantage of their Wi-Fi. To our delight one of the staff is holding a baby agile wallabee that she's rescued and is nursing, feeding it from a bottle. I pick up a brochure about an animal sanctuary that has koalas and John agrees we can go there as it's only about twenty minutes away.

The sanctuary reminds me of a place back home called Ipsden Zoo where I used to take my children. It's quaint and unsophisticated and I like it. There are birds, reptiles and kangaroos meandering on the grass. We also get to see at last, the elusive Cassowary bird, which looks like a cross between a turkey and an ostrich. Not the sort of creature you want to get too close to as it's one of the world's mostly dangerous birds. And then of course there are the koalas. I pay a daft amount of money for the opportunity to hold a koala but well worth it. His fur is soft and he's as cute as he looks. Used to hugging trees, the koala puts his arms around me as if he's hugging me and I fall in love with him immediately.

Back in our campervan we drive down to the coast and stop for a picnic lunch. This coastline has several long bays connecting with each other and we walk down to what I think may be Rosslyn Bay and walk its length.

Driving to our next campsite we pass some bush fires and whilst they're probably planned fires, they look very dramatic.

In contrast to last evening's campsite this one is beautiful, located by Causeway Lake. I grab some glasses and a bottle of wine and we take it to the lake's edge and watch the sun go down. In the tree next to us I spot two stunning rainbow parakeets, a real treat. This has been a lovely day.

## 25th July

### Day 7 Yeppoon to Hervey Bay (440 kms)

I wish we were staying here longer here. I maximise enjoyment of the campsite by carrying our breakfast back to the lakeside and I'm lucky enough to see the two colourful parakeets in the tree again. One of them is half in and half out of a hollow tree branch and reminds me of a cuckoo clock. I'm filled with the delights of this campsite, the birds are all making noises and the trees are exceptionally beautiful. I suggest to John that before setting off we walk along the Bluff which I saw on the drive in yesterday but he's keen to continue our journey.

To my delight, John changes his mind and says we can do the walk. It's a wonderful 2.4 miles with stunning views of the bays on either side, all in glorious sunshine.

Our drive today turns out to be longer than expected by 100 kms due to a miscalculation, so our comfort breaks are short. Our last stop is for provisions at the local Woolworth's. John finds a parking bay under a covered area and starts reversing into it when a sudden crashing noise brings expletives from his mouth. He's reversed into an unseen metal strut which unfortunately is enough to damage the rear window surround causing the back window to shatter. The incident seems especially bizarre, because on our drive today we passed a vehicle that had been in an accident and I noticed that the rear windscreen had been smashed.

Good fortune has it that we're in a place where John is able to buy some tarpaulin and tape to cover the space where the window should be. Thankfully our campsite, 'Big 4', isn't too far and from here we contact the campervan hire company and get advice how to fix our problem.

Our evening passes amicably with a jacket potato and broccoli meal followed by strawberries with yoghurt and honey and a glass or two of wine.

## 26th July

### Day 8 Hervey Bay

I love coincidences and today I experience a fun one. A man came to fit the new window but said that he couldn't do it because of the dent in the surround, so we have to wait for a specialist campervan 'fixit' person. I go for a walk along the esplanade while John waits for the guy to come.

On the way back from my walk I see a parked van with a trailer advertising that it fixes campervans. A man is sitting in the van so I approach him to have a chat. It turns out that he's the guy meant to come and fix our van, but (and here's the interesting part), he hasn't listened to the messages on his phone yet and doesn't know about us. If I hadn't spoken to him he would have moved on without coming to our aid!

He suggests I hop into the van, but first we have to encourage his gorgeous dog Mia who's occupying the front seat, to take a back seat. We drive straight to our campsite to look at the problem and I laugh at the look of surprise on John's face when I turn up with Adrian, the 'fixit' man. He can't replace the window because of the dent but he'll get some plywood and fit it in later so we'll be able to drive the campervan to Brisbane.

John and I hire bicycles for the afternoon and explore Hervey Bay. There isn't much to see, but we have a nice ride along the esplanade with the sea on the left and large houses along the right. The town isn't amazing either, it has a small beach with a few rocks and not much else. I finish the cycle ride with a very sore backside and wonder, not for the first time, how bicycle saddles are made to be so uncomfortable.

When we arrive back at the campervan Adrian hasn't been to fit the plywood but he has left a message to say he'll come tomorrow. This isn't a big problem because we have a flight to Lady Elliot Island planned, it simply means we'll need to take a taxi to the nearby airport.

## 27th July

### Day 9 Lady Eliot Island

We arrive at Hervey Bay airport and along with about twenty passengers we board the Cessna Caravan plane. John asks the pilot if he can sit at the front and he does. The flight to Lady Eliot Island takes forty minutes. Situated at the southern-most tip of the Great Barrier reef it looks like a beautiful disc sitting in the ocean. Looking out of the plane we spot whales on four separate occasions. They're very far away of course, but it's still exciting to see them.

Arriving on the island we're given a welcome drink and a briefing then we get kitted out with snorkels, flippers and wetsuits and our group is invited to sit in a small glass bottom boat to go looking for marine life.

Within a few minutes we see a green turtle, then a large manta ray, then a shark swims underneath the boat and we can see him through the glass. Further out to sea we see another whale. Back on the beach we can go into the sea to explore with our snorkels. This is a colourful underwater world but although the weather is sunny it's pretty chilly and I feel so cold I can't stay in as long as I'd like to.

Walking further around the island we come to another beach sheltered from the cold wind and while John lies on the beach I snorkel again. It's amazing, fish are everywhere and I'm childishly excited. I could stay here all afternoon, but an enticing buffet lunch has been laid on for us which means having to change out of wetsuits

After lunch we take a walk around the entire island which only takes about forty-five minutes. The shore is clean white sand covered in white dried coral, next to a stunning, aqua blue sea. The photos I take don't do it justice. It's a glorious blue-sky day and I feel lucky to be here.

On the return flight John asks the pilot if I can sit at the front and I enjoy the seascape out of the front windscreen and spot more whales. This has been an exceptional day.

Back at the camp site Adrian has patched up our van for us, so we're good to go to Brisbane tomorrow.

## 28th July

### Day 10 Hervey Bay to Brisbane (285 kms)

It takes more concentration driving without being able to see through the rear of our campervan, but we share the driving and make it to Brisbane. There are no problems handing over our damaged vehicle and the insurance covers the cost.

## Brisbane

Having spent a few nights sleeping in a campervan I thought it would be a treat to have a decent bed and I find the Park Regis Hotel has a room available for $119 instead of $170.

The panorama through the floor to ceiling bedroom windows is stunning, overlooking the Brisbane River and city. The last few days have left us exhausted. They've been fun but have also involved planning, decision-making, driving and patience. We buy ourselves a bottle of Oyster Bay wine and all thoughts of leaving our room in search of a restaurant go out of the window. We eat the bits and pieces of food I'd squirrelled away left over from our trip; fruit, boiled eggs, nuts and granola. A very odd meal.

## 29th July

After a disappointing hotel breakfast, we spend time pottering about in Brisbane, starting in the shopping mall then walking along the South Bank. We stop for a coffee and have a nap lying on the grass in the warm sunshine.

I'd previously learned that a friend of a friend, called Chris, lives in Brisbane. I met her a while ago, and she and her husband have offered to put us up for a couple of days and show us around. Chris very kindly comes to our hotel to take us to her home a few miles away in Nundah, where we meet the rest of the family, Jim and children Kate and Fraser.

## 30th July

I'm up early to go out with Chris and Jim walking their dog along the creek near their house. Later in the morning Chris and Jim, along with Frazer, take us both for a walk up high where there's a lookout and fabulous views across Brisbane. We then drive into the city to take a City Cat boat along the river and see the city from another angle.

In the evening we join some friends of theirs for dinner at an Italian restaurant. It should have been enjoyable but something has gone very wrong and we wait more than two hours for our meals. Everyone is fed up and annoyed by the time the food arrives and it isn't a good evening. I feel sorry for Chris, I think she's feeling uncomfortable although it wasn't her fault.

Frustratingly, I leave my much loved, coral cardigan in the taxi. It's been an absolute favourite and I'm going to miss it.

# *Fiji*

## 31st July

### Aeroplane to Fiji (3½ hrs)

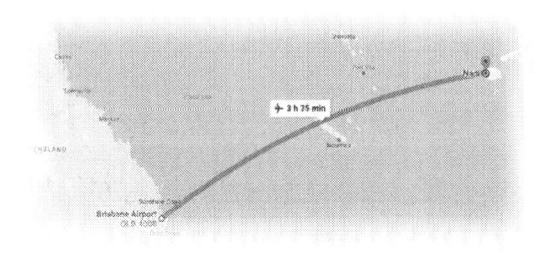

I'm excited. Today we're flying to Fiji. Chris has kindly offered to take us to the airport at 4.30 in the morning!

We land in Nadi International Airport just before midday. John and I are going separate ways in Fiji and it feels strange saying goodbye to him. He's joining a volunteer group and he's greeted at the airport 'arrivals' by his 'pick up'. I'm off to have adventures on my own again. With help from the 'Information Desk' I take a bus that is leaving straight away for the capital, Suva, on the other side of the island.

The bus journey is 200 kms and takes five hours. It's a very pretty ride, mostly along the coast and I keep dozing which is a shame because I want to look at the scenery.

By great good fortune, I have an introduction to the Archbishop of Polynesia and his wife, Sue. They're relatives of a dear friend from home and I've been invited to stay with them.

Fiji is hot and what should have been a ten-minute

walk to their address becomes a twenty-minute one because I take the wrong road. Just as I arrive, wondering if I've found the right house, I see Sue opening the front gate. At about the same time Archbishop Winston also arrives, so there are introductions all around.

I like them both immediately. Sue has made us a delicious meal and we chat, but Winston is clearly exhausted and he goes early to bed. Sue shows me their house, a large, homely, two storey property. The room that will be my bedroom is charming. I feel very grateful and very happy to be here.

## 1st August

There's a two-hour time difference from Australia and I wake up later than I'd intended. It wasn't a quiet night. The house is on a corner of a busy junction; my bedroom has windows on two sides and the traffic noises go on all night.

For lunch, Winston takes us both out to a vegetarian Indian meal but he's a very busy man and it isn't long before he leaves us to go to some meetings.

Sue and I go to the local cathedral and she introduces me to some ladies who are hand block printing fabric. I'm fascinated watching them. The cotton looks beautiful and I buy some that's printed white on purple, to show support.

Later in the day, Winston comes to pick me up and take me to St Christopher's Children's home in Nakasi where I might work as a volunteer. I had previously asked Sue if she can suggest some voluntary work I can do as I'd like to help in some way after the devastation of Hurricane Winston which hit Fiji earlier in the year.

After showing me around the home, Winston goes to a meeting and I have to wait for him. It goes on a very long time and I'm kicking my heels most of the afternoon. Fortunately, I have my electronic reader with me which helps to pass the time. I'm not feeling very excited about working at the children's home and whilst I could tell Winston this, I do want to be of use in the short time I'm here, so I think I'll give it a go and see what comes of it. I have faith it will teach me something. I think it odd that I'll be working with children again.

Winston and I eventually make it home to a rather cross Sue who hadn't been informed that we'd be late. I find it entertaining being with this endearing couple in their marital grumblings, Winston has a charming and gentle way of 'managing' Sue. I feel very comfortable sitting in their kitchen, eating a tasty home-made veg soup, accompanied by the cheese and bread I'd bought on the way home.

I go to bed feeling excited that I'm back on my 'adventures' again.

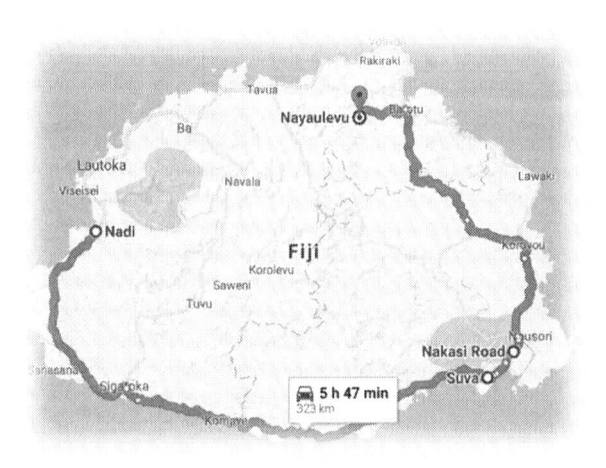

## 2nd August

## Volunteering at St. Christopher's Children's Home

It's hard to realise I've only been here two days as it feels longer. I have breakfast with Sue and Winston then walk the ten minutes into Suva town centre to buy some new sandals. The sole is coming off the ones I bought on my first day in India and they're also embarrassingly smelly.

After lunch, Archbishop Winston drives me back to St. Christopher's. It's been agreed that I'll work here as a volunteer until 14th August. I have a slightly heavy heart, this isn't what I was hoping for, but I'll get stuck in and do my best to be of use.

The home is located a forty-five minute drive from Suva in a residential area. The roads are wide, with one storey dwellings on either side and there's a parade of shops, a post office and a couple of supermarkets a ten-minute walk away.

When we arrive, most of the children are still at school, so I familiarise myself with the library and meet random people about the place. There's Merri who looks after 'the baby'; Naomi who's visiting from Tonga, and Anna, the cook. The home is basic but clean and painted in cheerful colours and surrounded by lawn and gardens.

When the children arrive back from school, I introduce myself and fetch a box of books to help some of them with their reading. We sit outside the kitchen at large wooden tables. There are about twenty-five children aged between six and sixteen, all very polite and friendly. I'm very grateful that English is the main language in Fiji, so communicating isn't a problem. Food however, might be a challenge. Our meal this evening is boiled cabbage and rice, but at least it's a vegetarian meal.

## 3rd August

I've been given a basic, small bedroom with accompanying bathroom which is perfectly fine but doesn't have hot water. I won't be taking many showers, the weather here feels warm during the day but cold morning and evening.

I'm up early to walk with the children to school. Sister Kalo asks me if I'll stop off at the bakers and buy four chicken pies. I'm grateful that the children can show me which shop I'm supposed to get them from. Returning with the pies there's much merriment because Sister Longo says she's very happy to see me, but from the hilarity around the table I'm guessing that she's more happy to see the pies which, it seems, are for breakfast.

At 9 am Sister Kalo shows me an archive office room and gives me some files to put away. Exploring the contents of the cabinet I realise they're in need of organising, so I spend the morning putting the files in order.

Early in the afternoon Naomi asks me if I want to come shopping for material with her, which I do. Naomi is probably in her thirties and I find her highly entertaining. First, we call on the home of a dressmaker who doesn't appear at all pleased to see us and only talks in Fijian which we can't understand, so although we can tell from her tone that she's grumbling, we don't know what she's saying. Our pleas that she speaks in

English are to no avail, even though Naomi is sure she can speak English.

We abandon the dressmaker and go to the fabric shop where Naomi chooses some brightly coloured cloth. I can't make out what she wants it made into, some sort of shirt-come-dress. We also get some provisions from the supermarket. Outside, a man is selling coconuts so I pay for two and he cracks them open for us to drink one each.

On the way back, we meet up with the children just out from school so Naomi asks one of them who speaks Fijian, to go back to the dressmakers with her and be an interpreter.

Back at the home I read with some of the children and hope to take them into the library but the Sisters want to go out and have made other plans, so there's nothing useful for me to do. Feeling frustrated, I step outside for a walk around the neighbourhood.

## 4th August

Today is sunny and I walk with the children to school at 7.15 am. They're getting to know me now and I enjoy chatting with them.

This coming weekend I have the opportunity to travel with a group of ladies from the Anglican Church. They're taking aid to a village in central Fiji that was devastated by Hurricane Winston. I want to take some food for them so, advised by Sue, I go to the supermarket to buy large tins of meat and fish.

I need to get back to the Bishop's house and Sister Longo tells me that she has to drive there anyway and she's willing to give me a lift. I'm glad to be back. Winston and Sue are both there and seem pleased to see me.

In the afternoon I walk down to the sea and along the path into Suva to buy vegetables from the market and a mop head for Sue.

Suva is incredibly busy and although the market is excitingly large and full of vegetable stalls, the crowds of people make me feel stressed. The supermarket is even worse, I don't think I've ever seen one as busy as this and I'm very glad when I find the required mop head and I can leave.

In the evening I get ready for the trip to Maniava. Sue and Winston will take me to meet the other ladies at the bus stop at the unsociable hour of 5.30 am.

## 5th August

The bus doesn't arrive until 6 am and I'm amazed to learn that some of the women have been standing waiting since five o'clock. It's still very dark. The bus is packed with large, boisterous Fijians, Tongans and Indians, about sixty-five ladies in total. I'm very happy to be with them. There's noisy chatter and laughter and the ladies sing gospel hymns which I join in with when I can.

The drive takes about four hours and the ever-changing scenery is fascinating. As we pass little dwelling places and villages, there's evidence of the hurricane where it has ripped trees out of the ground or stripped them of their leaves, and we see Unicef tents and tents from P.R. China being used as make-shift homes.

The bus turns off the road onto a narrow, bumpy, dirt lane, seemingly in the middle of nowhere, surrounded by lush green fields with hills and mountains in the distance. We pass a few dwellings and a school which I'm told is the one the Maniavan children attend. This must be a very long walk for them because the bus drives for another half hour before reaching the village.

When we finally come to a stop I'm entranced. The tiny village is set in a green bowl, surrounded by fertile land, trees and mountains. It all looks immaculately kept with cut grass surrounding each dwelling and planted shrubs and bushes. There are no paths or roads in the village, only grass.

A group of colourfully dressed villagers warmly welcome us and after off-loading people and goods from the bus we're invited to sit under some striped awnings and we're handed platefuls of home-made bread, cakes, pancakes and sweetmeats, together with a cup of lemon leaf tea.

Another mini-bus arrives as well as a truck, so we become a large crowd of about a hundred people, including the villagers. This is a lot of people to feed but there's plenty of food. It seems odd to me that the villagers are giving to us so generously when we've come to bring food to them and presumably ease some of their difficulties.

By this time I'm desperate for a toilet. Fijian ladies must have amazing bladders, I didn't see anyone appear to dash for a toilet when leaving the bus. I'm very grateful when I make enquiries to be unexpectedly shown a western toilet in an outhouse.

A long thanksgiving service takes place under the awning, with many people getting up and saying prayers or giving a talk, mostly in Fijian, all interspersed with hymns, beautifully sung. Some ladies from the village sing a hymn as a group. I find it very emotional and then a beaming Nun accompanies everyone on the guitar while we sing.

Walking around the village, I can see that thirty-two of the thirty-four dwellings destroyed by the hurricane have now been replaced with make-shift corrugated shelters which are neat and well organised. Some years ago, I lived in a hamlet that, by coincidence, also had 34 houses and I tried to imagine how it would feel if one day 32 of them, including mine, were destroyed.

I'm followed by a gaggle of giggling children and two seem to have taken a shine to me. They each hold one of my hands as I walk about. Nearby is a small river and waterfall and we go there with some of the women. I have fun taking photos and the children love posing for me.

I can't face lunch which is copious amounts of chicken and rice and hope no-one thinks me rude. Instead I play with the children and take photos. After lunch a man on a horse brings a couple of guitars along and a few people gather to make more music. I'm amused to notice a ukulele being played, it's battered and broken and doesn't have a full quota of strings but this doesn't seem to faze the musician playing it.

Around this time a brew called Kava is brought out. It's the colour of mud and I'm invited to try it. It tastes very earthy and leaves my mouth feeling slightly numb, like I've used an antiseptic mouthwash. After drinking the Kava everyone becomes even more jolly and several people stand up and dance, myself included, much to the delight of the onlookers who clap and laugh.

I have an interesting brief encounter with a young man called Jerome. He's also visiting the village and he has a very inspiring story to tell. He comes from an educated and wealthy family but during the 2009 recession, after some bad financial business decisions, his father lost everything, including their home. His parents didn't cope well with this and (long story short),

Jerome and his brother had to leave their parents and take care of themselves. He was only sixteen years old at this time! He tells me how tough this period was for him. For a while he and his brother are looked after by another family and during this time he 'finds' God and joins the Anglican Church.

Jerome has a fantastic, positive attitude and, like me, he believes in the 'Law of Attraction'. He has some great examples of how things work out for him. He's learned to ask for what he wants and he always asks for the best. When he needed a laptop, he asked God to provide an Apple Mac and less than a month later, a visiting Professor who had recently bought himself a brand-new Apple laptop, gave his previous one to Jerome.

Jerome has other amazing tales to tell too, all music to my ears. Like the time he and his brother had to leave the first family that had taken them in. They had nowhere to go and Jerome asked God to provide. On the day they had to leave, another family invited the boys to live with them. He had never met this family or known of them and they already had four daughters, which makes it even more amazing that they invited two boys to stay in their home. He's now been living with this family for the past three years.

Back at the bus and surrounded by waving villagers, we leave around 3 pm. The ride home is even more wonderful because the mist that had covered the mountains this morning has cleared and the scenery is stunning. I'm lucky to be sitting in the front of the bus and surprised the seat is available since I'm one of the last to get on.

The drive home is very long with only one stop for a leg stretch. The only available public toilet is disgusting but needs must. I buy a cauliflower from a street seller which will be lunch tomorrow. On the outskirts of Suva the driver stops no less than eight times to allow various passengers to get off. It's dark now and I'm tired. I'm wondering how I'll get back to Sue and Winston's home when a lady called Anni invites me to share a taxi with her.

Back at the Bishop's house, Sue is there but Winston is staying overnight in Nadi. I tell Sue my tales of Maniava, whilst eating her delicious pumpkin soup.

## 6th August

A day of frustration. I'm pleased to have the day at the Archbishop's house and time to use their good Internet, but today my computer is having none of it. It tells me *'the DNS server can't be found'*. It's raining and would have been the perfect opportunity to catch up on emails. I give in graciously, I'm not going to allow technology to spoil my day. Then I get a 'bonus', my son sends me a message, I'm able to call him back on my mobile and have a chat and I'm very happy to catch up with his news. Technology *can* be wonderful.

When I left the village of Maniava I was given a huge bundle of watercress and feel I must use it. The only thing I can think of is watercress soup so I make a large saucepan of it while Sue is out. We have some for tea, along with a cauliflower cheese I've made with the cauliflower bought from the street-seller on yesterday's journey home.

## 7th August

It's still raining, which makes me realise how incredibly lucky we were to have good weather on Saturday in

Maniava.

I have an idea to get the photos printed that I took of the village and find a photo shop in town that can do this for me. I buy an album to put them in and a 'thank you' card. When the pictures are placed in the album I'm delighted with the result. They really show the smiles, cheerfulness and colour of the day. I give the album to Sue who says she'll make sure it reaches Maniava.

While I'm out I buy a tin of coconut milk which I want to add to the watercress soup. I think it will make it much tastier and that proves to be the case. I'm especially happy because Winston walks into the kitchen during lunch and I'm able to give him some. He says he likes it. I have to laugh, who would ever have thought I'd be serving my home-made watercress soup to the Archbishop of Polynesia in Fiji!

Talking with Sue and Winston I'm excited to learn of a prayer written by Winston and produced by the Rev. James Bhagway. I'm able to find it on 'YouTube'. It's called 'A Prayer for the Moana' (Ocean), written and read by The Most Reverend Archbishop Winston Halapua of the Diocese of Polynesia, Anglican Church of Aotearoa / New Zealand.

This is the last time I'll see Sue and Winston as I'm going back to St. Christopher's. I had planned to take a taxi but Winston insists on driving me. He's just driven four hours from Nadi in the rain and I feel bad that he has to come out again. He's a very kind man.

When the time comes to say goodbye I'm not sure if it's okay to hug an Archbishop, but I do anyway. I've found him to be a very endearing man. Both of them have made me feel very welcome in their home. Sue doesn't spend any money on herself, she's very charitable, so I leave some money in an envelope on my bed for them with a note saying I'd like them to spend it on themselves, maybe have dinner out. This has come from my heart and I do hope it will be received well. It seems to me that where money is concerned we always have to be careful not to offend.

Back at St. Christopher's, the children are home from school and playing with a football or sitting on the front porch. I seem to be the only adult around. I'm reading a book with Samson when I hear a smashing of glass and in true classic cartoon style the football has smashed through the kitchen window. Mohammad, without any shoes on dives under the table to retrieve some broken glass and comes out with a piece lodged in his big toe. It bleeds dramatically so I locate the medicine box to get some bandages. I also find a tube of aloe vera in the box, perfect for healing wounds. I'm feeling very responsible that this happens when the children are in my care, but when Sister Kalo hears about it later she appears entirely unperturbed.

After supper, I spend time with two of the older girls who can play the guitar, showing them some chords on the uke. They play it easily and I'm envious of their excellent strumming style. Then I help Mileva with some homework on the topic of 'Aids'.

## 8th August

Sister Kalo has suggested that I spend time with little Milli, helping her learn to read. I think she's probably around four years old. She's as cute as a button, very cheeky and knows her own mind. She looks at picture books with me for a short while then decides she's had enough. There's nothing I can do to persuade her otherwise. She won't learn from me if she isn't interested, so I fetch my ukulele instead. This entertains her for a brief while and she likes strumming it but has no interest in being shown how. No activity I suggest captures her interest, she has more fun running from me and hiding. I think she's probably pretty smart and she certainly knows how to 'manage' me.

## 9th August

The rain is still coming down hard and has been for several days. I'm doing more admin and need to go into town to buy sticky tape. There aren't any footpaths and the rain water runs along the road like a stream, each time a truck passes by I get absolutely drenched and by the time I return to the home I'm soaked through to my knickers.

Sister Kalo has asked me to make a meal, she says she wants to eat the food I eat and the only thing I can think of cooking, with the ingredients available, is lentil pie. I have to use yellow split peas instead of lentils and there isn't any cheddar cheese available, but I do my best and it looks okay. We have the pie for lunch and then I'm completely thrown because Sister Kalo says can she have whatever I have for supper. I ask if omelette will be okay and she's fine with that, so I produce a tomato omelette with broccoli. I hadn't expected to be cooking for a nun as well as an Archbishop.

In the evening I help Vini with her reading. She's very keen and after struggling through three books she wants to read a fourth. I wish there were more books in the children's rooms, they're all desperate to read and love looking at the books but they're not allowed to keep them in their dorm. I decide to leave the ones I've brought with me and put them back in the library tomorrow.

I love the time I have on my own in my room and spend it doing yoga, learning Spanish and sending messages to friends and family. I do wish there was hot water though, I'm feeling too chilly for a cold shower. Maybe I'll boil a kettle tomorrow.

## 10th August

I'm going for a run. I'm very happy. I thought the rain had stopped, but when I go outside it's still coming down. Running down the drive I notice the gate is locked with its big chain and padlock, but on checking it realise it only *appears* to be padlocked, I can open it. My previously injured toe hurts more than I'd expected, but I'm still not thwarted. I only run for about twenty minutes, but I'm pleased with myself anyway.

I have a busy day. The Sisters go out and I'm left in charge of the phone and I've been asked to remove old files from a filing cabinet and sort them into different piles, one to archive and one to destroy.

When the Sisters come back they've brought a pumpkin so I make us all pumpkin soup. I add skinned tomatoes, onion, garlic, oregano, fresh parsley and roast the pumpkin first. Turning it into soup takes ages because there isn't a liquidiser, but the result is worth it, the soup is very tasty.

While I'm cooking, Illy comes into the kitchen. She's in her twenties and has been in the home for years. She spends her time wandering about and doesn't come to any classes, her head seems to be in another world. She wants to wash her hands and I turn on the taps for her. Then I take a tea towel and pat her hands dry. Illy smiles at me and says *"just like Mummy"*. It's a heart-stopping moment for me and I wonder what happened and where her mummy is now.

I read three more books with Vani, it's intriguing to me that she hasn't got the connection of sounds and how they make the words. I now realise that she hasn't been understanding *how* to read the words, she's mostly been remembering them. I've found a couple of books I think will be ideal to help her and will give her encouragement. If I keep going I'm sure the 'penny will drop' but I'm afraid we'll run out of time. Samson asks me to read to him at bedtime, he's a sweet boy. Roko comes and sits with us too, they're so very endearing.

## 11<sup>th</sup> August

I have another short run this morning. It doesn't feel so good today. I'm disappointed that the weather is still dull and there's some drizzly rain. After my run I go into the kitchen and see Anna. She's cooking and offers me some breakfast. I sit with her on the floor and we eat a delicious meal of roti with potatoes and vegetables.

The Sisters are out all morning so I man the phone again apart from a quick trip to the post office and bank to cash a cheque for the weekly wages.

During the afternoon a lady called Stephanie comes into the dining room to work on her computer, she has an external Wi-Fi thing and says I can borrow it. I'm really excited to get on line though my joy doesn't last long because it seems the world and his wife need attention. There are several phone calls and a bunch of people call in to see the Sisters and they're disappointed that they're out. It happens every now and then that random people call in with gifts of food and supplies for the home but a shame that they generally bring in the same things. The stores are filled with dozens of bags of rice, lentils and sweets.

I hear a vehicle pull up and go to the front to see who has arrived. A lady from Social Welfare gets out of the car, along with a small girl she introduces as Zafira. Without any warning, she's brought this young child to stay at the home. She leaves Zafira with me saying she'll phone Sister Kalo later. I'm very taken aback by this. I crouch down to Zafira's height and give her a hug at which point she bursts into tears and hugs me so tight my heart melts. Fortunately, a cat that visits the home from time to time turns up and for a while Zafira is distracted stroking and cuddling the cat. I fetch some books and we sit reading until Sister Kalo returns.

I haven't seen Tongan Naomi around for a few days and learn that she's been ill. I notice her coming out of her room and ask if she's feeling better. She says *"no, I'm not better"* so I reply *"oh, that's bad"* and she says *"no, it's not bad, its good, because it's a part of my life"*. I found her reply intriguing.

In the evening I again help Vani to read and I'm delighted with her progress, she seems more confident and is able to read a few more words without prompting. The boys want me to read to them too, so I do and I'm surrounded by all four of them, Roko, Samson, Mohammed and Philippe.

## 12th August

Today is a very big day for Fiji. The final of the Rugby 7's in the Brazilian Olympics is being played and Fiji are in the final against Great Britain. What are the chances! Here I am in Fiji and they're playing G.B. Fiji have never had a gold medal in an Olympic event before and now they have a strong chance. Everyone is super excited. The TV is put on in the Sisters' lounge and the children and a dozen other people pile in and arrange themselves on the floor. The game is very exciting and short. The Fijians score very quickly and the room erupts with jubilation. Every time Fiji score points, the folk who know I'm from Britain look at me, but I'm happy for them, my heart wants the lovely Fijians to win. The score finishes with Fiji on 43 and G.B on 7 amid much leaping up and down and shouts of joy from the spectators.

This is my last day at St. Christopher's. I'm feeling tearful saying goodbye to the staff. Anna in the kitchen cries easily and I don't want to say a long goodbye to her so I pick a time when she's busy cooking and give her an envelope with $50 in it. It feels right to give her something, she's a single mum with a very big heart (I put that bit in the accompanying note).

I help out generally during the day and take a group of children to the library for an hour and a half where we read together. I'm interested to notice how easily Zafira, who only arrived yesterday, appears to have fitted in. She's playing with the other children and seems very at ease. Children are amazing.

I'm asked to join everyone for prayers at 7pm in the Sister's living room and the children sing two hymns for me with Shalini playing the guitar. I feel very 'touched'. Sadly, Sister Kalo isn't here today because it's her day off, but Sister Longo is generous in her 'thank you' message and gives me a gift of two Fijian bags. Leaving is harder than I thought it would be because I've fallen in love with the children.

## 13th August

## Bus from Suva to Nadi (200 kms)

Sister Kalo drives me into Suva in the dark at 5.30 am to get the bus for Nadi. It's ready and waiting. The ride is a pleasant four hours and for once I'm sitting on the correct side of the bus to see the coast, although my attention is diverted when a young Japanese guy sits next to me. He's keen to chat, but it's quite challenging for me to understand his conversation because he has a Japanese accent and a stutter. When he gets off the bus, a young Indian lady sits next to me and she's keen to chat too.

I want to go to Wailoaloa and the conductor tells me I'll need to get off at the airport and he charges me an extra dollar. Then half way into the journey a different conductor gets on the bus and this one says I need to get off at Nadi Central and he gives me back my dollar.

I get out at the bus station in Nadi Central and find a bus stop which says Wailoaloa, but the guy at the Information kiosk doesn't know when the next bus is due, I could be waiting for hours. When a taxi driver asks me if I need a taxi I decide to take the easy route and I say *"maybe"*. He wants me to pay twelve dollars but I tell him I'll come with him if he makes it ten and he agrees.

My accommodation, called Beach Escape Villas is surprisingly nice. Surprising because the cost is only £7 a night. I have a relaxing time walking along the nearby beach and watching the sun go down.

The evening meal I order at the Villas takes a very, very long time to come but I'm in no hurry, it doesn't matter and it turns out to be worth the wait. A delicious meal of aubergines cooked in coconut milk.

Cara is the owner of the Villas and she invites me to join her. She's sitting with the musicians, two guitarists. One of them is called Sunny, we'd chatted earlier when he noticed my uke and he urges me to play. I really don't want to, I'm very embarrassed by my lack of skill, but I also don't want to disappoint them. After giving a brief rendition, one of the guitarists asks to have a go and I'm relieved to hand the uke to someone who can do it justice.

Everyone is sipping Kava and I have another small cup to see if it tastes any better than my previous experience. It doesn't. Cara is an interesting lady. She's from Australia and came to Fiji on a visit several years ago, she loved the place so much she gave up her life in Oz to start a business here.

14th August

John has arrived in Wailoaloa today, he's booked an up-market hotel nearby and suggests I join him. I'm reluctant to leave my fun accommodation, but the thought of a private room is appealing and of course I do want to meet up with John.

His hotel is disappointing, it lacks atmosphere and is a long walk from the beach. Even the restaurant is disappointing, there aren't any vegetarian options on the menu. We enjoy a glass of wine each and swap stories of our volunteering work. Just as we're thinking of walking down to the beach a monsoon rain storm comes 'out of the blue' so we have to wait. Fortunately, it stops in time for us to buy an ice-cream and head to the beach to watch the sun go down on my last evening in Fiji.

# New Zealand

15th August

Aeroplane to New Zealand (3hrs)

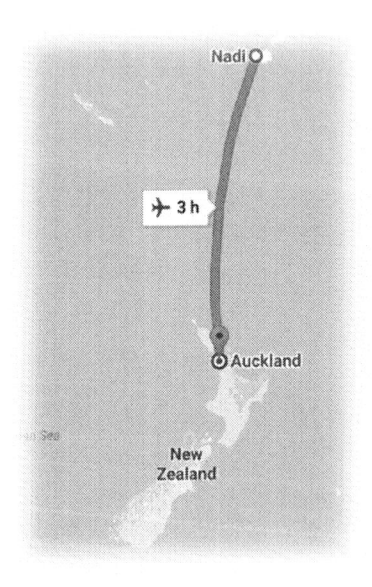

I'm leaving Fiji today ahead of John and we'll link up again later in New Zealand. The hotel offers a complimentary transfer to the airport from the hotel but I've been waiting for twenty minutes and the taxi still hasn't arrived. The receptionist tells me my taxi is here, he was late because he had to pick up bread for the hotel along the way but the bread wasn't ready. I'm amused, they're clearly on 'Fijian' time.

I make it to the airport in time although it's a rush and I grab a cup of coffee on my way through to

'Departures'. I'm perplexed that I'm not allowed to take a newly purchased sealed bottle of water on board the plane, but I *am* allowed to take my hot cup of coffee.

It's around midday when I arrive in Auckland airport. I change my Fijian cash for NZ dollars and buy a local SIM so I have a New Zealand phone. In a couple of days, I'm going to meet up with my good friend Carole, so I send a text to say I'm in NZ and to check the new SIM is working.

Getting a bus into Auckland is easy and it's a short walk to the YMCA hostel. I'm amused that YMCA stands for Young Men's Christian Association, I'm none of those! The hostel is excellent; clean and modern but lacking in atmosphere and I'm annoyed to learn that they don't offer free Wi-Fi. The 'Law of Attraction' is working for me though because when maintenance can't fix the broken handle on my bedroom window, the hostel provide me with free Wi-Fi to compensate.

How lucky that I've got Wi-Fi, an email has 'flown' in from Ben just twenty minutes ago, courtesy of his sister. I whack off a reply quickly in the hope he'll receive it straight away. Yay, I'm still on his radar.

It's now late afternoon and I walk downhill into the town to explore and find food. I'm aware that I'm again back in 'normal' land.

I haven't lost my love of tall buildings with a view, so I go to the Sky City Tower, an impressive 600 feet high. I sit somewhere near the top floor with a meal and a coffee, watching the sun go down over Auckland. The views are spectacular. At the entrance to the tower there's a Tourist Information office so I go in and buy a bus pass which will give me several hours of travel around New Zealand.

## 16th August

I savour the bliss of a leisurely lie-in, the bed is very comfy and there's only one other girl sharing the dorm, so it's peaceful.

Tomorrow I'm taking a bus to the Bay of Islands and because I like to check out bus locations before walking with my backpack, I stroll back into town to find it.

This is a beautiful day and I wander down to the port and dock area. This part of Auckland is very attractive, the area has been modernised and some of the old docks have been turned into trendy bars and cafes. There are some unusual large wooden sunbeds and seating that have been made from wooden wheeled pallets, presumably originally used to move cargo around. They look very cool. I also like an old container that has been turned into a 'book swap' store. It has trendy chairs outside and people are sitting in the sunshine reading the books. Such a good idea.

## 17ᵗʰ August

## Bus to Paihaia (250 kms)

The InterCity bus from Auckland to Paihaia leaves around 7 am. It's an enormous double-decker with very bouncy suspension and sitting upstairs I feel very queasy as the ride takes us through rolling green hills and forests. We arrive in Paihaia around mid-day. My hostel, the Haka Lodge, is right across the road, opposite the bus stop.

I can't believe how gorgeous the hostel is, right across the road from the sea, with stunning views through amazing floor to ceiling windows all across the living room wall. It's comfortable and has a well-equipped kitchen area and a cosy bedroom, such a contrast from the YMCA in Auckland.

Today is another gloriously sunny one and I'm not going to waste it so I go for a long walk along the bay. I'd seen a waterfall marked on a map and hope to reach it, but I've already walked further than I'm expecting. The path, through trees, is rather lonely and I start feeling uncomfortable. I don't want to still be in the trees when it gets dark so I decide to turn back.

At the hostel I discover good 'free food' in the fridge; eggs, cheese and potatoes, perfect for an omelette. It's a lovely idea some hostels have; when guests are leaving, they can donate their unused food to a 'free food' shelf for other travellers to use. I'm very excited to have good Wi-Fi here too. I'm in touch with my good friend Alan who lives in Matamata (Middle Earth) and I hope I can visit him while I'm in New Zealand.

## 18th August

I'm really enjoying soaking up the warm sunshine in Paihaia. Nearby, a ferry boat crosses the water to a place called Russell so I hop on board. Russell has a charming sort of 'old colonial' feel to it and a lovely walk takes me up high with amazing views. There's time for me to have a glass of wine before catching the ferry boat back and I find a quaint hotel on the front that will let me take my glass down to the water's edge. Sitting with a delicious cold Sauvignon Blanc, the sky changes to magnificent yellows and orange. A couple of young boys are playing in the water. This is so idyllic.

On the ferry back to Paihaia a perfectly round moon decorates the sky behind the boat, a magical sight.

## 19th August

### Bus to Whangarei (100 kms)

Getting the bus from Paihaia to Whangarei where Carole will meet me is easy; it stops over the road from my hostel and the journey is under an hour and a half. Arriving in the town I'm excited to see Carole with her four-year old grandson, Jarvis, walking towards the bus stop. The last time we were together was many years ago in England.

Sitting in a coffee shop by the harbour we catch up on each other's news. Carole is staying in Whangerai to look after her two grandsons while her daughter and husband are away for the weekend. The weather here is unexpectedly cold and walking around the town feels chilly, so I'm glad when the time comes to meet Jacob from school. Jacob is six years old and I like seeing how well the two brothers get on with each other. I've brought them each a gift of a small wooden robot with moveable arms and legs and their enjoyment of the toys surpasses my expectation.

Back in the warmth of Carole's daughter's home, we open a bottle of New Zealand wine and settle in for the evening.

## 20th August

The weather is not kind, it's raining hard and poor Carole has to take Jacob to play rugby with his school. I'm content to stay home and play games with Jarvis.

## 21st August

The weather is kinder today and we're taking the boys out. Carole drives along the coast to a rainforest where we walk, play hide and seek and feed the ducks along a river. Afterwards we drive further on to a vast, sandy beach which looks very beautiful because of the late afternoon light. There are sand dunes and grasses behind the beach and we have fun with the boys.

## 22nd August

Carole's 'babysitting' duties end today and after dropping Travis off at his Kindy (Kindergarten) she's taking me up to Kaimaumau, in the far north, where she lives with her partner.

We have a two-and-a half-hour drive and we stop on the way for a coffee in Kawakawa. Carole tells me this town is now famous for its toilets. Really? A visit to the Public Toilets reveal the explanation; the tiles around the whole toilet area were designed by a famous artist called Friedensreich Hundertwasser and they're crazy and spectacular.

We continue our drive through lovely scenery and as we turn down the road where Carole lives with her partner, it's a real 'wow' moment. Their large house is situated on the curve of a bay and the sea is on three sides, so there are incredible views from most of the windows.

We take a walk along the sandy beach which stretches for miles and there's no-one else on it. The sea is a gentle aqua blue colour and there are coloured seashells all along the shore. What a fantastic place to live.

## 23rd August

We leave Kaimaumau early because Carole has to go to work at Ahipara School where she's employed as their bursar. Happily for me, she also 'manages' a rental property on Tasman Heights and we're allowed to stay there for a couple of days while the house is empty. This is a stunning property with a large, open veranda and views of the surrounding hills with Ninety Mile Beach below stretching into the distance. It's all elegantly furnished and very comfortable.

I'm very content being here while Carole goes to work and could happily have stayed on the balcony in the sunshine drinking coffee all morning. It's been agreed that I'll go walking with Carole's friend Karen, who lives further up the hill. We met many years ago during my first visit to New Zealand. Karen and her husband are lovely people and invite me to have lunch with them on their own scenic veranda, which also has stunning views overlooking the beach.

After lunch, Karen and I walk down the road to the beach, then along the shore and around the coast. I love the walk on the sand and the rocks which are fairly flat. Occasionally a 4 x 4 vehicle drives past us, or we see someone standing near their car with a fishing rod in the sea. I find it odd seeing cars on the beach.

Karen and I are walking along casually chatting when I realise there's a seal in front of me. He's small and alone and Karen tells me that sometimes young seals get separated from the group because they don't have the energy or strength to keep up, and it's unlikely to live. It's a sad sight, but there's nothing we can do.

We walk a long way until we come to some massive creamy coloured sand dunes, and I mean massive! They soar up towards the sky. Walking up the dune is really hard work but funny, each step takes me up a little with a small slide down a little. I concentrate on putting one foot in front of the other without looking up and when I do raise my head I'm disappointed that I'm still only half way. With continuous plodding we make it to the top, hot and sweaty but now we've come out onto the most amazing landscape.

There's sand as far as I can see, with amazing sand sculptures and patterns, shaped by the wind. The sand is a creamy custard colour and with the bright blue sky behind it looks stunning. We walk to a 'rocky' outcrop and to my astonishment Karen pulls a flask of coffee out of her rucksack. She laughs at my surprise and says she's known for bringing coffee with her wherever she walks. It's wonderful to sit in such an extraordinary place drinking coffee.

This area is also the site where ancient Kauri trees once grow and every now and then we find a stick or part of a branch. They're a pastel creamy/grey colour and very smooth from being sand blasted and when I hold a piece in my hand it blows my mind to realise they're thousands of years old. I love pottering about here, the place is extraordinary. I'm very grateful Karen has shown me this.

Making our way down the sand dune feels weird because there's an almost vertical drop and the beach is very far down below. I've coped pretty well so far with my still poorly toe, but as we start walking again it feels very uncomfortable. When Karen tells me that it will take us about an hour to walk back I feel my heart sink.

A moment later a tractor pulling a trailer drives past and a guy on the back shouts *"would you like a lift?"*. I yell *"yes"*, possibly a little too hastily since I didn't even look to see Karen's response. We both clamber on in an ungainly fashion because the trailer is high and hang on tight. The drive across rocks and sand is very bumpy and uncomfortable on my backside but I don't mind a bit, at least my painful toe can have a rest.

I'm amazed to realise how far we'd come along the beach and in truth if we hadn't been given a lift I think we would have been walking for more like an hour and a half to get home.

## 24th August

This morning I'm having my hair cut and coloured. It occurred to me that Carole will know a local hairdresser and I want to take advantage of the opportunity. The 'salon' is in a garage attached to the house, not exactly salubrious, but she does a good job and I'm pleased with the result.

Afterwards I stroll back up the hill to Karen and Greg's home as she's invited me to join her on another walk while Carole is working. Karen suggests we take a drive over to the other side of the peninsula so she can show me around. I'd prefer to stay here and gently ask if there isn't somewhere more local we can walk, but Karen has already planned the trip, so along with a large flask of coffee, we set off in her car.

The drive seems long and when we come to the peninsular on the other side Karen drives up and down small roads and in and out of the bays to show them to me. I'm keen to get out of the car and walk and eventually we take a short walk to a bay where we sit and have the coffee. The weather seems to reflect my mood, it's grey and flat with quite a cold wind. Back in the car Karen takes us to another bay and concerned that we'll be driving about all day, I ask if we can get out and walk, which to my relief, we do.

After crossing some marshy grassland we come to a beach and I can't believe my eyes. I've come to shell heaven. The beach is covered with some of the prettiest shells I've ever seen, masses of them and gorgeous colours of pinks, yellows and blues. I would love to scoop them up and fill my pockets. I say a prayer of thanks to the Universe for showing me this incredible sight and a thank you to Karen for bringing me here. The sunshine has come back now too.

Karen drops me back at the house and I just have time for a shower and a quick bite to eat when Carole comes home. She throws herself through the door and says *"can we go for a walk along the beach?"*. There's some light rain and we take a fast-paced march along the shore line of Ninety Mile Beach. Carole clearly needs to expend some energy.

Karen has invited us round for supper this evening and we're expected at 5.30 pm, which doesn't give me time to pack my stuff ready to leave early tomorrow.

Carole says it's okay, we'll be back home early, but Karen and Greg are good hosts and we end up staying late.

## 25th August

## Three buses (180 kms), one aeroplane to Taupo (2hrs)

Carole drives me to the bus stop in Kaitaia and I'm sorry we're saying 'goodbye' I'd love to spend more time with her.

The InterCity bus arrives on time and takes me to Kerikeri where I change to another InterCity bus to Whangerai. It's a short walk across to a different bus station and I find one that will take me to the airport about fifteen minutes away.

At the airport there's just enough time for a cup of coffee before my flight and a short hop across to Auckland where I change planes. This one is bound for Taupo where I hope John will be waiting to meet me, since he's arrived there before me.

The plane lands at 5 pm. It's hammering with rain and getting dark so I'm relieved to see John waiting in the tiny arrivals lounge. He's hired a car and driven up from South Island.

We're booked into the Haka Lodge hostel, the same company as my Paihaia accommodation and although nice enough, it doesn't have anything of the 'wow' factor of my previous experience. In the evening we share a bottle of wine and have dinner out to catch up with each other's experiences.

## 26th August

Our reason for coming to Taupo is to trek the epic Tongariro walk, but at the moment this is not looking a likely prospect. The weather conditions on the Tongariro are not good and the walk is currently closed.

For something to do, we take a walk in an area known as 'The Craters of the Moon' where hot steam rises up through cracks in the land and it does look pretty weird.

We then drive to see the Huka Falls and happily the sun has come out. The falls are spectacular, I love the noise the rushing water makes. Walking up high above them we have fun watching a tourist speed boat circling in and out as close as it dares to the falls.

On the way back to the hostel we stock up on food and wine so we can eat in. Our menu is soup, ciabatta, cheese and tomatoes – delicious!

## 27th August

I've tried to remain upbeat about the weather and the walk, but we learn that the trek is again cancelled. With the possibility that the walk will re-open on Sunday, we book another night in Taupo. Today is very windy and I hope the wind will blow all the bad weather away. With another day at the hostel I want to catch up on Internet stuff but again the Internet goes down and I'm thwarted. How many times has this happened!

I spend time going through the stuff in my backpack, making sure I'm not hanging on to anything unnecessary. I still have the tiny Mother Theresa medallion, given to me by the charity and whilst it weighs nothing, I don't want to keep it because of the negative association it has for me. I've considered throwing it away before but ended up keeping it; this time I put it in the bin along with a few other bits and pieces. I don't know why, but it feels wrong to throw it away.

Later in the day we learn that the Tongariro trek won't be open in the next few days and as the Haka Lodge has kindly offered to refund the money we paid for the extra night in Taupo we decide to quit and move on. We'll go to Rotorua.

## 28th August

It's only about an hour and a half's drive to Rotorua and we have sunshine – yay!

We want to do something fun so book a zip line tour above a rainforest with seven zip lines.

The first time I experienced a zip wire was in Costa Rica with my Mum and I recall how nervous I was then, stepping from the safety of the platform into the void. John is playful on the zip wire and even turns himself upside down. I don't think I've seen this side of him before. I've gained confidence, but I'm not willing to turn upside down. We're up fantastically high and looking down over the tops of trees in a rainforest is amazing.

After the tour we have a couple of hours left and I suggest we go to the famous sulphur lakes and have a walk around. John wants to stroll around the lake by the town but is persuaded by me. The colourful brochure of the sulphur lakes shows spectacular colours and scenery, but the reality is less exciting and I'm disappointed.

The area is similar to the Moon Craters we'd seen a

couple of days early, only on a bigger scale and perhaps because the weather has been wet, it all looks a bit like a muddy quarry site. I'm sure that anyone interested in geology would have taken much more from the place. I apologise to John for persuading him away from his original preference. Adding to my discomfort is the cost of the entrance fee which seems exceptionally high.

Rotorua, in my opinion, is an uninspiring town and having decided to eat out, there's a lack of appealing restaurants, which seems surprising because there are plenty of motels here. We pick the best of a poor choice and with nothing vegetarian on the menu I order battered fish and chips, sweeping aside my intention not to eat fish any more.

We're staying the night in a motor lodge which boasts a luxurious spa bath. I think this is the first bath I've had since leaving home last December.

## 29th August

I've been in touch with my friend Alan via Facebook and John is willing to drive me to meet him. It takes about an hour and a half to reach Te Aroha, a quaint little town surrounded by green mountains. The area has become known as 'Middle Earth' because it features in 'The Lord of the Rings' films.

I'm very happy to see Alan who is such a dear friend from way, way back. We have coffee and catch up on our news. Our time together is short but somehow it feels right, more time wouldn't have made it any better.

I link up with John again and we drive to our next accommodation, called 'The Nunnery'. We've planned to walk up Mount Te Aroha to a 'lookout' and with grey clouds overhead we change into wet weather gear. The walk is about two hours and I'm very glad to have the exercise. From the top there's a far-reaching vista.

Turning back from the view to make our way down, my attention is caught by something bright red in a large bush. To my astonishment, dangling from a red ribbon is a Mother Theresa medallion, exactly the same as the one I'd thrown away only two days ago. I'm truly amazed to see it there and for a moment I wonder if I should take it down from the bush, but I decide to leave it and only take a photo, so I wouldn't think later that I'd imagined it.

## 30th August

John and I drive for an hour and a half to Auckland to return the hire car. A taxi takes us to another Haka Lodge, this one's good too.

Going in search of a coffee shop we come to the attractive arcade area I'd been to before and this time I treat myself to a very sticky, caramel and chocolate biscuit.

I'm keen to get back to our hostel to use their Internet which appears to be working well. I have admin to sort, but disaster strikes my laptop, the software has been invaded by an organisation called 'Kingsoft' who've 'hijacked' Microsoft Office and changed all my files. I'm feeling rather devastated, I've been trying to stay positive about all the banking dilemmas and not get overwhelmed by negative thoughts. Add to this mix my nervousness about my next trip and I'm struggling to rise above it all.

I close the laptop and set the problem aside, reminding myself that *"everything's always alright in the end"*.

John and I step across the road to an Italian restaurant and have a very tasty meal and probably more wine than is good for me. This is my last evening in New Zealand, we'll go our separate ways tomorrow.

# Santiago, South America

## 31st August

### Aeroplane to Santiago (12 hours)

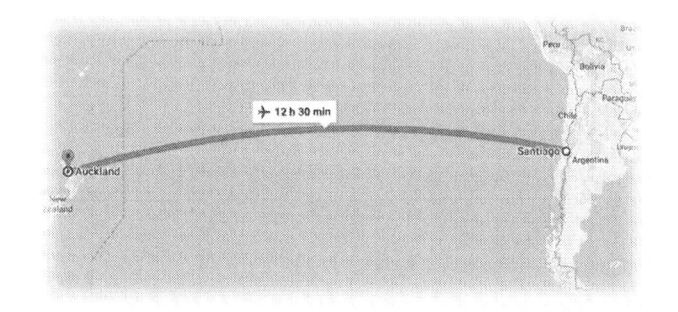

We have to check out at 10 am and I'm able to put my bag in the store room and settle myself into the hostel 'lounge' with time to spare before getting a bus to the airport. Several other travellers are quietly sitting with their mobiles or laptops. I pluck up courage and in the silent space ask if anyone is a computer expert and can help me resolve my problem. Oh joy, a man called Tom offers to take a look. He simply takes the invading program off my laptop, something I'd been afraid to do in case it removed Microsoft as well. My programs are restored to normal. I'm massively grateful and can't thank Tom enough. I give him the remaining several hours travel on my InterCity bus pass which is transferable, maybe he'll get some use out of it.

John leaves before me. He's staying in NZ a couple more days and has booked into a different hotel. Collecting my bag from the store room a young guy asks me where I'm going next and when I mention South America he says *"oh, you must go to Bariloche in Argentina, my dad has a bar there"*. He writes the address down for me. I expect I'll go there if I can.

I walk the ten minutes to the bus stop and don't have to wait long for one that will take me to the airport. The flight leaves on time at 6 pm and it's long, nearly twelve hours.

I think I'm very lucky that I enjoy the travelling aspect, whether on a bus, plane or train, I don't mind how long the journey is. On the plane I watch two good films, one is called 'Three Shades of Blue' with Juliette Binoche and it leaves me sad, the other, appropriately, takes place in my next destination, Chile. It's called 'Los 33', a true story of miners and that one leaves me uplifted.

Arriving in Santiago, I shoot through the airport without hassle, straight into a taxi to my hostel, all extraordinarily quick and smooth. I'd pre-booked Hostel Rado Boutique and it looks pretty good for a city hostel; comfortable, friendly and probably noisy because it's located on a busy main road. The timing feels very strange, I left Auckland at 6 pm, flew for eleven and a half hours, yet the time now is 2.20 pm *on the same day*. Can this be true, after all this travelling it's still 31st August?

By the time I've checked in then wander outside to take a look at my surroundings, the light is already fading. I'm excited by the area which is very 'buzzy' with some cute looking cafes and bars and colourful painted murals on the walls. I think I'm going to enjoy the next couple of days.

# 1st September

Well this has been a long night. Did I think it might be noisy? Noisy isn't the word. The traffic sounds as though it's coming right through the room and there's been drumming and chanting for several hours during the night. Not to mention the five occupants I'm sharing the room with who've been coming and going at various times. I'm tempted to remain in bed but don't want to miss out on breakfast, so at the last possible minute I dress hastily and locate the kitchen.

Breakfast is included in the room price and it's good; fruit, yoghurt, cereal and toast. I'm delighted with the view out of the window that shows the snow-capped Andes in the distance and a blue sky.

I'm keen to get out and explore this famous city of Santiago but find it impossible to resist one of the inviting cafés and I sit outside in the sunshine with a coffee, musing yet again how amazing it is to have such freedom.

A few streets away I find a bank and successfully acquire some cash, then I walk in the direction of San Cristobal Hill (Cerro San Cristóbal).

Somewhere in the middle of the city, it rises 300 metres above Santiago. The walk up takes forty-five minutes on a dirt path. The views all around are spectacular and I realise how lucky I am that the sky is a clear blue, the guidebooks warn that smog can get in the way of the view. I always love seeing a city from above and getting an overview of the scale of the place.

I spend a few more hours walking along different streets, meandering back in the direction of my hostel. The atmosphere is exciting, noisy and vibrant. Everything is colourfully painted with pictures; lampposts, doors, walls, even the street bins and there's graffiti everywhere, some of it exceptionally good, some of it dark and ugly. It's all very 'Santiago'.

When my feet and legs yell that they've had enough, I go back to the hostel and make myself some supper with the few provisions I'd bought at a local shop. I've had another wonderful day.

## 2nd September

I'm lucky that a lack of sleep isn't a problem for me because the noise again during the night is unbelievable. The drum band started up in the late afternoon and continued throughout the evening and is still going strong at 3 am. I've slept in some extremely noisy places but this tops the lot. Apparently, the drummers are promoting Escuela de Salsa, they're raising money. I'd have given them a substantial amount to be quiet. Two of my dorm mates, poor souls, left at 5 am, I doubt they had a wink of sleep before leaving.

After another excellent hostel breakfast, I potter about the streets of Santiago again and have fun taking photos for Facebook so I can do a "where am I now?" post. I call into the Museo des Artes and have a wander round. In my usual 'uneducated about art' way, I consider some artwork interesting or pleasing and some positively dull or weird.

There's another hill in the area called Cerro Santa Lucia, the remnant of a fifteen-million year old volcano. This is a very attractive place with some old, ornate stairs and facades and from the top there are more spectacular views over the city with snow-capped mountains in the distance.

## 3rd September

Some research on Trip Advisor yesterday suggested a good restaurant to visit is called Pelluqueria Francesca, 2789 Libertad, corner of Compania de Jesu, so at lunchtime I head off in search of it.

I've been walking for a long while and feel as though I've left the city behind. I wonder if I should keep going or give up, especially as I'm now in a residential area and I think I may be lost. The directions had seemed simple (don't they always!). I keep going and then I see it, on the corner of two streets, just like the picture. I should have guessed from the name that it would be French and I feel a bit silly going into a French restaurant while I'm in South America but once inside I'm delighted. It's decorated in antique style and very quirky with an air of affluence. I choose my table carefully and order a large glass of white wine. My meal is delicious, I eat slowly and relish every mouthful and every moment.

Tomorrow I leave here early to catch a 'plane to Puerto Montt. I've just finished a half bottle of red wine kindly given to me by my fellow room-mate, the one that left at 5 am. I hope the alcoholic effect will help me ignore the drumming which continues, I'd really like to get some sleep.

## 4th September

## Aeroplane to Puerto Montt, Chile (2hrs)

I've ordered a taxi for 5.30 am. It's been another raucous night and I'm intrigued to see that loads of youngsters are still on the streets. It's 5.30 am for goodness sake!

The flight is glorious because I'm able to watch the sunrise on the skyline and see the tops of snowy mountains, presumably the Andes. My destination this time is a tiny non-tourist place called Angelmo, by Puerto Montt and my intention is to have a few days out without feeling compelled to sightsee.

## Angelmo, Chile

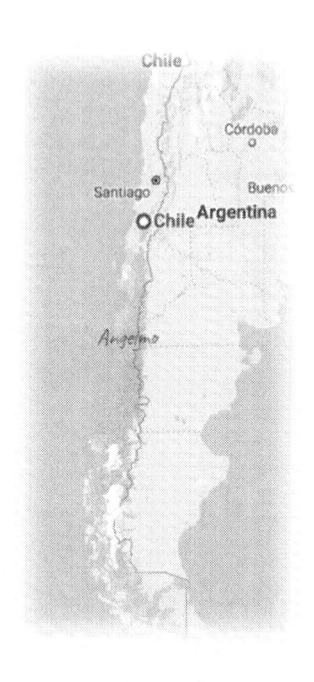

I've arrived at the very small Puerto Montt airport. Outside I find a taxi who will take me to Angelmo, a small bay about 2 kms west and where I've pre-booked a homestay called 'The Pink House'. Fortunately, the taxi driver knows where to go and he takes me up an unmade road on a hill. The house built into the hill, looks rickety and I hope it's safe.

Inside I meet my hostess Francisca. She's a young mum with a six month old baby called Nouhal. I've arrived early in the morning and ask if I can pay for breakfast and for 3,000 pesos Francisca provides me with fruit, bread and cheese and scrambled egg.

The accommodation inside is as quirky as the outside and I like it. It's cold here and I'm glad that my room has a heater. I dress up warm and walk outside to explore.

Angelmo is very messy and reminds me of India. There are as many dogs here too. I haven't walked far when I come to a small local market and a lake. Looking over the railing by the lake I'm taken by surprise. There are sealions. Dozens of them, playing in and out of the water. And lots of pelicans too. It's a remarkable sight. The market sells fish and I realise this is why so many sealions hang about the area, the fishmongers throw them their fish heads and scraps. Each time a trader comes out with a bucket, there's a frenzy of activity from the sealions and I have a very happy time watching them.

## 5th September

The more I potter about in Angelmo the more it grows on me. Although the temperature is cold, there's blue sky and sunshine. It isn't at all touristy and I think it's probably a place where locals come to enjoy a day out. It dawns on me that today is Sunday. At the market I buy some handmade chocolates, salad, avocado, fruit and cheese and a bottle of wine with an unrecognisable label.

Passing by a tiny craft shop my eye is caught by an attractive leather three-legged stool and I pop in to take a look. Hand crafted by the guy in the shop, the price is equivalent to £36. We try to have a conversation but our different languages make it impossible, so I do my best to indicate that I'll come back. I'd like to know how much it will cost to post to England because it will make an excellent gift for my son.

In the evening I settle into my room revelling in having the space to myself. I make a salad for my supper, drink wine, have a bath and feel very relaxed. I'm going to like being here for the next four days.

## 6th September

Last night I promised myself I'd go for a run this morning. It's 7.30 am and only just light. The air is very cold and although my body gets warm running, my hands are cold, I'll need to buy warmer gloves. Running along the water front to nearby Puerto Montt only takes about twenty minutes and I discover that Puerto Montt is a bigger town that I had realised.

After another of Francisca's filling breakfasts I head back out into the sunshine to walk into Puerto Montt, I need to get money. I locate an ATM and as always, I'm relieved to hear the reassuring ticking sound as the machine spews out my cash. I'm also very pleased to find a money exchange office where I can change Chilean pesos for American dollars. I feel more relaxed now because American dollars can be spent anywhere, they're my security blanket in case my last working bank card fails.

Back in Angelmo I go to the lakeside to visit the sealions again. A fishmonger is feeding them with a tray of fish heads and he's clearly enjoying flinging the scraps this way and that and causing a real scrum with sealions and pelicans. The whole scene is hilarious and along with a few other spectators I delight in the entertainment.

Back in my hostel I make myself an avocado salad and some pumpkin soup with enough left for tomorrow. The Chilean wine I bought has turned out to be excellent.

I've had another lovely day but I'm very aware that I'm far from relaxed. I have feelings of anxiety and last night the demons came and I had dreams about letting people down. I keep thinking up things I ought to be doing, which in the cold light of day is ridiculous – there's nothing I *have* to do. I came here with the intention of doing nothing but I'm already struggling with this. There's an island across the lake with a hill, I could go there and walk up it. There's a boat tour of the harbour I can take, it only costs £3. Or Osorno volcano, surely I shouldn't miss the opportunity to see this? And so my thoughts go on. I remind myself that this trip is about having experiences, not rushing to see one place after another.

7th September

I've got confused in my dates somewhere and now realise that I have one more day in Angelmo than I'd thought. It feels as though the universe has given me another day to relax. When I leave here I'm going to be a volunteer on a farm in Chile and my initial enthusiasm and excitement about the opportunity has gradually declined into anxiety and now mild terror.

Today is another glorious one and I start with a short run along the water's edge before breakfast. Francisca is out with her father for the day and I'm tempted to stay in and relax in the space and the quiet, but the sun is shining and I'm compelled to go out.

I walk to the market area to watch the sealions for a while then stroll again into Puerto Montt to find out about the postal service. I'm still thinking about the leather stool for Phil. Correos Chile can post a parcel to the U.K. but when they tell me the cost will be around £63 I wonder if I've made myself understood correctly, that's such a high price. I buy a stamp for a postcard for the equivalent of 66 pence,

I find a money changer again and change more

Chilean pesos for Argentine pesos. With these and my U.S. dollars I feel like an International cash machine. A small kiosk has a board nearby and postcards attached to it, so I ask if I can buy one and the guy behind the counter brings out a dated looking card from somewhere out the back.

Walking back to Angelmo, a massive container ship is in the sea being drawn in by a tug, it looks way too huge to be there. A couple of Chilean guys are sitting on the wall by the water, they appear to be drunk. One of them calls to me to take his photo and when I get my camera out they both make a daft pose. He tells me his name is Paulo and shakes my hand. I'm amused by their silly fun.

Near the fish market I again see an old man in a wheelchair. He's there every day selling CDs and plays them loudly with two large speakers, the music creating a jolly atmosphere. I catch his eye and smile and he nods an acknowledgement. I want to buy woollen gloves so I look for the old lady seller I noticed yesterday. Her wrinkled face makes her look anything between 70 and 80 years old although she walks pretty upright, so may be younger. She spends all day knitting and I particularly want to buy my gloves from her. The ones I choose are fingerless with a flap that folds over. They're woollen and warm and cost the equivalent of £1.11.

## 8th September

I'm up early again for another run and this morning the light is quite different. There are clouds and the sky is a soft silver grey colour, sort of monochrome. I didn't suffer so much from night demons last night and I'm feeling more relaxed.

Today I'm going to try out the local restaurant at the end of our road, recommended by Francisca. I can see it from my bedroom window, built from timber and painted pink and turquoise blue.

The restaurant inside is surprisingly 'up-market'. The waiters are smartly dressed and attentive and I like the décor. There's an attractive menu and I can't read a word of it. A waiter comes over to me and I say *"comido pescado, per no comido meat"* which translates as *"I eat fish but I don't eat meat"*. He comes back with a menu in English. I choose sea bass with duchess potatoes and sautéed vegetables and ask for a *"vaso de vino blanco"* which arrives in a glass so big I nearly fall in. I'm given some bread rolls and the tasty tomato, onion and parsley dish I'd had in Santiago. It's all absolutely scrumptious.

A group of four people come into the restaurant and sit near me, I notice two of them order a very pretty, frothy, pale green drink that comes in a champagne glass and I ask the waiter the name of the drink. He tells me it's called Pisco Sour and a few minutes later he hands me half a glass of the drink to try. It's delicioso!

## 9th September

My last day off and I can't deny I'm frustrated that I haven't been more relaxed here. It seems that when you travel the world you still 'take yourself' with you.

I walk into Puerto Montt again to buy some bits and pieces and I'm successful getting everything I want. Back in Angelmo, I visit the sealions for the last time. It's raining today and the atmosphere around the fish market is very different. I look for a café that sells hot chocolate where I can sit and write the postcard I've bought for Ben but there isn't anywhere, so I go back to The Pink House.

The postcard has been made from shiny photographic paper and is impossible to write on. By good fortune I have some white sticky paper labels with me, I can't recall now why I thought they'd be a good idea to pack in my rucksack, but right now they're exactly what I need to stick on the postcard so I can write on it.

I have an odd dinner of carrot soup that I make in Francisca's tiny kitchen, more like carrot puree than soup because I have to mash the cooked carrots with a wooden spoon. Dessert is the last of the home-made chocolates and a glass of wine.

# *Rupanco Farm, Chile*

## 10th September

Bus to Osorno (110 kms), Bus to Rupanco Farm (75 kms)

So here it is, the day I've been worrying about ever since committing myself to volunteer for a month at Rupanco Farm. After breakfast I say goodbye to Francisca and Nuelho and as I walk down the steps of The Pink House I realise sadly that I haven't taken a photo of the two of them.

I choose to walk the two kilometres to the bus terminal and as usual I have butterflies in my tummy. Approaching the first ticket counter they tell me their next bus is at 5.30 pm. What!! The next counter says a bus is due in 5 minutes.

On the journey I wonder how I'll know when to get off so ask the conductor to tell me when we reach Osorno Centre. About an hour and a half later he indicates I should get off so I do, but it doesn't seem to be the centre of a town, more like a suburb. I ask passers-by for directions to the centre of town and after about fifteen minutes walking I come to the bus terminal and of course this is where I should have got off the bus. Typical me, if I hadn't worried and pestered the conductor I'd have known to get off in the bus station and saved myself a long unnecessary walk with my heavy backpack.

I've emailed the farm at Rupanco for directions and they've given me very good instructions how and where to locate the rural bus stop and a lady who will sell me a bus ticket. I have a two hour wait ahead so I'm delighted that the ticket seller will also look after my luggage for 400 pesos. A café nearby is selling hot chocolate and over the next hour I drink two cups whilst reading 'Tuesdays with Morrie' on my electronic reader.

The rural bus is small and crowded. It's raining outside and warm and steamy inside. I can't see out of the windows. Again, I worry how I'll know when to get off and I ask the conductor to tell me when the bus arrives in Elvira. I have no idea if he understands what I'm asking or if he'll remember to tell me. There's a lot of coming and going on the journey, the bus becomes more crammed with people and youngsters from college and there's an ever-growing pile of bags, boxes and shopping piling up around my feet. I'm sitting at the back because the conductor put my backpack there.

Not long after getting on the bus my bladder lets me know it would like to be relieved of the two cups of hot chocolate and large glass of water that I've drunk. I hope the feeling will go away but it doesn't, and as my discomfort grows I wonder how I'm going to cope. This is a two-hour bus ride. I'm feeling miserable. I wonder if it's possible to wet oneself without people around you noticing. I'm imagining myself getting off the bus and diving into the nearest bush, while the bemused people who've come to meet me watch in astonishment. That is of course, if I get off the bus at the right destination, how will I know? Maybe no-one will come to meet me and I'll get off in the middle of nowhere in the dark and the rain.

When will I learn that everything always works out for me? The bus comes to a stop and ahead I can see some road repair workers have blocked the small country road with a load of dirt, we're going nowhere, for a while at least. I grab my opportunity. Clambering over shopping and gesticulating as best I can that I'm getting off the bus for a 'call of nature', I squat behind the bus for relief, praying that no other vehicle comes along. Even more amazing, as I get back onboard a young guy comes out of seemingly nowhere and gets onto the bus. He looks at me and asks if by any chance I'm going to Rupanco. He's just come from there and the truck waiting to meet me is on the other side of the road block. I can't quite believe how luckily all this has worked out for me. I thank him, grab my backpack and get off the bus.

True enough, a truck is waiting and I'm introduced to Andre, Cynthia and Luis. They're all very friendly and Cynthia embraces me and gives me a kiss on both cheeks. I am very happy. We drive maybe twenty minutes to the farm which looks even more wonderful than I'd been expecting.

Inside is a large, comfortably furnished communal room with a large fire in the centre. I'm going to be warm, that allays one of my concerns. Outside, the view of a lake and mountains looks stunning, even through the rain, so I know the scenery isn't going to disappoint.

I'm introduced to Jannes from South Africa who manages the volunteers and during the next hour or so I meet an assortment of about ten other volunteers, all young. A German lad called Max has also arrived today, he's 6ft 6ins tall, very charming and travelling alone. Age 17 years, he's younger than my grand-daughter.

The meal in the evening is laid out on large trestle tables and it's an absolute feast, a colourful variety of savoury dishes, all vegetarian. One of the volunteers has made a 'welcome' cake with 'Hazel & Max' written in icing sugar, a thoughtful touch.

## 11th September

Today is Sunday and no-one has to work. It feels wrong that I have the day off and I haven't even started working yet. Some of the volunteers have decided to take the farm's boat and row across to an island to camp overnight. This leaves only a few of us at the farm and I enjoy a quiet, relaxing day and the bliss that comes with being released from the anxiety of the past few days.

I'm going to be here for almost a month, so I spend time getting my bunk bed organised and cleaning the room I'm staying in. I'm sharing with three others, American Trish, an interesting character and closer to my age than the others, Sophie from Holland and Johanna who is just 17 years old and travelling alone in Chile. They're both delightful, but very untidy. There's a decent bathroom opposite our room with a shower but no hot water. The season is coming into spring and the weather hasn't warmed up yet so I'm unlikely to be taking too many showers.

## 12th September

Today is glorious sunshine and starts with a cooked breakfast followed by 'Morning Circle', a group meeting to share out the work. I elect to join Trish in the garden and have a very pleasant time planting seeds in a polytunnel, then building a low dry-stone wall around a garden 'bed'. The farm gardens are extensive with flower beds and lawns and the land reaches down to a massive lake with a snow topped volcano beyond it. The whole ambience of the place feels peaceful to me and I know I'm very lucky that I'm here.

We all work for five hours from 9 am until 2 pm when lunch is served. I manage to stave off serious hunger pangs with some nuts that I'd brought with me, but by two o'clock my tummy is very empty. A hand bell rings enthusiastically to let us know that food is on the table.

Lunch is another feast of different dishes and I eat loads. Afterwards we have free time, some sit around chatting or reading, everyone is very chilled out. Internet here is poor, we can request to use it for something important but I like not having to think about going online. I feel more relaxed than I've probably ever been. I'm getting to know my fellow volunteers and I like every one of them. I haven't yet met Greg who owns the farm, as he's currently away.

## 13th September

Another glorious day at Rupanco and I'm up early to see the sunrise. I'm working with Trish in the neglected vegetable garden called the Mandela Garden. It's a delightful ten-minute walk up a small winding path that comes out onto a grassy slope surrounded by bushes and trees. There are stunning views all around and across the lake to the mountain. Sophie is with us, and so is little Udi, an orphaned lamb who lives at Rupanco, who has followed us up here. This has to be the most idyllic place to work. We spend the next couple of hours in the sunshine, weeding the vegetable beds.

We need bamboo to make hoops for seed planting so I take the machete and walk down to the river and waterfall where the bamboo grows. The best bamboo is always just out of reach and I feel rather precarious leaning out from the bank across the water whilst wielding the machete, but I love being in this beautiful place and I feel very pleased with myself carrying the bamboo canes back to the garden.

Some guests arrive in the evening with Greg, the owner. I'm intrigued to meet him. He looks like Ernest Hemingway and he exudes warmth and assurance. He takes the time to talk to me and welcome me to Rupanco, which I appreciate. Andreas has been shopping for us and brought me the wine I requested, so I offer Greg a glass which he accepts with grace, even though he says he doesn't usually drink white wine.

## 14th September

I'm on 'housekeeping' today and I work hard and don't mind a bit. I hang laundry, wash up dishes, shake rugs, move furniture, vacuum, wash floors and clean bathrooms – phew!

Lunch has been made by Jaki from Iraq, he's an exceptionally good cook and I find him a fascinating man. He's quiet and solitary, choosing to live on his own in the woods and he has an endearing gentleness about him. I ask how he spells his name and it amuses me when he says he spells it Jaki, even his name is uncomplicated! I'd like to know him better.

In the afternoon everyone settles into their own different activities and I notice with some envy how comfortable the youngsters are with each other. Even though they've only recently met, they seem really at ease. Trish is doing Sophie's hair, Anna is massaging Martin's shoulders and Eugene is lying across Max's lap on the sofa. How admirable to have that level of confidence and personal freedom.

At dinner I'm sad to learn that Andreas is leaving in a couple of days, there's something very special about him and I tell him so. I said *"I haven't had time to get to know you"* and he replies in his quiet voice *"there's still time"*. Then I can't think of anything to say.

Each volunteer that arrives in Rupanco is invited to give a presentation to everyone and this evening is Anna's turn. She sings for us and teaches us three gipsy songs.

## 15th September

Anto, from Chile, a friend of Cynthia, has arrived with her baby daughter and we work together in the garden outside the house. She wants to learn to speak better English and I'd like to learn more Spanish so we can help each other.

Johanna is moving on today. I'm astounded by how extraordinary she is, her work ethic and her confidence at seventeen years. She's vacating the single bed in our room and I'm delighted when Jannes suggests I move down from the top bunk. I sweep and clean the room and make up my new bed.

A couple of hours later Jannes apologises and asks if I'd now mind moving to the room next door and sharing with Dorothy. Two new volunteers are arriving and they'd like to be together. I'm back in a top bunk again.

I'm going to miss sharing a room with Trish who is exceptionally noisy, but very amusing. She flounces into the room brandishing her toothbrush and toothpaste and says *"I once had a massage from a Venezuelan man, he had a beautiful penis. I said to him how can men be so strong yet so weak at the same time? He replied "coconut oil"!"*. Trish laughs and leaves the room.

Andreas is leaving tomorrow, he's been at Rupanco a few months. This evening after dinner we go outside to pay tribute to him. Everyone sits around a big bonfire by the lake and we're invited to say something about our personal experience of Andreas. He receives heaps of praise and I'm not surprised, I've only known him for a few days and yet feel emotional that he's leaving.

## 16th September

I've volunteered to cook today, along with Anna. This means we have to prepare food for approximately twenty people, lunch and dinner. I'm concerned about this, cooking is definitely not my forté, but I've been assured that Anna is excellent at cooking and I let go of my anxiety and trust that it will all work out.

Cooking in the farm kitchen is very different from at home. There's a wood burning stove that has to be constantly 'fed' with fuel and a large and very dodgy gas stove which I discover is difficult to light. Food is bought only once a week, the drive to get supplies is about an hour and a half from the farm, so we can only use ingredients that are available in the cupboard and this requires creative thinking.

Having checked out the supplies, I have in mind to cook lentil pie and maybe stewed pears and flapjacks. I'm keen to have the menu sorted in my head so I know what I'm doing but Anna assures me we've plenty of time and we can make it all up as we go along. I know this is a common approach but I find it difficult. Anna hears my concern and together we make a plan but as the morning progresses she changes the menu frequently. I'm not at all sure what's going on so I stick to the one thing I can do which is frying/roasting potatoes. They're tiny and there are hundreds of them and I scrub them all.

I ask Anna if we can start cooking early because things always take longer than expected and she agrees. But then we can't get the oven to light, the oven knob won't stay in and the oven keeps going out. The fire which needs stoking isn't hot enough to fry anything. By the time I get the fire hot there isn't enough time to fry all the potatoes which are laid out on a large baking tray and two big frying pans so I have to alternate with the oven and gas rings. I'm feeling miserable now. I can't see how this meal is going to come together.

Anna is getting stressed about the black bean burgers she's making and has decided to turn them into a tray bake. Time is running out. We put together a large and very attractive salad in between cooking other dishes.

We've been on our feet preparing and cooking for nearly four hours and at 2pm we have the food on the table. Everyone is very complimentary and I'm exhausted and relieved. Then I notice Anna isn't in the dining room or the kitchen. Looking down the garden I can see she's by some trees and she looks upset.

I go out to Anna and she's crying. I think it must be

my fault, thinking I upset her while we were cooking together. When I ask what's wrong, Anna tells me she had a text this morning saying that a dear friend has died, he'd been ill for a while, but it's still a shock. Bless her, she'd carried on in the kitchen all morning and not mentioned it, no wonder she found creative cooking difficult. All I can do is give her a big hug. Bless her, she apologises for being mean to me. She's a lovely girl.

So we're back in the kitchen again, this time cooking dinner. It's slightly less fraught as we're now working together. I am however, hugely relieved when the day is over and I hope I will never have to do this again.

## 17th September

I'm up at 8 am and discover, too late, that I was on the rota to be on breakfast duty. I'm very upset because I can't understand how I didn't know this. I've looked at the rota and didn't see my name there, I feel I've let people down. It reminds me of my recurring bad dreams about letting people down. I don't stay upset for long because other volunteers quickly stepped in and made breakfast and no-one seems to mind, they simply shrug it off saying it happens from time to time. What a kind attitude; no blame and no criticism.

Our bread is made by volunteers in an outside barn where there's another wood burning oven and I've asked if I can watch Casey (from Texas) make the bread. The barn is quite dark and cosy with the fire and I can sense Casey doesn't want to talk as he focuses on kneading the bread in a meditative way. It's hard to describe how privileged I feel being there, watching him. He's a handsome and extraordinary man and seems so wise it's hard to believe he's only 26 years old. I told him one time that I think he's an 'old soul' and he said many people have said that to him, which doesn't surprise me.

My job this morning is shifting a large pile of rocks to create a clear path to the chicken house and I love being outdoors and doing physical work.

While I'm working I'm thinking about what it means to volunteer and I have a 'lightbulb moment'. I've seldom been comfortable with volunteering in the charitable sense because it seems to me there's always someone *inferior*; the 'poor' person who needs help and the person 'doing good' becomes *superior*, so respect is lacking. Respect being the important word here. The volunteering that takes place at Rupanco is about give and take on both sides and mutual respect, and I realise that for charitable volunteering to be okay in my mind, it's necessary to make the receiver of the help feel respected.

In the evening the French girls show us a game to play which gives us a good laugh. We all write three nouns on pieces of paper and put them into a bowl. There are two teams and three rounds. In the first round each of us picks a paper out of a bowl and talks about the word while our team guesses what the word is. In the second round we get to say one word to describe the noun, and in the third round we have to mime it. It's amazing how hard this becomes, especially the miming part, and it causes much hilarity.

## 18th September

Christine has offered to teach Pilates to anyone that's interested, so I'm up early in the dark and join a handful of others. She's a brilliant teacher.

Brunch is served at 9.30 am and cooked by Jaki and of course, it's delicious. Then someone suggests we take the rowing boat and row across the lake to get up close to a waterfall and nine of us decide we'd like to go.

After a lot of faffing about to get organised we set off in the glorious sunshine, each taking an oar. Anto and her baby sit at the front and the two dogs come with us as well. I love rowing, I love the people I'm with and the scenery is stunning. I don't know when I've felt happier.

It takes over an hour to reach the waterfall and we tie the boat nearby and clamber and slither across the rocks to explore. All our best efforts don't get us very close to it, but we have fun trying.

Rowing back makes us laugh because inexplicably, we keep steering off course which is odd because we're on a lake and there shouldn't be a current. It takes a long time and I don't mind at all, I don't want this fabulous adventure to end.

Jaki's dinner this evening is spectacular, he's made a thick bean soup which he serves in bowls of bread, that is the bowls are actually made from bread, he's made four of them. I feel healthier just looking at them. We break the bread from the sides to dip into the delicious soup.

I'm on breakfast duty tomorrow morning and ask Jaki if I should use the left-over pastry-bread for breakfast and he suggests I make mashed pumpkin with herbs and layer it on top and re-bake. But then when I think about this my anxieties about cooking come up and I talk to Casey. He simply says if you're worried about it then don't do it, which makes me immediately relieved. At this point Jaki comes into the kitchen. He's very kind to me and seems to understand my anxiety about the cooking thing, absurdly I feel close to tears and he says not to worry and suggests that maybe I can cook with him next time and then I'd see that cooking is fun.

I'm happy again. I get things ready for tomorrow's breakfast and Jannes and Casey come in and help me. I open my bottle of red wine and we all have a glass, then Cynthia and Anto come and they have a glass of wine as well. We finish the bottle between us, it's been fun to share.

Today has been fabulous and wonderful.

## 19th September

I'm really touched that Jaki has turned up and is in the kitchen early to help me cook breakfast. I go out to the henhouse to get some eggs and when I reach underneath the hens I bring out nine eggs, still warm. For possibly the first time, I have an understanding of the 'life' we're denying by eating the eggs and it doesn't feel good. I talk to Jaki about it and he says that it's okay to take the eggs because we're looking after the hens. Jaki puts oil into a large oven tray and I break the eggs and cook them over two lighted gas hobs.

I've been invited to choose and read a poem after breakfast and I've found one that, although not strictly a poem, I feel is relevant. The words are by Dinah Maria Mulock Craik about Friendship from "A Life for a Life". It expresses something of how I feel when I'm with these 'safe' people.

> *Oh, the comfort*
> *the inexpressible comfort of feeling safe with a person*

*having neither to weigh thoughts nor measure words,*
*but pouring them all right out,*
*just as they are,*
*chaff and grain together;*
*certain that a faithful hand will take and sift them,*
*keep what is worth keeping,*
*and then with the breath of kindness blow the rest away.*

I'm gardening again today and the weather is warm. The work makes me hot and tired and I'm reminded of the two and a half hours rowing yesterday which was quite a workout.

I'm getting something of a routine to my afternoons, I have a wash, maybe wash a few clothes, practice ukulele, learn some Spanish and go for a walk. Tomorrow I'm giving my presentation, so I've also been working on that.

## 20th September

Casey is smoking fish outside. We've been given several large mackerel, caught in the lake, and he's made a fire inside an old oil drum. To flavour the fish, he's put aromatic tree leaves over the fire giving the smoke a distinctive smell. The fish are placed on wire mesh above the fire, then covered. He says they'll be there all night and he'll come back every couple of hours to keep the fire going, even through the night. Now that's dedication. There's a few of us standing around chatting, watching and learning from Casey, so I bring some glasses and a bottle of wine to share and it feels like a party.

This evening is my turn to give a presentation and I've chosen a talk I learned some time ago from the popular Life Coach, Anthony Robbins. The presentation is called 'The Six Needs for Happiness' and I can show how Rupanco Farm covers all six 'needs'. I'm disappointed that Greg hasn't made it back from his 'shopping' trip in time to hear it, he's gone to Osorno with some of the others, traffic has delayed them and they won't return until late this evening.

## 21st September

It's raining today so we don't work outside. Anto invites me to go with her for a walk through the woods to the barn. Because we don't know the way Jannes suggests we take Tonka, the dog, with us because he'll know which paths to take and he does, he leads the way for us perfectly, it takes about half an hour.

Jaki and Martin are in the kitchen of the barn and they make us tea. We stay a while, chatting and looking around. Several volunteers choose to sleep there but I wouldn't like this much, there's no view of the lake, no electricity and the only toilet is outside.

When Anton and I leave the barn there's a large bull standing in the lane. Anton isn't at all concerned, she says you can see he's docile. I'm not convinced and stand well back from him. Returning home, we take the wrong track and realise our mistake when Tonka starts barking to guide us onto the correct path. He's so clever.

## 22nd September

Casey is teaching Tai Chi to anyone who wants to learn. I feel privileged to have this opportunity, he's an excellent teacher and I get up early to join his class. It's still dark at this time of the day and cold too, so I'm wearing plenty of layers.

After breakfast, I take time out to watch Anto make bread, she's an amazing cook and we all agree her bread is excellent. I spend the rest of the morning digging in the garden, I work hard and feel good.

Today is Sophie's birthday and Martin has made her a birthday cake using bananas. I take a photo of her, it's a sweet picture, she looks so pretty and very happy.

Later in the day I join Christine's partner, Toby who has offered to do a meditation with anyone that wants it. With all this exercise, nutritious food, pilates, Tai Chi and meditation I feel incredibly wholesome.

## 23rd September

I'm having the most wonderful time here and shudder when I think that I was so anxious I nearly didn't come. Imagine, I might have missed all this. My day has started with yoga at 6.30 am, followed by breakfast, then a short video that Greg wants us all to watch. It's an enlightening world overview from space. We then disband into different directions to work for the next five hours and I join Eugene and Sophie in the Mandala Garden.

After another delicious and filling lunch, I go for a walk in the sunshine and find a quiet grassy glade where I can practice Tai Chi moves. I'm enjoying the Tai Chi because it's a form of 'moving meditation' and takes focus, it works better for me than sitting still to meditate, which I struggle with.

In the late afternoon a few of us go into the forest and light a fire. Toby and Christine have brought music for us to dance to and we take our shoes and socks off and dance in the forest. It feels slightly dotty but I'll try anything once. I would have liked it more if I wasn't in so much pain. Moving the large sofa this morning for the yoga session I crunched my middle toe and it's throbbing and sore. What is it about me and toes?

The day finishes with another beautiful sunset, supper, wine and good conversation. I enjoy listening to Jannes who has some hilarious stories to tell about his days in Korea. Can there be any more to life than this?

## 24th September

Another glorious day of sunshine. In the afternoon I go for a ramble across the farm's land. It extends for several hundred acres so there's no end to the exploring I can do. I walk up a path for about an hour and along the way I hear Udi, the lamb, bleating and see him in a field. The decision has been made to try and integrate him back with the flock and away from people, but having seen me, he squeezes himself through a small hole in the wire fence. Now I have a lamb on the wrong side of the fence, it has barbed wire along the top and I'm not tall enough or strong enough to lift him back over.

I'm looking for a gate to the field, when fortunately, Diego comes along the path with his bike. He easily picks Udi up and drops him back on the other side and we move swiftly away before he gets out of the field again.

I continue my walk and I'm returning on a different path, when I hear Udi bleating again. I call to him because I can tell he's not in the field any more, and he comes running up to me. This time I decide to walk him back to the house, he's clearly not going to stay in the field with the sheep. Udi is happy to trot along with me and clearly excited that he's back at the farmhouse.

I pour myself a glass of white wine and take it down the garden where there are wooden sunbeds and look with pure pleasure at the beautiful lake and the magnificent snow-capped Volcan Orsono. The sun is setting and the sky becomes a fabulous palette of pinks and oranges. Diego and Luis come and join me, they have their guitars with them and strum and sing. Tonka, the dog and Udi also join our party. I don't want to ever forget this moment; surrounded by nature at its best, two men strumming guitars, a glass of wine in my hand and a dog and a lamb at my feet.

## 25th September

Jaki and Casey are building a timber dwelling in the woods and a few of us walk across the fields and into the woods to find it. Everywhere is a feast for the eyes, the sky, the grass, the trees. This place feels exceptional, it reaches my soul and I wonder if it could be because it's so undisturbed. We reach Jaki and Casey who are in the woods working on the wooden frame. I can tell they've had fun building this project. Jaki heats some water over a camp stove and makes us coffee.

## 26th September

I have the feeling time is running out, two people have said to me *"I hear you're leaving soon"*. I don't leave until 7th October which didn't feel like soon, but now it does.

I've offered to take on the laundry duty this week

and there are several loads of washing to be done and hung out to dry. Rupanco provides shelves full of clothes that volunteers can borrow so they don't have to work in their own gear and there's a communal laundry basket where the dirty clothes can be dumped for washing. In between washes I sit on the lawn and help sort through a basket of sheep's wool which will be used to make yarn, the task is dull and I miss working in the vegetable garden.

## 27th September

This afternoon I'm on a mission to discover how long it takes to walk from the farmhouse to the gate onto the nearest road and bus stop. I want to know if I can make the journey carrying my backpack when it's time to leave. The dirt track is pleasant and I like the solitude and glimpses of the lake through the trees. It takes an hour and a half to reach the road which is a stretch too far for me to carry my stuff.

It's another hour and a half to walk back and I've come to the sheep field. A ewe and her lamb are outside the field. I try herding them in but when I approach they run further away, so I go back to the farm to get help. I find Casey, he was the 'shepherd' this morning and together we round them up. Back at the farmhouse I pour him some wine and we sit and chat, his conversation is always very enlightening.

## 28th September

I struggle to keep track of the days, especially since I rarely use my phone or Internet, I only need to know which day it is to remember whether I'm getting up early for Tai Chi or Yoga. I love both. Today is beautiful and sunny and after breakfast Greg suggests we have Morning Circle in the garden.

He has us do an exercise where we all walk around the inside of the circle and say a silent 'hello' to each person by taking their hand and looking into their eyes. It's very emotional. When I come to Luis I notice how exceptionally kind his eyes are, meltingly dark brown with the longest eye lashes ever. I hadn't realised until yesterday that he and Cynthia came here as a couple, but they're no longer together.

Cynthia is taking photos for a new website about Rupanco and she asks me if I'll be a 'model'. I dress in my running gear and have fun running up and down grassy slopes outside while Cynthia takes photos. Christine is with us and she wants to show us her 'special' place in the forest. We walk through soft tufted green grass across a neighbour's land then follow a path up high where we can see the beautiful lake. It looks so pretty and peaceful here that we spontaneously sit in meditative silence for a short while. I notice the white clouds in the blue sky have made formations like wispy angels floating above us.

I can understand why Christine loves this part of the forest, it has a magical quality. Huge leafy, trees reach up to the sky and they form a sort of circle. Something amazing in the atmosphere makes me feel very strong, I can't resist hugging the trees and I'm filled with a powerful feeling of courage. Next time I feel nervous or anxious I want to remember this.

After a delightful stroll back to the farmhouse in the company of these two lovely souls, I tackle the laundry then head off to the garden to get some work in before the lunch bell rings.

Still gloriously warm, I go for another walk in the

afternoon. Along the lane I encounter Teddy carrying a lamb in his arms. He tells me it ran off in fear when the dog barked and it was separated from the flock. The lamb is traumatised and I can tell Teddy is worried about it. Teddy has a very handsome face and with the lamb in his arms he makes a sweet picture. He gently places the lamb back in the field with its mother and we hope it will be okay.

In the evening I go outside with a glass of wine and realise the wind has got up, although not cold, it's quite blustery and it makes Kika the kitten very skittish. She makes me laugh scooting around the grass and up and down the tree. I have fun taking photos of her with the sun setting over the lake behind.

After dinner Tamara gives her presentation, she talks about the conflict between Palestine and Israel. It makes me think again of my ignorance of all things worldly and political. Is it okay to be so ignorant? Should I make more effort to become more knowledgeable? Many times I've thought "yes" and yet done nothing about it. Maybe my simple view of the world is alright.

Teddy is looking sad and I ask if he's okay. He tells me the lamb died.

## 29th September

My work today is strange, but fun. French Martin is making wasp traps and he wants some help. We fill old plastic water bottles with apple vinegar and hang them on trees all around the farm. Martin is also a quiet man and I like working with him.

With the job finished, I sort and hang the laundry and I'm about to do some gardening when I realise that Casey needs help.

The gas in the kitchen has run out, so he has to use the wood oven in the bakery some fifty yards from the kitchen. I help him carry trays of food back and forth from bakery to kitchen. The best thing about the wood oven in the bakery is that it creates hot water for the shower in the barn, providing the only opportunity to take a hot shower. I grab my chance before anyone else cottons on. It's bliss to feel hot water on my skin again.

I don't feel like walking in the afternoon so instead I offer to give Anto a break and look after her young daughter Arena while she cooks. I'm feeling quite virtuous because caring for small people is not my thing, but she's a sweet little girl and we look at books together sitting outside on the grass, until a light shower of rain sends us back indoors.

## 30th September

Today I've switched to the 'construction' team because I want to do something more physical and I thoroughly enjoy it, even though it's raining and I get soaked. Three of us climb into the back of the truck and drive to a massive pile of gravel, shovel it into the truck and bring it near the house. Then Anna and I dig a pathway creating masses of soil which has to be deposited around the garden. I love the work until other volunteers offer to help us and it gets crowded with everyone working in the same space, so I leave and help out in the kitchen instead.

In the afternoon I decide to make a 'poster' of the 'Six Needs for Happiness' that had been my presentation. Greg learned about my talk and has asked me to write it out for a display. Anna has kindly lent me her excellent paints and brushes and there's some poster size paper in the bureau I can use. Teddy and Lucy offer to help but their offer is challenging for me. The 'controlling' side of me wants to work alone, yet I want to be generous and more 'team spirited' so I accept. I'm fascinated to notice how difficult I find it to 'let go' of the outcome of the poster.

More volunteers have arrived today so we now number twenty-seven, I preferred it when we were a smaller team.

## 1st October

I'm having a fabulous day. A group of us are dispatched to plant potatoes and to my absolute delight we accompany Harvey, who's employed at Rupanco, taking two oxen up to the potato field. Leandro, a stunningly handsome new volunteer, holds the plough while Harvey leads the oxen. Leandro does a brilliant job and I love watching the plough turn over the grass with its rich brown soil underneath. Progress is slow, they go up and down the furrow three times and then five of us place potatoes into the furrow. It takes us all the morning to plant a small piece of land, but the work is rewarding.

In the evening after dinner, Jannes starts a drinking game. We sit round the table and each count out aloud in consecutive numbers, and with each round a number is changed, for example instead of saying '6', you have to say '99'. If a player forgets the 'number change' they have to have a drink and introduce another new rule changing another number so it quickly gets even harder. Then someone puts music on and the gathering becomes a party. Everyone spontaneously starts dancing around the living room, there's a lot of hilarity and laughter.

More alcohol appears from somewhere. The time is past one in the morning when I go to bed; the party is still going strong.

## 2ⁿᵈ October

It's Sunday and I wake with a hangover from too much red wine but I'm not alone. Out on the patio a few party-goers have gathered, nursing hangovers and waiting for brunch. As always, everyone is in a good mood and there's chatter and laughter as we talk over the events of last night. I learn that some people didn't make it to bed until 5 am. I have two large coffees and wait hungrily for food to arrive.

Brunch is amazing, Jaki even manages to produce some tasty small cakes and afterwards I go out into the sunshine intending to have a long walk.

This is another blue-sky day in paradise and after a while I feel a desire to snooze and settle in the grass, happily dozing. I have the beginning of a poem in my mind and while I'm lying there it sort of finishes itself. I wonder if this may be the first time I've been truly happy doing 'nothing'.

> *Do they know how beautiful they are,*
> *these gorgeous, warm, wonderful people,*
> *and how they fill my heart with love?*
> *And does the sparkling lake and the majestic, snowy volcano know how the sight of them fills my soul with wonder?*
> *And does the silent air and the gentle breeze know how they fill my mind with peace? And the tall trees and the soft grass, do they know that they make me feel*

> *safe and strong?*
> *And did the universe really conspire to bring all this beauty to my door? How can that be?*
> *And then the thought came to my mind, that if I am truly part of the whole, then this beauty is also in me.*

Walking back to the farm I know I can't leave without swimming in the lake at least once. Several of the other hardier volunteers, notably Danish Anna and French Martin swim regularly, but I've always wimped out because the lake is very cold. The sunshine is warmer today so I think this is my best opportunity. Down by the water I find the two Danish girls, Juliana and Therese also about to venture in because they want to wash their hair. It isn't just cold, it's freezing. I have a swim but don't stay in the water long, instead I sit near the edge and I'm entertained watching the girls.

Supper again sees the table piled with several dishes of food; pulses, lentils, rice, vegetables and salad but I'm aware that my tummy is feeling sore. I think it's complaining about being fed such large quantities, maybe I need to hold back this time and not fill my plate. I've never eaten so much food in my life before.

## 3rd October

Work today is different again, a group of us go with Greg to a field to plant seeds. He shows us how to divide the land and how to look at the camber to determine where the rows should be. He gives us excellent instructions on exactly what he wants done and how to do it. I'm working with Lucy, from the

States, she's good company and has a quiet confidence about her, she's trained in permaculture and I notice how frequently we all look to her for advice. I think she's a natural leader and I tell her this.

Returning to the garden from a lovely afternoon walk, several volunteers are relaxing on the lawn in the sunshine. It's a charming scene. Greg is there too, lying on the grass chatting with Christine. Toby is colouring in some pictures. They give me a warm welcome and I lie on the grass with them and marvel again at the pure pleasure of not having to do anything.

## 4th October

Work this morning is challenging. There's an area of land that needs to be dug over with a fork and cleared of roots. I'm working on my own here and although somewhat back-breaking I get great satisfaction from working hard.

After lunch a group of us walk through the forest to the barn. Greg is giving us a presentation about permaculture farming. I always like listening to him, he's so eloquent and the love he has for his farm, which has been in his family for generations, really shines through.

The word 'permaculture' comes from 'permanent agriculture', the philosophy behind it is one of working *with*, rather than against, nature. Greg says that permaculture can't be rushed, nature works very slowly, *"the slower you go, the faster you get there"*. It makes sense when he uses the analogy of a racing car – you go really fast, but you can only focus straight ahead, you lose your peripheral vision, yet solutions and good ideas will come up in the area of your peripheral vision. He says something else about nature that I like, he says *"nature is co-operation, not competition"*.

I could stay sitting in that cosy barn room listening to Greg for hours.

## 5th October

Generally, a few of us are willing to get up in the cold of the early morning and take part in Christine's yoga session, but this morning I'm the only one. I ask if she'd rather cancel, but she's happy to continue and I have personal tuition.

There's a sadness around us this evening because Casey, Teddy and Martin will all leave very early tomorrow morning, Casey and Martin are coming back but I'll have left by then so I won't see them again. They're all 'big' characters and have a tremendous presence at the farm, they'll be greatly missed. I find it hard to say goodbye, I feel oddly tearful. I'll be leaving here in a couple of days too and I don't want to face that reality yet.

## 6th October

I've woken feeling very emotional, these aren't feelings I'm used to. Still early in the morning I quietly leave my room and walk outside to watch the sunrise. The sky is a very pretty pastel pink which shines onto the snowy top of Volcan Orsono, reflecting pretty shades of pink, lilac and blue into the lake. I think for the hundredth time how magical this place feels.

Casey, Teddy and Martin will have gone now.

I see Greg as I walk back across the lawn to the farmhouse and he asks if I'm okay. I tell him I'm feeling sad and he gives me an affectionate hug.

I get lots of hugs today, I think everyone is emotionally sensitive. Jaki is around, which is unusual, he doesn't often stay in the farmhouse. He's making cakes in the kitchen and it gives me the perfect opportunity to talk with him and tell him how much I admire him and how inspiring he is. I have no embarrassment being honest about my feelings and he receives my words easily.

After lunch, he sees that Lucy and I have finished the poster about the 'Six Needs for Happiness'. He looks at the picture then quietly asks me *"why do you need to be happy? Isn't it enough to just 'be'?"* I laugh, because in a nanosecond he's blown holes in my poster! And I get it, I get exactly what he's saying; needing to 'be happy' is striving for something. We have an enlightening conversation and everything he says makes sense. I believe I will always remember Jaki, with his quiet wisdom and stillness.

In the evening after dinner I sit with Toby and Christine. It's the first time I've sought them out and had a personal conversation with them. They both have fascinating 'life' stories and they're both different from my 'pigeon-holed' idea of them. I kick myself for waiting until my last evening before getting to know these amazing people better. Am I really going to leave this oasis tomorrow?

## 7th October

Greg has arranged for a neighbour to drive me to the bus stop. Trish is going to come along too because she wants to visit Santiago to see a concert. My fingers are crossed the neighbour will arrive by 6 am as promised so we can catch the only bus. Trish, quirky as ever is smoking pot and drinking coffee.

I'm relieved when we see the lights of our car pull up. Trish is hilariously flirty with the driver who is lapping up the attention. We pay our fare and he leaves us at the bus stop.

It's very cold and dark but we don't have long to wait. This is a local bus at the beginning of its journey and there aren't many passengers yet, so Trish and I sit in seats near the front. When more passengers get on board they stare at us and Trish points out that it's likely we're sitting in somebody's usual 'place' and I think she's probably right.

When the bus comes to the main road I get off and wave goodbye to Trish, who's continuing to Osorno.

# *Argentina*

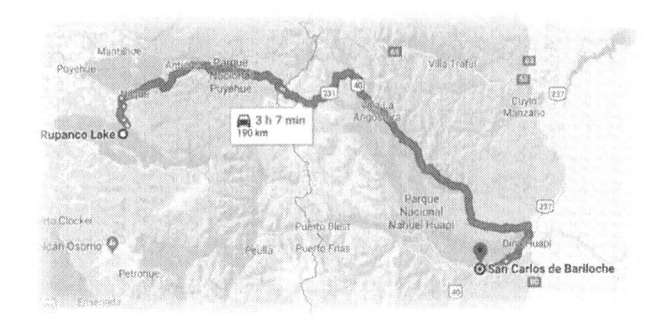

## Hitchhiking to Bariloche (190 kms)

I've taken advice about the best way to get to Argentina and there are just two options; go to Osorno and take transport from there, or hitchhike, which I'm told will be easy. Going to Osorno is going backwards, I came from there, so hitchhiking it is.

I look around to see where the bus has left me. Still early in the morning, the sun is peeping over the top of some distant mountains and there's a rising mist in the fields. Although the road is referred to as 'the main' road it doesn't look exactly major and there isn't a vehicle in sight. First things first, a call of nature has me squatting in a nearby ditch, it's as well there's no-one about!

I haven't hitchhiked alone before and I wonder where is the best place to stand? Do they use the same thumbs up gesture here in Chile? I realise that cars coming towards me in the direction I need to go are likely to have the sun in their eyes. Do I stand on the grass verge or leap out into the road so they'll see me?

Should I move further along the road away from the T junction? I giggle at all my questions which are currently irrelevant since there aren't any cars coming anyway.

This is a very strange experience. I'm curious that I'm not worried and excited that I've gained courage from Rupanco. A couple of cars and a truck have passed me now and although they don't stop, they do appear to acknowledge my 'thumbs up' gesture which gives me hope. A few more vehicles pass by, sometimes they gesticulate and I think they're telling me they can't give me a lift because they're turning off the road soon.

After about an hour with my thumb out, a truck indicates that it's pulling over and stops just past me. I approach the driver and he gestures to me to get in the back.

This isn't the sort of lift I was hoping for. I'm in a truck with three Chilean workmen, who don't speak a word of English, but I also don't think I'm in a position to be choosy. I smile a lot and manage a few short phrases of Spanish and it doesn't feel too uncomfortable. The drive is scenic and I'm starting to relax when the driver of the truck indicates that I must get out. I don't seem to have arrived anywhere, but I have no choice so with a *"gracias"* and *"adios"* I jump out clutching my stuff.

Looking up the road I can see a kiosk and some signage and I realise I'm at the Chilean border. I hand my passport to the man in the kiosk who takes a cursory look then waves me on. I'm not done yet though, because I then come to an area with office buildings and people and vehicles coming and going and I have to show my passport again. I locate the relevant office and I'm allowed to leave Chile. Now I need to hitch another lift.

With more vehicles about, my hopes are up, and it isn't long before a car pulls alongside me. I ask the driver if he's going to Bariloche and he says *"yes"* and more besides that I don't understand. I'm just relieved that I can get into his car. He introduces himself as Lucas and he can speak some English so conversation is easier, although it doesn't exactly flow.

We've only driven a couple of miles when he stops the car and says I have to get out. Looking around, it dawns on me that whilst I have left Chile, I haven't yet entered Argentina, this is the crossing point and until now we've been driving through the 'no man's land' in between the two borders. I again have to find the relevant office and queue, with scores of other people, to show my passport.

All the official stuff done, I walk down the road a short way ready to thumb for another lift. No sooner have I stuck my thumb out than Lucas pulls up again. I can't believe my good fortune that we should come through the border at the same time. This time I can relax and for the next hour I enjoy the drive until Lucas explains that his offices are just before Bariloche and he'll have to set me down then but I'll be able to take a bus into the town, which isn't far.

I consider hitching another ride but think better of it and I can see a bus stop a few yards away. I ask the young couple standing there if I can get a bus to Bariloche from here and they nod yes. At this point it occurs to me that I don't have any Argentinian money in my purse, I've packed it away somewhere at the bottom of my rucksack. I'm hurriedly pulling stuff out to try and locate the money when the bus arrives. The young couple urge me to get on but I shout *"nada cambiar",* "no money". The man grabs my bag and leaps onto the bus so I follow. Bless him, he pays for the fare for me.

I'm very grateful for his kindness.

The bus deposits me at the bus station on the outside of Bariloche and as I have no idea where my hostel is, I take one of the taxis waiting outside.

I'm again delighted with my choice of accommodation which feels homely and from an outside veranda there are views across the lake to the mountains beyond. I stand there and watch the sun going down which paints a picture of pinks and yellows across the sky. A couple of 'smokers' come out and join me and we chat.

Back in the hostel lounge I meet three physicians from Argentina travelling together, one is Mariano and another is called Alejandro and he tells me he's a magician as well as a doctor. I like them and we have an enjoyable conversation about travelling and how important it is to do what you most want to in life.

Re-connecting with Facebook I'm upset to learn that my lack of communication while on the farm in Chile was a cause for concern. I naively thought that people only noticed when I 'posted', I didn't think they would notice when I didn't. I feel bad that I hadn't considered this and that I caused some anxiety. There's good Internet available here and I take the opportunity to 'post' a video I made from the Chile farm. I need to allay any concerns that Ben has too as an email from his sister shows that they were also worried by my silence.

8th October

I've come to Bariloche mostly on a whim, after the brief conversation I had before leaving Auckland with the youngster who told me his dad has a bar here. I also noticed a brochure about Bariloche on a market stall in

Angelmo, which seemed out of place, and it prompted me to do some research. This is quite a good 'launching pad' to travel to El Calafate, because long distance buses leave from here and my mission today is to buy a bus ticket.

A traveller is leaving the hostel and I ask if I can share her taxi to the bus station. The weather is windy and rainy and I'm glad I don't have to walk.

Frustratingly, the bus terminal office is closed until the evening, so I end up walking 3 kms back to the town without having achieved anything. I pop into the Tourist Office who direct me to a company called Chalten Travel, but they're not at the address I've been given, so I walk back to the Tourist Office. They apologise, they've given me the wrong address. I finally locate the office in a very obscure location, only to learn they don't run buses to El Calafate and they suggest I try Via Travel. At Via Travel, a couple of roads away, they tell me they don't run buses to El Calafate either, I have to go to the bus terminal!

I feel frustrated, but not thwarted, so fighting the wind and rain I walk in the dark of the evening back to the bus terminal. I have a very difficult but funny conversation with the ticket seller trying to understand her and make myself understood. Eventually I buy what I believe is a bus ticket, to take me some 1,500 kms to El Calafate, for the pricey sum of 2440 pesos (about £120).

The reason our conversation is confusing becomes clear when I learn that there's a place called Perito Moreno which is different and a long distance from the glacier called Perito Moreno, located in Los Glaciares National Park. I'm glad I've found this information out. Outside the bus terminal I feel I've earned a taxi back, but there aren't any and I have another 3 km walk back to the hostel.

Very happy to be in the cosy warmth of the hostel, I find several travellers are sitting around the big table with alcohol and pizzas, they invite me to join them. The pizzas are home-made by one of the Argentinian guests and they are the best I've ever tasted, in fact I'd go so far as to say I've never really eaten pizza until now, this is pizza heaven. I fetch the bottle of wine I'd bought earlier and share it with a youngster from Korea called Soo, he's quiet and I like talking with him. The engaging, young Mariano invites me to visit him in Buenas Aires, I tell him how kind he is to ask me and I'm very touched when he says *"you have a lovely peacefulness about you"*, what a generous compliment.

## 9th October

The Internet at the hostel isn't working this morning so I can't do any research on line. I decide to visit Cerro Cathedral, a mountain about a forty-minute bus ride away.

It's a glorious sunny day and when I come to what I think is the bus stop, three of my hostel companions are already there. They tell me they've been waiting for twenty minutes already. I'm expecting the bus to arrive at 11.10 but at 11.30 it still hasn't turned up and I wonder if we're in the right place. There isn't anything we can do but continue to wait and after another half an hour Oliver and Cho from the hostel arrive. Oliver is from Switzerland and Cho is from Taiwan, they met travelling and have become good friends.

Cho speaks seven languages and talks to everyone in a most engaging way. He scolds us for not learning enough Spanish to read the bus time table which says that on the uneven hours the bus takes a different route, we have to wait until 12.10 for the next bus.

It turns out to have been a happy mistake for me, because Oliver and Cho invite me to spend the afternoon exploring Cerro Cathedral with them. I have the best time. Cho is hilariously funny, he interacts with everyone and is utterly delightful. We take a cable car up the mountain, there's plenty of snow about and people on skis. A chair lift takes us up even higher and we have incredible landscapes all around us. This isn't a novelty for Oliver who lives in Switzerland, but I find it amazing.

Before going back down the mountain, we stop at the café and each have a ridiculously sweet cup of hot chocolate. It's a slow afternoon pottering about and I start feeling anxious about getting back to check the Internet to do some forward planning. I scold myself for being ridiculous to think about anything other than spending time with these guys. At least twice during the afternoon Oliver says *"Ha, I love that guy"* as we fondly watch Cho saunter about taking a thousand photos or chatting with people.

There's still no Internet when we get back but the hostel says I can use their computer which works on a different system. It's tricky because the keyboard has Argentinian characters but I'm able to book my next accommodation.

# Patagonia

## 10th October

## Bus from Bariloche to El Calafate 31 hrs (1600 kms)

My bus for El Calafate leaves today, the company I'm travelling with is called Marga Taqs. I'm going to be on it around thirty hours so I'm relieved that the bus is a large modern looking one. I climb the stairs and bag a front seat which will give me a great view apart from the large crack across the window. A man called Claud sits next to me and we exchange greetings.

This journey is beginning to feel like a bad dream. The scenery is bland, we're on a straight tarmac road and there are large expanses of barren land either side with a few tufts of yellow grass and mountains way off in the distance. I like the colours; the sky, the road, the land are all shades of grey and the pale grass adds contrast. But the scenery simply doesn't change. I doze, I read, I study some Spanish and every time I look up, the view is the same. It's like someone painted this scene onto the front window!

Unlike other journeys I've been on, this bus rarely stops and not much is offered in the way of food or comforts. If I'd known they don't provide blankets or pillows for the overnight part of the ride I'd have brought my own blanket on board, unfortunately it's in my rucksack in the hold of the bus. The seats don't recline fully so the only way to sleep is lying on my back, which doesn't work for me, and it feels like a very long night.

I'm looking forward to breakfast, surely they'll provide some? They do, we're each given a paper bag containing a tiny carton of artificial fruit juice and a small cake.

About half way into our journey the bus pulls over at the side of the road and from the behaviour of the bus driver we can tell that something is wrong. He tries restarting the engine several times without success. This doesn't look to me like a good place to break down, there is nothing for miles in either direction, the nightmarish scenery is still no different. I laugh when my fellow travelling companion Claud says *"welcome to the real Patagonia"*. Then, oh joy, the bus starts. Smiles of relief all round and we pile back on board.

More hours in the bus and we arrive in the place called Perito Moreno which shares the same name as the famous glacier but isn't anywhere near it. Several people alight here, including the young couple that occupied the seats behind mine. There's nothing here and the couple look dismayed. They bought tickets to this place thinking it was the right destination to see the glacier. When they learn that it's another seven hours drive away they realise they don't have enough time to go there and get back for their flights home. I feel sorry for them and wonder how many people get 'caught out' in this way, as I might have done if the lady who sold me my bus ticket hadn't questioned my destination.

## 11th October

I reflect again how lucky I am that I never mind these long journeys, because this one is truly epic. The bus hasn't taken the most direct route and we arrive finally in El Calafate around 1.30 pm having travelled as a 'guestimate' some 1600 kms and thirty-one hours after leaving Bariloche.

El Calafate is in Santa Cruz province of Argentina and I'm now in the 'tail' of South America. It's sunny here, but very cold. A French lass called Anais, also with a backpack, gets off the bus. She hasn't booked anywhere to stay and I suggest she might like to try my hostel. The walk is further out of town than I'd expected, Anais walks at a cracking pace and I have to push hard to keep up. I try not to show how out of breath I am when we finally stumble through the front door.

The hostel is called 'American del Sur' and it looks inviting. My dorm room is cosy and has a warm radiator, always a bonus. The hostel staff are used to travellers wanting to visit the glacier and they have daily tours available, so I book one for tomorrow.

## 12th October

I have time for a good breakfast before the tour bus

comes at 8 am. There are about thirty of us on the bus, all going to Los Glaciares National Park, primarily to see the Perito Moreno Glacier. When the bus stops and we get our first glimpse of the glacier I feel excited. Everyone piles out and the mobile phones and cameras come out. It's a shame the weather isn't brilliant, there's some drizzle.

I had no idea what to expect of this tour, so I'm thrilled when we're taken right to the glacier. There's a long wooden viewing platform and we can stand quite close. The guide gives us about two hours to take in and appreciate this awesome spectacle and honestly 'awesome' doesn't do it justice. This is a vast frozen ice 'flow' that comes to an abrupt end as it reaches the water, the end of it looking like a huge cliff. The colours are stunning, the ice is a gorgeous aqua blue in places and I try to capture its beauty in my photos.

The platform meanders up higher and higher and every time I stop, the glacier looks more magnificent. Sometimes I hear the sound of cracking and see a large chard of ice tumble into the water, almost it seems, in slow motion.

It turns out that we've only had an introduction to the glacier, because now we're driven to the lake and board a boat which takes us out onto the Lago Argentino and right in front of it. Jaw-droppingly beautiful.

The boat lands us in another location where we're handed over to a hilariously funny guide called Diego. He walks with us along a boardwalk and across a short beach. Here we're each given crampons to attach to the bottom of our shoes so we can walk on the glacier!

This is an incredible experience. Who'd have thought I'd be walking across a glacier. The ice is shimmering brilliant white and clear aqua blues. There are narrow cracks and fissures and inside there's water as blue as ink. The sky is crystal clear blue. All totally amazing.

We're a small group and I feel like Scott of the Antarctic on an expedition trekking across the glacier. We concentrate on following Diego's experienced footsteps because he knows where the ice is safe, the thought of falling into a crevasse isn't a good one, possibly not life-threatening but I don't want to get a freezing cold soaking.

After maybe an hour of trekking Diego brings us to the end of the tour where a table has been set with glasses and bottles of whiskey. We're each given a shot of whisky complete with ice from the glacier, a nice touch.

## 13th October

I'm having today 'at home' to book my next adventure and make travel arrangements. Last night I had dinner with Australian Vanessa and another couple of girls called Kate and Allie and they'd shared some good travel tips.

The Internet can be the cause of a roller coaster ride of emotions; frustrating when it's non-existent or slow, but also amazing and awesome. I can book accommodation, tours and flights super-fast. I feel excited and scared at the same time, especially when I'm sometimes paying out a lot of money on a quick decision and the press of a button. I'm happy today that I've made progress and I think I've made some good decisions. I'm going camping and trekking in Torres del Paine in Patagonia, then I have two onwards flights booked from Punta Arenas to Santiago, then Santiago to Calama for the Atacama Desert.

However, not all transport can be arranged on the Internet and I walk to the bus terminal in town to buy a bus ticket for tomorrow, only to find the office is closed. Instead I go for a run, partly hoping to reach the lake but it's too far away. Another trip to the bus station later and I'm able to buy a ticket for Puerto Natales, located about 270 kms further south, and back in Chile.

In the evening I chat with five Dutch ladies who are all air stewardesses and very amusing. My room-mate from the past two nights is back at the hostel, he was supposed to have taken a flight back home but tells me his flight was cancelled because of a strike, poor guy. My room is also occupied by an Israeli man and an Argentinian man, three men and me. That feels a bit odd.

14th October

Bus to Puerto Natales, Chilean Patagonia, 5 hrs (290 kms)

After another satisfying hostel breakfast, I take the fifteen minute walk to the bus station. I'd considered waiting for Ness, an Israeli man who's catching the same bus. We met at breakfast, but I'm glad I haven't waited, he's a 'last minute' guy and leaps onto the bus just as it's about to leave. The ride is five hours and there's little change in scenery for the first three hours, then the landscape becomes more hilly and covered in snow.

We have a border crossing from Argentina into Chile, so have to get off the bus and go through the usual official rigmarole. It's relatively quick but I'm peeved because they take from me the avocado and kiwi fruit I'm carrying, they were going to be my lunch.

Arriving in Puerto Natales I can see that the town looks small. I ask a taxi to take me to Yaganhouse Hostel. It's run by the sister of Francisca, my host in Angelmo and I promised her that if I came here I'd stay at her sister's hostel. The building bearing the name Yaganhouse looks a mess, there's scaffolding and labouring work going on and my heart sinks. I tentatively opened the entrance door not feeling sure if the place is actually in business.

To my surprise Francisca and her father are sitting at a table inside having lunch. I'm greeted warmly, but this doesn't last long when her sister tells me she isn't aware of my booking and she doesn't have any rooms. I feel annoyed because I received an email response to my enquiry about room prices and I've already paid. My money will be refunded and the sister recommends another hostel a couple of roads away, so I walk there. The weather here is cold and beginning to rain.

The next accommodation is also full, but the lady who runs it is very helpful and recommends 'Mary's place' not far from here. She suggests I leave my rucksack with her while I walk to it.

Mary isn't at home, but her husband is and he invites me inside. They have a room available and he offers to show it to me, so I follow him up the staircase and past a parade of tired looking cuddly toys adorning each step. This is a homestay, not a hostel, but I'm not in a position to be fussy. Although tiny, the room looks comfortable and has a heater, I'll take it.

After settling in to my new accommodation, I take a walk out to explore Puerto Natales. It's on the west side of southern Patagonia and a port for boats touring the Patagonian fjords. The place is very plain and has an old-fashioned feel to it, there aren't many people about. I pass a restaurant that looks appealing called Le Bote, which turns out to be pleasant enough.

## 15th October

I like Mary's homestay. My room is warm and the bed is very comfy, I have a long sleep. Breakfast is bread, more bread, biscuits and cake.

After a 'pottering about' sort of day I go back to Le Bote, mainly because I want another glass of wine. I discover chips with eggs and onions on the menu, so I order it along with lettuce and mayonnaise and a glass of Sauvignon Blanc and I'm in tastebud heaven. The bottle of wine is Diablo Castillo and the waiter tells me this is the second largest winery in Chile. I've seen it in the U.K. but never bought it, I'll remember to try it when I'm back home. Sitting opposite my table I'm amused to see a guy wearing a T shirt that says across the front *"make people, not potatoes"*. What does that mean? He isn't English speaking and I wonder if he knows what his T shirt says.

## 16th October

### Five Day Torres del Paine Tour

### Day 1

This is an exciting day because I'm off to Torres del Paine. My tour is with Cascada Travel and Eco Camp and their offices are just around the corner from my homestay. When I arrive, I'm joined by the rest of the group and we all have lunch together at a restaurant next door. Afterwards we get into a minibus with our guides Daniel and a very cheerful female called Pad.

We have about an hour and a half drive to Eco Camp. As we drive into the Torres del Paine National Park I'm fascinated by the small bushes on the hills that have splashes of bright red, presumably small red flowers. From this distance they look as though they've been 'airbrushed' on one side.

When we reach the Eco Camp I'm delighted with the natural, rural setting. There are about thirty green eco-domes for sleeping accommodation and larger wooden domes for the communal areas. My dome is cosily warm from the sunshine and I can see the three towers (torres) in the distance. It's expertly fitted out with a wooden floor and natural materials. Although there are twin beds inside, I have the dome to myself. This is definitely 'glamping'.

We're given time to 'settle in' then our group meets up for a briefing, followed by a magnificent three course dinner and free wine. I remind myself to hold back on the wine as tomorrow will be a long hiking day.

## 17th October

### Day 2

Breakfast is a substantial buffet with plenty of good, healthy food to choose from. Another table is laid with bread where we can make our own sandwiches and take handfuls of nuts, dried fruit and muesli bars for a picnic lunch. They're looking after us extremely well.

My group comprises Don, an elderly looking man, Octavio who has done 'Iron Man' challenges, Ashley and Taylor from Connecticut, Eve and Ian from Australia, Anna who works for Cascada and our guides Daniel and Pad.

We set off in a small bus, then transfer to a catamaran that takes us across the stunningly beautiful Lake Pehoe. The air is cold but the sky is a perfect blue. Reflected in the gorgeous blue colour of the water are the surrounding mountains and rocks creating an incredible picture.

We arrive at Grande Paine Hotel where we leave some of our gear because we're coming back here later. And then our hike starts, along a natural path through grasses and across wild, undulating terrain. Daniel sets a very fast pace and I wonder if he'll keep this up all day. I'm glad that he stops when we come to an exceptional scene or landscape so I have time to take a photo and catch my breath. This is an incredible day of walking with steep uphill climbs and gorgeous countryside.

We climb up high to a flat rocky area and stop to rest. I'm over-awed to realise that I can turn 360 degrees and see three stunning and totally different landscapes. On one side there's a huge snowy mountain, another view is across a vast grassy plain to a blue lake and on another side there are two mammoth rocks, cream coloured at the base turning into dark grey at the top. Taking a photo of each scene, you would never believe I am standing in one spot.

We've been walking hard and fast for several hours and I'm somewhat daunted when Daniel says there's a three-hour hike to get back. Three more hours! I eat some nuts and a muesli bar. Maybe this helps my energy levels because a short while later I realise I feel great again and my energy is back. This makes me very happy.

By the time I can see our hotel in the distance my feet are pretty sore and no longer afraid of getting left behind, I dawdle and relax. The sun is beginning to set and it gives the grasses and hills around a warm golden glow.

I don't like the hotel much. It's basic and cold, the supper is mediocre and I share a room with four other people. We're given a sleeping bag and a clean white liner which is challengingly small. I squiggle into it but then can't move without getting all twisted up and considering I'm small, I wonder how larger people manage.

One of the guys sharing my room is also called Daniel and I have an enjoyable conversation with him. I love how quickly it's possible to 'connect' with a fellow traveller, especially given the difference in our ages, nationalities etc. Not for the first time I wish it was this easy in 'every day' life.

## 18th October

### Day 3

Daniel tells us that today we only have to walk 11 kms and I'm quite relieved because my feet are still sore. The trek takes us towards the Grey Glacier which from this distance looks very dramatic. We walk another four hours to the Grey Lake, from where the glacier gets its name, then we climb on board a boat which motors out right up close to the glacier. It has the same gorgeous aqua blue colours as Perito Moreno glacier.

On the boat we're given a drink of Pisco Sour, this one is called Campanario and it's delicious. The boats sets us back down on a sort of beach and we walk along the shoreline where massive chunks of ice, like huge ice sculptures, are floating in the water.

I'm very happy to learn that a bus is meeting us not far from here, so we don't have much more walking to do.

Back at Eco Camp there's an opportunity to join a yoga class. I think this will be perfect for stretching after a long walk but instead of gentle stretches it turns into a fairly tough work out, not quite what tired legs need right now.

Another excellent dinner and I've been given a different dome, this one has a double bed, very comfy and I wish I could stay here longer.

## 19th October

### Day 4

Today is a big hiking day, we're going to cover 22 kms. We set off on foot from Eco Camp in sunshine. We walk uphill a long way which gives us amazing views across the plains, then we come to a forest and for a long time we're walking through trees. The land changes again and we start climbing up rocks and boulders, up and up, for the longest time, clambering and climbing. Poor Ashley started the walk with bad knee pain and I wonder if she'll cope with this climb.

There's snow around us now, interspersed between the rocks, it becomes thicker the higher we climb. Suddenly we get our first sight of the three granite monoliths, the towers called Torres del Paine. They're magnificent sculptures created by nature. The three towers are called Torre Sur, 2,850 metres high, Torre Central at 2,800 metres and Torre Norte, 2,600 metres.

As we climb closer we see a turquoise blue lake in front of the towers. With huge stones and snow all around and a clear blue sky behind, the scene is extraordinary. The hike may have been exhausting but my goodness, it's totally worth it. I have a rewarding feeling of achievement as we sit on the rocks taking in the scenery and eating our packed lunches.

The trek back is long. The whole group are excellent walkers and Ashley is doing exceptionally well in spite of her horrible knee pain. I'm amazed to learn that Don is just a couple of weeks short of 79 years old, his energy and ability is phenomenal. Ironman Octavio shoots off ahead of us and heads back to the next Refugio to wait for us to catch up.

Relieved to have finished all 22 kms, back at Eco Camp, we all do 'high fives'. This has been a truly amazing day. There's another excellent meal in the evening with free Pisco Sour and wine and this time I don't have to restrict myself as there's no walking tomorrow.

*20th October*

*Aeroplane to Santiago (3½ hrs), Aeroplane to Calama, Chile (2hrs)*

## Day 5

My last excellent breakfast at Eco Camp, then I leave in a small bus with about eight others and depart back to Puerto Natales. I'm sad to say goodbye to our fantastic guides Daniel and Pad who revealed to us last evening that they are a 'couple' and they're engaged to be married. Pad tells me I can come back any time and stay with them, she says the sweetest thing *"the house is small but our hearts are big"*.

From Puerto Natales some of us, myself included, are continuing on to the airport at Puerto Arenas, so we have another three-hour drive arriving at the airport around 2.15 pm in plenty of time for me to catch my 4.40 pm flight back to Santiago.

The rather cramped aeroplane takes off as scheduled and the timing is perfect for me to see the sun setting over the Andes. From Santiago airport I'm flying on to Calama, but my next flight isn't until 6.05 in the morning, so I have all night to wait.

Fortunately, there's free Internet at the airport and I'm very happy that I'm able to talk to my daughter in England. She has her 40th birthday tomorrow and I'm sorry I won't be seeing her.

Having explored the airport I'm bewildered that there are very few chairs, however I manage to get two next to each other and I try to get comfy on them, tying my large rucksack to the seat and cuddling my front pack. Sleep here is impossible, I've picked an incredibly noisy area. Airport staff constantly wheel enormous trolleys along the corridor and located right opposite my chairs is a metal 'speed bump' which causes the metal trolleys to clang loudly each time they encounter the ramp. It's so noisy that I find it funny.

# *San Pedro de Atacama, Chile to Bolivia*

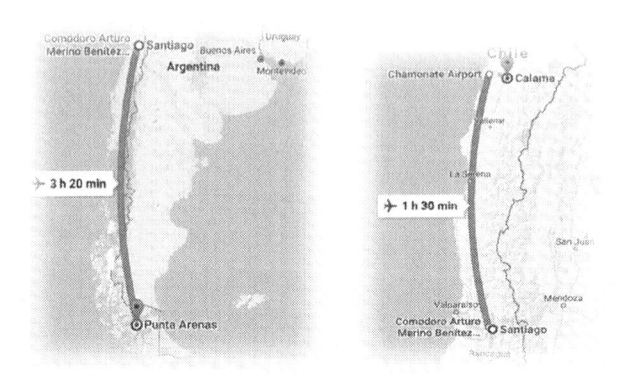

## 21st October

The flight to Calama is excellent, I have a wonderful view from the airplane of the sunrise and snowy mountains below. As we land it looks like there's nothing at Calama, it truly is in the middle of nowhere.

The heat hits me when I step out of the plane. I'm grateful that there are 'shared' taxis available to take me to San Pedro de Atacama for the not unreasonable price of about £14, and frankly I would probably have paid any price because I'm not sure there's any other way to get where I'm going.

It takes about an hour to drive across the desert and when we reach the small town of San Pedro de Atacama, I'm intrigued. It's quaint, hot and dusty with sandy roads and crude, single storey buildings, sometimes surrounded by red mud walls. This appears to be an oasis in a desert. The taxi drops me off at

Hostel Ayni which, compared to others we've driven past, looks rather charming.

I'm delighted to meet Natalie who runs the hostel, she's skinny as a rake and very sexy with masses of long dark hair. She's also very welcoming and helpful. The bedroom is charmingly decorated in lilac and pale lime and the bed looks comfy. I already wish I'm staying here longer than two nights. Natalie gives me a nutritious oaty milk drink which she makes in a blender and it staves off my hunger perfectly.

The hostel has a quaint balcony overlooking part of the town, and I sit in the warm sunshine feeling relaxed. The cleaner is working and her young daughter is curious about me, she comes over and we try communicating. I take a book about yoga off the shelf and we look at the pictures together, she's very sweet and giggly.

I've discovered that there's a sunset tour this evening to the Valley de La Luna and I have time to book it.

During the afternoon I walk into town and buy food; avocado, banana, kiwi, apple, cucumber, bread and milk and I'm relieved to find an ATM. Frustratingly, the most money it will let me have is 50,000 in 2,000 peso notes, which sounds like a lot but actually isn't. I get charged a high price by my bank each time I withdraw money, sometimes it can cost me £5 a time. I take some of the pesos to a money exchange and swap them for Bolivianos ready for my trip into Bolivia.

The 'Sunset Tour' comprises a group of seven, plus our driver, who takes us out of the town and across the desert sand. The whole area is awesome, the scenery takes my breath away, I want to stand and soak it in. As far as I can see there are swathes of sand, rocks, mountains, volcanoes all in rich reds, oranges, browns and creams. The sky is still a bright blue.

Our guide takes us into a cave which doesn't excite me much, until we come out the other side, then climb up. The landscape from here is truly spectacular and the evening light makes it even more so.

We drive further out across the desert to see different rock formations; three large upright rocks are known as the 'Three Mary's'.

For the final part of the tour we climb on foot up a steep and rather treacherous rocky site to reach the summit. This has to be the most stunning view ever, I'm so full up with the magnificence of the land and the colours I feel I may explode. We stay here until the sun disappears, but the incredible spectacle isn't over.

As the sun goes down the sky takes on glorious colours of purple, pink and orange, more amazing even than the sunsets I've already seen. The ascent down from our rocky outcrop is even more treacherous than going up and I wonder how many tourists this guide has previously 'lost'. Some of our group inch down on their bottoms rather than risk toppling over.

## 22nd October

The sun is searingly hot. I hire a bicycle and cycle up and down the dusty, narrow lanes of San Pedro to explore. There are a few streets with tourist shops selling brightly coloured garments and blankets. There's a holiday atmosphere here. I'm going to cycle to Pucara of Quitor and it should only be about 3 kms in the north. Typical of me, I cycle in the wrong direction for a while before I realise my mistake and turn around, so the ride is longer than I'd anticipated.

Pucara of Quitor is a massive, ancient, stone and red mud fortress, built by the Atacameño people to defend themselves. There are a couple of long paths leading to the top. I walk up slowly in the heat. The panorama is incredible, sand and rocks stretching out all around for miles into the distance with the little oasis of green that is San Pedro de Atacama. There are very few people about and I have an exhilarating feeling of awe that I'm here on my own surrounded by the vastness of this red land.

It's another hot and dusty cycle ride back into town where I've promised myself a coffee in the attractive square I saw this morning. Frustratingly I can't remember which of the many alleyways I need to cycle down to find it. At last, I spot the small church which was opposite and I'm rewarded for my efforts. The café is charming and I sit outside, people watching, with a tiny cup of cappuccino.

This evening I'm joining another tour, this one is an Astrological Tour. The Atacama is famous for stargazing and it's where the world's largest astronomical project is based. From here scientists are able to observe the birth of stars and planets and detect distant galaxies forming.

A French family is staying at Ayni Hostel, Mum, Dad and their two teenage boys and they're on the same tour as me. We're taken to the home of a husband and wife couple and, joining another group, we're invited to watch a video about stars and planets. Among the group I recognise Octavio from the Torres del Paine trek.

Outside is now pitch black and the sky decorated with stars. There are several massive telescopes each pointing at various planets and constellations and the guide gives us good information as we're each invited to look through the telescopic lens. I'm keen to learn about the different constellations, but I can't help thinking that the night sky I saw in Nepal was way better.

Chatting with the French family it turns out that we've also booked the same tour to Salar des Uyuni, which will be an early start tomorrow. We won't be getting very much sleep though, because it's gone 11 pm when the driver drops us back at our hostel.

## 23rd October

## Three Day Tour to Salar de Uyuni

### Day 1

A jeep collects the French family and me from the hostel and drives us to the Bolivian border and passport control.

I'm very amused by this border crossing which is a small shack in the middle of nothing and nowhere. We have our passports checked and come back to our vehicle to find that our guide has laid out a tasty looking breakfast, complete with table and tablecloth. There's mashed avocado, bananas, cake and coffee.

The temperature here is very different from San Pedro with a cold wind. We soon discover that this place isn't the only official crossing, we have to stop two more times to show papers before we leave Chile and enter Bolivia.

Our driver is called David and he only speaks Spanish. The French family, fortunately for me, speak English and some Spanish, so between us we're able to communicate. We're driving through the Eduardo Avaroa Andean Fauna National Reserve and the roads are at first poor, then non-existent. I don't know how David knows where he's going as we're driving across sand. I'm very happy that I'm sitting in the front seat and I take lots of photos through the windscreen.

During the morning David stops the jeep and tells us that we've arrived at a natural hot spring and we can put on swimming costumes and take a dip. The temperature outside is cold so we get changed quickly. Fortunately, the water is warm. It feels very surreal sitting in a pool surrounded by desert and distant mountains.

Oddly, when I go to change back into my clothes in the nearby changing hut, my pants have disappeared! There aren't many places I can look for them but they've definitely gone. I can't afford to lose any more, having lost a previous pair down the large plughole of the laundry sink at Rupanco Farm!

Driving across the National Reserve the scenery becomes ever more beautiful and 'other-worldly'. We pass spectacular lakes each with its own special colour, one is bronze-red, another lake is aqua blue. David stops the jeep often so we can get out and take in the scenery.

By late afternoon we arrive at Arbol de Piedra Hostel, a large, plain, single storey building, seemingly positioned in the middle of nowhere and we're given lunch. I meet a little girl who lives here, aged maybe 3 or 4 years old, her face has the rosacea red skin typical of this climate with its cold winds. It isn't warm in the hostel, we're all wearing coats, hats and gloves.

After lunch David drives us to see another lake and this one is exceptionally spectacular. It's covered in pink flamingos. I've never seen scenery like this before, nature really has used a palette of pretty pastel colours to create a stunning picture. The altitude here is 4,900 metres and we're all feeling a bit head achy and weird.

Back at the hostel we're given much needed hot tea and biscuits, then later they provide us with supper and I'm grateful that the meal is vegetarian. I notice David is outside washing down the jeep. He's not a young man and when I think of our early start this morning, the miles he's driven us across the desert and now he's cleaning the vehicle, I appreciate how hard he has to work.

The French family and I share a bedroom and sleep in our clothes because we're so cold.

### 24th October

### Day 2

Today is my son's birthday and I wish I could send him a message, but there isn't any Internet here.

We set off after breakfast with David driving the jeep again and travel for many miles and for several hours. Never have I seen scenery as incredibly beautiful and awesome as this and I hope I will always remember these colours of warm custard, soft creams, pale brick red with occasional bright green grasses, underneath a glorious bluer than blue sky. We stop frequently at lagoons and fantastic rock formations.

Our picnic lunch stop is truly magical. We've come to a gorgeous, vibrant green, grassy area and David sets up the table, complete with chequered cloth, and lays out an amazing spread of food, presumably prepared by last night's hostel. There's a tiny brook meandering between the clumps of springy grass. There's no wind here, it's quiet and relaxing. My French companions are suffering from the effects of the altitude and lie in the grass and doze, while I'm happy walking about and take photos.

We continue our drive in the afternoon, not without some concerns. There's something not quite right with the jeep and David is clearly worried. We stop a couple of times while he lifts the bonnet and tinkers underneath, but we continue to drive, David chews coca leaves all the while and offers me some now and again which I take. They taste pretty disgusting, but if they help ward off altitude sickness I'm willing to chew.

The problem with the jeep doesn't stop us arriving at our next hotel and I wonder what we've come to, it looks an ugly concrete building and appears to be unfinished. Stepping inside is a total surprise. The reception area is spacious, modern and nicely furnished and I'm delighted that I have a double bedroom to myself with my own shower and hot water.

We have a long wait for our evening dinner and I'm ravenously hungry but I utilise the time trying to connect with the Internet. I'm very excited when I'm able to talk with my son and wish him a happy birthday, although technically no longer his birthday because it's now one o'clock in the morning on the 25$^{th}$ October in the U.K. I marvel again at the wonders of technology, here I am in the middle of a desert in Bolivia and I can chat with my son in London.

This has been a truly memorable day.

25$^{th}$ October

Day 3

I wake feeling grateful that I'm well and not suffering from altitude sickness which seems to be afflicting the French family who all have headaches.

We leave the hotel at 4.45 am to catch the sunrise on the salt flats called Salar des Uyuni. I wonder how much sleep David has had.

Just half an hour's drive from our hotel, we've arrived on the extraordinary salt flats, covering nearly 11,000 sq. kms. The land is made from white salt and stretches as far as the eye can see. Underfoot it feels and looks like crunchy snow in a sort of crazy paving pattern. David drives across into the 'nothingness', there's nothing and no-one around but us. He parks up in the still dark morning and we get out of the jeep to 'play'. This is another surreal experience. There's nothing to see for miles in all directions but the outline of some dark mountains in the far distance.

The sun begins to show itself, pastel colours peep over the line in the distance, then it suddenly blazons its way across the horizon causing our bodies to make the longest shadows I've ever seen. The French family have silly fun taking photos of each other jumping 'over the sun' and creating shapes with their shadows. I suddenly feel a bit uncomfortable on my own.

We have plenty of time to experience this strange land, then get back into the jeep and David drives across the salt flats where we come to an odd looking small island of volcanic rock, covered in massive cactus. It looks strange and out of place here. David indicates that we can climb to the top while he prepares breakfast. As always, I love being up high and from the top there's a 360 degree view of the salt flats. Way into the distance I can see the occasional tiny black dot and realise these are cars driving across the land, it gives the vastness of the place perspective.

We're not the only tourists here. When we come down off the island, other tour groups and buses have arrived. I'm grateful that David has provided coffee. It's now fully light and the landscape looks different again with the whiteness of the salt against the bright, blue sky.

After breakfast David drives us back somewhere on the salt flats and again we're alone. We spend the next hour taking funny photos, the vastness of the horizon changes the perspective of everything which distorts things to look large or small by placing them a few feet in front or behind each other. Standing a few feet behind a can of Coke and positioning the camera correctly, it can look as though the can is bigger than you.

We've had several hours in the beautiful and strange Salt Flats and now David tells us we're going to visit a village. The village is small, and the dusty street we're on is lined either side with tourist stalls selling brightly coloured blankets, clothes and ornaments.

The traditional dress of the women is fascinating to me. The women tend to be stocky and short and they wear heavy colourful, pleated or gathered skirts which come past their knees and thick woollen stockings. Their black hair hangs in pigtails underneath a 'bowler' style hat which defies gravity, perched on the top of their head it looks as though it should fall off. One lady in particular looks such a character I want to take a photo of her, but I also don't like to be intrusive.

Our next destination is just 3 kms outside Uyuni and we arrive at the oddest place. A cemetery for trains. This has to be one of the strangest tourist attractions ever. Train lines had been built by the British at the request of the Bolivian government at the end of the 19th century. They were mostly used by mining companies and when the industry collapsed in the 1940's, the trains fell into disrepair and were abandoned, they now lie rusting in the desert. It's a sad and strange site to see so many magnificent engines and pieces of machinery left to decay.

Our last stop is Uyuni town. Marion is keen to buy a genuine antique blanket to take home and we spend some time at the market looking, but they are surprisingly expensive and she isn't tempted.

Our last lunch together is at a typical small eatery

with plastic table and chairs and a plastic table cloth. The meal looks awful; masses of sticky rice and tough looking meat swimming in a watery liquid. I have to be content filling the gap in my tummy with the rice.

The tour ends at the company's offices where I say my goodbyes to the French family. David kindly offers to help me locate the hostel I've pre-booked which I believe is close by.

The hostel turns out to be only a few yards away but tricky to find since it's located inside a railway station and up some iron steps. It feels like a furnace inside, swelteringly hot and there's no air. My bedroom is a wooden 'shoebox'. It has two bunk beds and barely room enough to walk alongside the bottom bed. There aren't any windows and I can't imagine sleeping with the door shut and surviving the night. Well I guess I'm going to make a poor choice of accommodation sometimes and this is clearly one of those times.

I walk from the hostel at the earliest opportunity, to explore Uyuni. Coming out of the railway station I'm in a wide and dusty road with a few plain square buildings either side. Just off this main road are smaller roads, one of them has a few bars and restaurants along it and there are other travellers sitting around chatting and drinking.

I need a bus to take me to La Paz tomorrow and this turns out to be something of a challenge. Along one street, I'm confused by the many different bus companies and bus 'touts', they all quote different prices and I have no idea if they're reliable. Then I have the idea of popping into one of the major tour operator offices to ask for advice. The lady working there kindly tells me the company they use, she says they're trustworthy, so I locate their offices and book a sleeper bus for the following evening, leaving at 8 pm.

## 26th October

Miraculously no-one shares my 'hothouse' bedroom and I survive the night by leaving the door open. A bit risky, but I decide I would rather be robbed, than die of suffocation.

I have another day to wander around Uyuni since my bus doesn't leave until this evening. I walk outside again and I'm fascinated by the colourful Bolivian people in their different clothes. The women wear a lot of layers and many of them have young children or babies tied to their backs with colourful blankets. All the women have the same styled black hair, always plaited and sometimes so long their plaits reach down the length of their back. It looks odd to see so many of these women walking along looking at their mobile phones, just like we do in the U.K. I manage to discreetly take a few photos of local people.

I'm looking for somewhere that I can buy food for the bus journey and I go into a small shop with a sign saying 'mini market'. Inside I pick up a packet of nuts and a young boy rushes over to me saying *'nierdo'* which I realise from his actions means 'closed'. I'm puzzled and look at the shop door that stands wide open, but he takes the nuts out of my hand and puts them back on the shelf, indicating that I should leave.

## Overnight bus to La Paz, Bolivia (550 kms)

The bus I've booked for the overnight ride is a tourist bus, not a local one and I think this was a smart decision. There's a toilet on board and they give us food. The seats are pretty good and as no-one occupies the seat next to me I'm able to get comfy and sleep fairly well.

## 27th October

It's a surprise to me when the lights come on at 5.30 am and we're told we're arriving at La Paz. I've woken needing the loo and frustrated to be told the toilet on the bus is closed. Closed, really? Now that seems mean, surely lots of us want a loo when we wake up! Another forty-five minutes pass before the bus pulls into the bus station, then the bags need to be off-loaded. By this time, I'm desperate for a toilet.

Grabbing my bag at the earliest opportunity I scurry into the terminal to find Los Banos. I have to pay first, then dash to the toilet area which is packed with people.

Trying to manoeuvre through the crowd with a front pack, back pack and ukulele is challenging and makes me laugh. Eventually it's my turn, a cubicle becomes available and I manage to squeeze myself and my stuff into the tiny space they call a toilet.

Now I have a decision to make. Enquiring about buses to Cusco I can get one at around 8 am today, which is appealing because I'm already here at the bus terminal, or I can take a taxi to the hotel I've pre-booked, take a look around La Paz and go to Cusco tomorrow.

I elect to do the latter and it has a lot to do with my desire to get my hair coloured again. I think it's likely that there will be a good hotel in La Paz that caters for European blonde hair. There are taxis outside the bus terminal and I ask the driver to take me to Latino Hotel.

I like the look of the hotel which is small, with character and pretty stained-glass doors at the front entrance. The receptionist, called Ricardo, shows me to my room and I'm grateful that he says I can use it now because the time is still only 7.30 am. I ask if I can have tomorrow's breakfast which is included in the room price, today, since I'll be leaving early tomorrow and will miss breakfast and Ricardo says I can.

My experience of Bolivians so far is they're not big on customer service, they don't smile much and the lady who provides my hotel breakfast is no exception. She still has her coat on which looks odd, though understandable because the hotel is cold. She puts a breakfast together and hands it to me without expression. The coffee is good but comes in a tiny cup so I go back for a refill. A few minutes later I'm handed a note that tells me only one coffee is provided on the room rate. I'll have to pay extra for the second cup.

I have the day to explore La Paz which looks like a

fascinating city, but my first mission is to go to an exclusive hotel in the hope they'll have an 'in-house' hairdresser. One of the top hotels here is called Europa and armed with a map from Ricardo I walk out to find it.

The Europa is on a busy city-style main street and enquiring at the Reception Desk I'm delighted to learn that yes, they do have an 'in-house' hairdresser. If I come back in an hour she can colour my hair. I return after enjoying a large cup of coffee and the receptionist phones through to the salon owner who comes out to meet me.

I cannot deny that my heart sinks when I see the hairdresser. I'm expecting someone stylish and young. The lady in front of me is stocky, plainly dressed and looks as though she's in need of a decent hairdresser. I hesitate momentarily wondering if I can make an excuse and leave, but of course I don't.

I don't speak Spanish or Bolivian and my hairdresser doesn't speak English. I want to tell her that I'd like my hair coloured blonde, similar to how it is now, but not more blonde, in fact if anything I'd like it to be a little darker and I don't want it to be brassy blonde, a gentle ash blonde would be nice and I want her to concentrate the colour on the roots, not all over. My message is conveyed to her using sign language, my mobile translator and internal prayers. When she opens the cupboard and shows me three pots of hair colour, yellow, red and black I'm not overly hopeful of the outcome.

I don't know how she did it, but this amazing hairdresser colours my hair perfectly. It's exactly the colour I want. This feels like something of a miracle. She's also manicured my nails and the total cost is 430 bob, the equivalent of £40, probably a lot of money by

Bolivian standards but a fraction of what it would cost me in the U.K. I give her a generous tip.

Now I have the rest of the day to explore. This is the highest capital city in the world, more than 3,500m above sea level and it sits in a sort of land 'basin' surrounded by hills and mountains. Every inch of the hillsides is covered in buildings, mostly red brick and with an unfinished look about them.

The roads, many of which are cobbled, are either a steep climb up or a long slope down. I come across a lively market area selling produce and buy some tomatoes, an apple and a mango. Women everywhere are wearing their quaint costumes and I want to take photos, but every time I ask if it's okay, they shake their head 'no'.

I'm curious about the bowler style hats the ladies wear and how they keep them on their head, so using some Spanish words and sign language, I ask a couple of ladies who are sitting together at a market stall. One of the ladies is willing to 'engage' with me and when she understands my question she tells her friend to take off the hat she's wearing. There's nothing to keep it in place, no elastic, no pins, no superglue. I'm amused to notice that she keeps things inside the 'bowl' of the hat, she uses the space as a handy receptacle for small items. I say *'grasias'* to the ladies, it's been a fun encounter.

The park area is busy with people, colourfully dressed and I'm able to take plenty of photos here. I wonder if there's something special going on because there are armed police about. It seems that yesterday was the President's birthday, so I guess there have been celebrations.

I take a long walk beyond the town to a viewpoint which shows the city sprawling up the surrounding hills. From here I walk to the bus terminal to check out the distance in readiness for tomorrow. By the time I'm back at Latinos I'm exhausted and quite breathless, which I assume is due to the altitude.

## 28th October

## Bus to Cusco, 12 hours (660 kms)

The walk to the big yellow bus terminal (Terminal de Buses, Lapaz) takes only twenty minutes, so I don't bother with a taxi and noticing how busy the morning traffic in La Paz is I think it was a wise decision. The morning air is cool, the traffic fumes are unpleasant and my luggage feels heavy, the altitude is sapping my energy and I walk slowly.

I'm relieved that terminal kiosk No.14 is open and the same lady that sold me the ticket is there. She checks me in and tells me where to find my bus. I only have to wait fifteen minutes and it arrives. The bus is a modern one, the seats, called cama, or semi-cama are reclining. Mine is upstairs, next to the window.

The scenery as we drive is pretty, the soil is almost pink with green tufty grass and we pass small villages that mostly look derelict but I now know from experience are probably not. Many buildings appear to be only half built yet people live in them, or they've never bothered putting a roof on, who knows! We pass small holdings with animals in fields, mostly sheep, donkeys, some cattle and a few llamas.

Now we have to cross the border again, this time from Bolivia into Peru. The bus parks up and we all pile out.

This is a big, chaotic and busy crossing. There are hundreds of colourful Bolivians walking or riding electric bicycle taxis. The bus driver has given us papers to fill in and several instructions, all in Spanish. I have no idea what's happening and follow the other passengers. There are three other English speakers; an Israeli, an Irishman and a girl from London and we chat together while waiting in the inevitable queues. The process of leaving Bolivia is long and then we have to weave through the crowds again to get through immigration and into Peru.

We muddle our way through the confusion and checked, signed and stamped, the bus driver is waiting to show us where he parked the bus and we can board again for the next leg of our journey.

Just outside the border crossing we can see Lake Titikaka and we drive alongside it for a while. I've been eating some fruit and bread which I brought for the journey and I'm glad I did. The first meal arrives five hours after starting the drive, meat, with rice. When I bought my bus ticket I was asked if I'm vegetarian and this information was written on my ticket but I'm told there aren't any vegetarian meals on board.

When we finally arrive in Cusco it's gone 10pm, which is actually past 11pm, the clock has gone back an hour here. Outside the bus station I take a taxi to my hostel called Intro Hostels. By the time I'm checked in, the people in my dorm are already sleeping so I can't do anything other than get into bed.

# Cusco, Peru

## 29th October

With the hour change, I wake early. The others in my room are still asleep so I have to creep out and hope I can get some hostel breakfast. The hostel is quirky and I like it. The communal area is a sort of internal courtyard and at this early hour its cold but happily for me, breakfast is available in a small indoor bar.

My friend from childhood called Diana, who lives in California, coincidentally is on holiday here in Cusco. I give her a call and she's delighted to hear from me but she's leaving today, so suggests I pop along to see her and her husband in their hotel before they go. They've been staying in luxury in a beautiful hotel just ten minutes' walk away. I haven't seen my friend for years and we have fun 'catching up' while sipping coca tea in elegant surroundings.

Cusco is quaint and full of character and I'm very happy walking in the sunshine exploring the narrow streets, lanes and the large square with its historic church. It's touristy but in a nice way. I choose to have coffee in Cusco's main square in a small cafe on the second floor. There's a little table in a rickety looking balcony with a good view. I think I'll be visiting this coffee place often.

In the afternoon I join a free walking tour which wanders around lanes I probably wouldn't have found on my own. Our guide shows us some plants that are used in the Ayahuasca blend, hallucinogenic spiritual medicine and he shares information about the practices of using Ayahuasca, very popular in Peru. The tour finishes with a walk up high and excellent views over Cusco.

I've bought some food from the supermarket to cook myself a meal this evening but the hostel kitchen is a nightmare. Putting a match to the gas stove sends a rocket of flames up and I only just avoid singeing my eyebrows. There isn't much in the way of kitchen pans or utensils either. I cobble together some pasta, tuna, sweetcorn and salad, but I won't be using the kitchen again.

## 30th October

My hostel room mates are annoying. I'm sharing with three men and they go to bed ridiculously early and get up ridiculously late, why so much sleep? It means I always have to creep to bed quietly in the dark and get up and out quietly, there's no opportunity to get organised.

Passing the reception desk on my way out, I overhear a woman asking for directions to the market; she sounds English. She's attractively dressed and looks interesting and I ask if she'd mind if I went along with her. Her name's Sandy and we walk together and chat amiably. At the market we go our separate ways but agree to meet up in the evening for dinner. We choose a small restaurant and have a simple but tasty meal with a delicious glass of red wine, my first glass of wine in Peru.

## 31st October

At breakfast, I chat with a guy called Neil, he looks a similar age to me and he suggests I join a free tour that he's going on this morning. There's a group of eight of us. I'm surprised to see that two taxis are waiting for us and they take us for a drive up high, then we get out and I'm told we'll be walking down. We've been driving for more than fifteen minutes so I'm slightly daunted that we're going for a long walk because I feel unprepared. I hadn't expected this and I don't have a jacket, water or food with me.

The weather and scenery are absolutely gorgeous and I'm very happy to realise that we're not walking back along the road, but across some grassy, undulating countryside. Our guide is a nice guy, but the passion he has for his country, its history and the many, many stories surrounding religion and the gods, causes him to talk incessantly and at great length and I'm suffering from an overload of information.

The open terrain we're walking across is my favourite kind with grassland and trees, sometimes sheep, goats and horses grazing and large rocky outcrops. The tour began at 10 am and we don't return back to Cusco until 2 pm, it's been a fabulous morning.

Someone in the group suggests we have lunch together and we find a restaurant. I choose spinach soup which tastes good but is served in a bowl so vast that I can only manage half of it.

Afterwards we go our separate ways and I wander about town exploring. I visit the church and climb up into the tower to see the square below. I've noticed several people, especially children wearing strange costumes and I wonder if they're celebrating Halloween here.

## 1st November

I have a difficult night, I went to bed too early, mostly because it gets dark early and I don't have anything else to do. The noise inside and outside the hostel went on until the early hours. Maybe Halloween frivolity, anyway, it kept me awake. In a hostel there's nothing you can do when sleep is elusive, unlike home when you can get up and make a cup of tea. I think I'm feeling unsettled, this hostel doesn't work for me. It's cold and with only a communal outside courtyard there's nowhere comfortable to spend the evenings and of course the kitchen, which is also outside, is useless.

After breakfast I walk once more to the main square and my favourite coffee shop with the intention of using my computer to make forward plans but I feel thwarted because the Internet here is as bad as at the hostel so I give up.

I've pre-booked a tour with 'G Adventures' to walk the Inca Trail to Machu Pichu and I'll join the group at the Cusco Pardo Hotel this Friday. I'll be walking to the hotel with my backpack, so rather than get lost carrying all my stuff I might as well locate it now. A hot half an hour later I've found it and take a look inside. They have good Wi-Fi here and I'm grateful they let me use their password and Internet. I make a good start looking up information, but it takes time and I really need longer yet don't like to outstay my welcome.

Whilst it goes against the grain for me, I've settled myself into 'Starbucks' coffee house in the main square because I know they'll have decent Wi-Fi and I really want to get more admin sorted. It costs me an orange juice and a cookie and I leave after two hours relieved that everything is sorted.

I'm hungry for dinner. There are plenty of small restaurants in Cusco and I pick one that looks especially inviting with its red interior and check tablecloths. The vegetable soup tastes delicious and just as I'm thinking what a shame they don't bring bread with it, a waitress emerges from the kitchen with some crusty garlic bread for me. Sitting here with a glass of red wine I think how often the small things in life can give such pleasure.

## 2nd November

It's decision day. I've gone around and around in circles in my head trying to plan where to go after the Machu Pichu trip. Getting out of Cusco is expensive and not easy, unless you're going south, which I'm not, because I've come from there. Finally, I decide to go to the Amazon Jungle city of Iquitos, still in Peru. It does mean two flights and I'll still have to come back via Lima, but I definitely want to go to some part of the Amazon jungle and the alternative is Manaus in Brazil. Whilst Manaus is also appealing, I'd have to fly first to Rio de Janeiro and this doesn't work for me as I'm going there at the end of my travels. Relieved at having made the decision I find a travel agent and book flights.

I've chatted with Neil at the hostel since doing the free tour with him. I suggest that he might like to join me for dinner this evening. He's willing and recommends a restaurant. I'm ready early and emerging from my room Neil is already waiting, looking a bit uncomfortable. I don't know what's going on for him, but he's clearly not at ease in my company. He doesn't have any problem talking, in fact he's quite a chatterbox but oddly, doesn't look at me when he's speaking. Maybe he's worried that I fancy him? After the meal, we step outside and he leaves me hurriedly, saying he's off to get a pint. Oh well, I enjoyed the meal and it makes a change to have some company.

### 3rd November

I have the hostel room to myself! All the boys have gone. I wake up happy and realise that I've stopped disliking my hostel. The bed is comfy and although I still wear gloves and socks while sleeping, I'm warm enough. It gets light early here so I wake early but that's not a problem.

Breakfast this morning is exceptional. Yesterday I bought mayonnaise and lettuce to add to my boiled egg and toast. Outside, the sun is shining gloriously and I wander along the busy Ave de Sol to get some cash from the ATM. I take lunch at 'my' café overlooking the square and the waitress anticipates my order of a triple sandwich of avocado, tomato and egg. I think she deserves a large tip.

Afterwards I pay to go inside the vast and ornately decorated Jesuit Church. There are some old steps I can walk up leading to an outside balcony overlooking the square below. Outside again I love exploring, in and out of alleys and streets but by the end of the afternoon I realise my feet are beginning to hurt in my sandals. Time to stop, I don't want any blisters before the Inca trek.

# 'Inca Trail' to Machu Pichu, Peru

### 4th November

### Day 1

I check out of Intro Hostel and walk for half an hour to Cusco Pardo Hotel. I'm hot and my backpack feels heavy and uncomfortable. The hotel is okay but having learned that it costs $60 a night I expected more luxury.

By 3.30 pm four girls have arrived who are also doing the trek and we meet up with the 'G Adventures' tour guides for a briefing. Meeting finished, the girls and I go into Cusco and find an Italian restaurant for a meal. They are all in their early twenties, two are travelling together, the other two, like me, have only just met. I think they're going to be fun.

Back at the hotel my allotted room-buddy, called Hannah, has arrived. She's also twenty something and comes from Henley-on-Thames, close to where I live. The other couple who will join us on the trek are called Neeraj, originally from India and his fiancée Teresa who lives in California. I wonder if Neeraj will cope, it seems he's the only bloke in our group.

It feels good to have reliable Internet here and free time to write an email to Ben, I haven't sent one for a while and I like spending time composing and 'chatting' with him.

### 5th November

### Day 2 Cusco to Ollantaytambo

I'm excited. This is the start of what I think will be an

amazing trip.

Our group is driven in a small bus to a village to meet local people supported by a 'G Adventures' project. Some Parwa community women have formed a weaving co-operative and make clothes and gifts for tourists, mostly from dyed alpaca wool. We're shown the washing, dying and weaving process and I marvel at how intensive the labour is. Now I understand why alpaca garments need to be expensive.

Back in the bus we drive past the Sacred Valley and although we have the opportunity to look down on the valley from our high vantage point, I'm disappointed that we're not staying in the area.

Our lunch stop is amazing, a stylish restaurant seemingly in the middle of nowhere, called Huchuy Quosco. We're treated like Royalty and given three excellent courses. There's an unfortunate incident though. Hannah is gluten intolerant and by mistake she's given soup with wheat in it. When she realises what's happened a look of alarm spreads across her face and she takes herself off to the toilets, presumably to throw up. She bounces back from the incident well and I appreciate that she doesn't make a drama out of it.

Our final destination for the day is Ollantaytambo, a quaint but very touristy town at the northern end of the Sacred Valley. The accommodation is rustic and quirky and I like it. After settling in, we all go for a walk to the ancient and atmospheric Ollantaytambo ruins and fortress.

I'm enjoying getting to know my companions. Neeraj and Teresa are travelling with her parents, Ernst and Ilse, although they won't be doing the trek, then there's Courtnay travelling with her friend Carmela, Felicity, Niamh who is very giggly and of course Hannah. We all have dinner together in the evening in a dull restaurant chosen by our guide, Victor.

Back in the bedroom an upsetting mishap occurs. The only socket I can plug my camera into for recharging is high up on the wall, so I balance it on the metal arm holding the TV. A few moments later the camera falls and unfortunately the lead detaches from the camera and it lands heavily on the tiled floor. Inspecting the damage, I realise the lens has been cracked and the camera is useless. It means that I won't have my camera for the Inca Trail. I have to find a way to be okay about this because right now I feel upset. I can't allow this to spoil the adventure.

6th November

Day 3 Ollantaytambo to Wayllabamba Camp

Today we start our trek. The girls are very amusing, they're all nervous and giggly and worrying about everything.

We drive early in the morning some 82 kms to the start of the walk. The weather is sunny and I'm happy with the thought that this will last for the next three days.

Another guide joins Victor, called Nick, and we have ten porters who will carry the stuff. We each have to carry our own personal belongings and the porters carry the tents, tables, food and drink for three days and everything else we'll need. My backpack feels heavy to me. I'm taking essentials, extra clothes and trainers but this is nothing in comparison to the 25 kgs each porter is carrying!

I tell the group about my mishap with the camera and ask if they would be willing to share photos with me after the trek. To my amazement, Teresa offers to lend me her camera to use for the duration. She says that Neeraj has a camera and she'll probably use her mobile phone anyway. I'm blown away by this extremely kind gesture and accept her offer with gratitude.

The natural rocky path takes us through beautiful scenery, the walking isn't difficult and we go at a gentle pace. At lunchtime we stop at a picnic spot and are amazed at the speed with which the porters set up camp and a kitchen and produce an excellent three course meal.

After lunch and a rest, our walk continues through more gorgeous scenery, surrounded by green mountains. The girls are delightful and I like chatting with them. By the time we reach our camp for the night, called Wayllabamba, we've walked about 12 kms and I've loved every step. The porters provide another excellent three course meal in a communal tent. I retire early to the tent I'm sharing with Hannah, primarily to get some 'alone' space.

Sleep is a long time coming. Fliss and Niamh are in the tent next to ours and they don't stop giggling and talking for hours after everyone's gone to bed. I think they don't realise that the 'walls' are canvas and their voices carry.

## 7th November

## Day 4 Wayllabamba Camp to Paqaymayo Camp

We wake early, the sun is up and the porters bring each of us a small bowl of hot water to have a wash, a thoughtful touch.

This is a tough walking day. We're climbing the

long steep, rocky path to Warmiwañusca, commonly known as Dead Woman's Pass. It's the highest point of the trek at 4,198m (13,769 ft) and hard walking, so everyone's elated when we make it to the top, there are 'high fives' all round. Rain clouds have gathered and the group fear our lovely clear weather may have ended, but I keep the faith and fortunately the rain holds off.

The wonderful trek continues to Paqaymayo Camp. Some of the time I choose to walk alone. I'm surprised how few people are on the path as I'd been told that the Inca Trail would be crowded. Just as we arrive at the camp the heavens open and it rains heavily.

We have an entertaining evening and night, trying to stay dry. The tents are pretty good but water will get in anywhere and ours has a few leaks so we pile our stuff into the middle and squish together when we sleep to keep dry.

## 8th November

### Day 5 Paqaymayo Camp to Wiñaywayna

The landscape becomes even more stunning as we cross two passes with Inca ruins along the way. The first pass is Runquraqay at 3,950m and we can see the Cordillera Vilcabamba mountain range. Continuing on through cloud forest and a gentle climb to the second pass of the day, we walk through original Incan constructions. The highest point of the pass is 3,700m showing us the spectacular Urubamba Valley. We pass the ruins of Phuyupatamarca, the "town above the clouds" and make it to our next campsite at the Wiñaywayna ruins located at 2,650m.

We've all been very appreciative of our hard-working porters and the girls have had fun interacting with them. We've made a collection of money and after our final meal we ask them to come into the communal tent and join us. Hannah does a great job of giving a 'thank you' speech, it's very sweet and they respond very appreciatively.

## 9th November

### Day 6 Wiñaywayna to Cusco

This is the final walking day and we're really excited that we'll see Machu Pichu. We're woken at the unsociable hour of 3.30 am so we can walk to the checkpoint that we have to pass through before reaching Sun Gate at sunrise. We're grateful our guides have got us to the checkpoint super early because a long queue of people builds up behind us while we wait for it to be opened.

Then we're off, setting out at a cracking pace and with no-one in front of us, it feels as though we have the path to ourselves. As promised, we reach Sun Gate before the sun has risen and then the ruins of Machu Pichu come into sight. It looks just like the pictures I've seen, only better, because now I can see the incredible mountains all around. We stop for a while taking photos then continue to hike down, and the view gets better and better.

I think we've walked for a couple of hours when we arrive at the site of the ruins. The place is amazing. We walk around for a while exploring in and out of the massive grey stones. We're given plenty of time and our guides leave us, explaining where we can get a bus back to Aquas Calientes when we're ready. The sun is now very hot and we're exhausted. We sit on a ledge near the ruins in the sunshine and take in the fabulous scenery.

When we've had enough, we take the bus into the town which isn't far, then we have a look around the market and tourist shops before meeting our guides at the agreed restaurant for a celebration meal.

After lunch we all get on board a train back to Ollantaytambo and from there we endure a very long bus ride back to Cusco.

It's dark and quite late when we finally arrive at the hotel and we've agreed to meet up in one hour's time at a bar in Cusco with our guides.

I'm disappointed by the chosen venue which is a down market bar with a poor menu. No-one seems interested in food, so it's drinks all round. We'd expected Victor and Nick to come, but only Nick turns up. I buy Nick a drink and the girls make a fuss of him. I'm highly amused when Hannah returns from somewhere with some comical party stuff, daft hats, spectacles and moustaches and we have silly fun taking photos wearing different attire. Nick is loving the attention and the suggestion is made that we move on to a club venue. This doesn't interest me and I'm content to leave the girls to it and walk back to the hotel.

## 10ᵗʰ November

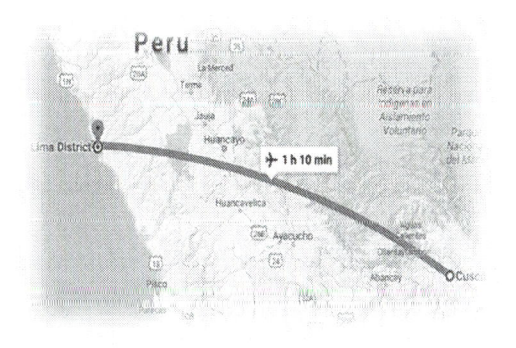

I shared the moment when I saw Machu Pichu with Ben via text message and this morning I received a witty and complimentary reply. It put a big smile on my face.

I'm leaving Cusco this afternoon to fly ultimately to Iquitos but this morning is free and I hope to find someone who can repair my broken camera. I've noticed a few camera shops along the Avenue and ask at each one, but none can help. A small kiosk and a man behind the counter looks promising and on enquiring he says he can fix my camera by 1 pm, which I've explained is all the time I have. This seems like something of a miracle, but then I ask the likely cost of the repair and he tells me it will be the equivalent of £200. This can't be right. That's more than the camera is worth and this is Peru, everything is cheaper here. I can't pay that much. He indicates that I shouldn't worry about it and feeling that I've probably miscalculated or misunderstood the amount he's asking for, I leave my camera with him.

Returning fifteen minutes before 1 pm to collect my camera he tells me that it hasn't come back yet. He's given it to someone else to fix. I'm not pleased with this news but he's confident it will be here in ten minutes, so I go next door where they serve coffee and order a cappuccino.

Back again I'm delighted that he has my camera. I check that the lens has been repaired and it looks clear. He again asks me for the equivalent of £200 for the repair. I can't believe the amount he's asking for and argue fiercely, explaining that I can't possibly pay that much. The most I'm willing to pay is the equivalent of £60 and even that feels like a lot. He shakes his head and says *"no lady, that isn't enough"* at which point I tell him to keep my camera, I'm not willing to pay the daft amount he's asking for. He looks unhappy. We have a heated discussion and I'm running out of time. We eventually settle on £80 which feels like way too much but I need to get to the airport now.

I leave feeling confused, was it me, or was it him? Could it really be that expensive to repair in Cusco? I know I'm gullible, but he still did come across as a nice man. I guess I won't know the answer.

Back at the hotel there are hugs all round and a final farewell to my Inca Trail group. There's no shortage of taxis, hailing one is easy but traffic is heavy so I'm glad the airport isn't far from town.

## Aeroplane to Lima, Aeroplane to Iquitos, Brazil (3½hrs)

My flight is on time and I arrive in Lima, with a quick forward flight on to Iquitos. On the plane I check out my camera and sadly realise that it's still broken. The lens may have been fixed but the photos are distorted. I've probably wasted £80.

## Iquitos, Peru

I'd pre-booked a homestay in Iquitos that offers a complimentary 'pick-up' service from the airport and emerging into the arrivals area of the tiny airport, I'm relieved to see a man is holding up a card with my name written on it. It's dark outside and pouring with rain.

My 'host' is called Victor. His English is limited but we manage to communicate a little. When we reach his homestay, he introduces me to his wife Yoley, who is very welcoming. I mention that I'm keen to visit the Amazon Jungle and to my amazement, within twenty minutes of our conversation, they're introducing me to a man from a tour company that runs tours into the jungle for a very reasonable price. Sandy, the woman I met in Cusco is keen to visit the Amazon too and she's going to come here and join me. I like the tour operator and I like that Victor recommends him, so after a quick message to Sandy and a reply from her, I book the tour.

### 11th November

Until now I've avoided taking malaria tablets, but it seems smart to protect myself if I'm venturing into the Amazon jungle, so I ferret them out from the bottom pocket of my backpack. I've been carrying several packs with me, each tablet individually wrapped in its own plastic bubble. Now I'm not sure whether to laugh or not. Opening the packets reveals that they've all disintegrated into powder, they're useless. I presume the changes of temperature through cold and hot has been their undoing. Oh well, I've survived this far and there's nothing I can do about it now.

I have a bedroom to myself with a double bed covered in a gorgeous red and multi-colour cotton fabric, it feels like luxury. Victor's wife makes me breakfast with coffee and an egg and bread then I leave the homestay through the double-locked security front door and gates, to explore Iquitos.

The rain from last night has gone and it now feels hot and humid. My homestay is down a side road, so I walk to the main road towards town and I'm reminded of India. The road is packed with speeding motos, old cars and numerous battered, colourful buses full of people. There is a difference though, these drivers are not using their car horns. I'm curious about the volume of traffic because there aren't any roads into Iquitos, the only way to get here is by plane or boat, so I'd imagined it to be a place without vehicles. Daft, now I think about it.

Iquitos is a port city and known as the gateway to the northern Amazon. The town looks poor, the buildings are mostly a bit run down. The walk into the 'centro' area is long but I'm fascinated passing the small shops along the way. I notice a shop selling TVs, the kind of analogue ones we used in the U.K. maybe twenty years ago.

Eventually I come to a road by the wide River Itaya and I love the area. It has the atmosphere of bygone times. There are some characterful old, derelict buildings decorated with mosaic tiles, one of them was probably once a grand hotel. I recall reading that the town was at one time full of wealthy Europeans because of the area's rubber production.

I'm approached many times by touts wanting to sell me something, mostly tours. I say *'hola'* to a man sitting by the river and I laugh when he says *'hello'* back in English and I stop to chat. He's American and has lived in Iquitos for three years. He tells me he came here with his wife 34 years ago and fell in love with the place. He 'adopted' two families and has supported them ever since, coming two or three times a year to visit them. Then his wife died and he decided to live here. Our meeting is fortuitous for me because he's able to help me with a tour to the Belen floating market, something I'm keen to do. He introduces me to a young boatman called Ryder who lives in Belen and we agree to meet at 8am tomorrow.

I choose a restaurant to have some lunch. It isn't cheap but I'd previously read that Iquitos tends to be a bit pricey because without roads, they have to import goods in by boat or plane, bumping the cost up.

It's a long walk back to my homestay, Posado Allpahuayo and I do my usual trick of taking a wrong turn and walking for a long time in the opposite direction. By the time I make it back, I'm hot and exhausted.

At the homestay I meet a new arrival, a lady from the States, she amazes me by telling me she's come to Iquitos specially to have an Ayouashka hallucinatory 'treatment', she has issues she wants to deal with and feels that this is the right way for her. She's going to see her 'Shaman' tomorrow. I've heard a little about Ayouashka and it sounds unpleasant.

## 12th November

Ryder is meeting me this morning to show me Belen market so I'm out early and hail a moto to take me down to the water front. He's there on time which is a good start and he's very amiable.

We stroll along the front to Belen market which is

closer than I'd expected. It's incredibly busy and I'm amazed to learn that this market is on every day. There's mostly fresh produce being sold, chicken and fish of many kinds, but there are stalls selling produce I've never seen on sale before such as turtle, cut into pieces, and small alligators. There are some distressing things I witnessed with live animals that I won't even write down because I'd like to erase them from my mind. I accept that all these things are part of the culture and it isn't for me to judge them right or wrong.

The dwellings in Belen are very poor, mostly rickety looking wooden structures, built on stilts because half of the year the area is under water. I can't imagine how life continues in these busy streets when the water comes in.

We come to a stall that belongs to Ryder's aunt. She sells natural products and I'm invited to try some of her homemade drinks. I have about three 'shots' of different drinks and hope they're not hallucinogenic. I'm pleased that I'm able to buy some natural mosquito repellent that Sandy has requested.

Passing through the market we come down to the river which is brown in colour. Ryder calls to a friend and we borrow his boat. He calls the boat a 'peka peka' because of the noise the motor makes. It's wooden, narrow and shallow and I pray it's river-worthy.

Pootling down the river is fascinating, there's so much to see of interest. There are rickety huts on tiny pontoons in the water and Ryder tells me these are bathrooms, this is where the families go to wash. On other floating platforms women are crouched doing the washing. Children are playing at the water's edge. We pass by many other boats, there's a lot of life on this river.

After a few minutes Ryder moors the boat by a river bank and says we'll go for a walk in the jungle. I've put my trust in Ryder up 'til now but I begin to feel uncomfortable. He wants me to swim in the river and says he'll do the same. It may be hot, but I'm very clear that I don't want to swim. Ryder persuasively says the water is nice and that it's clean. I'm not going to offend him by pointing out all the people that bathe in it, empty their rubbish in it, and the motor boats that chug up and down.

Back in the boat we sit for a while. Ryder wants me to put on some of the insect repellent I'd bought for Sandy. He takes it from me and smears some on my arms and neck. It's an odd thing to do, he seems to want to touch me. I've no idea if I'm making it up, I'm clearly much older than him. Maybe this is normal behaviour here or maybe he's not a good judge of age. He'd previously asked me to go to the disco that evening, being a Saturday, he said it's the best night to go. Anyway, the moment passes and we 'peka peka' our way back along the river to the market again. Ryder walks me back to familiar territory, I thank him and pay him.

After a visit to the bank for more cash, I find a moto to take me home. Sitting in a moto is akin to an exhilarating fairground ride. I don't know whether it's fun or terrifying. They're powered by motorbikes and the drivers accelerate as fast as they can until they have to stop suddenly at the next set of traffic lights, and there are many traffic lights, then they zoom off again at break neck speed. I don't know how they don't collide; or maybe they do.

I've been thinking about the next part of my journey and I've considered taking a trading boat along the Amazon to get into Brazil. Researching information, I'm changing my mind. It means travelling into Colombia first and I'm not sure I have the energy to cross another border. The trip takes seven days and passengers sleep in hammocks which is a step too far for me. With nowhere to keep your stuff safe on the boat, people talk about being robbed. Although reluctant to give up on the boat idea I've decided to fly to Brazil. When I tell Victor my plans he very kindly takes me into town to the LAN office where I can book my ticket straight away. It always feels good when a decision is made.

I'd like to eat out this evening, so brave another moto back into town and locate the 'Yellow Rose of Texas' restaurant, recommended by Yolla. A lady sitting next to me has just arrived here from Finland and we have an entertaining conversation.

Later in the evening I accompany Victor to the airport, to meet Sandy off the plane. There's a pretty young girl sitting on a low wall in front of me, she looks about five years old and is clearly waiting to meet someone. She keeps looking up at me and smiling, she's very sweet. Suddenly she leaps off the wall and rushes excitedly to greet a lady who's walking in from 'Arrivals', hugging her around the legs. The lady is talking on her mobile and doesn't acknowledge the little girl, it makes me feel sad for her.

Sandy arrives hot, she's wearing layers of clothes, including her warm woollen poncho and she's carrying several bags. She's pleased to see us and I'm excited to see her. We have plenty of chat to catch up on.

## 13th November

## Four Day Amazon Jungle Tour

### Day 1

After breakfast a Wimba tour guide arrives with a moto and drives Sandy and me, at great speed, to the riverside, where we climb aboard a largish wooden river boat. There are a few other tourists on board. Our guide is called Welly, short for something but I can't recall what. He has a nice smile.

The boat motors along the Itaya, passing the very busy dock area of Iquitos then joins the Amazon River and the place in the river where the two tributaries meet, the waters are different colours and we're told they never mix.

We're in the boat an hour or more and it's very relaxing. Everyone gets excited when we spot some pink river dolphins. We leave the main river and turn into a smaller tributary and the boat moors up to let us get off. From here, Welly takes Sandy and I on a short walk through a small rural village with wooden dwellings on stilts.

Sandy and I have been chatting as we walk and she says to me *"I really hope we'll see a sloth in the jungle"*. Near the wooden dwellings, a few villagers are standing around with some young children. One little girl dressed in pink is holding an animal and I can't believe my eyes. She's holding a sloth! She lets Sandy and I stroke the animal, he has a sad, wistful look about him.

Welly takes us to another smaller boat and we chug up a small river until we reach Wimba Lodge which will be our home for the next few days. There's a walkway from the river bank up to the wooden lodge which is built on stilts. It's quaint, rustic and basic, as we had been told it would be, but it also looks clean. There's a sparkling clean swimming pool too, very inviting in this heat, and there are wooden cabins around the raised walkway for accommodation.

It's late morning and we're told we have free time until lunch arrives. We're surrounded by jungle, tall trees and masses of vegetation, the sun is now searingly hot. We get acquainted with our accommodation; single beds in one room and our own bathroom. There are mosquito nets and coloured sheets but I may have to ditch the hard, lumpy pillow.

Lunch is simple vegetarian fare and Sandy and I are both happy with it, plus they provide coffee so I'm super-happy. There are a handful of other guests at the lodge but it seems that Sandy and I have the guide Welly to ourselves.

In the afternoon he takes us in a little boat down the river to an animal sanctuary and along the way we pass by some water lilies with giant green leaves like vast dinner plates.

I'm not sure that the place is actually a sanctuary or a tourist attraction, but it's quaint and appealing and full of monkeys that are fun. They jump on us and try to take things off us. There's also a snake, a couple of brightly coloured macaws and a toucan, all wandering about freely.

Back in the boat we pootle along a bit further until we stop at a sort of muddy 'beach'. There are a few people in the water swimming and we're invited to do the same. I decide that this time I will go in, just to say I've swum in the Amazon. The brown water is body temperature warm and feels squishy underfoot and I don't stay in long.

Fortunately, I always carry my cotton sarong with me and it comes in handy after my swim. It's a relaxing time, standing around, watching people and seeing little boats come and go along the river, the light is very pretty, especially as the sun starts going down.

Sandy and I are intrigued by the amazingly dense, white clouds that hang in the sky. Then the sunset takes over and lights up the clouds, the sky becomes exceptionally beautiful. With this gorgeous evening sky above us, Welly takes us back to the lodge in the boat.

There's a bar at our lodge but no wine, at least not as I know it, only jungle wine. But they do have Seven Roots which can be made into a Seven Roots Sour. Welly makes me one and it's delicious. This is such a relaxing place, I've had a truly lovely day. We retire to bed early and I sleep well in spite of the 'boulder' for a pillow.

## 14th November

### Day 2

I wake to jungle sounds and feel full of energy. This is the perfect place for yoga, followed by a swim before breakfast. Sandy isn't good in the mornings, she struggles to 'come to'.

Welly takes us for a walk through the jungle, I love the vegetation and the strange noises. Unsurprisingly in this heat we don't see any animals, but Welly shows us tree bats, a damsel fly, a stick insect and a large spider. The trees are amazing, some of them are vast with massive 'ropes' hanging down that we can grab hold of and swing on. Some trees have roots above the ground and are known as 'walking trees' because they move, sometimes up to three metres in a year.

In the late afternoon, Sandy and I go in the wooden boat with Welly to fish for piranha. He shows us how to do it by putting a small piece of raw fish onto a hook for bait then throwing the end of the line into the river. In no time at all Welly has caught one, he shows us the piranha's teeth which are numerous, small and vicious looking. Fishing is highly entertaining, although I'm not sure I really want to catch one. This becomes academic because I seem to be pretty rubbish at it and don't catch one anyway. Sandy catches two but makes Welly throw them back in the river. If I'd known yesterday there are piranha in the river, I wonder if I'd have gone swimming!

Welly takes the boat further down the river, until we come to a small community on the river bank with a few dwellings and we moor up for a while. The atmosphere here is tranquil and we stand and watch the sky and the river changing colour. Clouds have gathered, it looks as though it may rain. When the sun is partially covered by a cloud an amazing rainbow aura surrounds it, the effect is super-natural. Something about the whole scene, the river, the dwellings and the sky, is very surreal.

Time at the lodge goes incredibly slowly in a nice way, one hour seems like two. I don't think I've ever felt so relaxed in my life and I realise I'm becoming okay with doing nothing, though I'm hugely grateful to have Sandy for company and we have plenty to chat about. This evening we buy Welly a Seven Roots Sour and he sits and drinks it with us.

A night walk was planned for this evening but massive rains come. There's high drama with lightning and thunder and one thunder crack is so loud it makes me leap out of my chair.

## 15th November

### Day 3

I'm awake at 5.15 am ready for Welly who promised to take us for a sunrise boat ride, but he isn't about. The sky looks beautiful and I'm so excited to share it that I wake Sandy who leaps out of bed to come and look at it with me, but now the colours in the sky have changed rapidly into nothing of interest, so Sandy goes back to bed. Then Welly appears, looking sleepy, he'd forgotten to set his alarm but says we can still go out on the boat. By this time Sandy isn't in the mood for getting up again so I go on my own with Welly.

We both paddle the boat this time, it's quiet and tranquil pottering along the narrow river. We see colourful birds, a squirrel and a tree full of monkeys. When we get back to the lodge there's still plenty of time before breakfast is ready so I take a swim.

After breakfast we walk through the jungle to meet a traditional Amazonian tribe. Welly tells us there are forty-seven tribes in the Amazon jungle. It doesn't feel very authentic and is probably set up for tourists but the experience is entertaining and gives us a sense of how people live here. We have our faces painted and are encouraged to do a daft dance inside a massive straw hut, accompanied by some drums and pipes. Then we have a go at firing a dart out of a blow pipe to hit a target.

And, of course, there are the inevitable hand-crafted items to buy. I would love to have bought a large, decorated blow pipe. I do want to support the people though, so I buy a string bag and also choose a small bead bracelet to buy from a young mother. She indicates that she doesn't have change of the 10 sol I offer her, the bracelet being priced at 5 sol and she typically offers me a second bracelet instead. I feel annoyed now because I know she has change, this is a way of getting another 5 sol out of me and I feel used.

It doesn't rain this evening and we're able to take our night walk. Although not spectacular, I enjoy being in the dark and the cooler air and we see some tree frogs and a tarantula.

## 16th November
## Day 4

The planned 5 am sunrise boat ride happens this time, Welly has set his alarm. I don't get the glorious sunrise I'm hoping for, I think the sun probably rose around 4.30 am, but I love being out in the early morning light.

After breakfast we take the boat a short way, moor up and Welly takes us for another jungle walk. I've been noticing how Welly interacts with Sandy and I think he's keen on her. When she's bothered by mosquitos, Welly cuts down some ferns and sits and weaves a fan for her. We walk as far as a wetland lake then make our way back to the boat through a very muddy swampy patch that sucks our feet so hard it's difficult to keep the wellies on our feet.

Today is our last day at the Lodge and I think this is good timing. Some new guests have arrived with children, and the relaxing quietness of the place has altered in an instant.

Welly takes us in the boat back to the village where we started and this time there's a small truck for Sandy and I to ride on. A different larger boat takes us along the main part of the Amazon River to Iquitos. Sandy seems a bit low today but I think this may not be unusual for her.

A moto takes us the final part of the journey back to our homestay around 5 pm and Sandy packs her stuff ready to leave tomorrow, a day before me. Later we take a moto into town and have our evening meal at the same restaurant by the river where I'd taken lunch on my first day here. I've thoroughly enjoyed spending time with Sandy, it was comfortable and I felt we got on well, surprising in a way as she's not a dissimilar age to my daughter. I'm going to miss her.

## 17th November

Sandy leaves for the airport after breakfast. I revel in having the day free. My tummy has been dodgy for the past couple of days so I think I won't eat anything today. I spend time organising my photos and persuade Yoley to let me pay for my accommodation in U.S. dollars so I don't need to use the ATM again.

Staying in has become boring, so I go for a wander up and down some of the side streets, taking photos. I come to a shop that sells bread and unable to bear the emptiness in my tummy, I try to buy one small bun. The lady in the shop wants me to buy a whole bag of buns and I indicate that I only want one, it's just for me. Then she hands me a bun and to my surprise she doesn't want me to pay for it. She's giving it to me. I'm very touched. I know it's only a bun, but I've got used to sellers always trying to get money out of me. I blow her a kiss 'thank you' and leave the shop smiling.

## 18th November

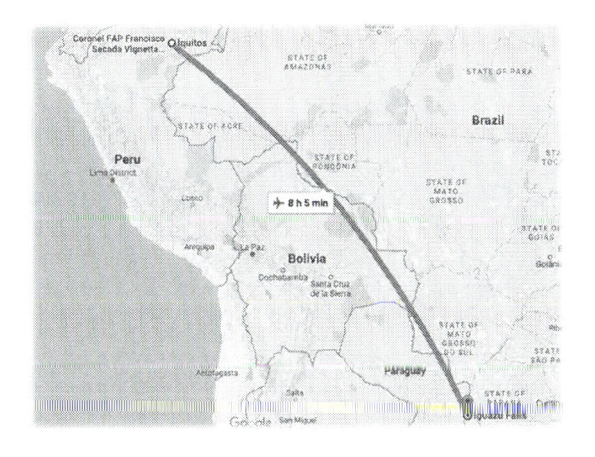

*Aeroplane to Lima, Aeroplane to Iguazu, Brazil (4½hrs)*

It's time for me to leave Iquitos. Victor drives me to the airport for my 8 am flight, which is on schedule. I land in Lima, Peru and realise this could be a good time to call my son. He's about to go off on his own sailing adventure and I desperately want to wish him well. I'm very excited that he answers my call, he's at Gatwick Airport ready for a flight to Portugal. I marvel again at how awesome modern technology is.

It seems odd that I have to walk outside of the airport and back in again to get to 'Departures' and the next leg of my journey to Iguazu in Brazil. The 2.30 pm flight is on time, I am incredibly lucky with my flights. Arriving in Iguazu I'm baffled to learn there's a time difference and I have to put my watch forward three hours.

# Iguazu, Brazil

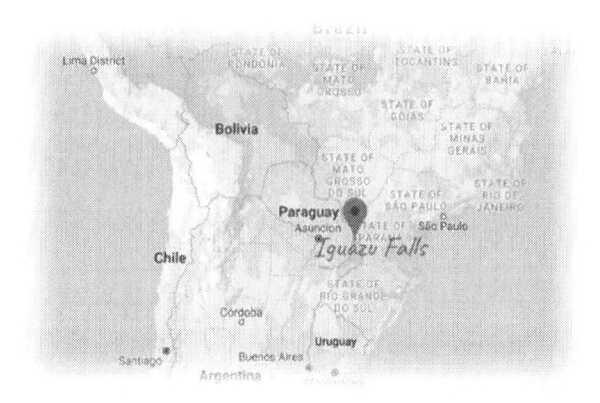

At 'Arrivals' in the airport I head straight for an ATM so I can take out Brazilian Real and pay for my bus fare into town. The cash machine charges me 24 Real for the privilege, about £5.30, but at least I now have money.

I ask a guy behind a desk if he knows where I can get a bus, he says *"where are you going?"* and to my amazement he knows the hostel I'm booked into and writes down the exact bus number and how to know which stop to get off. I have the feeling someone 'up there' is looking after me.

The green No.120 bus isn't long arriving. I've only just got on when the bus pulls away at great speed. The payment system requires that I hand the ticket money to a conductor who sits in the middle of the bus, making the aisle space very narrow, then I have to pass through a tight turnstile. Who devised this system? Trying to manoeuvre myself through this obstacle with back and front pack and a ukulele whilst handing over money and receiving change, on a bus that's flying along at breakneck speed, is tricky. All this whilst being observed by the other passengers.

The suggested bus stop proves to be correct, to my delight there's a big sign a few yards ahead shouting my hostel's name, CLH Suites.

The hostel is modern, with all the right facilities but I'm again sharing a bedroom with three men, I keep forgetting to book 'female only' dorms.

## 19th November

After a good hostel breakfast, I spend the day getting organised. My final destination will be Rio de Janeiro and I locate an office nearby that can book a bus to take me there, a twenty-four hour journey.

I'd like to do some volunteer work in Rio if I can because I'll be there for a few days, so I write some emails to a volunteer website called 'workaway.info'. Unfortunately, today is another of those days when the Internet doesn't co-operate and I only manage to send two emails.

I give up on the Internet and go instead to the local supermarket to stock up on food for the next three days. I've come to Iguazu to see the famous waterfalls and because they're located on the border of Brazil and Argentina, therefore officially in both countries, they can be seen from both sides. At the hostel I'm able to book a bus that will take me to see them from the Argentinian side on Monday.

## 20th November

It was a rough night, snoring in stereo from two of the men and a third gets up noisily, very early. That's hostel life. I sleep eventually, then don't wake up until 8.30, later than I'd intended, because today I'm going to see Iguazu Falls from the Brazilian side of the border.

The bus terminal isn't far and I take the same green 120 bus, this time to Iguazu Falls which takes about forty minutes. I've read that *"the Falls are located where the Iguazu River tumbles over the edge of the Paraná Plateau"*.

The area is very busy with tourists of all nationalities milling about. There's a queue to get a ticket, then a queue to take the bus to the falls, but the system is well organised and I don't mind at all, the sunshine is glorious and my spirits are high.

A sign indicates a path to 'The Falls' and then they come into view. What a sight! They're magnificent and not one waterfall, but lots, dozens in fact and several massive ones, they stretch out in a curvy line, cascading noisily. The walkway offers specially created viewpoints at intervals and continues right out over the Iguazu River to finish close to the main falls, where the noise of the water is deafening and I get a soaking from the spray.

Having completed the circuit, I love it so much I do it all over again. This time there are less people about and I take my time. Along the way there are cute furry animals scampering about that look like racoons and are called coati. Notices are posted with clear warnings that they bite.

I'll sleep well tonight, a text from Ben says he received my last two postcards, in the same week!

## 21st November

Today I'm looking forward to seeing the Falls from the Argentinian side. I've booked a tour rather than take a bus because it will make the border crossing easier, and it isn't expensive.

It feels different this side, much more rural. The vegetation is lush and green, there are footpaths that meander around the falls, one path along the top and one path nearer the base. There aren't many tourists and I feel very relaxed. The walk to Devil's Throat takes my breath away, it crosses vast expanses of river with green trees and vegetation around it, and in it, until it reaches an area where the river seems to fall into itself in the middle. There's huge drama here, it's thrilling, noisy and so spectacular it makes me feel emotional

I say a mental 'thank you' to the Irish pilot I met on Puerto Merino glacier. He told me he'd been here and said how amazing the Falls are. I remember thinking *"if a pilot who's seen so much of the world thinks The Falls are amazing, then I really should visit"*. I'm so glad I'm here.

In the evening I chat with Jima, who comes from Taiwan and he suggests we have dinner together. I'm not sure I want dinner but say yes anyway. The nearby restaurants are all fairly similar, with plastic tables and chairs and pictures showing plates of food on their windows. We choose one and sit outside on the pavement. I have to laugh because the only vegetarian dish on the menu is egg and chips with a side salad. Jima introduces me to a Brazilian cocktail called Caipirinha, made with Cachaca, a spirit made from fermented sugar cane juice, lime and ice. It's refreshing and delicious and after drinking two of these I notice he's grinning a lot.

Back at the hostel I'm very amused by the two Brazilian girls who now share the room with me. They want to connect on 'WhatsApp'. They're endearingly affectionate with me even though none of us can understand a word the other says. It's still a mystery to me why people I've met so briefly are keen to 'connect'. There's a lot of giggling and they send me many messages. It's 10 pm at this time so I'm surprised when they asked me through 'Google translator' if I will come out to dinner with them. Having now eaten twice already, I politely decline. The girls return late and come in noisily, then get up and leave early and even noisier.

## 22$^{nd}$ November

## Overnight bus to Rio de Janeiro 26 hrs (1500 kms)

I have to check out of the hostel this morning but I won't leave Iguazu until this afternoon. They let me leave my backpack in a store and I keep my front pack containing valuables and laptop with me. I need to find a bank to withdraw some money and ask at the reception desk for the nearest one. It's about four blocks away. When I get to the bank they don't have an ATM and on enquiring they direct me to an HSBC bank, seven blocks away.

I'm fed-up, I'm hot and my daypack feels heavy. I walk in the direction I'm shown and then stop to ask the way again, this time I'm told the HSBC is 8 blocks away. I've found the right street but walking up and down I can't see an HSBC, although there is a bank called Bradesco, so I go inside. It seems possible that HSBC has changed its name here to Bradesco.

In the lobby there are a dozen or so machines but none of them look like the familiar ATM. I try going inside the bank through their swivel doors but the doors block me and I'm stuck, I can't get in. The guard on duty simply stands and looks at me, stuck in the doors. I try swivelling the doors the other way but the same thing happens. Then the guard gesticulates me to back out of the doors which I do, but it means I can't go inside the bank.

I go back to the machines looking confused and a lady in the queue gestures to one, so I gave it a try. It declines my request for cash then clings on to my card. Losing my last working bank card has been my fear. I try pressing buttons, I can see my card but can't pull it out. To my great relief after a couple of minutes it does release it, but by this time I'm shaking and anxious.

I come out of the bank and notice another Bradesco over the road so try going in there but the same thing happens, I can't get through the doors. This time a banker comes out and I tell him I want an ATM. He tells me I can't use theirs and I will have to go to Banco du Brazil a couple of blocks away. I'm running out of time now and feel tired, hot and bothered. I don't go to the bank he suggests but start walking back in the direction of the hostel. On the way I pass a Santander bank, they don't have an ATM either, I've never experienced this before.

By the time I reach the hostel I have only ten minutes before the taxi is due and I still need to get my picnic ready for the long bus ride. I hastily throw four eggs into a pan and hope they'll hard-boil in time. I grab the remaining food I have from the fridge and scurry to reception to grab my rucksack, just as the taxi draws up to take me to the bus station.

The bus comes on time but getting on it is something of a palaver. Each piece of luggage has to have a sticker and be logged in a book, I've no idea why. About half an hour later we drive through a security area where armed soldiers come on board the bus and look us all up and down. The bus driver stands outside his bus and shakes hands with all five of them before we drive off. I guess this is why all the bags needed to be accounted for.

The journey lasts twenty-six hours, two hours longer than I'm expecting. We keep stopping at bus stations which means the bus detours off the main road and drives through towns. I'm not feeling particularly good on this bus, which is a shame because it means I can't read, study or use my computer. I doze or look out of the window and at least the scenery changes and there's plenty to look at.

For part of the journey I have the luxury of a spare seat next to me, then a passenger gets on and needs it. He's interesting to talk to, he's a professional footballer playing for Austria and this amuses me since one of the things I know about Brazil is they like their football.

## 23rd November

It's the second day on the bus and it's stopped again and everyone gets off. I assume this is a comfort break. These breaks are a problem for me because I never know how long the bus is going to wait and I always have the anxiety that it will leave without me. In all my bus journeys there's never been a head count to check all passengers are on board and of course no-one will notice if I'm missing. We're parked outside a large, modern cafeteria-cum-service station and I'd love a coffee, so hurry inside to grab a quick one.

This place has a 'system' and first I have to take a plastic disc which I put into a turnstile. The building is cavernous inside and I rush around trying to find the coffee area. There's a coffee machine, but it doesn't have any take-away cups, then a lady brings some, so I take one and fill it, then I try to pay. I can't pay here, I have to take my coffee over to the other side of the cavernous place. Over there I'm told to go somewhere else. This is getting ridiculous. I'm worried the bus will leave without me. When I come to pay I only have a 50 real note and the lady doesn't want to give me change for my large note. Frustration, anxiety and probably lack of sleep kick in and I'm close to tears. I just want to get out of here.

The joke is on me, the bus doesn't leave for ages. I feel an idiot. I've caused my own stressful situation when I could have had a pleasant time looking around and relaxing with a coffee. I scold myself for not having learned that everything always works out. The trouble with travelling is you still take yourself with you. And I laugh at how funny I must have looked, rushing around the cafeteria, getting annoyed.

## Rio de Janeiro, Brazil

Twenty-six hours after leaving Iguazu, the bus arrives in Rio, the time is 3.30 pm. I realise with some relief that I will probably never have to do such a long bus ride again.

My final destination is now Santa Teresa, an historic area on a hillside, on the outskirts of Rio. By great good fortune, one of the two hasty emails I sent out seeking voluntary work responded and I've been invited to help out at Villa Leonor Hostel in return for free accommodation.

A taxi driver agrees to take me there for 60 real, a better price than the 100 the first driver quotes. The address is R. Costa Bastos, but the driver can't find number 681 and we drive up and down and round steep cobble stone lanes looking. I give him the Villa's phone number and he's able to get directions.

Villa Leonor is very pretty; it's small, painted pale sage green and full of character, very historical looking. David, who works there, comes out to greet me, he speaks excellent English. I already know I'm going to love it here.

We walk down some steep stone steps and come out onto a semi-outdoor living area with tables and chairs, a bar and a balcony overlooking part of the town. David shows me to my room which is tiny, it has a bed, a window and a small ensuite shower room. He notices my uke and asks if I'll teach him how to play it.

Christian, husband to Erika with whom I'd communicated by email, arrives. He's young, has long dark wavy hair, a big wide smile and he's charming. About an hour later Erika turns up having finished work, she gives me a warm hug and we sit and chat. They've only recently bought the hostel and they're working hard to making it a successful business. They're a delightful couple.

There's time to take a walk around Santa Teresa while it's still light so I go out and explore the area, but I'm not feeling brave enough to have dinner out so instead I finish the food I've brought with me and retire early to bed.

## 24th November

I'm woken early by the sounds of a dog barking. Breakfast is provided on a buffet table; boiled eggs, bread, yoghurt, fresh mangoes from the tree and coffee. There are two other guests having breakfast too, so I'm not alone.

I'm keen to start working after breakfast to earn my keep, but Christian seems uncomfortable with this and doesn't give me anything to do. Erika has gone to work.

I walk down the cobbled lanes towards the town in search of a bank and oh joy, there's a Banco du Brazil. I try the ATM and it refuses my card, even though I have help from a friendly banker. He suggests Bank Itau over the road so I go there. I take a deep breath and put my card in the slot. It works, I hear the tick, tick noise of money being counted and spewed out and I get my card back. I can relax now.

There's a supermarket next door and I go in to buy a bottle of wine, fruit and rubber gloves in anticipation that I'll be given some work to do. There's quite a queue for the cashier and I enjoy watching how friendly everyone is as they chat with each other.

David arrives at the guest house in the afternoon and

I ask him if he can give me some work to do, but he's also reluctant and suggests that I might rather sightsee. Erika has told me that she wants some inspirational words painted in colour on the stone steps. They'll need to be scrubbed clean first so I persuade David to show me where there's a bucket and a scrubbing brush and I get started. The work is tiring and hot and I'm pleased when I finish about four hours later.

After a cooling shower I want to share my wine with David, but we're thwarted by the lack of a bottle opener, I'm baffled by a bar and a hostel that doesn't have a bottle opener!

So instead I walk out to find food at the Bar du Minervois, recommended by Trip Advisor and located in an area known as Guimaraes. I'm a little nervous walking in the dark; some of the streets are empty but following David's helpful directions I come across the bar some fifteen minutes later.

The Bar du Minervois is quirky and I'm not sure I like it that much, it's the sort of place that would be more fun with other people. There's only one vegetarian dish on the menu. A massive plateful arrives with rice, beans, mashed pumpkin and kale, I could feed David and Christian too with this much food. I walk home feeling very full and quite pleased with myself for venturing out alone.

25th November

I've slept for hours! I woke, then slept, then woke, then slept, until 8.15 and bearing in mind I went to bed pretty early that's a long time. I pester Erika to explain exactly what she has in mind for the steps and I'm eager to start. She wants inspirational words painted on each step in different colours and alternating English, Spanish and Portuguese. First, I'll need to paint the steps white.

Painting is enjoyable until the sun comes around and in the full heat I have to stop. Maybe I can come back to it later in the day.

There are a few interesting shops in the Guimaraes area, so I walk back there. I'd like to buy some small gifts to take back home. It takes about twenty minutes and all along the way are properties bursting with character.

One of the shops has huge, brightly coloured clay ornaments of Brazilian women for sale and I love them, one in particular is a black woman 'with attitude', I really wish I could buy her, but there's no way she'll fit into my backpack.

Just as I come out of the shop I see the famous yellow tram come past and I'm in time to jump on and catch a ride down into Rio de Janeiro.

It's a fun twenty-minute ride but I'm not in the mood to explore the big city yet, so I simply wait for the next tram back to Santa Teresa.

I've heard there's a popular drink here called 'acai' and I pop into a couple of cafes hoping to try it, without success, so I start walking back towards Villa Leonor. Ahead is a shuttered window and a signboard outside a small dwelling saying they sell food and acai, perfect! Acai is a fruit that looks a bit like a blueberry and the Brazilians make it into a sorbet, sometimes adding muesli, it tastes delicious and fills my tummy.

By the evening I'm keen to have a glass of wine and frustrated that Christian has again forgotten to bring a bottle opener. I tell David and Christian that I'll pop into town and see if I can buy one. It's getting close to 8 pm so this might be a fruitless mission. On the walk down, I reflect that it would be useful if I had a Swiss army penknife because they always have a cork screw and I've been caught out before.

Enquiring at the first likely shop, I'm told they don't sell corkscrews, then I come to the supermarket. One glance and I know I don't want to go inside, this is Friday night and there's an absolute scrum with long queues of people and shopping trolleys piled high.

Just beyond the supermarket an old lady is selling second hand bits and bobs from a trestle table. I give her my best impression of taking a cork out of a bottle complete with cork popping noise. She 'gets' what I'm asking for immediately but indicates that no, she doesn't have a cork screw, then she says something to a man standing nearby, who takes the penknife off his belt and shows me the corkscrew on it. Thinking he's asking if this is what I mean, I nod enthusiastically and say *'Si'* and then I realise he wants to sell it to me! I'm rather taken aback, he wants to sell me his penknife! It has several gadgets on it, but most importantly a cork screw. He wants 20 reals for it which is about £5 and I'm so amused I pay him.

I find this whole episode hilarious, especially as I'd been thinking on the way into town that a penknife would be useful. David and Christian are surprised how quick I've been and even more amazed when I relate my tale and show them the penknife. Erika arrives back at that moment and we share my bottle of wine.

## 26th November

The first set of stairs are now gleaming white and the sun is too hot to paint more for now. At Erika's suggestion, I take a taxi to Mirante Dona Marta, a cliffside lookout 1000 ft above sea level. From here I can see Christ the Redeemer, Sugarloaf Mountain and Rio spread out below. The taxi waits for me while I wander about enjoying the vista and then I ask him to drop me off at the Cantina Gaucha, a restaurant David has recommended to me, also because of the amazing views.

The Cantina is buzzing, it's very popular and it does have interesting views over the City. I order an acai and I'm disappointed when a pre-packed plastic container is hastily dumped in front of me. For 8 reals, about £2, I'm unimpressed.

From the Cantina I start walking down to Santa Teresa which I know is a long way, so I'm very happy when a bus comes in my direction and it takes me down to Guimaraes, the area I'm familiar with.

I decide to have dinner at the recommended 'Bar du Arnaud' and I order the only vegetarian dish available, beans, rice and pumpkin again. I'm very daunted when it comes, this is another massive meal, easily enough for four people. I do my best to do the food justice and leave the restaurant bloated.

Back at the hostel I'm not thrilled to discover a birthday party is in full swing, there are lots of youngsters in the bar area and very loud music. Christian seems to want me to join the party so I order a Caipurina, but not sharing their language I'm unable to talk with anyone and feeling uncomfortable I quietly sneak back to my room.

## 27th November

The party continues beyond midnight with raucously loud music and I wonder how their neighbours must feel, not to mention other paying guests. I doze on and off. At some point I'm aware of a scuffily noise that feels like it's in my room. My eyes don't want to open and the thought passes through my mind that probably a monkey is on the plastic roof outside my window.

I wake again just after 5.30 am, needing the toilet and I realise my bedroom door is wide open. Did I leave it open? I flush with embarrassment at the thought of the departing party guests, my room is hot and I don't wear anything in bed. Then I look around and I can't see my small rucksack. It's gone and I realise I've been robbed. I can't quite believe it and try to think if there's another explanation, but there's none.

I have to take stock of what's happened and with a flood of relief and gratitude I realise that my computer, my phone and my passport are all safe. I try to remember what was in the bag. I think I just have to mourn the loss of my purse and my prescription sunglasses and then, like a kick in my stomach, I realise my journal has gone. All my notes from the year are in my journal, names, places, recommendations, so much information. I take a deep breath and wonder how I can be okay about this.

It occurs to me that the burglar may still be on the premises, so I take a look around the villa, checking rooms. Then I realise that young Phillipe, employed by Christian and Erika for security, is sleeping on the sofa in the bar area. He wakes when I approach him and I tell him what's happened. Phillipe is no help at all, ha! some security guard. I ask him to unlock the front gate for me so I can take a look around the streets outside.

I've heard that sometimes, after taking the stuff they want, robbers will sling the unwanted bag, so I think it's worth looking. As I walk down the street I can't believe my good fortune; lying under a parked car is my cap and crouching down to look I also see my purse and *"oh, thank you God",* here is my journal. I'm amazed and delighted, the only thing missing from my purse is the cash, my credit cards are still there. I keep walking the streets and looking in trees and bushes in case I find my rucksack, without success. A shame, it's come a long way with me.

Erika and Christian are understandably concerned when they learn that I've been robbed. They trawl through pictures on the CCTV and we see the robber enter my room and leave with my rucksack over his shoulder, it feels very strange witnessing the deed.

Today's work is done, the second set of stairs are now also snowy white, so tomorrow I can start painting Erika's chosen words on them.

It's mid-afternoon and I'm back in Guimares hoping to get the tram into town but discover that it finishes at 4 pm and I'm too late. Instead I decide to walk into Gloria which doesn't look too far and should be by the sea. I start walking downhill and I'm wrong about it not being far. It seems to get farther away the more I walk and around every bend there's another bend.

I know I'm still not good at map reading but getting around Rio is proving tricky and the only map I have, has print so tiny I struggle to read it.

At last I've arrived in Gloria and find the marina only to be disappointed. There's a good view of Sugar Loaf Mountain, but apart from that I feel I've wasted my time.

Before walking all the way back, an attractive looking restaurant catches my attention. Sitting outside, I order an appetiser of mushrooms in cream sauce with bread. This is pure nectar for me and with a delicious glass of red wine I'm again content.

## 28th November

Another scorching hot day. I mix the paint Erika has given me to paint the words on the stairs but I'm not happy; the paint is poor quality and the colours are pastel, I feel they should be vibrant. I'd really like to buy new paint. It intrigues me that Erika has never asked if painting words on concrete stairs is something I feel capable of doing. I want to do a good job and ask for guidance from 'above' and it occurs to me to invite Michelangelo to help out, after all he was pretty good at painting and maybe he has nothing to do just now.

David asks if he can come out with me today, so, painting finished for now, we go together into Santa Teresa and his favourite coffee place where he introduces me to cheese balls. He has to go back to work afterwards and I take the tram into Rio to do some exploring.

David has told me to take the VLT train which runs through Rio but when I find it I'm thwarted. After queuing for a long time, it's my turn at the ticket machine and I struggle to comprehend the Portuguese instructions. A guy in the queue explains that I have to purchase a card first and load it with money, then I can put the card into the machine, I can't just buy a ticket. What a palaver, I only want to travel four stops. I wish things would be simple. I let it go and walk instead.

David is keen for me to pay a visit to the Museum of Tomorrow, a science museum, next to the waterfront at Pier Maua. It's vast inside and I can't muster up any enthusiasm, to me the museum is all 'something and nothing' and involves a lot of walking across big empty spaces.

## 29th November

Rio has an unusual conical shaped cathedral, called the Cathedral of St. Sebastian and I think it will be worth going inside. The cathedral is huge and can be seen from far away but I can't locate the entrance. I've walked along several roads always skirting around it. By the time I find the way in, it's getting late in the day and there are very few people about.

The stained-glass windows are floor to ceiling and stunningly beautiful, I feel as though I'm standing inside a kaleidoscope. As I turn to leave I realise the doors are being closed and I hurry over to them wondering if they would have locked me in.

Now I'm on the outside but I can't get out of the grounds. The gate I came in through has been padlocked. The man who was closing the door has disappeared. This is ridiculous, how am I supposed to get out. I remember that in my search for the entrance I had come across a car park which must be around the other side somewhere, I'll be able to get out there. Another very long, hot walk and I'm out.

Rio has exhausted me. I take the long meandering roads back to the Villa, purchasing a cheesy pastry thing along the way, and wonder how far I must have walked today.

## 30th November

It's the last day of November and I'm feeling anxious; my travels are drawing to a close. I don't sleep well, it doesn't help that it rains most of the night making a din on the plastic roof. I'm also feeling that I haven't done much work for the Villa, they still seem reluctant to give me jobs to do.

Coming out of my room I glance at the stairs to see how the newly painted words look and there's nothing there. The words have gone. I have to laugh when I realise the heavy rain has washed away my work. Well at least it proves a point, I need decent paint, or maybe Michelangelo needs decent paint!

At Erika's request I make drainage holes in colourful plastic flowerpots and attach wire hooks to hang them on a painted trellis. I'd like to buy some herbs and plants to fill the pots and ask Urma, a woman probably in her 30's and a long-term guest here, if she knows where I can buy herbs. She says she does know and offers to come with me.

I'm expecting a short walk to a shop, but as we walk it becomes apparent that Urma has no idea where we can buy herbs, in fact I'm now not even certain if she knows what herbs are. She stops to ask a shop keeper who sends us on a futile search further down the road, then she asks a trader who sends us further still, until we've walked the entire length of Rua Buenos Aires and we're now in downtown Rio. I protest that we've come too far and I need to get back, but she cheerfully suggests we try the next place. I'm struggling inside with a feeling of being 'hijacked', this quick jaunt is turning into a couple of hours.

We don't come across anywhere that sells herbs but I do find some gorgeous orchids and purchase one for Erika. I'm now very fed up and tell Urma that I'm going to go home. She says she knows a quick way back and after a brief argument because I'm not convinced she's right, I give in and we take her route. The route is the same one I've taken previously and it definitely isn't the quick route. On the way, we pass some antique shops and Urma goes inside and spends some time negotiating prices for various items but doesn't buy anything.

We eventually make it back to the town of Santa Teresa and Urma suddenly gestures to me to get on the back of a motorbike. What? Two guys are standing next to us with motorbikes and Urma tells me they're moto taxis. I clamber on the back of one and suddenly and hilariously I'm whisked up and around the cobbled streets back to Villa Leonor. It's a bumpy and treacherous ride as I only have one hand to hold on tight while the other clutches the orchid.

Urma redeems herself by cooking pasta for lunch and sharing it with me. As we chat she asks if I have children and I in turn ask her, to which she replies with a laugh *"no, I'm lesbian"*.

In the evening, Christian and Erika have gone out and I invite Urma and David to share my bottle of red wine, but when I try using the penknife corkscrew it buckles and doesn't pull the cork out, the metal is soft and bent and useless. There follows a very funny episode with three of us trying various ways to remove the cork, including using the power drill. Nothing works and desperation has set it. Last resort, I prize the cork out bit by bit with the pen knife leaving cork bits floating on the wine which I sieve through my newly purchased handkerchief. Finally, we're able to drink the wine and it tastes fine. We play some of Urma's excellent records on the player and dance to the music. It's been a funny evening.

## 1st December

Sleep is fitful again and I wonder if the robber episode has made me conscious of night noises

This morning I'm going to visit the famous Christ

Redeemer statue and work in the afternoon instead. Erika suggests a moto taxi which will take me to the bus pick-up point. My driver hands me a helmet that's way too large and just like in Vietnam I have to hold on to it, leaving only one hand available to secure myself on the bike. We weave in and out of traffic at speed and I partly love it and partly can't wait to get off and be safe.

Miraculously, there aren't any queues for the buses up to the Corcovado Mountain where the statue stands. The weather isn't great today and looks as though it may rain which could have kept people away. The first bus leaves us half way up and a van takes us the remainder of the journey. A short climb up some steps and there he is. The magnificent Christ the Redeemer statue.

I'm feeling very emotional as it dawns on me that a year ago I had to decide which airport I wanted to fly home from and I picked Rio de Janeiro. I could see myself standing at the foot of Christ the Redeemer looking down over Rio as the finale to my journey – and now here I am. I cried. I would like to have cried loudly and a lot but surrounded by many tourists I manage some restraint.

The statue is of course amazing. It isn't white as I had in my mind, but a greyish, stone colour. There are tourists all around and they're very funny, taking daft photos of themselves, standing with arms spread out like the statue, or lying on the ground to get a good photo angle. Rio spread out below us looks amazing and I spend a time soaking up the atmosphere and being with my thoughts.

I decide to take a taxi home, but approaching one, the driver wants 30 reals which seems too much considering I'd only paid 10 to get here, so I walk. For once I follow the map successfully and I'm pleased when, along the way, I see a selection of herbs for sale which are perfect for Erika's coloured plastic pots.

To my delight Erika has bought new brightly coloured paints and I spend some time in the late afternoon painting words on the stairs, starting with *'Sea Feliz'* in Spanish, *'Seja Feliz'* in Portuguese and *'Be Happy'* in English. I'm pleased with the result so far.

I'm going to eat out this evening and leaving my room I see Urma, Erika, Christian and David at the bar and they invite me to join them drinking 'shots'. Looking for dinner I walk in a different direction up the hill and come across a quirky little restaurant on a street corner. The only vegetarian food on the menu is a salad sandwich so I order it with a glass of white Chilean wine, musing that all meals taste better with wine.

## 2nd December

More inspirational words painted this morning, *'Be Brave'* and *'Be Patient'* and now I feel as though I'm doing a fair share of work at the Villa.

When the sun has become too hot to paint, I walk down the road to take a taxi to Sugarloaf Mountain. December is known as the taxi drivers thirteen month, they all charge more, sometimes double, but the fare is still very cheap at 34 reals, less than £8, and we drive quite a way across town.

A cable car takes me to the first stage on Sugarloaf and again I feel lucky that there aren't any queues, it seems I'm 'out of season' everywhere I go which really works to my advantage. The views from the first stage are stunning and I'm grateful the weather is dry although it is quite sultry and the sky is more grey than blue.

I like it here, there are some musicians playing and a couple of places to eat, also some tourist shops but tastefully done. There's another cable car which takes me up to the top at 396 metres. The mountain is situated at the mouth of Guanabara Bay on a peninsula that juts out into the Atlantic Ocean, so there are incredible views of the sea with beaches and bays all around.

Back down to earth again I get another taxi and ask the driver to take me to Copacabana Beach. I can't leave Rio without seeing Copacabana. The beach has a big expanse of soft white sand and large ocean waves. The city of Rio stands behind. I take off my sandals and walk along the shore paddling, it surprises me how few people are here. When the sun appears from behind the clouds, sunbathing seems like a good option.

I've only been lying on the sand about ten minutes when I hear a guy shouting, something about drinks he's selling. I ignore him but he comes over to me anyway. I pretend to be asleep but that doesn't deter him, he's chatters away in Portuguese. I open my eyes and give him a very firm *"no, nada, there's nothing I want"* and he still doesn't go away. The cheeky man then prods me in my tummy and I realise he's telling me that he thinks my pale skin shouldn't be exposed to the sun.

Before too long I'm bored on the beach so I look for a bus to take me to Rio Centro. I hop onto one that seems to be going the right way and hang on tight, my goodness they travel fast. Some of the places we pass are on my map, so I think I have a good idea where I am and then we come to Gloria Marina and because I know this place I ring the bell, but the driver doesn't stop. He keeps driving and I ring the bell again. This time he gesticulates but I've no idea why.

The bus whizzes on some more miles and eventually

comes to a standstill. I wait for the doors to open but they don't. The people around me are all telling me something in Portuguese and I press the bell gain then pull on the string thing. Then it dawns on me that I have to use the doors at the back of the bus to get out. I bet the driver is glad to see the back of me.

Looking around to see where I've landed I'm relieved that the area is familiar. It's a long walk back to the Villa but I think I know how to get there. On the way I give in to temptation and buy a big Panettone cake which has been advertised everywhere I go.

My legs are weary but I've made it back to the Villa and I share my Panettone with everyone. There are some new guests, Pedro, Gabriel and Liticia. Pedro is especially friendly and reminds me of the comedian, Mr Bean, he has a very intense way of talking. They're all here to see Black Sabbath who are playing in Sao Paulo; this amazes me, a band from my era, playing here.

## 3rd December

I'm still waking up often in the night and early hours but never for long and I'm grateful that I can go back to sleep easily. I feel very content. Getting up for breakfast is pure pleasure, sitting under the awning I take my time, enjoying the sunshine and entertained by little monkeys that scamper about the mango tree and along the colourfully painted wall.

I'd like to stay at the Villa today and finish painting the stairs and I'm doing well until people keep arriving to set up another party, they need to come up and down the steps, so I have to give up painting. It's a shame because I've almost finished. *'Be Yourself'* and *'Be Playful'* have now been added.

## 4th December

The party is another noisy one and goes on until the early hours. My bedroom is above the bar and the music. I can hear torrential rain and feel concerned that it will rain tomorrow preventing me from finishing painting the stairs.

The weather in the morning is fine and I'm relieved that I can finish the lettering. The final words read *'Be Silly'* and I've added tiny red dots around the lettering for a *'silly'* touch. I'm very happy with the result which may not be quite to Michelangelo's standard, but I think Erika is genuine when she says she's really pleased.

I'm back in the little shops in Guimares looking for more gifts to take home, when I see the huge ornament of the black Brazilian lady 'with attitude' and I have a mental battle. *"You can't take this back to the U.K., it's too heavy!" "But she's so colourful and so Brazilian and encapsulates the fun I've experienced here."* Heart wins over head and I buy her. I'll find a way to take her home.

It rains again in the evening so I don't go out, instead I have a pizza at the Villa with Chris, Erika and Urma. Back in my room I realise this has been the last full day of my travels and I feel sad that I'm not doing something special. Then I laugh at myself. As if being here at the quirky Villa Leonor with views over Rio de Janeiro and these amazing people isn't something special!!

## 5th December

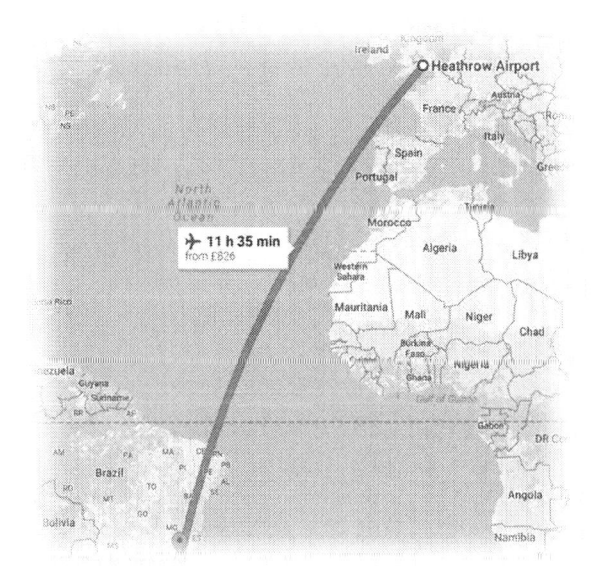

### Aeroplane to London (12hrs)

It's the end. I have mixed emotions about returning home. It's hard to say goodbye to everyone. A taxi comes to take me to the airport. The driver shares interesting information with me about Brazil, stuff I don't know, he's very politically aware. I feel sad for him, he loves his country but works his socks off to educate his children so they can leave it. He says they'll never have a good life in Brazil because of all the corruption.

At the airport my flight is delayed by an hour, the only occasion in all my flights that I've experienced a delay. Maybe the universe knows I'm reluctant to leave. The flight lasts eleven and a half hours and I'm not happy with British Airways. They don't offer any vegetarian meals and when we're woken in the morning they don't provide coffee. Enquiring why, I'm told that because of turbulence they are unable to serve it.

## 6th December

The transition through Heathrow is easy, I grab my backpack from the luggage conveyor belt for the last time and still clutching my ukulele, walk through customs into the 'Arrivals' area where my friends John and Fliss will be waiting for me.

At this moment I'm hit by the thought that *"I'm alive, I've made it"*. When I set out a year ago I didn't know what was ahead, I had no idea what might happen, I'd heard horror stories about ladies travelling alone and now I'm back and all is well.

To my amusement, John and Fliss are looking the other way expecting me to come out of a different entrance and I take them by surprise. I'm very happy to see them.

## Postscript

The delicate silver necklace Ben gave me survived intact and so did our relationship.

If there are any questions you'd like me to answer you're welcome to email, hazel.loutsis@gmail.com

*Photos can be seen using this web address:*
http://www.photobox.co.uk/creation/4763191048

And remember…

"Everything's always alright in the end,
and if it isn't alright, it isn't the end"

Adaptation of a quote, attributed to John Lennon
"everything will be okay in the end, if it isn't okay, it isn't the end"

Printed in Great Britain
by Amazon